D1008842

VALUES
MATTER
MOST

ALSO BY BEN J. WATTENBERG

The First Universal Nation
The Birth Dearth
The Good News Is the Bad News Is Wrong
Against All Enemies (with Ervin S. Duggan)
The Real America
The Real Majority (with Richard Scammon)
This U.S.A. (with Richard Scammon)

BEN J. WATTENBERG

VALUES MATTER MOST

How Republicans or Democrats or a Third Party Can Win and Renew the American Way of Life

THE FREE PRESS

New York   London   Toronto   Sydney   Tokyo   Singapore

To my children,
RACHEL, SARAH, DANIEL, and RUTH
to my grandchild, EMMA
and to my brand new grandnephew, HENRY ISAAC

To RICHARD SCAMMON

In memory of ERWIN GLIKES (1937–1994)

Copyright © 1995 by Ben J. Wattenberg

The Free Press
A Division of Simon & Schuster Inc.
1230 Avenue of the Americas
New York, N.Y. 10020

Printed in the United States of America

printing number

1 2 3 4 5 6 7 8 9 10

Text design by Carla Bolte

Library of Congress Cataloging-in-Publication Data

Wattenberg, Ben J.
    Values matter most : how Republicans or Democrats or a third party
can win and renew the American way of life / Ben J. Wattenberg.
        p.   cm.
    Includes index.
    ISBN 0-02-933795-X
    1. Social values—United States.   2. Public opinion—United
States.   3. Political parties—United States.   4. United States
—Politics and government—1993–   I. Title.
    HN59.2.W38   1995
    303.3′72—dc20   95–34915
                                                         CIP

CONTENTS

Part One

FROM THEN TO
NOT QUITE NOW

Chapter 1

PROLOGUE

This book is about the politics of values and the value of politics. I tell a story and advance a thesis, intertwined.

There are facts and opinions here. I think it is clear which are which. When dealing with facts, I try to be fair and accurate. I like to think my opinions have come from the facts, and not the other way around. I will demonstrate that as best I can, but will not pursue it at length. In politics it is difficult to keep facts and opinions separated. After all, I have been known to criticize others for squeezing facts in the service of partisanship or ideology, wittingly or unwittingly.

And so it seems I ought to begin by offering readers some of my relevant political biography. Readers can then intelligently discount what I say here, if such discount is deemed necessary. Moreover, as we shall see, my political hegira can be seen to have an extra bearing on the tale. After all, I am a so-called Reagan Democrat; at least I was when I started writing this book. And Reagan Democrats are extra-important people these days.

I was born in the Bronx, in August 1933, which makes me sixty-two plus a little as this book meets its publication date in late 1995. I have

3

always been a Democrat. I grew up in a Jewish neighborhood where at age seven I found a Willkie-for-President button, and no one knew what a Willkie was.

In 1952 I was a student at Hobart College in Geneva, New York, and if nineteen-year-olds had been eligible to vote for president I would have enthusiastically cast my ballot for Adlai Stevenson. It would not have made much difference: Dwight Eisenhower won, big. On the day after the election, a college professor of mine told the class that General Eisenhower's ascendancy would lead to military fascism in America.

On election day in 1956 I was living in San Antonio, Texas, while I served in the air force. I cast my first presidential vote for Stevenson. Ike won by an even bigger margin than in 1952. Fascism never did arrive.

By 1960 I was living in Stamford, Connecticut, to where I had come to edit a trade magazine, *Rivers and Harbors*. This time I was able to work for Stevenson; I sat at a table on a downtown Stamford street gathering signatures for a "Draft Stevenson" petition for the Democratic convention. Senator John Kennedy was nominated. I voted for him and came to admire him greatly. Anyway, all we reflexive Democrats knew enough to know that Kennedy's opponent, Richard Nixon, was a bad, bad man.

Of course, in 1964 I voted for Lyndon Johnson. After all, Barry Goldwater was a very, very bad man, and a hundred psychiatrists had signed an advertisement certifying him as crazy. None of them had met Goldwater, which may tell you who was crazy.

In 1965 my first adult book was published, *This U.S.A.*, in collaboration with Richard M. Scammon. That led to a call from the White House office of Bill Moyers, which led to a job as a White House speechwriter for President Johnson. (When the first phone call came from Washington I was not at home, and my six-year-old son told me when I returned that "Mr. House" had called.)

By that time I had run twice for minor local office, as a Democrat, in Stamford. I lost twice. But it wasn't until I got to the White House in August of 1966 that I realized that it was more than just running for office that I didn't understand.

Shortly after I began my distinguished public service as a presidential scribbler, I got into a conversation with the late Peter Lisagor of the *Chicago Sun Times* and Hugh Sidey of *Time* magazine. The conversation soon turned to Vietnam, about which I knew little, and something called the DMZ, about which I had not heard. I nodded sagely about that old DMZ, learning only later what was under discussion. (Young readers: It was the demilitarized zone between North and South Vietnam.)

I thought President Johnson was quite a piece of work, and I liked him. In any event, I soon learned something about Vietnam and, along with the majority of other Americans at that time, agreed with what we were trying to do there. (In fact, despite its tragic ending and great complexity, I think that case might still be made, when seen as one losing campaign in an epic and victorious cold war.)

Soon, many—but not all—liberal Democrats in Congress opposed the president in Vietnam. Allegedly learned liberal professors were attacking the way LBJ ran the War on Poverty, saying money was siphoned from that war to pay for the other. I knew that charge was wrong-headed; much of my speechwriting was about the poverty war.

In August 1968, the whole world was watching as Democrats raucously and sometimes violently played out opposing sides of a cultural revolution at the Chicago convention. I was at the LBJ ranch drafting a speech for President Johnson to deliver to his riven party. He decided not to attend. And I have wondered since why the ACLU didn't condemn the demonstrators who tried to disrupt the free meeting of the most important political party in the world.

After LBJ left the White House in early 1969, most of the remaining liberal hawks turned dovish on Vietnam and soon metamorphosed into ostriches on foreign policy—all while the cold war was still white hot. In 1970 Richard Scammon and I published *The Real Majority*, which warned that Democrats were heading into big trouble. More about that will follow.

In 1972 I realized that I could not vote for the Democratic presidential candidate, George McGovern, who thought America was guilty of too much and preached "Come Home America" while there was still an evil empire out there. In the 1980s most liberals refused to see the Soviet hand in Central America. Speaker Tip O'Neill was against helping the Contras in Nicaragua because (he said) he had always taken guidance from the Maryknoll Sisters (by then a very radical organization), and because he remembered that, fifty years earlier, a friend had told him that the United Fruit Company had exploited the peasants in Central America. All this in a party where many ethnic voters supported Captive Nations Week because they knew what was happening to their relatives behind the Iron Curtain.

By my lights, the domestic policy views of the liberals weren't much better. I grew up in a Democratic party that was a political home to many immigrants and their offspring. They did not spend a whole lot of time thinking about American guilt. Maybe racists and company bosses were guilty, but not America. I grew up in a Democratic party where liberals denounced quotas. After all, that's what was keeping Jews and blacks out of many colleges and medical schools. By the early 1970s the same party was too often endorsing new forms of "affirmative action" that came to be seen as the functional equivalent of quotas.

My Democratic party was tough on crime; the cops were Irish Democrats. Support for public schools was inviolate; they were temples of tough discipline and good behavior, where the melting pot bubbled innocuously and powerfully among multicultural student populations. This effect of the public schools was regarded as a good thing; it helped smooth out the tensions between whites and blacks, Catholics and Protestants, Jews and Christians. That Democratic party was a workingman's party that stood for vigorous economic growth replete with smokestacks. The pinched environmentalists of that time, called "conservationists," were Republicans.

During the 1970s my elderly mother was robbed on the street, and my father was mugged in the lobby of his apartment building. In the 1980s my former sister-in-law was murdered in Philadelphia. The killer was never apprehended. Crime was no longer an abstraction.

Over the years, so many traditional Democratic themes not only were abandoned by the liberal and most vocal part of the Democratic party but were picked up by the Republicans. The GOP became the party of internationalism, merit, economic growth, and domestic order. I would like to call it the biggest heist in American political history, but in truth the Democrats weren't robbed: they gave away those issues, gratis.

After the Democrats went down in flames in 1972, I helped start, and later became chairman, of a Democratic anti-McGovernite factional group called the Coalition for a Democratic Majority (CDM). I had become an ideological Reagan Democrat before the term was cool, or even known.

I tried to vote and work for Democrats whenever possible. I had been happy to vote for Hubert Humphrey in 1968. I worked as his speechwriter in his 1970 Minnesota Senate campaign. I found my champion in Senator Henry M. "Scoop" Jackson and worked in his campaigns in the 1972 and 1976 Democratic presidential primaries, but he lost both times. Jimmy Carter got my vote in 1976; after all, he had run to Scoop Jackson's right in the primaries. But I couldn't vote for Carter in 1980, by which time he had announced that America had "an inordinate fear of communism" and had generally shown himself as just one more instrument of the liberal "New Politics."

By 1984 I had moved into the District of Columbia, where, in effect, a voter's presidential ballot doesn't count because the city typically goes about five to one Democratic. I voted for Fritz Mondale, who was a decent man and a friend, despite the lefter-than-thou primary campaign that had captured all the Democratic candidates. (If I thought my vote would determine who would be president, I would have voted for Reagan, not because of Mondale but because of what had become of Mondale's party.)

I had another reason for voting for Governor Michael Dukakis in 1988. I still thought I might again be active within the Democratic party, and I wanted to be able to say truthfully, if challenged, that I voted for the Democrat. Anyway, I knew he was going to lose. My general theory was that sooner or later, for good or for ill, Democrats would recapture the White House, and it would be best for all if the party still had a moderate wing.

The 1992 election was different. Governor Clinton had run his campaign as a dynamic moderate who preached, "No More Something for Nothing," a slogan that resonated in my political soul. He hadn't burned his bridges to the liberals, but he seemed more than halfway on our side, and that was enough to keep me hopeful. He was saying what I had been waiting to hear from a Democratic presidential candidate for many years. How could I not support him? And the cold war was over. How much harm could a Democratic president do, even if he ended up captured by the liberals, as Carter was?

So I wrote a column endorsing Clinton over Bush. It was the first time in a dozen years of column writing that I had publicly come out directly for a candidate. (It is included as an appendix to this book.) I first started thinking about this book as a way to assess neutrally how far Clinton and the Democrats had moved toward that "No More Something for Nothing" idea. You will see how I came out.

I think the polling evidence is clear that Clinton won in 1992 largely because he was able to gain the votes of many Reagan Democrats, or as we called them in my cell, CDM Democrats. We potential swing voters had become very important people for either party. That became apparent during the congressional elections of 1994. Such voters will be around in 1996.

If all that needs discounting, then discount.

There is a personal political epilogue to this book, which tries to look ahead.

Chapter 2

HOW A THEME GREW

This story and this thesis start bubbling during a Houston summer at the 1992 Republican Convention when the most potent political issue in America, values, came steaming back into play, for the first time as a negative. What some foolish Republicans did in Houston, how the mostly mindless, mostly liberal media reported it, and what the traumatized Republicans did not subsequently do about the values issue, led in some large measure to the election of Bill Clinton. (It was not just the economy.) For an extended moment it looked as if the Democrats had at least leveled the playing field regarding this values situation, by far the scariest and most urgent part of our politics, and our lives.

Not unrelated, Clinton's election in 1992 was the first one captured by a Democrat by a margin of more than a whisker since 1964. That was twenty-eight years and seven presidential elections earlier, a long time by any standard. Clinton's victory in 1992, and how he won, opened a once-in-a-generation window of political opportunity for the Democrats.

9

Then, remarkably, Clinton and the Democratic Congress profoundly mishandled the values issue. And so, on election day 1994, despite a reinvigorated economy, the Democrats were decimated. It seemed that the magic grail of values had passed back to the GOP, there to rest for a long time. We will learn more about that in the presidential election season of 1996.

Here is my take on what's going on: I believe that the values situation in America has deteriorated. I believe that government has played a big role in allowing values to erode. I *think* that values are our most potent *political* issue. I *know* that values are our most important *real* issue. I believe that in the governmental arena, most of the blame for what has happened goes to liberal guilt peddlers whose remedies almost invariably involved what has been called "something for nothing." This erosion is not irreversible; it does not involve reraveling a sweater. I believe that what government has caused, government should cure, through politics. I believe that what liberalism has caused, conservatism can cure. I believe that liberalism, which has contributed so much to America, might still change and help lead.

The values situation is bad stuff, striking at the heart of a decent life, for blacks and whites, males and females, in every area of the country. We are talking about mothers without husbands and children without on-site fathers, hurting financially, often fearing violence, often causing violence, learning too little, worried about morality, too often hustling to gain group victim points, and possibly cleaving what is still a remarkably successful and patriotic society. It's worse by far than most plausible bad-news economic scenarios. Moreover, eroding values create bad economic news, so much of it, for example, keyed to the low income of the growing number of female-headed households. (Paradoxically, the values issue may well be exaggerated, but even at half strength, it's terrible.)

I suggest here that whichever political party, whichever political candidate (including perhaps a new party or two, with a third or fourth presidential candidate), is seen as best understanding and dealing with that values issue—will be honored. Honored at the polls. Honored at the polls at national, state, and local levels. Honored at the polls in

1996 and, I bet, for a long time after that. Honored at the polls in a way that will likely realign and refashion the existing American political landscape.

More important by far, the current combined partisan opportunity can also serve as a great opportunity for America itself. In a more direct way than one might imagine, it can help shape the rest of the world, also in a salutary manner. Not bad for some issues that not long ago were scorned as "demagogic."

How all this plays out, from Houston to now, and beyond, will be explored in this book. To do so wisely and well requires some discussion of theory and history, now.

BEGINNINGS, 1968

For me all this started in the autumn of 1968 as I sat at lunch with Richard Scammon in the White House Mess, a dining room burnished in glistening dark wood and staffed entirely by male Filipino U.S. Navy stewards. (A different era.) Scammon and I talked about the year that was, and quite a year it had been.

We chatted about some of the events of 1968 that would come to gain near-mythical proportions: the bloody Tet offensive in Vietnam, a campaign within the Democratic party to dump President Johnson from office, the tragic assassinations of Martin Luther King, Jr., and Robert Kennedy, racial riots in 120 cities, a tumultuous and bloody Democratic political convention in Chicago, student insurrections, and George Wallace's third-party candidacy which had raised the issue of race in a way never seen before in American politics.

But as Scammon and I talked, we noted some other things that were going on. Contrary to popular belief, the polls showed that young people were more hawkish on Vietnam than their elders. Young people were also more likely to be pro-Wallace than their elders, which did not exactly fit the common portrait of the dawning of the Age of Aquarius. The Gallup Poll asking Americans to identify "the most important problem" revealed that crime and race relations shared top billing with Vietnam, and, if combined, those social concerns outdistanced Vietnam, by far. And, how strange! Voters were disaffected with

Democrats, the incumbents, something that is not supposed to happen when the economy is doing well, which it was.

It was a mix of conditions that would elect Richard Nixon by an apparently thin margin but a margin that, when examined, was ideologically much wider than it seemed. (Surveys showed that the Wallace vote would have split heavily for Nixon.)

Scammon had witnessed 1968 from his position as director of the Elections Research Center, where he held forth as America's most prominent psephologist. I was serving as a thirty-five-year-old speechwriter for President Lyndon Johnson. I had been told the year before by some other staff members that LBJ wanted me on his 1968 campaign plane, and for a special reason. Why? I quote what they said he said, because it will become relevant later: "That Wattenberg," LBJ overstated, "he really hates Republicans."

With all this in mind, Scammon and I talked about collaborating on a new book. Two years later it was published, entitled *The Real Majority*. It received great attention, neon cover-story type of attention, op-ed praise and op-ed scorn, climbing to the very bottom of the best-seller list.* One cliché about *The Real Majority* was that it had become "the Bible of both political parties." That may even be true; elected officials in both parties have since told us it was their bible. It even established an abstract folk heroine. Scammon and I wrote that the typical voter was a "forty-seven-year-old wife of a machinist living in Dayton, Ohio"; she was "unyoung, unpoor and unblack," "middle aged, middle class and middle minded"; and it would be wise to know that "her brother-in-law is a policeman and she does not have enough money to move if her suburban neighborhood deteriorates." (*Life* magazine located a very nice woman who met most of these criteria.)

Our central theme in *The Real Majority* was elemental. In the 1960s, we said, a new tidal political issue had reached shore in America, washing across the most important spot on the political spectrum: the

---

* Which is pretty good for a work of political analysis, and at a time when only ten, not fifteen, books made the *New York Times* list and how-to books were included in the nonfiction lists.

center. We called that tide "the social issue," a coinage that has since come into general usage. We believed that the SI had become *coequal* with an earlier tidal concern, the economic issue. We believed, too, that the SI had contributed heavily to Nixon's 1968 victory.

We further said that unless the Democrats paid serious attention to that socially turbulent center, they would likely keep on losing in the national arena. They didn't, and they did.

We published in 1970. The book dealt principally with voting behavior in the 1960s, a decade of social tumult and social turbulence. On the face of it, then, it should not have been surprising that Scammon and I placed such a high priority on social concerns. Everything seemed to be coming unglued.

But *The Real Majority* was not designed as a book just about the sixties. We had modestly set out to write a general theory of elections, of which the social issue was one very important part.

A long political generation has now gone by. The social issue is now often called "values," sometimes "cultural issues," and sometimes still the "social issue." (I use "values" here as the superior rubric, for reasons that will be explained soon.) Many of the conditions that Scammon and I had written about have since evolved.

I've written several books since then. Most did not concentrate on politics but on our material well-being and on changing social demographics. By most of these measures America is doing quite well. But regarding the values-social-cultural concerns brought up in *The Real Majority*, there has been deterioration. New social maladies have emerged. At best the situation is unhappy; at worst, perhaps combustible. I have come to the conclusion that the values issues are no longer merely *co-equal* with economic concerns. *The values issues are now the most important.*

This book is an attempt to marry what I have learned about politics with what I have learned about social demographics. It is an optimist's book of deep concern, with a suggested direction for plausible partial political remedies. Optimists still think there are remedies.

UNDERSTANDING VALUES

To get a preliminary flavor of what's going on in America, consider this much published, much believed, and phony poll of teachers.

Top Problems In Public Schools, Identified By Teachers

1940	1990
Talking out of turn	Drug abuse
Chewing gum	Alcohol abuse
Making noise	Pregnancy
Running in halls	Suicide
Cutting in line	Rape
Dress code infraction	Robbery
Littering	Assault

It turns out it wasn't a survey at all. It was one Texan's *opinion* of what had happened in his lifetime. (T. Cullen Davis, of Fort Worth.) But the fact that so many Americans believed it to be true may make the list more important than if it were a reliable public opinion poll. Do we really think that our young people today are drunk, pregnant, and suicidal; that they are junkies, rapists, robbers, and thugs?

Now, I am not now, nor have I ever been, one of those who believes that "America is going into decline." This country self-corrects. But, I hesitate to bring it up, even I do not know the future. This, though, I predict: Should America founder, it will founder not on economics but on values.

I believe we should try to learn something from what has gone on in the past twenty-five years as politics and policy have played themselves out sadly in the realm of government.

I say this with some sorrow. I am not now, nor have I ever been, antigovernment, or even anti big government. In fact, one has to believe in government to believe as I do. As I said, and will say again, what government has caused, government can cure; what government has done, government can undo; what government has screwed up, government can unscrew up. I don't think most Americans hate government, but they surely hate some of what government has done recently.

That can change if we create a different kind of politics in this very new moment of the mid-1990s. And then let this fresh politics work its magic. After a generation of politics bashing, there is something we forget: American politics, when it works right, can be magical.

Just what is this values issue, this social issue, this cultural issue? It is hard to define with any precision. We shall have to pick up pieces of it as we go along. Offered first is a dictionary definition. Then comes a lazy tactical description of what it mostly is not. Then a list. And finally an attempt at an operational typology of terms, which sounds grander than it is.

Here is how *Webster's New World Dictionary* defines the gauzy word "values":

> *The social principles, goals, or standards held by an individual, class, society etc. That which is desirable or worthy of esteem for its own sake; thing or quality having intrinsic worth.*

(As used here "values" can be assumed to be "traditional values," or "the values of virtue." After all, there could be "bad values.")

Seen another way, from the tactical and rather parochial point of view of a political campaign consultant in the heat of a campaign, the values/social/cultural issues might be seen best as a string of negatives. That is, these are the issues that are mostly *not* the bread and butter economic issues that surface in a political contest: *not* taxes, *not* spending, *not* unemployment, *not* deficits, *not* wages. These are the issues that are *not* usually associated with foreign policy: *not* Haiti, *not* Kuwait, *not* the defense budget, *not* Russia, *not* NATO, *not* Bosnia.

Excuse the fudging here—I say "mostly" and "usually"—because there are times when the values issues impinge on classic foreign policy and economic concerns. (For example: Is antiwar draft dodging a social issue or a foreign policy issue? Don't high crime rates have a huge negative economic effect?) In general, however, in this narrow political campaign sense, it might be said that the values issues are what are left over after economics and foreign policy have been taken off the table.

Here is a list, alphabetized but surely incomplete, of some of the items that, in the last generation, have been seen as social/values/cultural issues:

abortion	illegitimacy
amnesty	infidelity
bra burning	movies and television
busing	multiculturalism
capital punishment	"Murphy Brown"
condoms in the classroom	patriotism
crime	permissiveness
dependency	the pledge of allegiance
discipline in schools	political correctness
disparagement of America	pornography
disruption	prayer in school
draft dodging	promiscuity
drugs	quotas
elitism	race
family values	rap music
feminism	school discipline
flag burning	sex education
Gennifer Flowers	Troopergate
gays in the military	values
gun control	welfare
homelessness	Willie Horton
homosexuality	work ethic

That's forty-four items, not an inconsiderable number, and it is much less than a complete list. It's worth examining. It is very, very broad: from prayer, to crime, to homosexuality, to welfare, to music. It is, in fact, too broad for some of the purposes here. And so, some different nomenclature is offered to keep things simple.

The overarching term "values" is used to describe everything included above, aspects of which are seen by some or many voters to violate "the (worthy) social principles, goals, or standards held by an individual, class, society etc."

And we shall then subdivide values into two separate categories: social issues and cultural issues. Graphically, thusly:

VALUES ISSUE

Social Issues   **Cultural Issues**

There are some important distinctions between the social issues and the cultural issues. The **social issues,** as used here, are (1) important, (2) harmful to society as a whole, and (3) agreed to be both important and harmful to society as a whole by a vast consensus of Americans. Further, I particularly concentrate on social issues that (4) hold out the possibility of plausible governmental reform because (5) these issues were in some large measure engendered by governmental action, and (6) they are issues that President Clinton and/or Democrats promised to do something about, opening up a possibility of some real political action.

Crime clearly fits these criteria as a social issue. Almost everyone agrees it's terrible and that we can do something about it. Americans are fearful, and not just in areas where crime is highest. If you don't believe that, come talk to the folks in my affluent neighborhood, in Northwest Washington—liberal, well educated, and frightened.

Welfare fits too. Almost everyone agrees it is malfunctioning in a serious way, harming us and harming recipients. A woman on welfare said this to an interviewer in 1990: "Public aid made the problems with my older girls worse. If they knew they wouldn't get no help, they wouldn't be having all those babies."*

Education fits, certainly educational discipline fits, and it's a lot easier to fix than welfare or crime.

And I argue here that preference, proportionalism, quotas—that is, certain aspects of affirmative-action-as-now-practiced—also fits. That is a harder argument.

---

* Respondent interview, recounted in Susan J. Popkin, "Welfare: View from the Bottom," *Social Problems* (February 1990).

Those four big social issues—crime, welfare, educational discipline, and quotas—are examined here as the prime examples of what's wrong and what ought to be done about it.

The **cultural issues** are quite different. There are monumental arguments about whether this subset of the values issues are *important* or not, *harmful* or not. Accordingly, there is certainly no broad *consensus* about whether they are important and harmful. This makes it hard to figure out what to do about them in a governmental context and, in any event, many of these issues are not government-driven. The Democrats haven't promised to do anything about them, reducing the possibility of serious political action to slim, at best.

I do not mean to downgrade the cultural issues; they are powerful and potent to many voters. I am offering mostly a tactical distinction between the social and cultural issues. It is in the social arena where there is a strong possibility of remedial action on important matters.

For now, consider again the earlier incomplete big list of forty-four values items and note only that there is a massive political point to be drawn from that compendium of a quarter of a century's worth of turbulence. As the political scientists say, many of those issues are salient. Using those issues, sometimes demagogically, usually not, Republicans won five of six presidential elections between 1968 and 1988, most of them by solid margins, some by landslides. The sixth case, Jimmy Carter in 1976, also showed the force of the issue in its own way.

The 1992 presidential season will be examined in the next chapter. Later, we will observe how Clinton and the Democrats governed, see what happened in the congressional elections of 1994, consider extraordinary developments in 1995, and divine what the future holds.

GROWING GUILT, 1972

Let us pick up the values trail back in 1972, almost a quarter of a century ago, the first presidential election after the publication of *The Real Majority*. It was the year that showed clearly that the social concerns were not just a political mutation that had flowered evanescently in a hothouse moment now known so conveniently as the sixties.

In the early 1970s the war in Vietnam was winding down, certainly in terms of American combat involvement. When Senator George McGovern was nominated for president at the Democratic convention in Miami in July 1972, American troop strength in Vietnam had already been reduced by more than 90 percent, to 47,000, with *none of those troops serving in combat roles*. The phasing out of the Selective Service draft had already begun.

What happened at the Miami convention that year was a walking advertisement that the values issues were not out of season, despite the wilting of Vietnam. In fact, those issues were only reaching full bloom. The surface stuff was easy to see, and it was broadcast prominently and with purposeful verve, on television, into 50 million American homes.

There were some long-haired shaggy delegates in shorts and sandals, apparently straight from Central Casting. There were hippies, and Yippies Jerry Rubin and Abbie Hoffman, surrounded by cameramen. I watched the chairman of the Democratic National Committee, the late Lawrence O'Brien, hounded out of a public meeting by black welfare mothers, hooting loudly.

There was the bitter fight over which group of Illinois delegates would be seated at the convention. The high symbolism was shown right out front: The boss of bosses, Mayor Richard Daley, the putative villain of the tumultuous 1968 Chicago convention, was dumped as a delegate, in part by Jesse Jackson, a young activist minister. I had occasion recently to watch the old 1972 film clips of Jackson—militant, surly, dashing, dashiki clad, sporting an outsized Afro. The film gives fuller meaning to the idea that American politics tends to moderate and absorb even the thorniest of players.

(The McGovern campaign coordinator for Texas was a young man from Arkansas, Bill Clinton. He was helped by a young woman named Hillary Rodham.)

But the politics of 1972 were not just show biz, symbols, and video. Serious ideas were bubbling, particularly in the social sector. Institutions were crumbling; new ones were forming and solidifying. New laws were being passed. Old ones were being been reinterpreted, with the force of new law. Reflecting these new ideas were new regulations, directives, court orders, and guidelines. Conditions were changing, driven by, and driving, all of the above. And it would intensify as the years unfolded.

Consider briefly some of those ideas, institutions, rules, regulations, and conditions.

Much of the left wing of the Democratic party—adored and widely chronicled by most of the media—had signed on to the notion that America was a sick society. America was said to be racist, sexist, sexually repressed, environmentally retrograde, imperialist, corrupt, arrogant—and guilty.*

Such a harshly negative view of America tends to see the unfortunate as victims. That view changes things: The unfortunate *need* our help, may *deserve* our help, but victims are *entitled* to restitution. It was America's fault! Accordingly, it was maintained, victims were entitled to more than they were getting, even though federal social welfare spending had more than tripled in real dollars during the 1960s, and doubled during Nixon's tenure.

And so liberal special interest groups—civil rights, feminist, gay, environmental, consumer, civil libertarian, welfare, peace (to only begin a list)—formed or expanded. Their goal was to diagnose America's sickness for Americans, and then to gain political entitlement or reparations for victims, each group in its own way. If that case is accepted, the victims were getting something in return for something done to them. If that case is not accepted the victims were getting something . . . for nothing.

In pushing this guilt-laden view, the so-called cause groups took some good old American ideas, quite properly tried to extend them, and then extended them over the line—in many cases far over the line. Some of those ideas would be pushed to a point where a solid majority of Americans would see them as alien to the American experience, alien to the American way of life. Sooner or later these views came to be seen as value-busting, and often budget-busting as well.

---

* In 1974 I wrote a book entitled *The Real America*, which challenged the "Failure and Guilt Complex."

For me, and for tens of millions of other Democrats, this trash-America process was itself sick. It was getting rather easy not to hate Republicans.

Looking back, there are three important observations that should be offered about the liberal cause groups that erupted in the sixties and seventies. They were remarkably successful in their own terms. They were a long-term tactical disaster for the political party in which they assembled. And they leave a mixed legacy to America, some quite good, some very bad, and with many of the deleterious features concentrated in the realm of values.

Now, in the mid-nineties—an extraordinary moment of political opportunity—we ought to sift out the bad from the good.

In those early hothouse years, the blossoming left-liberal ideas set in motion a number of social issues, upon which we concentrate. Here is a brief rundown:

Welfare

Americans believe in the value "work equals reward." But in *Goldberg v. Kelly*, in 1970, the Supreme Court ruled that before a state could cut off an individual's welfare grant, the recipient was first entitled to a "pretermination evidentiary hearing." As Justice Hugo Black noted in his dissent, the ruling had the effect of freezing welfare into a constitutional structure.

That was the idea. In the late 1960s, the dynamic welfare rights leader George Wiley pushed the idea that welfare was indeed a right, that it should not be a stigma, and that receiving welfare was a noble condition. That case was pushed by Wiley's organization, the National Welfare Rights Organization, which issued studies and papers maintaining that welfare ought to be regarded as highly as work, that more people ought to seek welfare payments, that benefits ought to be much higher, and that welfare recipients were owed whatever they got. On the action side, the NWRO recruited eligible people to the welfare rolls.

Wiley's vision concerned a value where no additional work was required for additional reward. For a while that view resonated among potential recipients and in state and federal legislatures.

Facts:

- In the ten years from 1970 to 1980 welfare rolls went up from 7.4 million to 10.6 million, a 43 percent increase.
- The rate of illegitimate births, for all races, went from *11 percent* in 1970 to *18 percent* in 1980, a 64 percent surge.

Crime

Most Americans believe in the value "crime does not pay," or at least "crime *should* not pay." But new, and soft, court decisions, often pushed by civil libertarian groups, had the effect of making it easier for crime to pay off. For that reason, and a variety of others, it became harder to arrest, to convict, and to incarcerate. For criminals there might be something for nothing out there. Government had acted, unwisely.

Facts:

- In 1950, of all reported robberies, 14 percent resulted in a prison sentence. In 1983, the rate was 2 percent.
- From 1957 to 1993 the violent crime rate soared by 538 percent.

That was bad enough. But there is the matter of public rhetoric to consider as well. It plays a powerful role in our politics, and in our life. It can elevate us, or depress us; it can make us believe that our government is on our side, or against us. As a former speechwriter, I believe in the Public Scrivener's Code, whose first item is, "Rhetoric yields reality," or, at least, "You can't change reality without first changing rhetoric."

How did most Americans view the crime situation? The public saw the police as mostly heroic and understood them to be the thin blue line between chaos and civilization. But while the criminal law was being at least partially unraveled and crime rates went up, the radical left spoke out. They called the cops "pigs," who enforced an ugly thing called "law 'n' order," which, they said, was nothing but a "codeword for racism." That figured: America was guilty.

Such language originated from a small fringe group. But, alas, under the apparent doctrine of "no enemies on the left," mainstream liberals rarely repudiated the extremists in public. In fact, in some instances, as in "law 'n' order is a codeword for racism," there was often rhetorical agreement.

Merit

This may be the most powerful and unifying American value. The idea of individual merit, was, in fact, the organizing principle of the modern civil rights movement. Segregation and institutionalized discrimination had been an evil stain on American life, in large measure because the principles of separation thwarted the idea that blacks could move ahead based on merit, just as whites did. The stated civil rights goal in the 1950s and early 1960s was to create a "color-blind" society.

But the second phase of the civil rights movement, which was roughly coincident with the advent of the McGovernite cause groups, went beyond such "equality of opportunity." The new goal was "equality of results."

In the realm of employment, as in many other areas, this change started with long-overdue new laws, and then developed in strange ways, mostly outside the legislative process. Title VII of the 1964 Civil Rights Act properly and finally prohibited discrimination in hiring, promoting, firing, transferring, training, and pay. But affirmative action did not come about through an act of Congress. In its modern connotation it surfaced a year later through President Johnson's Executive Order 11246, which required government contractors to pursue affirmative measures, like outreach and advertising, to promote the hiring of blacks and other minorities. It did not mean, not even close, numerical standards by race; it did not mean preference, proportionalism, or quotas. In fact, the Order specifically prohibited preference.

But in 1970 a federal court ruling, *Contractors of Eastern Pennsylvania v. Schultz,* held that "goals and timetables" were required to implement affirmative action. Then, in *Griggs v. Duke Power* in 1971, the Court held that high school diplomas or test scores could not be used as a prerequisite for employment because in such competition blacks as a group did not do as well as whites as a group. The proof was in the pudding: If minorities didn't have their proportionate share of jobs, if there was "disparate impact" from hiring policy, even if caused by tests that were fair, a company could face legal challenge and penalties (as well as adverse publicity).

The emerging formula was apparent: Affirmative action + goals + timetables + sanctions = racial proportionalism (commonly called "reverse discrimination" or "quotas"). The value of "merit" was under attack. And the new civil rights line maintained that those who stuck with merit were racist: Americans were as guilty as ever.

Many aspects of the recent history of the feminist movement are not dissimilar from that of the civil rights movement. Feminism, too, was a noble fight against discrimination, followed by a demand for equality of results, challenging merit.

Education

There was, once, a clear value expressed implicitly and explicitly throughout our schools: "work plus discipline equals reward," which was a long way of saying "merit." That has been diluted, by government. As we shall see later, it involves "social promotion," "grade inflation," "student warehousing," as well as the growing inability to discipline rowdy students. All this was necessary, we were told, because poor student performance wasn't even the fault of the students; it was America's fault. And so, students were entitled to reward without hard work. There was less of an apparent payoff for merit.

In a somewhat different sense, the diminishment of merit and the elevation of guilt can also be seen at the root of the epic political argument about "busing," or more specifically "busing to achieve racial balance."

The decision *Brown* v. *Board of Education* (1954) had stated that it was unconstitutional for children to be assigned to schools on the basis of race. With a remarkable display of legal legerdemain, a series of subsequent court decisions, pushed by civil rights groups, legislated an opposite principle: that children *should* be assigned to schools on the basis of race.

And so many white parents who thought they merited and earned their place in a decent neighborhood, where their children could go to decent schools, suddenly found out otherwise. Their children were to be transported each day from such neighborhoods. Perhaps it should not be called a value, but the idea of the neighborhood school, particularly for younger children, had been hallowed in American life. Suddenly, for millions of Americans, it was gone, while liberal politicians said "busing isn't a real issue, it's demagoguery."

Facts:

- From 1960 to 1980 per student spending on education went from $1,700 to $3,835 in constant dollars.
- From 1967 to 1980 the average combined Verbal-Math SAT score fell from 958 to 890.

Homelessness

The list could go on and on. A 1972 ruling (*Margaret Papachristou* v. *Jacksonville, Florida*) overturned a municipal statute dealing with vagrancy. No longer were "beggars," "drunkards," "vagabonds," and "rogues" to be prohibited from plying their trade on public streets. In the 1970s a series of court decisions, brought about in part through the efforts of a determined group of civil liberties lawyers, made it more difficult to hospitalize the mentally ill. The deinstitutionalization of hundreds of thousands of mental patients followed.

Legal rulings had helped create more unstable people on the street and less legal ability to deal with them. Not long after, the number of homeless people soared, which was blamed on a lack of jobs and housing for poor people.

Drugs, Sex

These days we tend to forget that there was a serious intellectual movement in America that was pro-drug. Drugs were said to be "consciousness raising" and "mind expanding." There was that nifty item called the "drug culture." How nice. "Feed your head," sang the Jefferson Airplane, avatars of the Bay Area druggie scene. "Tune in, turn on, drop out," exhorted ex-Harvard professor Dr. Timothy Leary. Some, like Ken Kesey, the Merry Prankster, speculated that LSD might form the basis of a new worldwide body of religious thought.

There was the issue of "sexual liberation," which could lead to sexual promiscuity. There seemed to be something for nothing out there.

Facts:

- The incidence of cocaine use among young adults more than doubled in five years during the 1970s. How many Americans ended up dead or brain fried? No one knows.
- The incidence of sexually transmitted diseases—principally syphilis and gonorrhea—climbed by 64 percent from 1970 to 1980.

Rhetoric

Always, there were the inflammatory words, even about issues that made a great deal of sense. Most Americans, for example, harbor nothing but good feelings for the environment, but they also have strong feelings in favor of economic growth and material comfort. When some environmentalists described the sum total of American goods and services as the "Gross National Pollution," that was a problem. The environmentalists looked at energy consumption and condemned the "single-family home ethic," which happened to be just the ethic where most Americans hung their hat.

Beyond all that were other issues, cultural ones: abolition of the display of Christmas symbols in public places, pornography in the open marketplace, taxpayer funding of allegedly pornographic and/or blasphemous art designed to shock and offend taxpayers, the abolition of the death penalty, the discontinuation of prayer in the schools, and many other items—each of which had high symbolic value and offended large majorities of Americans.

Abortion is also a values issue, subcategory cultural issue. It will receive special discussion later on. So will gun control.

Note that the social issues mentioned here, and many of the cultural issues, had a governmental base to them. And so as values were seen to erode, an American political countertheme grew: Values matter most.

Democrats had dug themselves a deep hole on the values issues. It does not take a learned election expert to know that a national political party associated with an agenda that is seen to be against the neighborhood school, against single-family homes, against work, against prayer, against merit, and against Christmas—and perceived to be in favor of vagrancy, murderers, crime, promiscuity, drugs, pornography, and quotas—will soon be in deep trouble. (It enables their opponents to say that Democrats are not the party of "normal people," to use Speaker Newt Gingrich's unfortunate phrase.)

Politicians in both parties knew this. I worked in the 1972 Democratic presidential primary campaign of the late sainted Senator Henry M. "Scoop" Jackson. The campaign slogan was "Common Sense for a Change."

Nixon made a similar case in the general election of 1972, running against McGovern. Republican senator Hugh Scott, then minority leader of the Senate, made the argument with a particular flourish. McGovernites, he said, favored the "three A's," that is "Acid," "Abortion," and "Amnesty." Liberal Democrats retorted, "Nixon is a white-collar Wallace," perhaps forgetting that Wallace had received as many votes in the 1972 Democratic primaries as McGovern did. (Abortion and amnesty became the law of the land, but in politics, as in life, timing matters.)

Nixon beat McGovern in the biggest landslide of American history. He lost only one of fifty states, Massachusetts, often called "the most liberal state in the union." Even there the Democrat's proportion of the two-party vote sunk from 63 percent in 1968 to a less-than-robust 54 percent in 1972.

Now, one can argue about the merits of some of these issues. Some of them made sense, at least in a moderate form. But there can be little doubt that the tonality, symbolism, and cost associated with them were a political disaster.

Let us move on from 1972, bearing in mind two thoughts about this governmental, legal, and institutional value-busting activity: (Mostly) government did it. (Mostly) liberalism did it.

Interestingly enough, social liberalism proceeded at flank speed during Republican, nonliberal administrations—Nixon's and Gerald Ford's. Why? Regardless of who won the presidency, Democratic liberals ended up highly influential in a Congress with a Democratic majority. They were entrenched in the courts. They were ensconced at the regulatory agencies. Young liberals were disproportionately represented at staff levels in the Congress, the courts, and the regulatory agencies. The media had a liberal tilt.

CARTER'S TEMPORARY U-TURN, 1976

For a time, in 1976, it seemed as if the Democratic party had understood the error of its ways. A cover of *New York* magazine in 1976 carried the headline, "The Dawn of an Old Era," and featured the smiling visage of Scoop Jackson, my hero. The piece called Jackson the frontrunner. And Scoop Jackson, it should be noted, was called "conservative" by many other Democrats.

But it wasn't to be Jackson's year. The prize went to the man who gave the nomination speech for Jackson in 1972 and someone who in the presidential primaries of 1976 ran to Jackson's conservative side in many ways: Governor Jimmy Carter of Georgia. We tend to forget, but Carter surfaced first as the anti-Washington candidate—a position alien to Scoop Jackson's New Deal view that government could often be a solution, not a problem.

As Carter opened his campaign early in 1976 he was almost totally unknown to American voters. That is obviously a problem for a candidate, but it can also be a blessing. There is sometimes a golden moment in political life, when a candidate begins to look like a contender but before the press begins exposing his frailties, and before the candidate's image is shaped in the public mind. In that brief and shining interval, the candidate can paint his own portrait, from his own palette, on fresh canvas, in colors of his own choosing.

When Carter's campaign gained overnight credibility with a stunning victory in the Iowa caucuses in February, Carter had that magic moment. And how did he paint himself? As a very religious man, a southerner, a military man, a farmer, a nuclear engineer, and a strong family man. Talk about values. His big pledge (in the aftermath of Watergate) was that he would never tell a lie (a prevarication the moment it was uttered.)

Carter won in Iowa and then took the New Hampshire primary, where he again stressed his anti-Washington theme. He made the cover of *Time* and *Newsweek*. Suddenly he was the front-runner and a national and international superstar.

The Massachusetts primary was next, on March 2, 1976. For a variety of political reasons, Scoop Jackson had decided not to run in either Iowa or New Hampshire. But Jackson shoved in his whole stack in Massachusetts, campaigning there at length, conducting telephone banks, and buying extensive and expensive television advertising. His campaign slogan was "Jackson Means Jobs." He had heavy union support. He opposed school busing to change racial balance, which had been imposed on the city of Boston by a federal judge.

The allegedly conservative Jackson solidly won the primary in the allegedly most liberal state of the union. But, interestingly, Jackson did not carry Boston, the major liberal city in that most liberal state. That prize went to a man who based almost his entire campaign on busing, the social issue that had plagued Boston. The winner in Boston, no liberal he, was—George Wallace!

Carter ran fourth. But one night during that Massachusetts campaign, I chatted with Carter's campaign press secretary, Jody Powell, over a drink at the Parker House in Boston. After a while he said, "Carter's going to beat Jackson because we're going to take votes from Jackson's well." That is just what happened.

Scoop Jackson was competitive in the North. After winning Massachusetts, he carried New York. He lost a crucial contest to Carter in Pennsylvania. Then, as the primaries moved to the South, any hope of Jackson's recouping was doomed. Carter, a Georgian, cleaned up. In a critical race he nosed out George Wallace in Florida (which Wallace had won in a landslide in 1972). Then, in blitzkrieg fashion, Carter mopped up the rest of the South.

There was an interesting and revealing detour in the Carter campaign. On April 8, 1976, Carter was interviewed by the *New York Daily News* about "scattered site" federally subsidized housing that could bring poor minority populations into middle-class neighborhoods. Carter said, in language that would cause a media firestorm, that he saw "nothing wrong with ethnic purity being maintained."

When the press pursued him on the ethnic purity issue in the course of the next few days, questioning whether Carter was playing a sneaky race card with Goebbels-like language, he defended his language thusly: "I have nothing against a community that's made up of people who are Polish or Czechoslovakian or French-Canadian or blacks who are trying to maintain the ethnic purity of their neighborhoods," and "I think it's good to maintain the homogeneity of neighborhoods if they've been established that way." Offering an example of such homogeneity he used phrases like "black intrusion" into white neighborhoods, of "alien groups" in neighborhoods, and of "injecting" a "diametrically opposite kind of family," or "a different kind of person," into such neighborhoods.

Carter complained about the press coverage of the ethnic purity flap, and also sounded a more liberal theme. He "would not permit discrimination against a family moving into the neighborhood," he would "never condone any sort of discrimination against, say, a black family, or any other family, from moving into that neighborhood," and he would rather "withdraw from the race" than use "racist" appeals to win.

(What would have happened if George Wallace, or Ronald Reagan, or George Bush had used the phrase "ethnic purity"? Or, for that matter, Pat Buchanan?)

The press regarded the ethnic purity flap as a great gaffe. Perhaps it was. But there is no evidence that it hurt Carter in the subsequent primaries. In fact, it probably solidly positioned him as a nonliberal on racial matters, not a bad place to be. My sense at the time was that Carter was screaming at the unfairness of being put in a politically profitable briar patch. He ended up getting it both ways: He had beaten the racial ogre of the Democratic party, George Wallace, in the South, with the heavy support of the black community. Then he sent out code to the "inner urban ethnic peripherals" that he wasn't going to countenance blockbusting.

Ultimately he apologized for using "ethnic purity" but still insisted that he "would not arbitrarily use federal force" to change the ethnic character of a neighborhood.

After a while the issue went away. Carter, with his anti-Washington, never-tell-a-lie, pro-family-military-southern-agrarian image, gathered enough delegates to be nominated without a fight at the New York convention in July 1976. After the love-in, Carter led President Gerald Ford in the polls by thirty-three points, 62 to 29 percent, a monumental lead, even after discounting the massive, and massively favorable, positive television exposure that Carter received during the convention.

But as Carter campaigned, he became more closely identified with the perception of the national (and liberal) Democratic party. Carter's lead shrank. In late August, after the Republican convention, his margin was fifteen points. In early October it was down to six.

Carter won the election, but by a mere two points, and for an interesting reason. Southern whites, the most socially conservative part of the electorate, voted their southernness, not their conservatism. He carried ten of eleven of the southern states of the Old Confederacy, something no other Democrat had done since 1944.

Carter was elected because he was (barely) able to cross the threshold and be seen as a social moderate.

But running for office and running a country are not the same. As president, Carter's governance was seen as liberal, certainly on the social issues. Here is what Dick Scammon and I wrote about Jimmy Carter in 1978, little more than a year after he took office, in the American Enterprise Institute's *Public Opinion Magazine*:

> But quite a different picture emerges when one examines the sub-cabinet and sub-sub-cabinet appointments. Perhaps unwittingly, perhaps wittingly, it is not moderate technocrats who most prominently populate these slots. Ideologues live there—ideologues from every one of the activist movements of the last decade. Environmentalists, consumerists, civil rights and women's activists, veterans of the peace movements have moved en masse from their ginger groups to large federal offices controlling massive budgets and armies of bureaucrats. A recent *Fortune* article names *sixty* high-level appointments made from activist groups; beneath them are a small army of their cohorts.
>
> ... The Democratic Party now has a large and militant flapping left wing, nurtured by activists who are veterans of a decade-and-a-half of civil rights, anti-war, environmental, consumerist, and feminist causes. In a party that is slightly to the left of the people, the activists are to the left

of the party and the apparatchiks are often to the left of the activists. They are part of the Carter coalition, they have moved into government and no one knows what their long-range effect will be. It is fair to ask, however, "upon what meat doth this our Caesar feed?"

Don't get confused: The quotation refers to Carter in 1978, not Clinton in 1994.

REAGAN DUMPS DEMS, 1980–1984

Carter had problems when he came up for reelection in 1980. The economy was in poor shape; interest rates were sky high; Americans were held hostage in Iran; Ted Kennedy had run primaries against him for not being sufficiently liberal. Worse still, he was attacked as too liberal and too permissive by the man who knew how to attack liberalism better than anyone else, before or since.

That candidate was Ronald Reagan. Recall how he ran. His five watchwords were work, family, neighborhood, peace, and freedom—which may be a better formulation of the values issue than any offered here. He talked, on rare occasion, about welfare queens. He trumpeted Milton Friedman's mantra that there is no free lunch. (Say, doesn't that sound like Clinton's "No More Something for Nothing"?)

And Reagan said (quite interestingly in the context of this book) that "Government is the problem, not the solution." Reagan's was a near-plenary case: he thought most big government was harmful in its essence. The brief presented here is less simple: At the least, *some* government is hurting us, grievously. At the least, we ought to try to change those aspects of government that are hurting us. If we agree on that, let's have an extended dialogue about whether big government is harmful by its nature.

Reagan won by ten points.

———

As Reagan's first term moved toward its end in 1984, the Democrats again moved willingly into the liberal trap that gave out something for nothing to victims, cause groups, and special interests. A few years later I interviewed Gary Hart, one of the major players in the 1984 primary season. Here is how he described what went on:

Candidates going around to constituency groups which included labor, included minorities, included environmentalists, included arms controllers, and having to take an oath to a litany of their demands.

Hart, in fact, tried rhetorically to run against those special interests in the Democratic party, although his opponents believed he was as much in their thrall as they were, if not more so.

And 1984 saw the first and formal political presence of Jesse Jackson, who had moved beyond his militant activist phase and presented himself as a presidential candidate. There is something quite revealing about Jesse Jackson and the 1984 campaign. There were about twenty separate public debates during the 1984 election season and seven other major candidates in the race: Walter Mondale, John Glenn, Ernest Hollings, George McGovern, Gary Hart, Alan Cranston, and Reuben Askew. All were, or had been, elected office-holders, ranging from moderate, to moderate liberal, to liberal, to quite liberal.

Jackson, who had never been elected to anything, ran in 1984 from a fairly radical position, in terms of both optics and substance. He was supported by the antiwhite, anti-Semitic minister of the Nation of Islam, Louis Farrakhan; he went to Cuba and saluted the communist dictator, saying, "Viva Castro"; he hugged the PLO terrorist Yassir Arafat; he got snarled in an apparently anti-Semitic episode ("Hymietown" was what he called New York City); he called for a massive defense cut. His economic and international views came close to socialism in many respects. His views on the values issues were almost without exception the most unpopular ones available: pro–increased welfare, pro-quotas, pro-busing, pro–set-asides, and anti–death penalty.

In the course of those twenty-odd public debates, not one Democrat candidate directly and publicly disagreed with Jesse Jackson. (When you talked to them privately, it was clear they did disagree with him.) There were, of course, political reasons for this: Jackson wasn't going to win so why antagonize him? Jackson was black, and who needs a race fight? Jackson's delegates might come in handy in the convention, Jackson could help get the black vote in the general election, and so on, and on.

Against this, of course, was a quaint notion: If voters saw that Democrats didn't disagree with Jackson, might they not think that they were cowed by him, and that perhaps they might well partially agree with him?

The eventual nominee, Walter Mondale, is a fine man and an able public servant, but he put yet another nail in the Democratic coffin. Feminist groups demanded that he choose a woman for his vice-presidential nominee. He did. She was Geraldine Ferraro, a three-term congresswoman, quite able, quite decent, but by no stretch of the imagination credentialed to be vice president by any conventional standard. She said to me in a television interview:

> If I were not a woman I would not have been the candidate. . . . Because my experience—is obviously—as a third term member of Congress. . . . I mean how many third term members of Congress are on the national ticket? I would not have even been considered if I were not a woman . . . if I were Gerald Ferraro from New York. . . . I'm realistic and honest enough to admit that.

The message Mondale sent was clear: Merit didn't matter most.

Perhaps the most pathetic political sight I have seen was the final night of the San Francisco convention in July 1984. Democrats passed out an estimated 30,000 plastic American flags. On cue, everyone in the Moscone Convention Center flapped their little plastic flag.

The message, as I sensed it, was, "Yes, America, we know you have perceived us as cavalier about patriotism, work, religion, crime, and discipline, but, really, America, we're Americans too, and we really share your values." They believed that, and for good reason. It was true. Alas, they could neither campaign nor govern that way. Such has been the power of the liberal special interest constituencies.

So completely had Democrats dug themselves into a hole that Reagan didn't even have to do much attacking. Surrogates could drive home the point. Former Democrat, former Hubert Humphrey brain truster, U.N. ambassador Jeane J. Kirkpatrick, addressed the Republican convention in Dallas in prime time and excoriated the "San Fran-cisco Democrats." Speaking in a foreign policy context, she said that Democrats "always blame America first."

But "blame America first" can be seen in a context beyond foreign policy. If there is a sick society and it is creating victims, who of course need greater entitlement, then it is intellectually consistent to blame America first about our domestic situation. There are at least two problems with that view: most Americans didn't believe it was true, and it is a political loser.

Reagan floated serenely above the Democrats' self-inflicted bruise, the sort of injury that comes from continually banging a head into a stone wall. Not only had Mondale been unable to dodge the values bullet, he impaled himself on another Democratic bugaboo: higher taxes. (Mondale's famous convention quotation: "Mr. Reagan will raise taxes, and so will I. He won't tell you. I just did.")

Higher taxes is not a great issue for any politician. (Flash!) It is a particularly bad issue for Democrats, who are known as tax-and-spenders. But taxes are not a single bullet theory of politics. Taxes are important, but they are seen by voters in a context of other issues, very much including the social ones, and particularly in the context of *how the tax money is spent*. When government programs are seen to be not only expensive, not only wasteful, but also *harmful*, then taxes hit vot-ers several times: once when their dollar leaves their pocket to go to Washington and once again when it comes back home in a way that hurts.

Reagan beat Mondale in 1984 by 59 to 41 percent, right up there in landslide country. The theme, that values matter most, was strong.

BUSH CAPTURES THE ISSUE

Perhaps the quintessential values issue candidacy of our time was George Bush's in 1988. Of course, as was their habit, the Democrats presented him with a setup. Their Atlanta convention, which nomi-nated Michael Dukakis, was designed to show harmony. It displayed plenty of that. But harmony on what theme? All year long, once again, no Democrat running for the presidency dared to criticize second-place finisher Jesse Jackson. In Atlanta, Reverend Jackson was lionized and was frequently proclaimed to be "the conscience of the Democratic party."

With the ball properly teed up, Bush picked up his driver. To begin, he didn't blame America first; he didn't think it was a sick society. In fact, he reveled in America:

> This is America: the Knights of Columbus, the Grange, Hadassah, the Disabled American Veterans, the Order of AHEPA, the Business and Professional Women of America, the union hall, the Bible study group, LULAC,* "Holy Name"—a brilliant diversity spread like stars, like a thousand points of light in a broad and peaceful sky.

Not a victim in a carload. These were Americans helping America. And, as could have been predicted, Bush drilled home the social issues. The liberal media said that the theme was demagogic, but that is a charge that should be examined more closely. It bears much relevance to the thesis of this book.

Consider three prominent examples from the 1988 race: (1) the ACLU, (2) the pledge of allegiance, and (3) Willie Horton.

ACLU—the American Civil Liberties Union

The Democratic nominee, Governor Michael Dukakis, from liberal Massachusetts, said, rather proudly, that he was "a card-carrying member of the ACLU." Now, readers may agree or disagree with the positions put forth over recent years by the ACLU, but they should also accept that the ACLU deals with issues of serious public policy, worthy of political discourse. Moreover, the ACLU, almost by definition, is in the business of defending minority rights. Politicians are in the business of assembling majorities.

It is the ACLU that pushes the idea that a Christmas creche or a Hanukkah menorah on a public square is unconstitutional, that voluntary/silent/nonsectarian prayer in public school is unconstitutional, that the death penalty qualifies as cruel and unusual punishment, that

---

* AHEPA stands for the American Hellenic Educational Progressive Association; LULAC is the League of United Latin American Citizens.

violent criminals deserve a better break from both the courts and the police, that use of marijuana is constitutionally protected, that suicide should be legal, that homosexuality should not be taken into account in a child custody hearing, that the distribution of child pornography should be free of state interference, that metal detectors at airports are unconstitutional, that the word "God" should not be in the pledge of allegiance, and so on. They do sort of specialize in sociocultural matters.

Isn't it legitimate for one candidate to nail another who proudly announces his membership in an organization with such a public policy agenda. If not, why not?

Pledge/Flag

While governor, Dukakis had vetoed a bill stipulating that Massachusetts students would begin each school day by reciting the pledge of allegiance. Dukakis didn't say he opposed the pledge, nor did he say he supported it, only that he vetoed the law because he believed the state courts would not uphold it. Maybe so.

But the pledge is something special. While of relatively recent vintage (written in 1892, appearing first in the magazine *Youth's Companion*), it is has become the ultimate symbol of American patriotism. And politics deals in symbols as well as substance. Symbols often drive substance.

Transnational opinion polls show clearly that among the modern industrial democracies, Americans are by far the most patriotic people. For twenty years Americans had been served up a bunch of liberal blame-America stuff, including the peace movement flying the flag upside down. They were sick of it.

Bush, of course, made the pledge an issue and put an exclamation point on it by visiting a flag factory in New Jersey. Demagoguery? Why? Because it is not a real issue? Readers: It is voters who decide what real issues are, in the context of the times. They thought it was real. So did I.

Willie Horton

This was the most interesting one. Republicans said Horton showed how far Democrats and liberals had strayed from understanding the potency of the crime issue. For Democrats, Horton showed how mean-spirited and demagogic the Republicans were, and how, when they chose, they would "play the race card."

Recall the facts: Horton was a convicted murderer, serving a life sentence. His sentence allowed no possibility of parole. Notwithstanding the fact that such a no-parole prisoner had little incentive to return, Horton was given a series of weekend furloughs. On one of them, he traveled to Maryland, where he raped a woman and assaulted her husband. Horton is a black man.

Republicans attacked. Two different television commercials were aired, a harsh one sponsored by an independent committee (allegedly without the knowledge or approval of the Bush campaign) and a somewhat gentler one by the Bush campaign itself.

Dukakis, and the Democrats, then attempted to explain Willie Horton. Furloughs were fine, they said. It was good prison policy. Lots of states had such policies, including California under a governor named Reagan. (But there was a crucial distinction: No other state offered furloughs for lifers with no potential for parole.) Democrats denounced the Bush campaign for "injecting race into the campaign," which they deemed to be divisive and cynical.

The Horton-crime and the Horton-race issues deserve some separate thought. "Willie Horton" was a perfectly valid metaphor for how far social issue Democrats had moved from common sense on the issue of criminality. It was a metaphor, too, for how public policy affects the crime rate and private lives: The assaulted couple were direct victims of a policy decision by an elected legislature.

The race issue is more complex. The Horton hot button, interestingly enough, was first used against Dukakis by Senator Albert Gore when he ran in the New York State primary in April 1988. When questioned about it later—when Bush was accused of demagoguery on the issue—Gore said, in effect, that he didn't know Horton was black. Some liberals said that was different, Gore had a good civil rights record.

Therefore what? Nonliberals can't touch the issue? Do blacks get a free pass on crime, even though the violent crime rate among blacks is five times higher than the white rate, and most of the victims of black crime are other blacks, and it is black inner-city neighborhoods that are being made into free-fire zones? Would it have been all right to run the Horton ads, but without showing the Horton picture? (The independent committee commercial did show Horton's picture. The Bush campaign ads, running after the independent committee spots had aired, did not.)

I think the Horton issue, with photograph, was legitimate. If he had been white and looked like a thug—which Horton did—his photograph would have been used.

Horton turned out to be even more important than it seemed in 1988. In some ways, Horton, or Hortonism, or the values issue, ended up helping defeat not one but two candidates for president: Michael Dukakis in 1988 and George Bush in 1992.

After the Democratic convention in Atlanta in July 1988, Dukakis was leading Bush in the polls by seventeen percentage points. That was a solid lead, even though pumped up by the bounce from the convention. The Republicans unsheathed the values issue. Bush closed the gap, moved ahead, and won moderately, 54 percent to 46 percent, as befits a moderate. The theme grew: It could help moderates, too.

The most surprising aspect of the 1988 campaign was that the Dukakis Democrats were surprised by the nature of the Republican campaign. Anyone with a whit of political common sense knew it was coming. About how Bush was hurt by Horton—we shall soon return to Houston and the convention of 1992.

Chapter 3

1992: DEMOCRATS
GET THE MESSAGE,
REPUBLICANS LOSE IT

Remember 1992. It could have been the beginning of the beginning of a new Democratic party.

Slowly, it seemed, Democrats—even some liberals, even on some of the most tender issues—began to get the idea. For a portrait of a party in change, consider this March 1992 statement from a liberal senator, John Kerry of Massachusetts:

> But there is a negative side and we can no longer simply will away the growing consensus of perception within America's white majority. We must be willing to acknowledge publicly what we know to be true: —that just as the benefits to America of affirmative action cannot be denied neither can the costs. . . . By that failure, we send a message to many of those who feel alienated or abandoned by their government that we simply don't care about them, and that we don't realize that it is they, far more than we, who have borne the burden of compliance to the law. The truth is that affirmative action has kept America thinking in racial terms and as Yale Law professor Stephen Carter has recently and so provocatively

asked: "is it a good thing, is it a safe thing, to encourage America to think in racial terms?"

Among those Democrats who understood very clearly what had happened to his party in 1988, and what had happened before that, was Governor Bill Clinton of Arkansas.

Starting with his announcement speech in the fall of 1991, then drummed upon in his stump speeches, echoed in the Democratic platform, reinforced with television commercials, and restated in the presidential debates, Clinton made certain points, again and again:

- That he was a "different Democrat," that neither liberalism nor conservatism was working, that we needed a "third way" in order to "reinvent government," and that both parties were "brain dead."
- That government programs had to be based on "reciprocity" honoring those who "played by the rules," which meant "No More Something for Nothing," an astonishing line coming from a Democrat with solid ties to liberal Democrats.
- That he believed America should "end welfare as we know it."
- That he believed that an erosion of "personal responsibility" was at the root of so many of our national problems.

As the campaign wound on, other things became known about Clinton. He believed in the death penalty. During the primary season he twice returned to Arkansas to hear, and deny, last-minute pleas for clemency in capital cases. One concerned the death sentence for Rickey Ray Rector, who was black and mentally impaired. In 1988 Michael Dukakis had told a national television audience that he would not seek a death penalty for a criminal even if that criminal had raped and murdered his wife, Kitty. In 1992 Clinton flew home to (in effect) personally wield the syringe that would end Rickey Ray Rector's life by lethal injection.

Unlike earlier Democrats, Clinton understood that catering to the whims of Jesse Jackson was politically suicidal. In May 1991 the Democratic Leadership Council, whose chairman was Governor Bill Clinton, met in Cleveland and purposefully and publicly broke an earlier precedent: they did not invite Jackson to speak. That gained positive national publicity for the DLC.

In June 1992 Clinton appeared at the Rainbow Coalition meeting in Washington, D.C., and denounced rap singer Sister Souljah for suggesting that blacks should start killing whites rather than blacks. Reverend Jackson thought Clinton's denunciation in poor taste. Clinton, in effect, told Jackson to stuff it. That too gained positive national publicity for Bill Clinton.

Of the five Democrats who entered the primaries, Clinton was the only one to stress the social issues, although former Sen. Paul Tsongas ran to his conservative side on economic issues. In fact, Clinton had intended to run an even harder-line campaign, to distinguish himself better from the liberal positions of Governor Mario Cuomo, whom he had assumed would be his principal opponent. (Cuomo never entered the fray in 1992.)

Clinton amassed enough delegates for the nomination. As a perceived southern moderate he was expected to choose a northern liberal as his vice-presidential running mate. Instead, he tapped another perceived southern moderate, ironically the man who raised the Willie Horton issue first, Senator Al Gore. He is a sensible man, who seems to have briefly gone bonkers on some environmental matters, as seen in his book *Earth in the Balance*. ("Owls Matter Most?")

The 1992 Democratic Convention in New York was not a perfect work of art, but it worked perfectly. The idea was to get across one message: The Democrats had changed; no longer were they cause group–special interest liberals; no longer were they preaching guilt to assuage victims; no longer would they be defenseless on social and cultural issues; no longer would they be vulnerable on values. No more. They were moderates!

In a departure from practice, the Clinton convention managers offered not one but three keynote addresses.

The magisterial Barbara Jordan, who can make a McDonald's menu sound like Shakespeare, opened up the proceedings and delivered the goods. She denounced white racism *and* black racism. She decried separatism. She censured the doctrine of political correctness, which endorses the ideas of victimhood, entitlement, and hyper-multiculturalism.

Senator Bill Bradley of New Jersey took the podium next. He tried some silly convention rhetoric: George Bush, he said, as a refrain, "waffled, wiggled and wavered." But when he got serious, he got quite serious. He spoke to the theme enunciated by the black poet Langston Hughes: "Let America be America again. Let it be the dream it used to be." Bradley's eloquent plea for traditional pluralism and upward mobility sounded like this:

It is sometimes said that Americans lack a tragic sense of life. It would be more correct to say that Americans are not content to let tragedy have the last word. The United States is history's greatest experiment in the elimination of despair. It was built on the belief that though there are many men, women and children among us who have been victims of injustice, we are not a nation of victims; built on the belief that we are free men and women who cannot be reduced to our social and economic circumstances, but can alter those circumstances; built on the belief that scars do heal, that change is possible, and that the present can free itself from the grip of the past; built on the belief that adversity is not fate but a dare, a challenge, an opportunity to show that all of us—all races, genders, ethnicities, and religions—can live together, strive together, work together, prosper together, and achieve a better America, achieve a better world.

Let America be America again. Let it be the dream it used to be.

Let America be the dream it can be.

The keynote address of Governor Zell Miller of Georgia reminded Americans that real Democrats are not limousine liberals:

My father—a teacher—died when I was two weeks old, leaving a young widow with two small children.

But with my mother's faith in God—and Mr. Roosevelt's voice on the radio—we kept going.

After my father's death, my mother with her own hands cleared a small piece of rugged land.

Every day she waded into a neighbor's cold mountain creek, carrying out thousands of smooth stones to build a house.

I grew up watching my mother complete that house from the rocks she'd lifted from the creek and cement she mixed in a wheelbarrow—cement that today still bears her handprints.

Her son bears her handprints, too.

She pressed her pride and her hopes and her dreams deep into my soul.

So, you see, I know what Dan Quayle means when he says it's best for children to have two parents. You bet it is. And it would be nice for them to have trust funds, too.

(Cheap shots at Dan Quayle are permitted at Democratic political conventions if the language is so artful.)

The platform itself was a solid document, reiterating much of what Clinton had said in his announcement speech, and during his campaign. Here are some excerpts, not standard Democratic fare.

We honor business as a noble endeavor.

Governments don't raise children, people do. People who bring children into this world have a responsibility to care for them and give them values, motivation and discipline.

Welfare should be a second chance, not a way of life. . . . No one who is able to work can stay on welfare forever.

The simplest and most direct way to restore order in our cities is to put more police on the streets.

The United States must be prepared to use military force decisively when necessary to defend our vital interests.

We reject both the do-nothing government . . . as well as the big government theory. . . . Instead we offer a third way.

Hmm . . . A third way. One need not be a rocket scientist or a political scientist to understand that the concept of a third way, when pushed forth by a party that had produced one of the earlier two ways, is a rejection of existing tradition. *The Democrats were saying that they would change.*

What was Clinton up to in that platform? He rebuked the social science radicalism that has suffused the modern Democratic party. He cut down the arrogance and sanctimony that went with it. That allowed him to try and marry earthy, commonsense American values to what he (not me) believes to be the redeeming aspects of European-style social democracy.

But do platforms matter? One school of thought says platforms contain glittering generalities, absurd alarmism, painless pieties, boring bromides, and kooky contradictions (all of which were present in the Democratic document, mixed in with some standard liberal goo). When the platform draft was issued, many experts reminded us that presidential candidates are not bound by platforms, and neither is the Congress. And so, it was said, ignore it.

But there is another view, and I share it: Platforms count. I have served twice on the Democratic party platform-drafting subcommittee, and I can tell you that at the very least platforms tell you what the presidential candidate wants you to believe.

Bill Clinton wanted Americans to believe that he knew the Democratic party had been wrong and that it would be different under his stewardship. That Clinton ran on such a platform, and won on it, didn't mean that it would happen. But would it be plausible that any serious change in direction could happen in a party that is too afraid of its constituencies even to speak the right words?

We saw in New York that candidates who wanted to be seen as Different Democrats could make speeches and platforms about a values-driven government. Only later would we find out whether they would have the courage, commitment, and savvy to take the fight to the most hostile terrain imaginable, a Democratically controlled Congress.

There was also plenty at the Democratic convention that remained troubling. There was the standard salute to victimology personified by glorified appearances of professional victims: gays, lesbians, poor people, the homeless, minorities, and single parents. There was the repeated statement that Democrats are "the party of women." That went generally uncriticized, but one must ask how would it have been regarded if Republicans bragged that they are "the party of men."

America could have managed without the lectures on family values from—who?—Senator Ted Kennedy and Representative Joseph P. Kennedy, Jr.! Jesse Jackson's statement that Dan Quayle was like the baby-killing King Herod was plain ugly. The statement by AIDS activists that Ronald Reagan killed people with AIDS was unconscionable—more so than anything we would hear a month later at the Republican convention in Houston. Clinton's let-it-all-hang-out psychobabble about how his drunken stepfather, lacking self-esteem, beat up his mother was icky.

The idea that Governor Bob Casey of Pennsylvania, who is pro-life, was not able to get a time to speak at the Democratic convention was outrageous. Equally outrageous was that the press did not make an issue of his muzzling. (I say this as a prochoice supporter.) But in 1992 the mainstream press did not seem prepared to acknowledge that there are two sides to the abortion debate.

There was also enough liberalism in the platform for Jesse Jackson to note that it contained so many of the views he had championed over the years: big investments in the cities, D.C. statehood, national health care, defense cuts, "motor voter" registration, gay rights, and so on.

Still, by the end of the Democratic convention in 1992, two things were quite clear:

1. Bill Clinton, more than any other recent Democratic presidential candidate, clearly understood the nature of the values issue in America, and he had constructed formidable defenses against a standard Republican attack on these issues.
2. His party, upon whose support he depended, was less than wholly convinced or disciplined on these issues.

It seemed obvious how the Republicans would campaign against that combination. First, they would say Clinton doesn't really mean it; he's just putting it on for show. And then they would say, even if by chance he does mean it, his party doesn't support it, and the liberal Congress and the liberal interest groups will force him to bend to their will.

That is what one expected to hear in Houston, at the Republican National Convention, in August 1992. It is what one expected during the Republican campaign after Houston. It's not what happened.

We turn now to the Republican side of the political coin. Something very important went on at the Houston convention: attempted ideocide. An idea was almost murdered, or was almost aborted, or contracted a severe disease, or all of the above.

As a result, America suffered. We ended up without the debate we deserved in 1992. We ended up with only a sideways glance at our serious problems instead of a square look in the eye. We ended up with half an agenda for change. In short, we ended up without the full blessings that our hurly-burly, sometimes ugly, national elections can often provide.

Luckily, unlike homicide, the crime of ideocide is not a permanent matter. It occurs, after all, in the arena of politics and public affairs, an arena where near-death experiences occur all the time.

The almost-murdered idea concerned values (or the cultural issues or the social issues). It was unfortunately phrased in Houston, surfacing as "family values."

The actual formulation was thought up on an airplane flight by a secretary of one of the GOP platform officials. She reported her brainstorm when she returned to the office. As happens, a small idea grew, took root, spread, and emerged full-blown.

Family Values became the stated theme for the third night (Wednesday) of the Republican National Convention. (The themes for the other nights were Foreign Affairs, The Economy, and Leadership.) But by Sunday evening August 16, the night *prior* to the opening of the Republican convention, Family Values was already dead meat, an idea destined for full-time trashing. The swarm of 15,000 journalists covering the convention were already in a classic media mode, a manner of ritual group behavior memorialized in the title of political scientist Larry Sabato's book, *Feeding Frenzy*.

How this came to happen is worth some speculation. It gives a sense of the playing field as it existed in Houston and offers some hints about the possible nature of the current playing field, for 1996 and beyond.

During the week preceding their convention, the Republican party had held platform hearings in Houston. The word went out: the platform "had been captured by the religious right," it was a "right-wing platform," and "the right wingers had taken over the party."

Now, the first thing to be said about the 1992 Republican platform is that it is a long document. Long platforms are almost always a political mistake. Nitpickers have more nits to pick at. Reporters often don't read it and often end up relying on the word of partisans.

I do not believe many reporters actually read the 133-page Republican document. The attacks always characterized the platform as right wing, but with the exception of the plank regarding abortion, almost no specifics were offered with such characterizations, and when any were put forth, they were typically wrong or silly.

It was said, for example, that the platform endorsed Pat Buchanan's anti-immigration views, including his idea that America ought to build a high fence along the Mexican border. In fact, the platform goes out of its way to endorse and salute continued *legal* immigration:

[America] accepts immigrants and is enriched by their determination and values.

Regarding *illegal* immigration, the platform was far more detailed, resembling the old laundry list sort of document:

Illegal immigration . . . undermines the integrity of border communities and already crowded urban neighborhoods. We will build on the announced strengthening of the Border Patrol to better coordinate interdiction of illegal entrants through greater cross-border cooperation. Specifically, . . . we will equip the Border Patrol with the tools, technologies, and structures necessary to secure the border.

Exactly what is the problem with that? I am a pro-immigration superhawk. That is language I could endorse without blinking an eye.

But Bay Buchanan, the failed candidate's sister and political campaign chairman, was at the Houston platform hearings running spin control for the Buchananistas. As soon as the plank was voted upon, with the word "structures" in it, she was briefing the press, declaring victory for Pat's proposed fence. "Fence," "structure": What's the difference? It was all code for Brother Pat's program, she intimated, and many journalists swallowed it whole.

Of course, regarding the key broad areas where Buchanan disagreed with President Bush—protectionism, isolationism, nativism—the platform rejected the Buchanan views with quite remarkable vigor. Without doubt the GOP platform is a free trade, internationalist, pluralist document.

To be sure, in the great abortion debate, the Republican platform does endorse "life" over "choice." I am prochoice and always have been. But it is absurd to make the case that "life" is right wing. Wouldn't it then be fair to characterize "choice" as left wing?

It was said that the Republicans showed their repressive tendencies by not allowing the abortion plank to be brought to a floor fight for an open argument and a vote. It is true that the plank was not brought to the floor for debate. Petitions from a majority of delegates from five states are necessary in the platform committee to bring an issue to the convention for a floor fight. Such majorities were not forthcoming in Houston.

But there was no debate about abortion at the Democratic convention for just the same reason. I was at the Democratic Platform Committee meeting at the Mayflower Hotel in June 1992. And in an unclose vote, not enough *pro-life* delegates cast their ballot to put the abortion issue before the convention. At the Houston convention the Republicans at least allowed speakers to make prochoice statements during their general remarks, which is not something the Democrats permitted pro-lifers to do in New York.

In Houston, the press was spun a mighty spin. The GOP prochoice leaders, among them Ann Stone and Mary Crisp, had indicated during the runup to the platform hearings that the abortion plank stood a good chance to be amended, eliminated, or toned down. The prochoice forces made their case to the platform committee—and lost decisively in a fair fight. Whereupon, in keeping with time-honored political tradition, Stone, Crisp and others went to the press claiming that the verdict was "unfair" and "discriminatory," that they had been "shut out," and that they faced a "closed door."

In any event, one central fact was underemphasized in the debate about abortion: The 1992 plank was just about identical to ones in 1988 and 1984 and very close substantively to the one in 1980. If the antiabortion plank made the GOP a right-wing party of religious zealots, why didn't we hear much about it in 1988, 1984, and 1980?

Beyond abortion, I don't find much that can be fairly characterized as right wing in the platform. I made that statement on a radio call-in show shortly after the convention, and an outraged caller said that the platform was "fascist." He said that the "prayer in the school" plank proved it.

The options now in play on that matter concern "silent prayer," "voluntary prayer," and "nonsectarian prayer." Are those ideas such a big deal in a country with "In God We Trust" on its coins? With a chaplain to open the proceedings of the U.S. Senate? With mandated prayer in school permitted for most of the course of American history? In a country where the president closes his inaugural address, "God bless you" (Bill Clinton, 1993)? That's fascism?

The Republican platform did not even come out against the funding for the National Endowment for the Arts. It did favor discretion in grant giving at the NEA. Just imagine: Those crazy right-wingers did not think that tax dollars should be used to fund *Piss Christ!* Or a photo of Robert Mapplethorpe's bull whip in his own rectum! Nor do I, and I believe I am prepared to go almost to the last mile against censorship. But what was at work in the great NEA contretemps of 1989–1991 confused the ideas of censorship and sponsorship. We should not censor Mapplethorpe's bull whip, but why fund him? Why give government funding to anti-Christian paintings? Does anyone think that anti-Semitic, antiblack, misogynic, homophobic, or pro-Nazi paintings could get funded?

In my judgment the so-called arts community made a major error in the early 1990s when it went to the wall on the issue of "anything goes" at the NEA. Ultimately (and wisely) they backed down.

Beyond that there is not much of a disputatious nature in the Republican platform. It is hard to believe, but it calls for diversity, inclusion, internationalism, tolerance, pluralism, and free trade. It is more pro–free trade in emphasis than the Democratic platform. It calls for a reform of the welfare program, but so does the Democratic platform. It calls for America "to fight and win a new conservative war on poverty." It says America is made stronger by immigration.

The immigration-diversity issue is particularly interesting. The carefully designed cover of the Republican platform has a photograph of an awestruck immigrant family, circa 1900, arriving on a ship and gazing at the Statue of Liberty. It is clearly a family of European origin but not from northwestern Europe.* That is not a conservative image, not in a party, or a country, that once had non-Anglo anti-immigration deeply embedded in its political inventory.

Moreover, the photographs in the platform book are instructive: Asian faces, Hispanic face, black faces, black and white children playing together, even some occasional WASPs. The optics of the platform make it look like a book published by the League of Women Voters or Common Cause. Exclusive? No matter. The word was out: It was a right-wing platform, the product of a right-wing takeover, run by religious zealots.

Against that background, the events of Monday evening began to unfold. There were three prime-time major speeches scheduled. The first one was by Condoleeza Rice, an elegant young black woman, a former Kremlinologist on President Bush's National Security Council staff. Dr. Rice gave a brilliant address, presenting an incisive defense of America's (and Bush's) assertive internationalism—just what Pat Buchanan had been campaigning against. She said:

> Today, as yesterday, power in the international system comes from permanent engagement in it. To turn inward now would be sheer folly. . . . In 1989, I was privileged to stand in Gdansk, Poland, when President Bush addressed 70,000 Polish citizens. I can still hear them chanting "Bush, Bush, Bush, freedom, freedom, freedom." How proud I was to work for

---

* Says Bill Gribben, editor in chief of the platform, "After all these years, I finally got my Czech grandparents into the party."

George Bush! How proud I was to be an American! Through their eyes, we see that much of America's greatness is in her generosity, the willingness to look beyond our shores to make the cause of others our own.

The three major networks did not air Rice's prime-time speech. (It was shown, live, only by C-Span, CNN, and PBS.) Amazingly, there was almost no press coverage of it the next day. Too bad. A black, female internationalist in prime time, just before Pat Buchanan; might that have been an attempt to send a message?

The third of the three speeches was Ronald Reagan's, the Republican party's greatest vote getter. The Gipper had the ability to say tough things in a gentle way. Talking about the Democratic convention, he said:

They put on quite a production in New York a few weeks ago. You might even call it slick. A stone's throw from Broadway, and how appropriate. Over and over they told us they were not the party they were. They kept telling us with a straight face that they're for family values, they're for a strong America. They're for less intrusive government.

And they call me an actor!

And, in the middle of the Rice-Reagan sandwich, appeared Pat Buchanan.

———

There were thirty-nine Republican primary elections in 1992. Buchanan was on the ballot in thirty-six of them. He lost all thirty-six. His high-water mark was in his first campaign, in New Hampshire on February 18, where he lost to Bush by 53 to 37 percent, a 16-point spread. Under normal conditions this could be characterized as a landslide, or a near landslide.

Buchanan, however, was jubilant after New Hampshire. He had challenged a sitting president. He had made his case—tinged with nativism, isolationism, and protectionism. He had captured the media spotlight. He had surfaced a constituency—not a huge one, but there.

He said it was just the beginning; just wait until the message gets out; just wait until the Buchanan Brigades go into high gear.

The Buchanan message did get out. And from New Hampshire onward, Buchanan went downhill. On March 3, he lost by thirty-seven percentage points in Colorado, but that was understandable because he was concentrating on Georgia. He lost Georgia by twenty-nine points. He also lost Maryland by forty points and South Carolina, another target state, by forty-one.

Then on Super Tuesday, March 10, the Buchanan campaign suffered one of the starkest collapses in the history of recent American primaries. He lost Florida (by thirty-six percentage points), Louisiana (by thirty-five points), Massachusetts (by thirty-six points), Mississippi (by fifty-six points), and a state he devoted much time and energy to, Texas, by forty-six percentage points, 70 to 24 percent.

After Super Tuesday, Buchanan pretty well packed it in, but he promised one more fight, in troubled California, the last big primary and a state in a deep economic recession, with a boiling immigration issue. California was said to be ideal for Buchanan's message. Bush beat him there by forty-seven points.

This was not a great showing. As Eugene McCarthy once remarked in an era prior to the advent of political correctness, a candidate gets about fifteen percentage points from palsied voters hitting the wrong levers in the voting booth. Bush, coming off his glory highs of the Gulf War, was sinking rapidly in the popularity polls, writhing in what seemed to be a recession, unsure whether to campaign against Buchanan or ignore him. Bush had alienated many conservative Republicans who were steamed because he had broken his tax pledge, endorsed what they regarded as a quota bill, dithered about the National Endowment for the Arts, and promoted some big government programs like the Americans with Disabilities Act.

Clearly, Buchanan got much of his vote as a catch-all protest against Bush. Still, after New Hampshire, Buchanan lost in huge landslides, which the press chose to cover as showing Bush's weakness, rather than Buchanan's. The media case was that a sitting president should get almost all the votes in a primary. But that is not what happened in 1980 when Edward Kennedy challenged Jimmy Carter, and it is not likely what would have happened had Lyndon Johnson chosen to engage in 1968. In 1972 a then-popular Richard Nixon was challenged in the New Hampshire primaries by Congressmen John Ashbrook and Paul McCloskey, who (combined) got almost 30 percent of the votes cast.

Still, Buchanan did get nearly 3 million votes in the course of a long and sometimes bitter campaign. His apparent price for endorsing the Bush-Quayle ticket at the Houston convention was a quite conventional one: a prime-time slot on the convention program.

Offering goodie bags to defeated candidates is traditional political practice. The defeated candidate is supposed to endorse the winning candidate and bring his followers into the big tent. To prevent any slipups, the speaker's remarks are usually reviewed by party officials.

The Republicans clearly made a mistake by scheduling Buchanan on opening night, notwithstanding the Rice-Reagan sandwich. Buchanan's speech ran long, cutting into Ronald Reagan's prime-time window, which displeased the Gipper, who was looking nervously at his watch offstage.

Buchanan's speech was vetted in advance by Rich Bond, chairman of the Republican National Committee. It was approved in part because the speech—in Buchanan's terms—was on the moderate side. He simply did not bring up most of his red-meat issues. There was no talk about immigration. He did not sound his isolationist trumpet. He did not trash the North American Free Trade Agreement; nor did he sound his other protectionist themes. He barely mentioned blasphemy and pornography at the NEA.

But even in a nonconfrontational mode, Buchanan can still be too harsh:

My friends, this election is about much more than who gets what. It is about who we are. It is about what we believe, it is about what we stand for as Americans. There is a religious war going on in our country for the soul of America. It is a cultural war, as critical to the kind of nation we will one day be—as was the Cold War itself. And in that struggle for the soul of America, Clinton and Clinton are on the other side, and George Bush is on our side. And so, we have to come home—and stand beside him.

Buchanan was talking about something real when he used the terms "religious war" and "cultural war." There has indeed been a divisive struggle in America, between the secular and the religious, between the traditional and the hypermodern (condoms versus abstinence, prayer in the schools, gay activists disrupting prayer at St. Patrick's Cathedral, and so on). Some of this book is about that. There are times when that battle has taken on harsh aspects and harsh tones, on both sides of the divide.

But "religious war" and "cultural war" is what Europeans have, not Americans. "War" is an overstatement of what is going on in the United States, culturally or religiously. Buchanan is one of the premier speechwriters of our time. He could have made his points and kept the language in bounds. He had already been in the soup for that kind of insensitivity. Whatever he gets, I thought at the time, serves him right.

What I did not expect was the transference of Buchanan's views to the Republican party. But transferred they were, in a way that would resonate for a long time. To the press pack Buchanan's harshness became a symbol of the 1992 Republican party. The shrewd and active Clinton campaign was happy to throw logs on the fire.

After the Buchanan speech, for example, it was said that Republicans were into an orgy of gay bashing. But what actually did Buchanan say? He quoted Bob Hattoy, a homosexual with AIDS, who spoke at the Democratic convention and said, quite accurately, that "Bill Clinton and Al Gore represent the most pro-lesbian and pro-gay ticket in history."

———

What was quite amazing in 1992 about the issue of homosexuality was not that it was raised by Buchanan in Houston but that it remained almost unchallenged during the whole campaign.

The issue had long before graduated from an argument about nondiscrimination to one also dealing very directly with other quite specific aspects of public policy. Many gay activists, for example, wanted it taught and stressed in public schools that homosexuality is a value-neutral alternative lifestyle. One can agree with that, or disagree with that. But it is a public policy issue, dealing with the curriculum of public schools, taught to the children of voters and taxpayers. Disagreeing with the gay activist view should not brand one either a demagogue or a homophobe.

The Republicans should have been ready to deal with the issue. Back in December 1991 the Human Rights Campaign Fund, the biggest gay political action group, sent a questionnaire to all the Democratic candidates for president. One question was:

> As president, will you sign an executive order ending the Department of Defense's policy excluding qualified men and women from the armed forces simply because they are gay or lesbian?

Candidate Bill Clinton's answer was straight to the point and phrased in the lingo of gay activists:

> Yes, I believe patriotic Americans should have the right to serve the country as a member of the armed forces, without regard to sexual or affectional orientation.

If there was doubt that the politics of affectional orientation would be public and that it was about legitimate public policy, not gay bashing, that should have changed on May 18, 1992. It was on that evening, *three months before* the Republican convention in Houston, that Clinton, speaking at a huge gay fund raiser in Los Angeles, promised to do away with the federal ban on homosexuals in the military. Reporter David Maraniss described the scene on the front page of the *Washington Post*:

> There stood Bill Clinton on the stage of the Palace Theater, jaw set, eyes glistening, as he reached the conclusion in a speech in which he promised that as president he would lift the federal ban on homosexuals in the military and launch a Manhattan Project–style effort to combat the AIDS epidemic. He lowered his voice and spoke slowly, looking out at a crowd that national candidates once shunned or ignored.

An estimated 15,000 to 20,000 videotapes of Clinton's speech were distributed throughout the gay community. Substantial monies were raised by gay activists to support Clinton's campaign.

Clinton's endorsement of gays in the military gave the Republicans a remarkable opportunity. If they had raised the issue of homosexuality first and frontally, their actions could well have been trashed. One can conjure up the comments: "a new Willie Horton issue," "there goes George Bush taking the low road again."

But Clinton opened the matter as a clear issue of policy. The president, as commander in chief, could change military policy by the stroke of his pen (at least temporarily, unless and until the Congress tried to undo it). Clinton said he would wield the pen in just that manner. Bush disagreed. That is a clear policy choice. It would be hard (not impossible, only hard) to accuse Bush of demagoguing the gay issue if Clinton was the one who raised it, as he had.

When questioned, Bush said he opposed Clinton's position. And that was about the end of it. It was not revisited in a serious way, not made the subject of a campaign commercial, not grouped with other values issues, or social issues, or cultural issues, to show a pattern, not dealt with in any serious way. (For example: Does a society that becomes value-neutral on homosexuality change? Do some young sexual "waverers" go gay instead of straight if the society is value-neutral on the matter? One man who believes that may be the case is Professor E. J. Patullo, who served at Harvard University as director of the Center for the Behavioral Science, director of the Psychological Laboratories, and associate chairman of the Department of Psychology. Do we even know much about any of this?)

There was only Republican silence on the matter—until *after* the election, when President-elect Clinton said that he meant what he had said about gays in the military and that he intended to act on his campaign promise. As we shall see much later, that remark ignited a political firestorm that Clinton will have to deal with as long as he is president.

Remember only this: It was not Buchanan who raised the gay issue. It was Clinton.

————

On the second night of the convention (Tuesday) two major prime-time speeches were offered. One, the official keynote address by Senator Phil Gramm, was well less than a spellbinder. Still, it had authority to it. The keynoter states the party's sanctioned message. Gramm's theme concerned free market economics and big-spending Democrats, topics that unite and inspire Republicans. There was a potential press lead in Gramm's remarks: "Republicans Sound 1992 Theme—Capitalism."

That was not to be. The press, particularly the talking heads on television, kept talking about what they referred to as the "intolerant" and "exclusive" nature of the Republican convention. But based on what? It surely could not have been based on the other big Tuesday night speech, delivered by Jack Kemp. For my money, Kemp's address won best-of-show award. He explained how the free market was not only a ticket to prosperity for the rich but could be just such a ticket for the poor as well, particularly if the government got out of the way. Kemp made the point that big government has done much to create the values problem in America's poorest communities:

> For 50 years, the Democratic Party has dictated most of the policies governing our cities. Higher taxes. Redistribution of wealth. A welfare system that penalizes people for working, discourages marriage, punishes the family, and literally prohibits savings. It's not the values of the poor that are flawed; it's the values of the welfare system that are bankrupt.

Kemp is interesting. All during 1992, he was saluted by the mainstream media. Exactly how this came to happen is somewhat obscure. He hadn't changed his views much from the times when he was regarded as a supply-side "zealot." He always thought free enterprise was good for poor people, and he gained a podium to express it when he became Secretary of Housing and Urban Development in 1989. He was, and is still, prolife and moderately pro–prayer in the school. Yet he is now regarded as both inclusive and tolerant. Indeed, he is both.

Moreover, at convention time in 1992, Kemp was the darling of the Houston Republicans. Here is a strange thing: They polled the delegates at the Houston convention, the very ones who made up the gang that was routinely described as zealous and right wing. Their number one choice for the 1996 Republican nominee was Jack Kemp, he of tolerance and inclusivity! Kemp got 39 percent of the delegate-respondents. His closest rivals, James Baker and Phil Gramm, received 6 percent each, with Dan Quayle at 4 percent.*

In theory the Wednesday morning lead story might have run something like this: "Tolerant Speech Gains Massive GOP Support; Buchanan Tide Reversed." But media, gorging in a feeding frenzy, are not easily diverted. The Kemp speech was mostly ignored.

The story quickly swung over to the topic of Wednesday evening: "Family Values."

I have reread the by-now-infamous speeches of Reverend Pat Robertson and Marilyn Quayle. If that's the right wing, we are safe.

Robertson's talk mostly flailed the welfare state generally and LBJ's Great Society programs specifically. I worked for LBJ and think much of the original Great Society legislation was necessary for America (although some of it was selectively and harmfully distorted later by liberals). But no one who knows anything about public policy would ever suggest that attacking the Great Society makes anyone a zealous right-winger!

Actually, there was not much that was offensive in Robertson's address. He was against abortion. No surprise there. He was against the Clinton "litmus test" for the appointment of prochoice Supreme Court justices, but that mirrored exactly the liberal position on litmus tests when it was thought that *prolife* justices might be appointed by a Republican president. He opposed Clinton's position on homosexuals in the military. He opposed Clinton's alleged view to make "sexual preference a privileged minority under our civil rights laws," which the Clinton campaign says Clinton never endorsed. And Robertson noted sorrowfully that the Democratic platform didn't mention the name of God, not even once.

Robertson was not the only one who had noted the absence of the deity. Earlier in the year it had been brought up at Democratic platform hearings in Albuquerque by the moderate Democrat Senator Joseph Lieberman (D-Conn.), an observant Orthodox Jew. Lieberman thought it would be appropriate to mention the Almighty in Albuquerque and suggested a reference to God in the platform. Lieberman's view was rejected.

---

* Washington Post/ABC News Poll, July 29–August 7, 1992.

The one Robertson paragraph I found offensive was this one:

When Bill and Hillary Clinton talk about family values, they are not talk-ing about either families or values. They are talking about a radical plan to destroy the traditional family and transfer its functions to the federal government.

That is wrong and over the line. There is no such plan. It may be the effect, but not the plan. What Robertson said is at least as bad as Demo-crats' saying that Republicans don't care about poor people.

But why should Robertson have mattered much? He is a minister with a large electronic flock who ran unsuccessfully for president in 1988 and chose not to enter the fray in 1992. He has organized a grass-roots political action group, the Christian Coalition, which has some in-fluence. He sometimes goes too far, or is perceived to go too far. Does that sound familiar? Does the description not equally apply to Reverend Jesse Jackson, another man of the cloth? Jackson, too, has an organiza-tion, the Rainbow Coalition, which has some influence. Jackson, too, spoke at a national political convention, the Democratic one. Jackson, too, said some outrageous things (that the baby-killing King Herod was "the Dan Quayle of his day who put no value on the family").

But did the media coverage of the Democratic convention say that Jesse Jackson represented the Democratic party? Of course not. Why did the media coverage say that Robertson represented the Republican party?

Or consider the case of the former governor of California, Jerry Brown. In 1992 he challenged his party from the left, just as Pat Buchanan challenged his party from the right, each with a populist fla-vor. Like Buchanan, Brown spoke in prime time at the national con-vention. Unlike Buchanan, former Governor Brown actually won a few primaries and caucuses. Yet the mainstream media in no way ever sug-gested that Brown's convention speech represented the views of the Democratic party.*

---

* Brown was not *scheduled* by the convention to speak; he got platform time under the rules per-mitting challengers to talk on a point of order. But the reason he was not granted convention-authorized time concerned his refusal to endorse Bill Clinton publicly, not because of his beliefs, which in some respects may be seen as extreme as Buchanan's or Robertson's.

The baseline media story of the Democratic convention was short and mostly accurate: The Democratic ticket was moderate. But why did the media emphasize the "ticket" at one convention and the "party" at another? The attack on the Republicans, recall, was on alleged Republican zealots like Buchanan and Robertson, not on the candidates, Bush and Quayle.

The frosting on the cake of family values was served up on Wednesday night by Marilyn Quayle, attorney, mother of three, promulgator of family values. Well, one may properly ask, what on earth was she doing up there? The strategy was not very subtle: Put the spotlight on Hillary Clinton, whom Republicans sought to portray as (a) very liberal and (b) very influential. (How could they have believed that?)

One passage that gained great attention in Mrs. Quayle's speech was this one:

> But remember, not everyone joined the counterculture. Not everyone demonstrated, took drugs, joined in the sexual revolution or dodged the draft.

It was, in many ways, an unexceptionable statement—if anything, understated. Not only did every young American not go down the countercultural road, by far the overwhelming majority did not. That is one reason that Richard Nixon won in America's biggest landslide, over George McGovern in 1972, *and carried the majority of the votes of young people.*

It was said, by feminists and liberals, and echoed by the talking heads, that Mrs. Quayle attacked single mothers, female-headed households, and working women. An examination of the text of her remarks shows that she did no such thing. I argued some with Marilyn-bashers after the speech. When informed that she didn't say what they said she said, their reply was near uniform: "Well, it was all in the tone."

That was most of the case against the Republicans: a platform called right wing that wasn't, a speech by a thoroughly defeated candidate from 1992 (Buchanan), another one by a thoroughly defeated candidate from 1988 (Robertson), and the ear-of-the-beholder "tone" of the vice president's wife, not theretofore a major statutory position in American public life.

This is not to apologize for the Houston Republicans. Beyond teasing Democrats about family values, Republicans did little to explain the essence of social deterioration in America, the best issue they had, albeit a complex one.

The values fire raged, and it was not until Wednesday night that a prime-time GOP speaker, William J. Bennett, made some sense about what was under discussion. Bennett continually explained what he was *not* talking about:

> When we talk about traditional family values we are not using "code words." We are not seeking a political "wedge" issue. And we are not seeking to demean or belittle others. Rather we are seeking to honor and affirm the "better angels of our nature" and of our children's nature. . . .

> We do not disparage the good, noble and sometimes great effort of single or divorced mothers. [Bennett was raised by a single mother.]. . .

> Let me address the issue of alternative lifestyles. Heaven knows, there are a lot of them. This is a free country. Within very broad limits people may live as they wish.

Bennett, a former professor of philosophy, also managed to get the priorities straight:

> Plato understood that, in the end, there is only one fundamental political issue: how we raise our children.

Plato, not having our range of received wisdom, did not know that it was the economy, stupid. Bennett was on the right track. It was the best we were to hear on the issue, in prime time, in Houston, in 1992. But it was a short talk, actually a nominating speech for Dan Quayle.

It spoke elegantly about marriage, motherhood, fatherhood, and parenthood. It had a couple of paragraphs about education, but mostly about school choice and condom distribution rather than educational standards and stakes. It barely touched on crime and welfare. It did not mention quotas. It implied that Democrats were at fault for the social issues but did not really make the case that what government had caused, government might cure. After all, it was only a short nominating speech for the vice president.

Here are some items that were not presented forcefully in prime time in Houston: quotas, welfare, crime, educational discipline. These are all legitimate grist for political discourse, all are harming America, all can be, arguably, laid at the feet of the recent liberal impulse in America, and all of which Bush had addressed at one time or another.

I left Houston stunned. I asked myself: Are these Republicans idiots? Foreign policy was mostly off the table because of victory in the cold war. The economy was limping. And they ignore a huge part of the issue that had won for them a series of national elections! The very issue that any damn fool knew was causing great grief in America, and bubbling within a troubled electorate, sometimes below the surface, often above.

I wasn't the only one surprised. In the Clinton war room in Little Rock, Clinton campaigners had expected attacks on him based in some large part on values issues, leading to the idea that Clinton was "a liberal in a moderate's disguise and that he was just too liberal for average Americans."*

Is there an excuse for the Houston Republicans? In retrospect, perhaps. The values issues are difficult to lay out before the public and the press. One misstatement and the argument about affirmative action becomes proportionalism, becomes race, becomes racism. Talk about crime, and it's "police brutality" and "law 'n' order." Talk about welfare, and it's blaming the victim and racism. One verbal misstep regarding homosexuality and the perception of conservatives goes from traditional values to gay bashing. A miscue about what sort of art the federal government should fund, and the press banshees start yammering about an assault on the First Amendment. These are difficult issues, often compounded by Republican tone deafness.

---

* Reported in Peter Goldman, Thomas DeFrank, Mark Miller, Andrew Murr, and Tom Mathews, "Quest for the Presidency, 1992," *Newsweek.*

Beyond that is the very nature of the modern national political convention. It is designed to be an exercise in tight control by the winning candidate. Often it is. But not always. When it gets out of control, as Republicans saw in 1964 and Democrats saw in 1972, it can get very much out of control. At such a point the image of the convention, the party, and the candidate is pretty well driven by the press. Houston went out of control. Most of the journalists hailed from a sensibility far from conservative; they were pretuned to believe stories about the alleged zealotry of the religious right. Moreover, these journalists were not just making it up; they were being fed raw meat by Republican moderates, still smarting from bruises sustained in committee fights and in selected local intramural defeats inflicted by the religious right and/or conservatives.

What happened next is less excusable. A *convention* out of control, directed in effect by 15,000 journalists on the warpath, cannot easily be put back on track. But a *campaign* for the incumbent president, with sufficient funds, run from the White House, in a party with skilled political operatives, is another matter. It is not asking too much to expect a reasonable plan of action.

After Houston, the Republicans were in trouble, but probably not insurmountable trouble. The Republicans did not get the big bounce that is expected from a national convention. Obviously, the foolish convention and the simplistic and snotty reportage about it played a role in such bouncelessness. After both major party conventions, the major polls showed President Bush trailing Governor Clinton by about ten points, give or take a few.

At the end of August 1992, Secretary of State James Baker and his team from the State Department arrived at the White House to run the campaign. There were ten weeks remaining before Election Day. Could Bush get even, and get ahead? It has been done before, including by Bush in 1988.

The campaign that Baker & Co. inherited was a mess. After the election, I chatted with Robert Zoellick, Baker's chief lieutenant, and asked him what the Baker team found when they arrived in the White House. He said, roughly, this:

> There was nothing there. There were no campaign commercials. There was no media strategy. There were no agreed-upon themes. There was an inadequate scheduling and advance operation. We didn't even have a plan for the economy.

Why? One can make a long list of prominent Republican campaign officials who might be blamed for that situation. In addition, the death of Lee Atwater was a major blow; he had displayed a pitch-perfect ear for the values issues when he ran the winning Bush campaign in 1988. But in the end, the blame goes to the one man who let the nonorganization nonorganize: President Bush. After all, he was the leader of the party that had developed what had been regularly described as an unbeatable national political operation, replete with political superstars and just plain stars.*

At the root of the problems of the Bush campaign, not surprisingly, was the question that plagued the Bush presidency: Just what did the candidate stand for, or, more cynically, what would the candidate say he stood for? Until that question was answered, there was little hope that a coherent campaign could be developed. It never was.

It was decided, probably correctly by that time, that the first thematic issue Bush had to address was that fabulous invalid, the American economy. After all, the world's most prominent sign, scribbled in the Clinton campaign war room, included the line "It's the economy, stupid."† Whenever the election dialogue moved to any other topic, Clinton and his spokespersons said it was " a diversion."

Indeed, in late 1990 and early 1991 America had lived through a moderate but stretched-out recession that seemed to recover and then started to do a double-dip. The ensuing 1992 official recovery appeared to be very slow. It was regarded as laughable when George Bush declared the recession was over, even though it was, as retrospective figures show clearly.

---

* Marlin Fitzwater, in his 1995 book *Call the Briefing*, relates that Bush felt both sick and tired at the time owing to side effects of medication for a thyroid condition.

† The first issue listed on the sign was "Change Vs. More of the Same." The economy was second. Third on the list was "Don't Forget Health Care." And fourth was, "The Debate, Stupid."

The late eighties and early nineties had been a tough patch in the economy. It was a time of recession, a big deficit, corporate layoffs, and a wrenching global economic transformation. The unemployment rate climbed to 7.7 percent in June 1992, not at all bad for a recession but still no picnic. More important was the impression of massive job churning within the labor force as major corporations stripped down to the waist for international competition. (A probably incorrect notion, as will be noted in Chapter 4.)

It had been said, all through the election year, that the three big issues were "jobs, jobs, jobs." In Washington it was said, endlessly, and accurately, that "people were hurting." And Clinton said, endlessly, that "the economy" would be his highest priority because the United States was in "an economic crisis," that he knew how to "grow the economy," and that he would focus on it "like a laser beam." (The economic drumbeat was so constant that even a flustered Bush apparently bought it for a brief moment, alluding to an economy in "free fall"—when the indicators had already turned up.)

Let me tell you a story about "jobs, jobs, jobs." All during the election year I gave speeches, as is my wont. As I began my remarks, I would take a short survey of the audience. I would ask how they voted in 1988 and how they intended to vote in 1992. I asked the polling staple: "Is America on the right track or the wrong track?" The overwhelming response was "wrong track," from every kind of group, just as with the public as a whole.

Then I would ask my sneaky question: "When you look at America today do you think our principal problems are in the realm of 'jobs, jobs, jobs,' or 'values, values, values' ?"

I offered no explanation of what I meant by "values," just as I offered no explanation about what, in fact, "jobs" might mean. I asked my questions at the very start of my talk so that my exposition would not influence the respondents. Every audience I spoke to gave at least a solid majority to values—typically in the 65 percent to 75 percent range. (One small audience, of New Jersey hospital administrators, gave values a 100 percent vote.)

How strange! Everyone in the politics trade was saying that it was the economy, stupid. The Republicans were to show, in Houston, that values could turn into political quicksand. And yet to me, audience after audience, throughout the election year, said the basic American problem was not jobs but values. How could that be? Of course, my sample was not representative. Still, a perfect batting average usually tells you something.

In any event, by late August 1992, after both conventions, Bush had to address the economy and come up with "a plan." (It was a big year for plans.) Zoellick wrote a good speech, which Bush delivered to the Detroit Economic Club on September 10. The new Bush plan received very favorable reviews.

But that was playing defense. The economy was Clinton's issue. Surely, I thought, the Republicans would offer a high-profile twin to the Detroit speech, saying, roughly, this: "Look, Americans, what happened in Houston was mispresented and misreported. Here's what we really meant to say." Surely the Republicans would play the values issue, their trump card. Surely they understood that values mattered most, or at least a lot, and the most logical values issues to deal with were the ones that are described here as the social issues, intermixed with a few of the easy cultural ones.

Suppose, for example, the Bush campaign had run commercials with the president saying,

- Bill Clinton says he's for getting people off welfare, and for getting tough on crime, and for discipline in the schools, but it is his party, and the liberalism that drives it, and the Democratic Congress that promotes it—that has created the mess we're in.
- In the summer of 1990 every Democratic senator voted in favor of a quota bill. Bill Clinton supported that action. But I vetoed it, and a year later we ended up with legislation that is fair to all. (Subject to argument.)
- Now that Governor Clinton has raised the issue, and because it is an issue that the commander in chief must resolve, let me be clear: I agree with General Colin Powell and Senator Sam Nunn that gays in the military is a bad idea.

- America faces a moral crisis. Can Bill Clinton deal with it? [Laughter. Soundtrack, lifted from Democratic 1988 commercials that asked "Dan Quayle for Vice President?"]

They didn't do any of that, or anything like it. To the contrary, by mid-September, leaked stories from White House sources came out in the newspapers saying that the Bush campaign would "back off" the values issues.

Back off! Why did the Republicans abandon their best set of issues? Why didn't they even try it in a calm way, in the controlled environment of the national media campaign?

A number of reasons have been put forth. (1) The media-public reaction to Houston made it difficult. (2) It had been trivialized by the Dan Quayle/"Murphy Brown" episode. (3) The Bush campaigners bought the line that the issue had passed its prime; it was hot some years earlier, but its time had passed; young, modern Americans wouldn't be taken in by that social stuff. (4) It fell through the cracks; the campaign was so disorganized that no one quite got to it. (5) The economy was too sour.

But as all this was going on in the fall of 1992 something was buzzing in the back of my mind. It all seemed so familiar to me, as if I had lived through this peculiar ceremony once before. I wondered: What ritual pattern of behavior was being played out?

The answer that came to mind surprised me: Vietnam. I came to Washington in the summer of 1966 to work for President Johnson. For almost two and a half years I served on his staff, principally as a speechwriter, mostly dealing with domestic matters, but on a few occasions on foreign policy issues as well. That meant Vietnam.

It is hard to remember it this way, but opinion surveys show it: The American public supported the policy of both Johnson and Nixon during the Vietnam War. I remember lunching most days at the White House mess at the big round table in the back, where the president's staff gathered. I didn't hear dovish talk at that table or in private conversations with my colleagues. When I left the White House at the end of Johnson's term, I did not believe that America would, as the saying then went, "bug out" on Vietnam.

Clearly I had missed something. Liberal Democrats in the Congress had abandoned Johnson before he left office. When a Republican took over in early 1969, most mainstream elected Democrats became doves as well. Soon most of the American elites, of both parties, turned against the war.

Of course, Vietnam was a highly complex situation. Sensible arguments can be made on all sides of it, certainly in the light of its tragic outcome. But what interests me here is not the substance of the issue but how American officials came to act as they did, particularly in the light of (grudging) public support.

I believe that the elites abandoned the assertive American role because they were bombarded by the media and, most importantly, by their own children. If "Hey, hey, LBJ, how many kids did you kill today?" was an acceptable chant, what did that make Daddy? Could Daddy be a war criminal? What we learned in that time is that, under such pressure, daddies wilt.

I do not mean to make the case that Vietnam and the values issue are of the same class. But the way minds change, the process of policy formation, seemed similar. Capture the culture, capture the policy.

Ultimately I believe it was the dominant liberal media culture that eroded the Republicans' will to fight it out on values in 1992. If, as the press reported, Republicans were really homophobic right-wing zealots in Houston, what does that make you, Daddy? If Horton bashing was racist, what does that make you, Daddy? By the time a decision had to be made, the country club Republicans had lost their nerve. And so had George Bush.

They backed off. Leaving them with what to run on? Not foreign policy and defense. Not jobs, jobs, jobs. Not values, values, values.

And so, in 1992, we had twin Republican themes. One was the old standby, taxes, which is all right but not great when your own candidate had broken his pledge and gone along with a tax increase. The other was trust, as in, "Bill Clinton eats at the Waffle House." Bush's attack on Bill Clinton as a waffler was strained. From George Bush? Whose career, while quite distinguished in many ways, also includes a long stack of waffles and switches, including not only on taxes but also on little items like civil rights and abortion?

So the Bushies, Vietnamized, Hortonized, and traumatized, backed off and ran the worst presidential campaign in the history of the world.

Now, no one knows for sure how important a role a campaign plays in the outcome of a presidential election. Few analysts believe it is large. If a large electoral tide is in motion, it is doubtful that a good campaign can change a loser into a winner. Barry Goldwater in 1964, George McGovern in 1972, and Walter Mondale in 1984, who lost by 23, 23, and 18 percentage points, respectively, would not have beat Lyndon Johnson, Richard Nixon, and Ronald Reagan, no matter how skillfully crafted their campaigns.

On the other hand, most political professionals agree that better campaigns could have made it possible for Richard Nixon in 1960 (margin of loss 0.2 percent), Hubert Humphrey in 1968 (margin of loss 0.7 percent), and Gerald Ford in 1976 (margin of loss 2.1 percent) to win their contests.

But there are elections that fall in the middle of these polar extremes, elections that are fairly close. In 1988 George Bush beat Michael Dukakis by 7.8 percent. Could a better, smarter, tougher Dukakis campaign have taken 3.91 percent of Bush's vote, to gain a popular vote majority? Perhaps.

As the election returns came in on Tuesday night, November 3, 1992, several things were clear. The Bush-Clinton race was (1) not a blow-out landslide, (2) probably closer to a "squeaker" than to a "medium," and (3) plausibly winnable for Bush.

Clinton beat Bush by a margin of 5.5 percent. In theory, if only 2.8 percentage points worth of Clinton voters had switched to Bush, Bush would have won the popular vote, which almost always yields an electoral college victory. Actually, in 1992, the number of necessary switchers would probably have been somewhat fewer. The English psephologist David Butler, who spent the election autumn of 1992 in America, pegged the necessary swing vote at the very slender level of 1.9 percent.

Why so? Because Clinton ran up particularly big margins in the biggest states: California (1.473 million), New York (1.004 million), and Illinois (.661 million). Under such circumstances, if the race tightened by 1.9 percent across the board, Clinton would have a huge accumulation of so-called wasted votes, while Bush would have tipped close contests in Ohio (margin of 0.088 million), New Jersey (margin of 0.057 million), and Georgia (margin of 0.014 million)—that is, 13,714 votes, which is pretty damn close. In short, according to Butler, even had the two-party popular vote been 50.5 percent for Clinton and 49.5 percent for Bush, then Bush would have probably won the electoral college and the presidency.

Might an intelligent values issue campaign by Republicans have made up that difference? Ah, that's just rubbing it in. The problem is not that Bush didn't win; he didn't deserve to win. The problem is that by not raising the issues that he might have won on, he robbed the American people of a needed debate.

Ironically, by not raising the issue, he may have destroyed Clinton's presidency. That's what can happen if it is believed that voters no longer really care much about those old-fashioned issues of values.

Part Two

WHAT IT'S NOT

Chapter 4

IT'S NOT THE ECONOMY

Recall that we began with a title, *Values Matter Most*. But if values matter most, what doesn't matter most? In the chapters here in Part Two, it is explained (1) that economics *does not* matter most, (2) that within the values issues, the *cultural* issues do *not* matter as much as the *social* issues, and (3) that concern about values is *not new* in American political history and consequently should *not* be feared. Three *nots*.

America, by almost any serious measure, is the most successful nation in history. The "Who's Number One?" argument has turned from silly to absurd. America is number one. America is the most potent economic, military, geopolitical, cultural, educational, scientific, demographic, ideological, and linguistic power in history. America is likely to remain number one for a very long time. This is so not only because by any measure America is a great nation, and a dominant civilization, but there is no one in second place as either a nation or as a civilization. An earlier book of mine, *The First Universal Nation*, spells out some reasons for this view. Now, as we have seen Japan stagger, Europe struggle, and the Soviet Union wipe itself off the map, that case has become stronger.

But successful nations can have problems, lots of problems, problems most everywhere, even big problems, even threatening problems. Indeed, it would be unusual if any human society, institution, or organization were not beset by grief or potential grief. That comes with the territory.

The task in public policy is to determine not whether there are important problems but which problems are most important and most pliant to public interventions.

America's principal problems today are in the somewhat amorphous realm of values. To put that in proper context, it is necessary to deal first with the "compared-to-what" argument. And so we look now at the economy. After all, the case has been made in recent decades, and sharpened in recent years, that our main problems are economic. Not only was the plenary case made, but it was bought, whole hog, particularly in the high-profile political arena. The famous campaign sign in the Clinton campaign's famous Little Rock war room of 1992 said it all: "It's the Economy, Stupid."

Of course, there is a big argument about what has actually happened in the economic realm. There are those who maintain that "since 1973" or (alternatively) "thanks to twelve years of Reagan-and-Bush," the American middle class has taken it in the neck, that real wages have actually gone down, or that real wages have not gone up, and that because of something called "trickle-down" the rich got richer while the poor and the middle class got poorer, or at least not richer, yielding an increase in "income inequality." All of that showed that America was in decline, or that it was all quite "unfair," and it took place mostly in a high-profile moment called "a decade of greed."

In a political context, this view was expressed most publicly and politically by an author and fellow provocateur whom I have known for many years. Recently I have come to think of him as named Even Kevin Phillips (as in: "Even Kevin Phillips, a conservative Republican, says . . .").

The case Even Phillips made in his very influential book, *The Politics of Rich and Poor*, went something like this: American politics operates principally on an economic axis, and it moves in cycles. When Republicans take the power of the presidency, they show their naked greed;

they are sleazy, gluttonous, arriviste folks; they believe in terrible things like markets, free trade, deregulation, capitalism, lower taxes, and less federal spending. Consequently other Americans, that is, the middle class and the poor, *suffer.* And suffer we did, said Phillips—during the Reagan-Bush years and, indeed, for an entire generation.

Phillips's book was published in late 1990. Democrats, looking toward the 1992 election, with a recession at hand, jumped at the opportunity to endorse such a case, particularly when it came from Even, because he is so regularly described as a conservative Republican. (Actually he is more of a nonpartisan acerbic populist. Many professional Republicans do not regard Phillips as a Republican anymore.)

Has the middle class really made no economic headway in a generation? Were the 1980s bad news for the middle class and poor? Are the poor getting poorer? Did the greedy rich make out like bandits? Is the economy therefore properly the preeminent concern of the voters?

And another question, central to this book: Insofar as some of that economic view is valid or partly valid, might it have been "values" that played an important role in causing economic hardship?

The essence of the case that middle-class working men and women are economically beleaguered rests principally on wage and earnings data from the Bureau of Labor Statistics that came out in the mid-1980s. (See the Indicators on pp. 83–89.) Using such data, economist Frank Levy, then at the University of Maryland, wrote in *Dollars and Dreams:* *

> The second [economic] period [since World War II] extended from 1973 through at least 1985. Over this period inflation-adjusted wages have stagnated and, in many cases, declined. This stagnation has led to a kind of quiet depression that is responsible for many of our current problems.

This notion surfaced more colorfully in sentences in Phillips's book, such as this one:

> For much of Middle America, the Reagan years were troubling and ambiguous as the contrast intensified between proliferating billionaires and the tens of millions of others who were gradually sinking.

---

* Russell Sage Foundation, New York, 1987.

The BLS data on weekly and hourly wages that supported such a case is presented in the first chart in the Indicators section concerning income. It is presented roughly as it has been popularized in the political dialogue, showing a flattening out during the mid-1970s and then a decline from the 1980s onward. Those BLS data sets on which the chart is based are titled "Real Average Weekly Earnings of Non-supervisory Employees in Private Industries" and a twin series, based on "Hourly Earnings." But these data series are but two of a multitude used in the income-measuring trade. A headline in *An Illustrated Guide to the American Economy*, a remarkable volume by Herbert Stein and Murray Foss, shows these same BLS series under a headline that reads:

SOME COMMONLY USED MEASURES GIVE
AN INACCURATE PICTURE OF THE COURSE OF
REAL WAGES OVER THE PAST SEVERAL YEARS.

Yes, inaccurate. Stein and Foss have it just right.* They point out that the measurement concerns cash only, ignoring benefits. These measurements are applied to a time when employees (and their unions) much preferred to take benefits rather than cash, thereby

---

* The Stein-Foss book, first published in 1992 and then updated and revised in 1995, has a lot else right in it also. It ought to be made mandatory reading for all who ply the public policy trade. With clean charts that tell stories, buttressed by lean backup prose, Stein and Foss lay out "A Hundred Key Issues" (the subtitle of the 1992 book). They write: "We have tried not to make a book of Republican or Democratic, conservative or liberal, optimistic or pessimistic data. . . . We have not looked for things that would surprise the reader."

It is, above all, credible, flowing from the experience and mission of the authors. Stein, age seventy-nine, is a former chairman of the Council of Economic Advisors. Foss, age seventy-seven, was editor of the *Survey of Current Business*. Jointly they have worked in the tangled vineyard of statistical economics for more than a hundred years. They are now my colleagues at the American Enterprise Institute. I would describe them as eclectic liberal conservative economists, or perhaps the reverse. In the 1980s, Stein publicly hammered Reaganomics and supply-side economics with clarity, wit, and gusto, particularly on the op-ed pages of the *Wall Street Journal*, where supply-siders hang out.

But that's not the idea in the *Illustrated Guide*. It is to lay out the data understandably, and impartially, in an arena that is too often obfuscated and partisan. I cite Stein and Foss's book here frequently because it has such credibility. (The book is published by the American Enterprise Institute.)

avoiding taxation on the cash value of the benefits. It is strange. We complain about the high cost of health care but neglect, in our political discourse, to count the same health care as income to those who get it "free," and then moan that it constitutes an erosion of their living standards when it is somewhat reduced and rationalized. Nor do the BLS earnings figures account for any private pension benefits or public pension benefits, although both went up substantially "since 1973" and/or during those horrible "Reagan-Bush years."

Health and pension benefits represent an important relative part of middle-class income and a much lesser relative share of upper-class income. A rich person doesn't have much problem paying hospital bills and doesn't worry much about making ends meet during retirement. A middle-class person worries, a lot, about both. Thus, when medical and pension benefits are increased substantially, as they were in the 1970s, the middle class gains real security it previously did not have.

Moreover, the oft-cited BLS data (of "non-supervisory employees in private industry") do not take into account the rising earnings of government workers during the time period cited, or the rising numbers of people who work for themselves, or the earnings of supervisory personnel, or the rise in the "underground economy" which provides much unreported income, or the sharp increases for poor persons in the form of food stamps, housing subsidies, Medicaid, and the rest of what is called here "Greater Welfare." In some cases (but not in the Indicator section that appears at the beginning of this chapter) the BLS series is shown with a flawed inflation index that substantially understates earnings and has been generally abandoned in many other statistical federal series. Other than that, it's useful.

Stein and Foss show other data series, partly to counterbalance the omissions from the straight cash earnings material. One series is also from the BLS and deals with employee compensation per hour, which includes benefits as well as earnings or wages. That line is clearly trending *upward*, as shown in the Indicators.

Other statistical series show mostly similar trends. Bureau of the Census data from the Current Population Survey and the decennial census—family income and household income—showed an *upward* trend during the 1980s: mildly for medians, solidly for averages. Per capita income and per capita GDP jumped up. And these measures do not include noncash income such as health care, employer pension deposits, or noncash benefits for the poor. (See Indicators.)

As economist Marvin Kosters of the American Enterprise Institute points out, "At the time of the great political debate, the ascendant data was generally ignored, while the only negative series, a somewhat misleading one, was stressed. Most economists, from across the ideological spectrum, would accept that."

Of course, the economy has not been all roses. Stein and Foss make the point, correctly I believe, that although there was real income progress during the seventies and eighties—certainly the eighties—such growth was slower than in the earlier postwar decades. Kosters notes that the wages of less skilled and less experienced workers went up, but at a lower rate than for the average worker. Some groups, he notes, actually did experience real declines. There was real pain.

It is also true that many Americans felt unusually scared about the economy. The great American perestroika was proceeding apace, restructuring with a vengeance. Industries were going lean and mean—"downsizing" and laying off employees—all highly publicized. Losing a job is a difficult situation in any circumstance but is made more pointed by the possibility of losing employer-related medical care. Losing a job and not finding another one can surely be a disaster. More typically, workers were laid off and, after an interregnum for job seeking, found new work. That is also no picnic. Add to that those Americans who *feared* a layoff in a highly charged atmosphere. And so, the political tub thumping about a poor economy resonated among legitimately anxious voters.*

---

* On December 18, 1991, General Motors announced 74,000 layoffs. The headlines were scary. "General Motors to Close 21 Factories and Cut 74,000 Jobs" wrote the *New York Times*. The headline in the *Washington Post* was: "GM to Jettison 74,000 Workers, Shut 21 Factories." The reality was somewhat different. The GM press release said all layoffs were to be made "through attrition and a new special early retirement program." Jettison?

Moreover, despite the perception of great job churning, the actual data concerning "job duration" may well reveal just another politico/media frenzy. In December of 1994 a paper by Henry Farber of Princeton takes on the topic. His conclusion, based on Current Population Survey supplements from 1973 to 1993: "There has been no systematic change in various measures of the overall distribution of job duration over the last two decades." (As with almost everything in the economic world, there is an argument about this.)

A pair of charts in the Indicators section give a sense of whether the rich have made out at the expense of the not rich. There has been some change toward greater inequality in a time series that is normally quite stable, particularly for the wealthiest and poorest cohorts. When tax policy and benefits are included, the growing inequality may have stopped in the past few years. (Since the mid-1980s federal income taxes have been eliminated for low-income Americans, and a progressively higher Earned Income Tax Credit has provided additional cash well up into the lower end of the middle-class bracket.)

Why have the most poor fared poorly? Stein and Foss offer two clear reasons: (1) a "widening gap between the incomes of people with little education and of people with more" and (2) the "increase in the proportion of all families that are headed by women without a husband present, who tend to have below average incomes." This will be discussed in a moment, stressing that (2) often causes (1). Yes, social conditions harm the economy.

Perhaps you are not yet convinced that our economic situation is somewhat less than grievous. There are, after all, these ongoing arguments about how to measure income and income distribution, and further arguments about what kind of jobs we have now, how to measure unemployment, the role of the two-earner family, and the number of jobs created—only to begin a long list that cannot be fully explored here. (I suggest that such further digging does not much change the picture I have sketched.)

But there is another way to look at our economic situation. Let us ask this question: *What do we have?*

After all, if there is an argument about how much income we earn, why not take a look at what *we have*, or have not, been able to buy with those earnings. Won't that give a solid clue as to how we're making out?

The handy Indicators in this chapter and some others offer solid evidence. There has been an explosion in the consumption of goods and services—that is, an explosion in what our money is buying. We live in more space, with more television sets, traveling more, with more cars,

with a wide array of new electronic marvels. The rate of home owner-
ship has stayed about the same, at a very high historic level, but we
spend a somewhat smaller fraction of our incomes for our larger homes.
And: In the 1980s, that putative decade of greed, charitable giving
soared.

There is also the matter of international comparisons. We have the
highest standard of living, by far, as measured by Purchasing Power Par-
ities, which is the U.N.'s best index.

––––––––––

What about the politics of economics? The American economy is a
big, dumb, irregular, green machine. It grows, and falters, and then
grows some more. It has yielded a jagged but ascendant national trend,
regardless of who is president, regardless of which party is in power.

Of course, that doesn't mean that presidents, and their respective
political parties, don't claim credit when the economy does well.
Ronald Reagan and George Bush said they created 20 million jobs. My,
weren't they creative! When the economy briefly hit a wall in the early
1990s, the Democrats charged that Republicans weren't creative at all,
that the Republicans believed in that terrible idea of trickle-down, and
that only Democrats knew how to make an economy bubble up. As we
pulled out of the recession in late 1992 and onward, Democrats
claimed credit for the new jobs. My, aren't they creative!

As Stein and Foss note, most jobs are created by energetic, innovative Americans, not by presidents or political parties. Our free and
open economic culture allows Americans to work hard for their own
account. Economic policies that encourage such openness over a period of time tend to expand those opportunities.

Rhetorical differences aside, the economic options available are
constrained by reality, no matter which major party is in power, and
would remain constrained with a third party as well. There is a global
economy. There is a budget deficit and huge national debt. Inflation
does happen. The infamous bond markets impose a discipline of their
own. The Federal Reserve Bank has real autonomy. Unlike, say, welfare
or affirmative action, the American economy is not a federal program.

Did some people get hurt economically in the last generation

INDICATORS: ECONOMICS

Average money earnings have declined since 1973.

Index of Average Hourly and Weekly Earnings Using 1973 as Base Year, 1947–1994

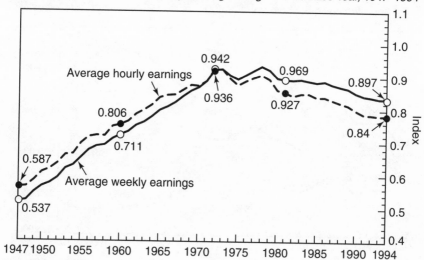

Note: Data for 1994 are from third quarter. All measures are adjusted for inflation using Consumer Price Index-UX1.

Source: Bureau of Labor Statistics.

Though monetary pay has declined since 1973, compensation, including benefits, has grown.

Index of Hourly Compensation Using 1973 as Base Year, 1947–1994

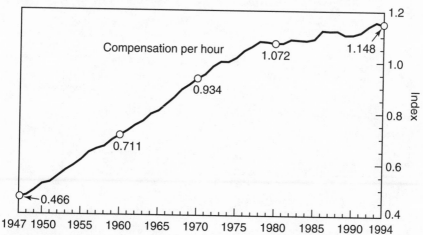

Note: Data for 1994 are through third quarter. Measures are adjusted for inflation using Consumer Price Index-U X1.

Source: Bureau of Labor Statistics.

Income for families and households has increased mildly according to the Current Population Survey.

Mean and Median Household and Family Income, 1967–1993 (1993 Dollars)

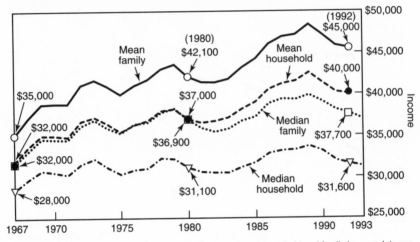

Notes: Income adjusted using 1993 CPI-U-X1 adjusted dollars. Household and family income data are unavailable for 1993.

Source: U.S. Census Bureau, Current Population Surveys.

Decennial census data provide a positive perspective of America's economic growth.

Mean and Median Household and Family Income, 1969–1989 (1993 Dollars)

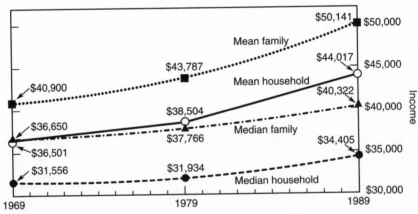

Source: U.S. Bureau of the Census, Decennial Censuses: 1970, 1980, 1990.

84

Per capita income almost doubled in three decades.

Per Capita Income, by Decade, 1959–1989 (1993 Dollars)

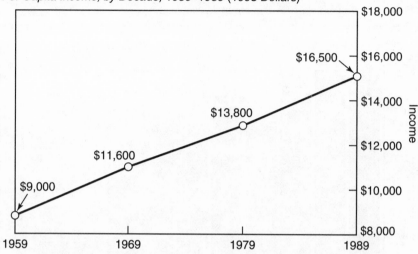

Source: U.S. Bureau of the Census, Decennial Censuses: 1960, 1970, 1980, 1990.

As measured by per capita gross domestic product (GDP), the trend is also solidly positive.

GDP per Capita, 1960–1993 (1993 Dollars)

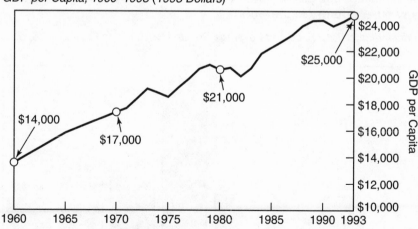

Source: U.S. Bureau of Economic Analysis.

Measured by what Americans can buy, the United States is the richest country in the world.

Purchasing Power Parity (in Thousand 1993 Dollars)

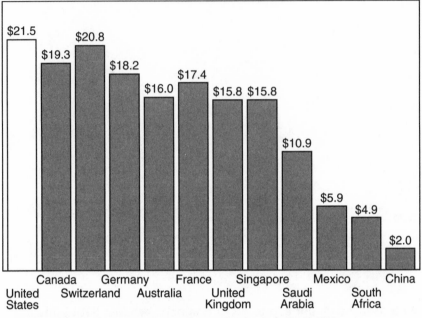

Source: United Nations, *Human Development Reports: Freedom in the World,* 1994.

America spends proportionally less on food and beverages than any other country in the world.

Percentage of Total Food and Beverage Private Consumption Expenditures, by Country, 1990

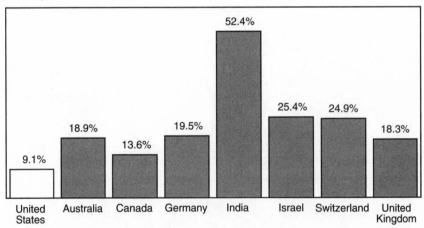

Source: U.S. Department of Agriculture, Economic Research Service. Based on United Nations, *National Accounts Statistics Annual;* 1994.

In the past decade, many luxury items have become common conveniences.

Household Distribution of Selected Items

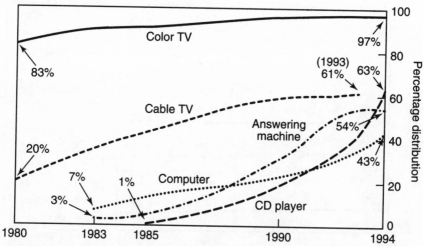

Note: Cable TV measured as a percentage of households with televisions (excluding Alaska and Hawaii).

Source: Electronic Industries Association; Consumer Electronics Group; cable television subscription from Television Bureau of Advertising. CD players for 1994 reached by adding "portable" and "home."

While costs have stayed fairly flat, American homes are continuing to increase in size.

Average Square Footage of New Homes, 1955–1993

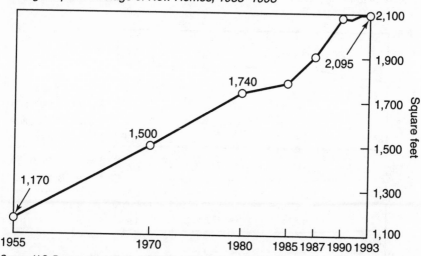

Source: U.S. Bureau of the Census and U.S. Department of Housing and Urban Development, Current Construction Reports C25.

In recent years there has been some change toward inequality in the shares of pretax, prebenefit income.

Shares of Total Income of All Families, 1967–1992

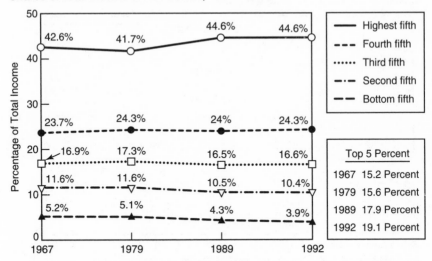

Source: Congressional Budget Office tabulations of data from *Current Population Survey,* 1968, 1974, 1980, 1990, and 1993 (1994 *Green Book,* published by the House Ways and Means Committee).

In recent years there has been slightly less change in shares of total income when taxes and benefits are included.

Shares of Total Income of All Families After Taxes and Benefits, 1979–1992

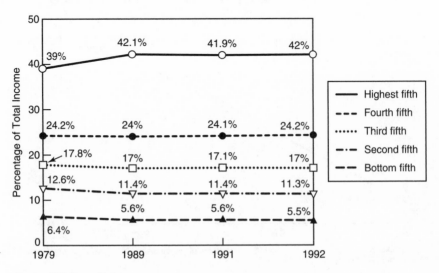

Source: 1994 *Green Book.*

Corporate and individual charity increased sharply since 1960.

Corporate and Individual Philanthropy, 1960–1992 (1993 Dollars)

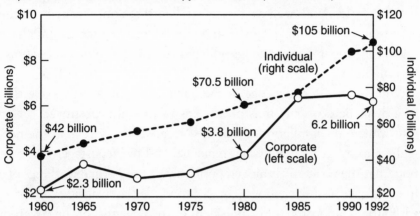

Note: Amount for pre-1970 individuals reached by adding "living donors" and "charitable bequests."

Source: AAFRC Trust for Philanthropy, *Giving USA;* 1994.

of economic turmoil? Of course they did. Should we feel sorry for them? Of course we should. Should we try to smooth out some of the bumps? Sure. Will we see plenty of heartbreaking scenes on the television news about people losing jobs? Sure. Will we see much on television about simultaneous job growth in a dynamic economy? Not much.

Will we ever acknowledge in the public and political dialogue that in a dynamic economy tens of millions of jobs are "destroyed" every year while tens of millions of jobs are "created" every year, in the normal course of events? Will that dialogue, and the reportage of it, ever note that the economy is moved positively by the normal workings of a free and successful economy, by a proud, self-activating workforce, with little relationship to the president or the Congress or the governor or the mayor, unless those elected officials do something monumentally stupid to screw it up? Will it ever be accommodated into the rhetoric of unfairness and inequality that there is enormous mobility, decade to decade, of the real people who are in the "lowest quintile" and move on to higher quintiles? (The medical intern in 1980 is a well-to-do doctor in 1990; the hamburger flipper of 1990 will repair copying machines in 2000. Most people go *up* the income ladder as they grow older, bringing both more experience and seniority to their jobs.)

Do not count on such media balance. Rest assured that the bombardment of economic bad news will continue and that politicians of both parties will blame each other. I can tell you one thing from writing about it for about a third of a century: It never stops.

There is another way to look at it all. The plausibly bad scenario is roughly this: Having become the richest people in all history, Americans are growing somewhat more prosperous very, very slowly, and this causes relative pain.

(Although, when one listens to the economists get into the details, the essence of the great, complicated, boring, tax-deficit/budget-spending debate—running time so far, about fifteen years—seems to be whether the American economy will on average grow by a "sluggish" 2 percent per year or at a better 2.75 percent per year. An American economy growing at 2 percent doubles in about thirty-five years and, even discounting for population growth, shows a 50 percent increase in per capita income in twenty-two years.)

———————

It was said during the campaign of 1992 that the values issues were not "real" issues. They were called diversionary or demagogic. The economy, according to many pundits—now that was a real issue, with some real answers.

Get real.

I do not want to offend the economics profession. Mostly honorable and intelligent persons inhabit the realm, and do useful work. But economics is not exactly hard science.

Consider: Regarding the deficit, there are some serious economists who think we should cut spending, and some who think we should raise taxes. But there are some who believe we need more economic growth, which they say is harmed by raising taxes *or* cutting spending. Some economists say we should cut taxes. Some economists say the deficit is way too high. Some economists say the deficit isn't really high. Some believe it doesn't matter much if it's high or low. Some say the deficit doesn't even exist because we measure it wrong. Democratic economists criticized Republican economists for saying that deficits should be measured as a percentage of GNP, which is what Democratic economists now say. Serious economists all. (I think we should cut the deficit, substantially, mostly because we're spending too much money in ways that hurt us.)

What about productivity? It is generally understood that the root of slow economic growth is slow productivity growth. Productivity in the manufacturing sector has soared (while the number of manufacturing jobs has remained about level). It is productivity in the service sector that has been mostly flat. But most economists concede that the profession just doesn't know how to measure productivity in services. (Don't computers increase productivity in offices? Don't automatic teller machines increase productivity in banks? So where's the measurable rise in productivity in the service sector?)

What about jobs? Surely we need more jobs, and good ones too. But many serious economists stress that 19 million new jobs were created from 1980 to 1990, and that the new jobs were mostly good ones, not mostly hamburger-flipper service jobs. The occupations with the fastest rate of growth over recent decades have not been in the service sector, but among professional and technical workers.

(When I first started writing about this sort of material in the early 1960s, critics were saying that manufacturing jobs were so very boring and unfulfilling and that we really should try to get people into other kinds of work. And that's what happened. I also wonder this about the ongoing economic debate: If everyone is supposed to get a good job, who will do the bad jobs? Will learned economists live without chambermaids in their hotels and busboys in their restaurants? If there are no illegal immigrants in California, who will do the yard work for Californians who complain about illegal immigrants?)

And so it goes. Arguments by serious economists everywhere. The rich got a tax ripoff in the eighties. No they didn't. We're overtaxed. No, we're undertaxed. Poverty is understated (because the methodology has not been updated). No, it's overstated (because we don't count noncash income). A strong dollar is good. No, a weak dollar is good. Trade creates jobs. No, trade costs jobs. Lower deficits will lower long-term interest rates. No, they won't. New infrastructure stimulates the economy. No, it doesn't. The trade deficit hurts us. No, it doesn't.

Want more? The budget deal of 1990 was a failure; no, it was a success. The budget of 1993 was a failure; no, it was a success. Foreigners are buying up America; no, America is investing too much abroad. We're losing our work ethic; no, we're working harder than ever. We need more regulation; no, we need less regulation. We have/haven't lost manufacturing jobs. Immigrants help/hurt the economy. America can't compete in the world market; America is the world's largest exporter. And, of course: Income has gone down, income has stayed flat, income has gone up.

Voodoo anyone? It's not the social issues that are phoney baloney. The economy is the snake-oil issue, the smoke-and-mirrors issue.

On the other hand, in the realm of social issues, the issues are real, and some consensus lives. Almost everyone knows that crime is too high, that it is a cancer on this society, and that we ought to be tougher on it. Almost everyone, including welfare mothers, knows that our welfare situation is a tragedy and we ought to change it drastically. Almost everyone knows we have dumbed down our schools and have to undumb them. Not everyone, but almost everyone, knows that preferential treatment is a threat and that we ought to stop it.

Even if, despite my cogent arguments so far, you have not at least amended, in your mind's eye, the commonplace ideas that (1) middle-class income has shriveled and (2) the rich are getting richer while everyone else gets poorer, I will give you a powerful reason to help you make your case, not mine.

Much of what is bad about our recent economic situation happened because of changing social conditions. It did not happen primarily because "we're not investing in people," or because "we're losing factory jobs to a global economy" or, more recently, because "this was a different kind of recession."

Some long-term numbers from the Census Bureau shed light on these matters. In 1993 married-couple families with children under age eighteen had a poverty rate of 9 *percent*. Families with a female head, no husband present, with children under age eighteen, had a poverty rate of 46 *percent*! And the *number* of such female-headed households soared from 2.6 *million* in 1960 to 8.8 *million* in 1993, a 238 *percent* increase, while married couples with children increased by only 8 *percent*.

The median income of a *husband-wife* family with children under age eighteen in 1993 was $45,548. For counterpart *female-headed* families, the median was $13,472.

Such numbers show how social issues drive economic data. Family breakup is a very big reason why poverty rates aren't falling, stalled between roughly 12 and 15 percent for almost thirty years. It's a big reason why income inequality has increased, slowly, for several decades.*

---

* Income inequality is usually measured without including the array of noncash benefits that goes to poor people: including food stamps, Medicaid, rent supplements, and more. The Census Bureau has been issuing a data series that factors in such considerations. In 1993 the poorest quintile received 3.5 percent of all private income when measured by cash only, but 4.9 percent when adjustments were made for noncash benefits.

And it's a big reason why both median and average incomes have gone up only grudgingly. You don't have to understand what a regression analysis is or what the GINI coefficient means, in order to know that a mom and a pop raising children will do better than a mom alone.

A study by three Census Bureau economists shows that the rise in female-headed households is the single largest component in the slow-down of income growth and the increase of income inequality from 1969 to 1989. The median income for *all* households would have been 11 percent higher if family composition had not changed negatively during those years. (And since 1989 the process of family decomposition has continued.) They write:

> At issue, of course, is whether the U.S. economy in recent years has been so transformed by world competition and other developments that it can no longer assure the ever-increasing standard of living American house-holds have become accustomed to. This theme has been popularized by a number of writers and economists during the 1980's. For example, Barry Bluestone and Bennett Harrison (1982) argued that "deindustrial-ization" was impeding the growth of the middle class. Robert Kuttner (1983) and Lester Thurow (1984) speculated about whether the Nation was becoming one of "have and have nots." And Frank Levy (1987) warned that the increasingly unequal distribution of incomes was creat-ing "an inequality of prospects" for the attainment of the American mid-dle class life style.
>
> One of the common threads running through all of their arguments was the belief that the source of the greater income polarization was the labor market. Economic forces, whether they be low productivity and wage growth, the soaring trade and fiscal deficits, the decline in union membership, and so forth, were all taking their toll on the traditional jobs of the middle class. On the other hand, demographic changes, such as the maturing of the baby boom generation, and social changes in living arrangements, were usually given lower importance in the explanation for the growth in income inequality among households. . . .
>
> The greater incidence of marital disruptions and births out of wed-lock, along with the increasing age at first marriage in recent years, has had a profound effect on the living arrangements of society. The Nation's

divorce rate climbed steadily from the late 1960's and into the 1970's, only to level off in the 1980's. Births out of wedlock more than doubled as a proportion of all births between 1970 and 1987 (from 10.7 percent in 1970 to 24.5 percent by 1987). And the median age at first marriage for men went from age 22.5 (years) in 1970 to age 25.1 by 1986. The resulting impact on the proportion of all households composed of married couples over these years [was]: In 1969, 70 percent of all households were made up of married couples, by 1979 the proportion had dropped to 61 percent, and by 1989, it was down to 56 percent. . . .

*Married couple households have much higher incomes than other types of households and the impact on income levels and the incidence of poverty is obvious.** (Italics mine.)

Thus: The values issues and social issues are important in their own right, but they also have an enormous impact on the economy.

Does anyone seriously contend that a child who believes in hard work and ambition will not do generally better economically than one who doesn't? Does anyone seriously contend that a child growing up in a family with a mother and a father will do better economically than a child growing up in a family with a mother only? Doesn't an erosion on the social side erode economic progress, as when predatory teenagers kill foreign tourists in Florida and harm the tourist industry? Or when American businessmen vacate the inner city because they don't like being shot at? Or that the cost of police, courts, and prisons during a high crime era raises taxes and diminishes after-tax income? Even Kevin Phillips knows all that.

Or, most poignantly, isn't it obvious that health care costs much more because of corrosive social conditions: drug abuse, teenage pregnancy, injury by crimes of violence, crack babies, sexually transmitted diseases, alcohol abuse, and smoking. Some medical economists have estimated that *about half* of our total health care bill comes from behavioral antecedents.

---

* Paul Ryscavage, Gordon Green, and Edward Welniak, "The Impact of Demographic, Social and Economic Change on the Distribution of Income" (paper presented to the Conference of the Association of Public Policy Analysis, 1991).

A case has been made that a sour economy causes unemployment and poverty, leading to a variety of social plagues: criminality, illegitimacy, welfare, female-headed households—and the consequent erosion of values. I doubt it. Scholar John DiIulio of Princeton and the Brookings Institution notes that neither criminality nor illegitimacy soared during the Great Depression, when economic conditions were far, far worse than anything we see now. He says: "There was a tripling in the murder rate among young black males since 1985. These kids are not economically deprived; they are criminally depraved because nobody ever taught them right from wrong. It is a calumny to say that poor people have poor values. It is not true."

Those young murderers typically end up in prison where they do not pay taxes, do not produce goods and services, and eat tax money for their incarceration. The erosion of values causes an economic cost, not the other way around.

———

Do economics matter most? This chapter should at least establish the case for an open mind on a matter that has been largely closed off in recent years. Values matter most. Social issues are where we can change things most easily, even some economic things. Through politics.

Chapter 5

THOSE DARN CULTURAL ISSUES

The values issues are subdivided into two categories: *social* issues and *cultural* issues.

The *social* issues may be characterized as follows: (1) They are important. (2) They are harmful. (3) There is some consensus about them: Americans, by huge majorities, are scared about crime, furious about welfare, irate about lack of discipline among school-aged children, and angry about preferences. Americans typically believe in a fairly tough response to these corrosive concerns. Further: These important, harmful, and consensual *social* problems are caused to some important extent by government and politics. They all seem to revolve loosely around the idea of "something for nothing."

The *cultural* issues are also a subset of the values issue. They are neither economic nor international. They concern "the social principles, goals, or standards held by an individual, class, society . . . that which is desirable or worthy of esteem for its own sake." The cultural issues can be found scattered prominently in the list on page 16.

How are the cultural issues different from the social issues? There is often *no consensus* about them, that is, Americans often don't agree about what to do about them. When they do, there are often constitutional blockades that prevent serious action. The cultural issues *may not* be important. They *may not* be harmful.

There is often no consensus because there is no agreement about the very nature of what they represent. Liberals often see the cultural issues as related to liberty and leeway. Conservatives often see them as related to license and libertinism. (Some examples: gays in the military, sex education, abortion, the pledge of allegiance, flag burning, and pornography.)

Are the cultural issues *important*? That too depends on who is doing the looking. Many First Amendment liberals think there is no big problem with pornography, and that it should not be censored even if there were.* Many social conservatives think pornography is evil. Some cultural issues—remember the flap about "Murphy Brown"?—were seen by liberals as positively trivial. Many conservatives thought otherwise.

Are the cultural issues *harmful*? Prochoice people view the availability of legal abortion as a great social advance for women. Prolife people think it is murder. Some Americans see homosexuality as an alternative lifestyle. Others think that teaching such a view to young children in public schools is an abomination.

IS THERE CAUSE AND EFFECT?

Despite the conflicting views, the cultural problems are highly relevant to the thesis of this work. They can be potent in the political arena. More important, beyond straight politics, many conservatives (and some liberals) believe the cultural problems may be a root cause of the social issues discussed here—crime, welfare, education, and preference. That makes them pointer stars toward the social issues about which most Americans do agree, and by that reasoning the cultural issues can often provide a good reason for voters to cast their ballots for or against a given candidate.

---

* For the record, about half the pay-per-view movies selected in hotel rooms are soft-porn. The average viewing time per soft-porn film is fourteen minutes. (Hmmm . . .) Of course, most hotel guests watch free television on over-the-air and cable channels.

Thus, many conservatives have said that when you take prayer out of school, when you teach sex education and then make condoms available in school, when criminality is seen as sociology not morality, when you teach that homosexuality is a valid and equal lifestyle, when abortion and pornography are made legal, when promiscuity is countenanced or not discouraged, when moral relativism is saluted, when "judgmental" becomes a bad word, and so on, a tone is set that pushes politicians and government to go down the wrong route on bigger social issues like crime and welfare. Many cultural conservatives (and some liberals) believe that when "Anything Goes" becomes the national cultural mantra, the "anything" that goes on is usually harmful far beyond its immediate effects. Many of these conservatives also say that a society that believes in nothing will soon give away something for nothing— welfare checks, diplomas, jobs by pigment, freedom for criminals.

Something for nothing in sex, many conservatives say, is a long step on the path to the welfare trap and the soaring rate of illegitimate births. Conservatives (and some liberals) have asked: when rap music glorifies cop-killing or misogyny, when the coarsened pop culture purveys sex and violence, isn't it obvious where so much of the crime, rape, and promiscuity come from? Many conservatives see a seamless web between social and cultural issues. I believe there may be a small amount of truth in all that, but I do not come out where they come out.

CULTURAL POLITICS

These cultural issues will remain powerful political weapons, as well they should, although the very idea of cultural politics is often scorned. It is a glory of our system that whatever people are angry about—including pornography, permissiveness, or prayer—can become big political issues. That happens even when the elite observers say they are not "real" issues or they are "demagogic" issues. What's real in politics is what the voters decide is real.

These issues will likely surface in the political campaigns of the future. Near as I can tell, the separate cultural issues—with the probable big exception of abortion and the possible exception of gun control—will help Republicans and conservatives, and harm Democrats and liberals.

I doubt, however, that much serious change will come about within the federal political arena, which requires not only joint action by House and Senate and a presidential signature, but often subsequent validation by the courts. The real changes wrought are often minimal. Abortion and homosexuality have been illegalized at some times and in some places—but certainly not stopped. Similarly, not much should be expected from Clinton's bold foray into the culture wars in mid-1995. Restraints on teenage smoking may be good politics, particularly when coupled with a self-congratulatory visit to a Baptist convention. But teen smoking, of course, is already against most state laws. So, too, Clinton made a dramatic mid-1995 speech supporting many forms of prayer in the schools, *noting that it's already legal.*

That's what often happens when there is not much consensus concerning private behavior. Nor is consensus around the corner. It is unlikely that pro-lifers will suddenly change their mind. It is unlikely that pro-choicers will change their mind. Nor the pro-gays, nor the anti-gays, nor the pro-tolerance-but-antiglorification-of-gays contingent.

Insofar as serious cultural change is possible, it is mostly a retail trade, person to person, within families, often attuned to religious values. I deal here with social issues. You can get those wholesale. Government did big things wrong. Change government, and make big changes.

Rest assured: We will all continue throwing sand at each other in our *cultural* playpens. Debate is useful, even unresolved debate. It is useful even if we don't know whether there is a strong relationship between cultural erosion and social problems. Meanwhile let us simultaneously and principally concentrate, laserlike, on *social issues* about which Americans agree, such as crime, welfare, merit, and education. We can make headway on these problems.

I tend to side with the cultural conservatives on some of their issues because I do not think that these days most of what they want is so very radical, and in fact what they want often makes quite good sense. I would surely rather send a child of mine to a school that praises abstinence than to one that gives out free condoms. (Why aren't free condoms means tested?) I don't even have too much of a problem with voluntary nondenominational silent prayer at the beginning of a school day. I don't want creationism taught as science, but I am amused when liberals go ballistic about the very thought that there is conservative pressure to change textbooks. Liberals, after all, have remade American textbooks from top to bottom in recent decades, too often in ways that have denigrated America and taught permissiveness and hyper-diversity as if it were religious doctrine.

POPULAR CULTURE AS A HEALTHY CASE IN POINT

There is something often missed in this cultural argument: Many aspects of our cultural situation are healthy.

As this book tries to drive home, values do matter most, and we should act boldly and dramatically on the *social* issues. But I am dubious about the idea that we will get much done by slaying fire-breathing *cultural* dragons. Some of those dragons are friendly critters.

Let us look at pop culture, a big cultural issue. Movies and television make up a large and contentious part of that issue of pop culture. I concede that too much tawdry, violent, promiscuous, and evil material is being purveyed. Still, I suggest that American movies and television, deservedly subject to much criticism, are monumental American assets.

Is culture, not law, the prime mover in social erosion? For example, has the rise of something for nothing been caused by the popular entertainment culture? If so, are there remedies available that are better than the disease?

The distinguished director Sydney Pollack (*Tootsie, Out of Africa, The Firm*) reminds us that American movies, with all their flaws, almost invariably have a common theme: "The hero shapes destiny," he says. That is quite far from something for nothing, and pretty close to that old American value of individualism. S. Robert Lichter, co-director of the Center for Media and Public Affairs, concurs: "Our studies of television programming have been coded for individualism, but it is so pervasive in American entertainment that we have never even published the material."

Would the incidence of violence, sex, and intoxication seriously diminish if those topics disappeared from our screens? That seems to be the apple-pie view of most psychologists (and of Lichter). But it is not a point that has been proved. Indeed, how could such a proposition be seriously validated? In a television-drenched society, just where do the subjects for comparison come from? Social scientists would need two groups similar in home environment, heredity, and school environment—except that one control group would have been fed a wholly different diet of television fare. Would the violence found in news and cartoons be counted? Does on-screen violence that is punished on-screen reduce or increase the incidence of violence off-screen? Is the violence portrayed rewarded or punished? Is the sex displayed wanton or loving?*

Professor Jonathan Freedman of the Department of Psychology at the University of Toronto reviewed the literature in 1984 and concluded that "there is little convincing evidence that in natural settings viewing television violence causes people to be more aggressive." In 1992, he wrote that "research has not produced the kind of strong, reliable, consistent results that we usually require to accept an effect as proved. It may be that watching violent programs causes increased aggressiveness, but from a scientific point of view, this has not been demonstrated. Our public statements should reflect this."

But suppose there was some direct relationship between popular entertainment and the apparent eroson of cultural values. What could we do about it in any public way? We could try to return to censorship. Some conservatives talk wistfully of the good old days of movie censorship. There would be legal hurdles, but perhaps not impossible ones.

But do we want broad censorship on sex and violence? How much good could it do? No, and not much.

I do not refuse to see movies with naked women in them—realistic ones, arty ones, and not-so-arty ones. Nor do scores of millions of other Americans. In the recent past, that number included a lot of good ole boys, and their wives, in pickup trucks, watching X-rated movies at the drive-in on Saturday nights, getting home early because, after all, they had to be in church the next morning. These days they may get the same sort of movies in the corner video store.

---

* Based in part on Eric Minkin in the *Washington Journalism Review.*

I do not happen to like much violence in drama. But, market-tested, lots of Americans do. Shakespeare understood the popular lust for blood, and so did Sophocles, in whose plays characters tear each other's eyes out, on stage. (I grant that the works of Shakespeare and Sophocles had redeeming value not readily apparent in the ugly violence of today's late-night movies.) Cartoon violence, horror shows, cowboy and gangster shoot-em-ups were around long before the current argument started.

Now, Hollywood does not deserve a free pass on this debate. Many Hollywood people make the case that what appears on the screen is only reflecting American reality, and it is what Americans want to see. Perhaps. But critic Michael Medved was correct when he said a few years ago that for a long time Hollywood pretty well ignored a potentially large family audience by concentrating mostly on themes that were violent or sexually driven. (More recently there has been an abundance of such family fare.)

Further, I have become convinced by Daniel Wattenberg, my son the writer, that Hollywood is missing a big bet by not doing movies that are heroic and serious. These days, he notes, we see biographical movies about Jimmy Hoffa, a criminal labor leader; Jim Garrison, a discredited city district attorney; Bugsy Siegel, a gangster; and Jim Morrison, a rock singer who died from a drug overdose. But in an earlier time the film industry did pabulum movies about Lincoln, Edison, and Alexander Graham Bell. Couldn't they now do modern movies, warts and all, about remarkable Americans? Where is the incredible story of George Washington? Or Hamilton versus Jefferson? Or Teddy Roosevelt? Or Henry Ford, Clare Boothe Luce, Einstein, Eisenhower, Salk, Marian Anderson, Frederick Douglass, or Harriet Beecher Stowe?

WHAT'S HAPPENING IN AMERICA

America, and America as reflected in pop culture, is often denounced as shoddy and coarse. It is also vibrant and may well be making the world better. That may be a paradox, but it is no less true for being paradoxical.

What is happening in America is no hopeless case. We talk about the corruption of youth by the popular culture. But look at our young people, all of them.

Not long ago—in this horrible era of obscenity, salaciousness, violence, nudity, drugs, alcohol, pornography, and evil music—I noticed a hand-printed sign in the room of my young daughter. It was this: "On my honor, I will try to serve God and my country, to help people at all times, and to live by the Brownie law." There are today almost 9 million children in America who are members of Boy Scouts, Girl Scouts, Daisies, Brownies, Tiger Cubs, Cubs, Cadettes, and Explorers—all apparently regularly pledging to serve God and country, to obey the law, and to help others.

America sociology has changed. The female-headed household is more prevalent than in earlier times, and that is not a healthy indicator. Still, most everyday Americans—young and not young—in single-parent or two-parent households—remain patriotic, religious, ambitious, law abiding, and family oriented. (There are some data in the public opinion Indicators.)

We are told, too, that our young people can't read, can't write, can't add, can't compete, don't have discipline, come from broken homes, and can't find Brazil on a map. I do not wholly reject this argument, as will be seen. But in early 1991 those same troubled American young people found Kuwait on a map. They manned (and womaned) the most complex machines in history (aircraft carriers); they worked seven days a week, sixteen hours a day, in 100-degree-plus temperatures. Viewed on television around the world, they showed themselves to be bright, innovative, and patriotic. Moreover, they prevailed. If what we saw was the symptom, perhaps we need more of the disease. We might take time to salute the military, which is interracial, merit oriented, and disciplined.

Let's talk politics. There too we are told that a corruption of spirit is taking hold, that special interests are working overtime, distorting our lives. We are told that in politics, as in culture, we are flaccid, have no discipline, and seek only instant gratification. Again, I do not wholly reject that argument; it is part of this book. But do not forget that we seek reform from a high plateau, not a sordid slum. Indeed, our unique elevation is what makes this struggle so important. Adlai Stevenson once said in the United Nations, "America can gag on a gnat, but we swallow tigers whole." Remember that for forty-five years, amid constant bickering, the American democratic political system cobbled together the most mighty and most successful alliance in history. It was the Liberty party and included democratic governments that traveled under conservative, liberal, social democratic, and socialist banners.

American voters chose freely to stay the course—a long, expensive, and disciplined course—in order to engage a threatening and evil empire. Americans taxed themselves, drafted their children, and won the cold war. Americans are not made of cotton candy, nor are they intent only on instant gratification. The argument of the deficit hawks that we have mortgaged the future of our children is precisely wrong in some important respects. America paid a price to ensure liberty for our children. We went into debt for it. We adults paid some of the price, and our children, who will benefit most, will pay some of it. That's fair.

During our time, some conservatives mournfully said that America had lost its nerve. The hell we did.

A POP CULTURE IMPERIUM

There is a split-level view of America around the world. There is one thought in the air that notes what we've been doing, and demands it at home. There's a revolution of ideas going on. Its buzzwords are "democracy," "markets," and "individualism." People everywhere want to participate. But where do those ideas originate? In their most modern incarnation, they seem to come from something that in an earlier, less bashful moment was called the "American way of life."

A major purveyor of that American culture is our visual pop culture industry, the same one that we regularly flay at home. Today that industry operates in a climate that is more free than ever, more popular than ever, and more global than ever. Incredibly, in Europe, 80 percent of the movie box office receipts come from American movies. In 1990 in Japan, twenty-one of the twenty-five top movies were American. Beyond that, American television programs and VCR tapes are in living rooms around the world. In 1994, for the first time, American companies received more than 50 percent of their theatrical revenues from foreign sources.

And what are people in America and around the world watching? The dozen biggest movie hits released during the 1980s were *E.T.*, *The Return of the Jedi*, *Batman*, *The Empire Strikes Back*, *Ghost-Busters*, three *Indiana Jones* movies, *Beverly Hills Cop*, *Back to the Future*, *Tootsie*, and *Rain Man*. This is not exactly your run-of-the-mill dirty dozen of pornographic violence.

And so too in the early 1990s. Among the top ten movies in each of the five years from 1990 to 1994 were: *Home Alone*, *Terminator II*, *Dances with Wolves*, *Boyz N the Hood*, *Thelma and Louise*, *Silence of the Lambs*, *Hook*, *Beauty and the Beast*, *Aladdin*, *A League of Their Own*, *Dick Tracy*, *Ghost*, *Jurassic Park*, *The Firm*, *Sleepless in Seattle*, *In the Line of Fire*, *Mrs Doubtfire*, *Teenage Mutant Ninja Turtles*, *Naked Gun 2 1/2: The Smell of Fear*, *Forrest Gump*, *The Lion King*, *The Santa Clause*, *Schindler's List*, *The Fugitive*, *True Lies*, *Lethal Weapon*, and *Wayne's World*. Yes, there is surely some violence, some sex, and some stupidity in the list, even, in *Lambs*, some creative cannibalism. Yes, there is some political subtext, and, alas, it is rarely conservative. But mostly these are enjoyable, well-made stories, just like in the good old days. They appear in theatres around the world and then are re-aired on television, along with American television dramas and sit-coms, some good, some not. (About half of all movie revenues in a given year are earned by the top thirty movies.)

During the 1994 Moscow summit meeting Bill Clinton met with Boris Yeltsin. But Russians, like Americans, were not paying much attention to issues of NATO or nukes in the Ukraine. Across eleven time zones Russians were talking about "Twin Peaks."

THE NATURE OF THE PRODUCT

The new global entertainment situation is a *market*, perhaps one of the purest around. The television zapper may be the most democratic market-oriented instrument in history. Zap! Zap! Out of my house! And because of cable, satellites, privatization, and deregulation, more people have access to that market than at any other time in history. The coming information superhighway will make that market much larger still, even if the reality turns out to be one-tenth of the hype.

Free markets offer people choices. Free markets make consumers into voters. Free markets force purveyors to offer what people want.

There is an aspect of the cultural conservative argument that sometimes drifts dangerously close to that view, elitist to the core, as elitist as the New Class, as elitist as limousine liberalism: *The public ain't got no couth.* You can hear those old-fashioned elitist wheels spinning: Maybe we need a few government regulations to deal with the couth shortage.

What are those audiences buying, all over the world? Action, adventure, violence, sex, conflict, obscenity—surely. All that's been in the deck since Aristophanes; since Chaucer; since Shakespeare. In a famous scene in *Born Yesterday*, the late Judy Holliday berates her crude boyfriend. She screams: "You ain't got no couth." Is there less couth than before? Is the couthlessness more available? Perhaps so.

But we also will do well to notice what is so often attached to these standard themes, often hidden and latent: American views and values. That's a very big reason why American entertainment is so popular everywhere. Audiences see upward mobility in *Working Girl* and *Boyz N the Hood*; see the fight against the bureaucratic establishment in *Beverly Hills Cop* and *Dirty Harry*; see pluralism in *The Shawshank Redemption, Smoke, The Joy Luck Club,* and *Jungle Fever*; see populism in *Rocky*; see individualism in *Dances with Wolves* and *Clear and Present Danger*; see patriotism in *Top Gun*; see technical virtuosity in *Terminator II, Jurassic Park,* and *Apollo 13*; see what goes wrong in places where values are very different, as in *Schindler's List*.

Audiences around the world have paid more than a half a *billion* dollars to see *Forrest Gump*. Its theme is not complicated: Traditional values trump modernist sophistication.

BE CAREFUL: THE WORLD IS AT STAKE

So I offer only certain cautions, applicable across the board, but particularly to cultural conservatives. Conservatives, like liberals, can blame America first. Condemning the product can too easily condemn the people who purchase the product. Conservatives can fall victim to the liberal disease: trash-America exaggeration in the cause of tactical victory. Conservatives, like limosine liberals, can think the public ain't got no couth.

You can hear those old-fashioned elitist wheels spinning: Maybe we need a few government regulations to deal with the couth shortage. Maybe we need a super V-Chip so that the government will do what parents ought to do.

Why worry?

Because there is a second view of America. You can hear the retrograde voices around the world: Who are these Americans to tell us how to live? We know best, our people aren't ready for liberty; we know best, liberty brings pornography; liberty brings alcohol; liberty brings crime; liberty brings dependency; liberty breeds separatism. Modern conservatives should not be bolstering that case.

Americans care a great deal about telling their story and changing the world. Once this tendency was labeled manifest destiny. At times that harbored racialist overtones. We understand now that we can't clone the world American style. But the American missionary idea lives on. It is as old as John Winthrop's *City on a Hill* and as recent as Ronald Reagan, who kept quoting Winthrop. (So far, President Clinton's on-again off-again democracy-oriented foreign policy has usually been in the same tradition, sort of.)

American movies, television, music, books, and magazines have such pervasive worldwide influence that it is asked: Is the world Americanizing? That trend toward Americanization is also driven by immigration, tourism, language, advertising, and international commerce. Harvard's Joseph Nye calls it "soft power" and ranks it high. Our foreign policy is Kissinger and Schwarzenegger.

Is all this good for America? Of course it is, if we think we have something to offer. Is all this good for the world? I think so, but the peoples of the world will have to decide that for themselves. They, and only they, will ultimately decide whether the individualist, democratic, pluralistic, and marketplace values offered by the American cultural imperium are of some use as the world reshapes itself into ways we cannot yet foresee. More so than at any other time in history, people have a choice: A menu of views and values is available.

Many reasons for American pop-cultural primacy are offered: We started the movies. Our technical virtuosity is supreme, from film, to audio, to publicity. Our home market yields an economy of scale. English is the universal language. Americans have the universal demography. There are European filmmakers who will tell you, "Only Americans know how to tell a story." (That from the soil that nurtured Dickens and Balzac.)

It is more than that. People everywhere want to share the American experience. They too want to be heroes shaping their own destiny. They get that idea in part from our visual popular culture. Trashing American popular culture, putting it in tight quarters here surrounded by a V-Chip programmed by cackling congressmen, tends to dilute or muzzle that export. A government rating system will be either a farce or a tragedy.

What does all this globalism have to do with a book about social issues in America? I believe that democracy American-style, with all its flaws, is still the last, best hope of earth, as Lincoln said. But if our flaws aren't fixed, if the flaws get worse, America will cease to be the model of what can be. It will be the model of another thought: that democracy leads up a blind alley.

We are not the only nation with crime or welfare problems. We are not the only nation troubled about the education of our children. We are certainly not the only nation struggling with the problems of pluralism.

But we are the only nation to which everyone else pays attention. If America works fairly well, there will be a model showing that free expression doesn't yield decadence, that pluralism doesn't yield chaos, that there can be order and liberty, that there can be compassion without dependency—all visible and influential on a billion screens around the world.

If we cannot do that, the rest of the world is in for trouble. When they're in trouble, we're in trouble.

Chapter 6

IT'S NOT NEW, IT'S NORMAL

Having noted that it's *not* the economy, and that cultural issues are *not* as important as social issues, consider the case that the primacy of values issues is *not* new. It's normal, and it's back.

There can be a rich argument about whether social or economic issues had primacy during the presidential election of 1992. There is much less doubt about the earthquake election of 1994, whose seismic wave rumbled right over some old political thinking. Suddenly pundits and pollsters were forced, at least momentarily, to rediscover the potency of the values issues.

Just forty-two days before the 1994 election, an NBC/*Wall Street Journal* poll asked:

Q. *Please tell me which of these statements comes closest to your point of view:*
   A) *The social and economic problems that face America are mainly the result of a decline in moral values.*
   B) *The social and economic problems that face America are mainly the result of financial pressures and strains on the family.*

Results

Moral values: 54 percent.
Financial pressures: 34 percent.*

* NBC/*Wall Street Journal* taken by Peter Hart and Robert Teeter, September 24–27, 1994.

So, by about five to three, Americans said in 1994 that our problems are not due to financial causes, but that our problems, financial and otherwise, are caused by a deterioration of moral values. Then, a *Newsweek* poll taken eleven days before the election asked:

How much do you blame each of these people and groups for the problems that make you dissatisfied? Do you blame [BLANK] a lot, somewhat, only a little, or not at all?

Results (those answering "a lot"):

"Republicans in Congress" 25 percent
"Large corporations" 28 percent
"President Clinton" 32 percent
"Democrats in Congress" 36 percent
"The news media" 43 percent
"The moral decline of people in general" 57 percent.†

† *Newsweek*, October 27–28, 1994, taken by Princeton Survey Research Associates.

Morality, again, was in first place by a big margin. Only a partisan Republican knave would point out that the blame for the moral decline referred to above goes primarily to (perceived) liberal items: the news media, the Democrats in Congress, and President Clinton. The least blameworthy are congressional Republicans and large corporations.

A *Washington Post*/ABC poll in early September of 1994 showed 68 percent of the public regarded social issues as "the most important problem," while only 13 percent said it was economic issues. And a front-page story in the *Washington Post* headlined, "Disillusioned Public Puts Social Issues at Top of Campaign." Remember "Disillusioned": It's a most important word.

Moreover, almost every survey showed that in 1994 crime was head and shoulders the number one issue (as shown in the Indicators section).

This notion of social primacy didn't quite sink in with the mainstream media. The first interpretation of the 1994 election results dealt with the idea that the real theme was "antigovernment." That was not a bad call, except that it was usually expressed as an abstract notion and mostly unrelated to just what it was that government was doing that made voters "antigovernment." It was also said that the election concerned "angry white males," without much specifying what the angry white males were angry about (except perhaps affirmative action). It was hardly noted that a majority of *white* women also voted Republican, apparently also angry at something. It was further said that the psephological tidal wave was "anti-Clinton," principally because of health care and taxes, that is, non-value issues.

Soon, predictably, much of the political dialogue returned to economics. We were told that it was really "economic anxiety" that was troubling people. After all, there was that new global economy, real wages hadn't gone up, people were bouncing from job to job—and that's why the 1994 elections had come out so peculiarly. By mid-1995 the big political issue was said to be "the budget," or the budget-busting Medicare specifically, or "the deficit." Again, we were served up a description of a mostly disembodied economic concern, with little attention paid to the idea that Americans hated big government spending not just because it was in deficit, but because it was doing harmful things.

This tropism toward economics should come as no surprise. It has become an article of faith that in elections, economics matters most. Recall, it had been said in the 1992 election that America had outgrown those demagogic values issues, and the three main issues were "jobs, jobs, jobs."

So pervasive is this belief in the economic primacy of elections that a variety of academic models have been built upon that rock. Each purports to be able to predict a forthcoming presidential election on the basis of economic indicators, usually the unemployment rate, or the rate of growth in the economy, or the inflation rate, or some combinations thereof, like the "misery index" (which is the sum of the unemployment and inflation rates).

Until 1992, the most prominent of these theories had been put forth by Ray Fair of Yale University, who over the years has applied his own economic formula evenhandedly to Democrats and Republicans alike. In mid-1992, using his never-miss, sure-fire formula, Professor Fair showed that George Bush would be reelected to a second term.

In its modern incarnation, seen case by case, the economics-is-everything argument goes this way:

- Incumbent Nixon won in 1972 because he put on price controls and fixed the economy.
- Challenger Carter beat incumbent Ford in 1976 because the economy was bad.
- Challenger Reagan beat incumbent Carter in 1980 because the economy was bad.
- Incumbent Reagan beat challenger Mondale in 1984 because the economy was good.
- Republican Bush (identified as an incumbent Republican) beat Dukakis in 1988 because the economy was good.
- Challenger Clinton beat incumbent Bush because the economy was bad.

It's a simple theory. And suspect. A short history lesson is in order. Social primacy is not new.

First, economic primacy may not even have been in the saddle during the runup to the 1992 election while America went into a recession and then began climbing out of it.

Go back to late 1989 and early 1990. The first "Latino National Political Survey" was in the field.* As is the custom in these sorts of

---

* *Latino Voices*, de la Garza, DeSipio, Garcia, Garcia and Falcon (Boulder, Colo.: Westview Press). The study was funded by the Ford, Rockefeller, Spencer, and Tinker foundations. The Temple University Institute for Survey Research did the actual polling. This was a large project, with a sample of 2,817 Latinos and an additional control sample of 456 Anglos. Both samples were drawn principally from the major metropolitan areas of the United States, that is, central cities and suburban areas, with little rural representation. Not a perfect sample, but a pretty good one in a nation where 80 percent of the people live in such metropolitan areas.

omnibus surveys, a question was asked about the "most important national problem." Here are the results:

Q. *What do you say is the most important problem facing people in the country today?*

	MEXICANS	PUERTO RICANS	CUBANS	ANGLOS
Economics	23%	11%	18%	20%
Social problems	56%	73%	64%	44%

In an interview with me, the director of the study, Rodolfo de la Garza, explained that the principal responses that were coded into the rubric of social problems were "crime," "drugs," and "family breakup."

The social issue responses were much higher for the Latino respondents than for the Anglos, but even for Anglos social concerns were twice as important as economic concerns. So, just two years before the election, the voters said social concerns were more important than economic concerns.

Of course, at that time—late 1989 and early 1990—the official recession of 1991 had not quite begun, although the economy had already slowed down.

A little later, in April 1990, with a struggling economy, the Gallup Poll showed that "drugs/drug abuse" was the number one problem in America (with 30 percent of the respondents so indicating). "Poverty/homeless" was in second place at 11 percent, and "economy" was third at 7 percent.

In 1991 the *Washington Post*/ABC News poll (shown in the Indicators on page 117) conducted two askings of the economic-social split; both showed "social" as the most important problem. In the election year of 1992 there were three askings: one showed "economic," one showed "social," and one (just before the elections) showed a dead heat.

Other polls showed it somewhat differently. As the recession arrived for real in 1991, the economy went up as the "most important issue," achieving first place in most polls through the election year of 1992. Still, it was no blow-out. In April 1992 the Gallup survey aggregated all the economic concerns and reported a 73 *percent* response, and at the same time aggregated what they termed the noneconomic issues and came up with 62 percent—not a vast difference.

Each month in 1992, pollster Richard Wirthlin asked the "most important problem" question, grouping the responses in a three-way split: economic, social, and international. The international response ran last, never higher than 6 percent. The economic answer usually ran well ahead. Still, in May, June, and July 1992 the social and economic issues ran roughly in a dead heat, each getting about 35 percent of the respondents. That was when the fury about the economy-stupid was at a high point and just when the candidacy of Ross Perot, keyed to economic concerns, captured the fancy of the nation. And in fairness, it was also the time span that encompassed the riot in Los Angeles.

Moreover, once the talking heads in television-land bought the proposition that the economy-stupid and jobs, jobs, jobs was so obviously the most important issue, some poll respondents almost surely responded in the manner expected of them. After all, respondents don't want the interviewer to think the respondent is stupid. This is a common phenomenon in the survey research trade, called a "social response." Certainly after the Houston convention, when persons who were concerned with so-called moral issues were publicly portrayed as zanies and zealots, one can assume that it was somewhat harder for voters to tell pollsters that values issues were more important to them than economic ones.

It can be argued that had the Republicans run something better than the world's worst campaign, they might have succeeded, at least partially, in keeping the economy as a somewhat neutral issue. Remember: The official numbers had shown that America had actually emerged from the recession more than a year prior to the election. The real gross domestic product actually grew by 2.6 percent in 1992. What economic problems existed were not solely American: Both Europe and Japan were in the tank. It had been almost a full decade since a recession. There was a Democratic Congress to lay blame on. Bush made a stab at explaining all this but did a rotten job of it, by his own admission.

I do not make these points to show that the economy was not the major election issue during the poor economic climate of the 1992 election. Perhaps it was. But the Bush campaign didn't press values issues after the Houston convention. And Clinton was able to capitalize on the economic issue only because he had been able to certify himself as tough on the social issues.

INDICATORS: PUBLIC OPINION

Americans have become increasingly pessimistic about the course the country is taking.

Percentage of the Public Who Think the Country Is on the Right Track and the Wrong Track

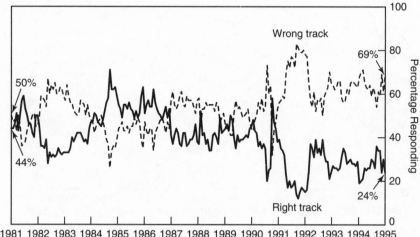

Source: The Wirthlin Group.

Since the late 1980s (with one exception in 1992 out of three askings), social issues have been a bigger concern for most Americans than economic issues.

"What do you think is the most important problem facing this country today?"

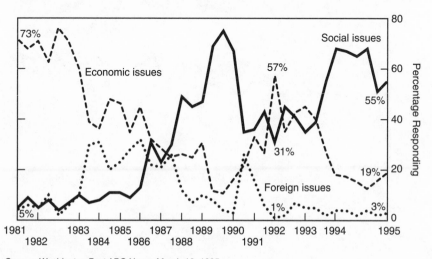

Source: *Washington Post*-ABC News, March 16, 1995.

117

Most Americans view themselves as moderates or conservatives.

"Generally, do you think of yourself as a liberal, moderate, or conservative?"

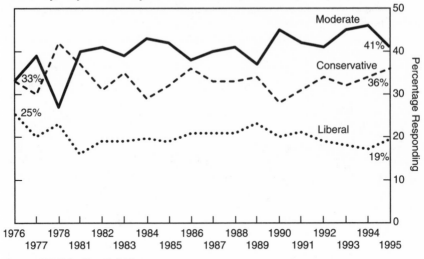

Source: CBS News/*New York Times.*

For the first time there are more independents than Republicans or Democrats.

Self-identification by Party, 1937–1995

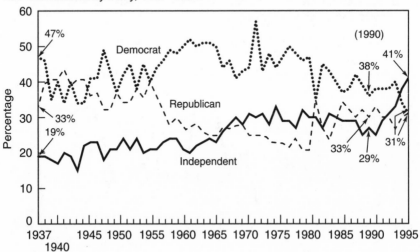

Source: Gallup Organization.

118

Americans would like to see more money spent on crime and education but less on welfare.

"We are faced with many problems in this country, none of which can be solved easily or inexpensively. I'm going to name some of the problems, and for each one I'd like you to tell me whether you think we're spending too much money on it, too little money, or about the right amount."

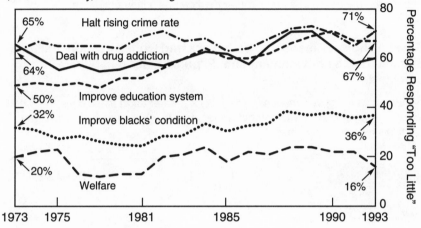

Source: National Opinion Research Center.

Americans say crime is the most serious problem facing our country today.

"What do you think are the two most serious problems facing the country?"

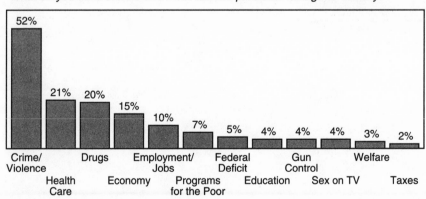

Source: Harris Poll, 1994.

119

PUBLIC OPINION ON CRIME

There is a strong consensus among the American public that crime is the most important issue facing the country today. Americans are worried about the rising crime rate and fear walking the streets in their own neighborhoods.
Most people believe more emphasis should be put on punishment, mostly through increased incarceration, rather than on prevention programs.

Given a choice, Americans, both black and white, are more inclined to think that the government should punish, not rehabilitate, criminals.

"Where does the government need to make a greater effort these days: in trying to rehabilitate criminals who commit crimes or in trying to punish and put away criminals who commit crimes?"

RESPONDENTS	PUNISH	REHABILITATE
National	49%	32%
White	49	32
Black	46	40
Hispanic	56	30

Source: Los Angeles Times, 1994.

Both whites and blacks favor tougher anticrime measures.

"For each of the following, please tell me whether you favor or oppose it as a way of dealing with crime in the United States."

	FAVOR*	OPPOSE*
Making parole more difficult	82%	17%
Whites	84	15
Blacks	74	24
Restricting bail	75	24
Whites	78	11
Blacks	58	39
Imposing more severe sentences	79	18
Whites	78	19
Blacks	76	20
Putting more police on the street	80	19
Whites	80	18
Blacks	76	20
Limit appeals in death penalty cases	60	35
Whites	62	34
Blacks	43	48
Enact tougher gun laws	64	33
Whites	63	34
Blacks	67	28

* "Favor" encompasses "strongly favor" and "favor" responses. "Opposes" encompasses "strongly oppose" and "oppose" responses.
Source: Gallup Poll Monthly (December 1993).

Americans think crime in their neighborhoods is rising. They are becoming more uneasy.

| | CRIME IN YOUR AREA COMPARED TO LAST YEAR | | | HOW UNEASY DO YOU FEEL ON THE STREETS COMPARED TO LAST YEAR? | | |
	INCREASING	DECREASING	SAME	MORE UNEASY	LESS UNEASY	SAME
National	54%	5%	39%	42%	5%	51%
Whites	55	4	40	43	4	51
Blacks	50	15	33	44	9	43
Hispanics	46	8	43	33	11	52
Central city	53	5	41	42	5	51
Suburbs	53	5	41	42	5	51
Small town	67	2	29	48	4	46
Rural	38	6	39	37	5	55

Source: Louis Harris and Associates, 1993.

Although black and white response rates differ, most Americans have solid confidence in the police but not in the criminal justice system.

| | CONFIDENCE IN THE POLICE | | | CONFIDENCE IN THE CRIMINAL JUSTICE SYSTEM | | |
	GREAT DEAL/ QUITE A LOT	SOME	VERY LITTLE	GREAT DEAL/ QUITE A LOT	SOME	VERY LITTLE
National	54%	33%	12%	15%	35%	49%
Whites	57	33	10	14	35	50
Blacks	34	35	30	26	25	50

Source: Gallup Organization, 1993.

123

Americans think that the government is spending too little on halting crime and that the courts do not deal harshly enough with criminals.

"In general, do you think the courts in this area deal too harshly or not harshly enough with criminals?"

			"NOT HARSHLY ENOUGH"		
	1980	*1983*	*1987*	*1990*	*1993*
National	83%	86%	79%	83%	81%
Whites	84	87	81	84	82
Blacks	77	74	70	77	86

"Are we spending too much, too little, or about the right amount on halting the rising crime rate?"

			"TOO LITTLE"		
	1980	*1983*	*1987*	*1990*	*1993*
National	69%	67%	68%	70%	71%
Whites	68	66	68	68	70
Blacks	79	75	70	78	76

Source: National Opinion Research Center, 1993.

PUBLIC OPINION ON WELFARE

Americans have little sympathy for welfare recipients but favor more initiatives to help the truly needy, even if they require more spending. About ninety percent of Americans think the welfare system needs to be reformed but only a very small percentage think welfare should be eliminated altogether.

Although the number of Americans who favor reducing welfare has more than doubled since 1972, by wide margins Americans want to reform the system even if it means spending more on certain items.

	FAVOR	OPPOSE
Reforming the welfare system	90%	7%
Take money out of the paychecks and tax refunds of deadbeat dads	93	5
Spend extra money to provide free day care for working mothers	92	7
Require all able-bodied people on welfare to work or learn a job skill	87	11
Increase the minimum wage	74	24
Replace welfare with a system of guaranteed jobs	70	25

Source: Times-Mirror Poll, May 13–14, 1992.

125

"Do you feel the amount of tax money now being spent for welfare programs to help low-income families should be increased, kept at the present level, reduced, or ended alltogether?"

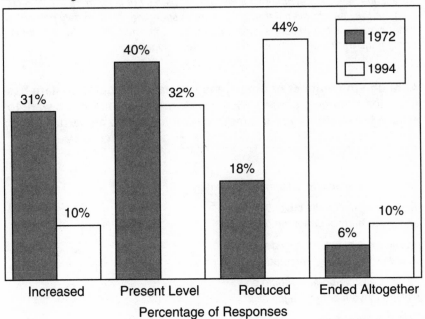

Source: Gallup Poll, April 16–18, 1994.

Americans are quite skeptical of welfare recipients.

"Do you think that most people on welfare are using welfare for a short period of time and will get off it eventually, or do you think that most people on welfare are so dependent on welfare that they will never get off it?"

	TOTAL	REPUBLICANS	DEMOCRATS	INDEPENDENTS
Off eventually	11%	8%	15%	10%
Dependent	82	84	77	84

"Do you think most welfare recipients really want to work, or not?"

	TOTAL	REPUBLICANS	DEMOCRATS	INDEPENDENTS
Want to Work	27%	25%	28%	27%
Do not want to work	63	54	58	64

"What do you consider a more serious problem in America today—families not getting enough welfare to get by, OR families getting more welfare benefits than they need?"

	TOTAL	REPUBLICANS	DEMOCRATS	INDEPENDENTS
Not enough	21%	10%	25%	21%
More than they need	58	62	54	59

"In your opinion, do you think that most people who receive money from welfare could get along without it if they tried, or do you think that most of them really need this help?"

	TOTAL	REPUBLICANS	DEMOCRATS	INDEPENDENTS
Really need help	35%	30%	40%	35%
Can get along without help	48	57	43	45

Source: CBS/New York Times Poll, January 15–17, 1994.

PUBLIC OPINION IN OUR SCHOOLS

High school students are mostly worried about social issues like crime and violence. More than a fifth of students fear personal violence in their schools.

High school seniors worry about social issues most.

"Of all the problems facing the nation today, how often do you worry about each of the following?"

Percentages Responding "Often" or "Sometimes"

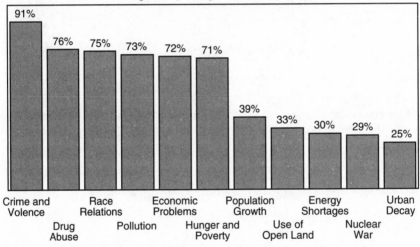

Source: Survey Research Center of the Institute for Social Research, 1993.

One-fifth of white students and one-third of black students fear for their physical safety while at school.

"When you are at school, do you ever fear for your physical safety, or not?"

HIGH SCHOOL STUDENTS	YES	NO
National	22%	78%
Whites	20	80
Blacks	30	70

Source: Gallup Organization, 1993.

Surveys of high school students indicate that a majority of young people think that traditional values are important.

Views of High School Students, 1990–1991

VALUES ISSUE	PERCENTAGE WHO THINK ISSUE IMPORTANT
Religion in life	59% (seniors, 1991)
Work/success	85% (sophomores, 1990)
Marriage/family	83% (sophomores, 1990)
Giving their children better opportunities	82% (sophomores, 1990)
Friendship	73% (sophomores, 1990)

Source: University of Michigan, Institute for Social Research, *Monitoring the Future,* various years; U.S. Department of Education, National Center for Education Statistics, High School and Beyond, Base Year Survey, "1980 Sophomore Cohort"; National Education Longitudinal Study, 1988.

PUBLIC OPINION ON
AFFIRMATIVE ACTION

Whites and blacks both believe that "ability" should be the principal criteria for advancement. Phrased less starkly, whites and blacks disagree about preferential treatment.

"Some people say that to make up for past discrimination, women and members of minority groups should be given preferential treatment in getting jobs and places in college. Others say that ability, as measured by test scores, should be the main consideration. Which point of view comes closer to how you feel?"

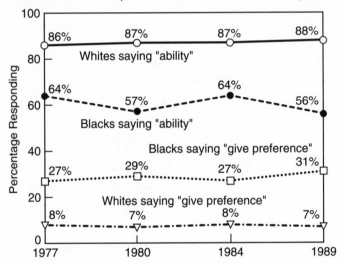

Source: Gallup Poll. Numbers from 1977 and 1980 are for nonwhites.

130

"We should make every possible effort to improve the position of blacks and other minorities, even if it means giving them preferential treatment."

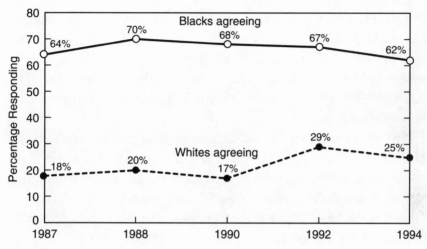

Source: Times-Mirror Poll, October 1994.

It is important to look at the economic versus social situation from a longer perspective. Today there is a commonly held notion that economic issues—not just in and around 1992, but almost invariably—are the primary ones that determine national elections. Until the Republican sweep in 1994, which recreated divided government, many analysts looked ahead to the 1996 election and said, "It all depends on how the economy is doing. If it's doing well, then Clinton wins; if it's bad he loses." Some pundits still say it. I didn't believe it then; I don't believe it now.

The perception that economics is everything, says political scientist Everett Carl Ladd, is just not correct.* Ladd notes that the idea of ongoing economic primacy in our elections didn't come into our political thinking until the elections of the 1930s. So horrific was the economic impact of the Great Depression, Ladd says, that for a while economics did indeed become the largest voting issue. But he stresses that such a condition was the aberration, not the norm, in American history.

Historian/Columnist Michael Barone looks back to before the Depression and writes in his book *Our Country* (Free Press, 1990) that: "The major struggles in American politics in the two decades before 1930 were not over issues that split the nation on economic lines, but over noneconomic cultural issues." Barone cites four big noneconomic issues of that time: racial segregation, Prohibition, immigration, and the intense argument about American participation in World War I.

It was also true before 1910. The famous "realigning" election of 1896 was won by William McKinley, who drubbed William Jennings Bryan, partly on economic issues (as in the "cross of gold") but on cultural issues as well. Religion played a big role in Bryan's several defeats; he was the last hope of the rural fundamentalists in their battle against the growing numbers of more secular and metropolitan voters. Going back to 1824, Andrew Jackson won not just on economic policy but on regional and cultural attitudes—the frontier beat the eastern establishment.

---

* Ladd is Director of the Roper Center for Public Opinion Research and professor of political science at the University of Connecticut. He is the author of a premier textbook, *The American Polity: The People and Their Government*.

And, of course, the issue of race has played a powerful role in many American elections. This was true prior to the election of Abraham Lincoln, it was true for Lincoln, and it was certainly true through to the time of Franklin Delano Roosevelt, whose majorities were solidified by the Democratic "Solid South," still driven by memories of a civil war caused by race. Bill Moyers recalls President Johnson's morose thought in his White House bedroom late on the sweet night that the Civil Rights Act of 1964 passed the Congress: "We've turned the South over to the Republican party for the rest of our lives." And today it is said that Republicans often win because they "play the race card," and Democrats often lose because their party is seen as "too black."

In recent decades, at least until the end of the cold war, international issues have been powerful in the presidential arena. Just fast-forward some hot issues from 1944 onward: "Don't Change Horses in Midstream" (World War II), "Who Lost China?" (1948), "Communism, Corruption and Korea" (1952), Hungary and Suez (1956), "The Missile Gap" (1960), Vietnam (1968), Vietnam (1972), hostages in Iran (1980), and cold war spending (1984). I do not believe it was an accident that whenever Democrats nominated a hawk—Roosevelt, Truman, Jack Kennedy, Johnson, and Carter (in his first incarnation)—they won. Noneconomic issues.

Many pundits say that what wins are the "bread 'n' butter" issues. But in recent years (at least until the silliness in 1992), Republicans have not cooperated in allowing economics to drive elections. Voters do not live by bread and butter alone.

A moment ago the economic interpretation of recent presidential elections was put forth. Fair is fair; here is another way of looking at the same elections.

- The 1968 election is a classic case in point (often ignored by bread 'n' butter economic theoreticians). The economy was healthy, inflation was still at moderate levels. And Hubert Humphrey, vice president of the in-party, lost the election. Technically, it was a close contest. But with the George Wallace vote properly factored (recall that about two to one would have gone for Nixon had Wallace not been in the contest, according to exit polls), it was a solid Nixon victory. Humphrey and the Democrats lost *despite* a strong economy. There was racial turmoil, a war in Vietnam, an ugly reaction to the war in Vietnam, and a cultural split within the Democratic party, symbolized by bloodshed at the Chicago convention. Values issues, and to a lesser extent, issues of foreign policy.

- It is true that the economy was in good shape for Nixon in 1972. But even if the economy was sour, it seems clear (at least to me) that the identification of McGovern with counterculture activists would have poisoned the McGovern campaign, even if the economy had been in trouble.

- Did Gerald Ford lose because of economics? Well, there was indeed a recession in 1975, and by election day 1976, the recovery was not complete, although clearly moving in the right direction. Did Ford lose because of economics? Remember, he lost to Carter by only 2.1 percent of the vote. What about Watergate? Did that harm the Republicans? What about Ford's pardon of Nixon? Did that harm Ford? What about the famous gaffe about a free Poland? Might that have cost Ford a point or two? (Ford was actually trying to say something true about the Poles: that in their hearts they did not regard themselves as Soviet satellites.)

- Reagan did indeed run principally on the economy in 1980. He asked: "Are you better off than you were four years ago?" (By the way, some serious economists say that the correct statistical answer was yes.) Why shouldn't Reagan have run on the economy with the prime rate at about 15 percent and the inflation rate at over 13 percent? But his social buzzwords were at the public root of his campaign, and there for all to see: "family," "work," "neighborhood," "peace," and "freedom." He ran against liberal negativism. And on the theory that the Soviet Union was an evil empire that deserved to go on the scrap heap of history, where it could be put by building up American armed forces. Not just economic issues.

- Having established his bonafides on values, when good economic times came about on his watch in 1984, Reagan was unbeatable.

- In 1988 Bush returned to the social issues to come from behind and beat Dukakis. (Curiously, analysts who say Bush won because the economy was in good shape are mostly the same analysts who now say that the eighties had been an economic disaster for the middle class!)
- And then in 1992 Clinton, because he had co-opted the values issues, was able to get 43 percent against an opponent who first butchered the values issues and then ignored them during a slow economic moment.

If we must make rules about national elections, try this one: If the economy is perfect and has been so for quite a time, (say, 4 percent growth and 2 percent inflation), and the president running for a second term has been involved in no scandal, and America is at peace with honor, and solid progress is being made on the social problems—that president is likely to win. Remarkable.

Add this: If the nation is in dreadful shape, with a deep and lasting recession, runaway inflation, public scandal, and losing a war—that incumbent will likely lose.

But neither of those two scenarios comes about too frequently. Most national elections, to one degree or another, take place in a much grayer area.

Because I doubt that the 1992 election was simply about "the economy," because I am certain there is no rule that says subsequent elections will be determined simply on economics, because I believe America's biggest problems are social ones, I think—and hope—the next election will be fought out on social grounds rather than on economic grounds. America would be better served. Let the voters rank the issues.

Dick Scammon and I wrote in 1970 that, as voting issues, the social issue had become co-equal with the economic issue. That was regarded (by a generation that had matured during the Depression and immediate postwar years) as something unusual and, to some, even unclean. Issues of crime and race, for example, were said to be "demagogic." The only "real" issues were economic ones, from tax rates, to union working conditions, to social security (and sometimes foreign policy). Elections, we were told, were essentially issues of big guys versus little guys.

That, of course, is a good, and legitimate, strategy for Democrats in America, and for social Democrats and democratic socialists elsewhere. Such a concentration, however, may have also led to a condition wherein social issues were swept under the rug, or trivialized, or demonized—leading us into the fix we are now in. It is one big reason why Americans are fed up with the current political scene, why they profess to be independents, why they seek third parties of the center, as shown in the Indicators in this chapter and discussed later.

I believe it was true that social issues had reached rough political coequality at the time *The Real Majority* was published. Times have changed. A quarter century later I believe that those same sorts of no-more-something-for-nothing values issues are the *most important* in real life. Because elections tend to mirror reality and because the data show it, I further believe that those issues are the most important *voting* issues as well. The values issues, particularly the subsidiary social issues, *have moved from coequality to primacy.*

First Republicans (1992) and then Democrats (1994) mishandled those issues. I believe that either major party can devise a social battle plan for the presidential election year of 1996 that can lead to a stronger electoral position and a better country. (It will be easier for the Republicans.) Moreover, a third or fourth party or candidate could score heavily with these issues. I will offer some game plans for all after a while. But first we had better understand in greater depth just why those social issues are even more important now than in the recent past.

Part Three

WHY THESE VALUES MATTER MOST

Chapter 7

THE CRIME WAVE

Six percent of any group of 18-year-old boys in London; Copenhagen; Stockholm; Philadelphia; Racine; or Orange County, California, get in trouble with the law. . . . So the problem, therefore, is, can we address what is going on in the lives of the six percent at the same time that we tighten the cultural constraints and the legal constraints around them? . . . The best we can do is make credible threats of punishment. This country for 20 years reduced the credibility of any serious threat of punishment.
—James Q. Wilson, interviewed on "Think Tank," January 1995

It is time now to end this on-the-other-hand sissy stuff. The economy is not so bad; on the other hand, it can surely be better. The cultural situation is troubled; on the other hand, it is a great American asset. Values issues have been most important in American political history; on the other hand, so have economic and international issues been important. That degree of other-handedness cannot be maintained as we move for a closer look at our social situation.

139

There is some very bad stuff out there, probably worse than ever before, and it is driving public opinion, which drives politics, and had damn well better drive public policy.

We grapple in this part of the book with four big social issues. Two—crime and welfare—are rotten disasters. The other two, education and quotas, offer a more mixed situation. On balance they are only disappointing and corrosive. So, we ask now: What happened? Why? How did the public react? How did politicians react? Does it hurt us?

―――――――――

Crime is probably the worst of the worst. It should be acknowledged that crime is a complex issue. Thus, once over lightly: Many good jobs have left the inner city, an exodus that might well yield a sense of hopelessness, which breeds crime. Crime may well be related to welfare, female-headed households, and a lack of male role models. It would be good to have more rehabilitative drug programs, in prison and out. More walk-the-beat community policing makes good sense. Criminals are getting younger, and more violent. Crime is going up in most of the modern nations of the world. The crime rate is disproportionately high in the black community. The biggest increase in crime has occurred in grim inner-city neighborhoods, not in neighborhoods where most readers of this book are likely to reside. Yet.

But there is something simpler and more important that transcends much of that complexity: *Crime is deeply related to punishment.* Further, punishment yields incapacitation of criminals. Those are useful prisms through which to open a discussion of what has been happening in America on the crime front.

Back when it was thought—to recall an old value—that crime does not pay, there was much less crime than now. Why did crime not pay? In some large measure, because heavy punishment was associated with it, and such punishments were relatively certain to be applied to a transgressor. When it became more plausible for a potential predator to believe that crime does pay, or even that crime might pay, crime went up.

If the diminishment of punishment is at the root of much of our ugly criminal situation, let us not forget where punishment comes from: the law and law enforcement. That is put into place by elected officials—

governors, mayors, state legislatures, the Congress, the president—or by appointees or hired hands of these elected officials—police, parole officers, sheriffs, judicial and prison personnel. They all serve, directly or indirectly, by the choice of the governed. We elect them. And so on the punishment side, let us not forget that if we don't like what's going on, we have in some large part been doing it to ourselves, through our federal, state, and local governments. Remember: Politics runs government, and what government causes, government should cure, or try to.

———

There is one chart, the lead-off one in the crime Indicators section, that tells the recent story of crime, punishment, despair—and then perhaps hope. Developed with some flair by Morgan Reynolds of Texas A&M, it deals principally with the concept of "expected punishment." (It was originally published by the National Center for Policy Analysis and has been updated for use here.) That concept, expressed as an index number, is linked to the number of days served in prison and to the probability of events that must transpire before a criminal actually does time in prison.

To get to prison, a criminal must be arrested. Then indicted. Then prosecuted. Then convicted. Then actually sentenced to serve time. It takes all five to get a criminal into the slammer. (A sixth aspect of punishment then follows, which concerns whether the criminal's stay in prison is diminished by parole and/or time off for good behavior.)

The chart shows that from the early 1950s to the mid-1970s the "expected punishment" rate sank like a kryptonite anchor. And so (say Professor Reynolds and others) serious crime went up because there was less on the loss side of the ledger for a potential criminal. Crime became a better deal. Then, starting in the mid-1970s, the "expected punishment" rate stopped sinking and actually *climbed* somewhat. That at first *flattened out* the crime rate and then began pushing it down.

So, by Reynolds's calculations, here is where we stand now: The level of expected punishment is still almost two-thirds less than in the early 1950s. And—no surprise—we still have very high levels of crime, somewhat lower than the peak and probably diminishing somewhat.

There are, of course, complicated and offsetting factors in the crime equation; a menacing explosion of crack cocaine in the mid-1980s is probably most significant. Still, the essence of the dazzling "X" in the Reynolds chart is confirmed by a variety of other federal statistics found in the Indicators.

Clearly, the popular notion that crime has gone up is correct. The FBI's violent crime rate has increased sixfold (!) from the late 1950s to the early 1990s.* We should pause momentarily to stress what these data stand for. Every integer represents a human being who was murdered, raped, robbed, mugged, or subjected to an aggravated assault. These are numbers drenched in blood; they represent traumas forever imprinted in the minds of the surviving victims and their loved ones.†

It is terrible. But something else has been going on in the data that (mostly for political reasons) has been generally unstressed in the argument about crime: Violent crime has been going up at a *decreasing* rate and is now probably actually *declining*.

Thus, from 1960 to 1970 the violent crime rate went up by a stunning 126 percent. Then, from 1970 to 1980, the rate climbed by 64 percent, about half the previous level but still surging. And from 1980 to 1990 the increase was 23 percent, up still but at a much lower rate of increase. Not insignificantly, these data are prominently cited in *The Case for More Incarceration,* published by the Bush administration's Justice Department in late 1992. And these data remain a central root of the Republican/conservative/hard-line philosophy of how to deal with crime.

---

* Reynold's data deal with "serious" crimes, which include burglary; the FBI's data deal with "violent" crimes, which do not.

† There are two methods for assessing violent crimes in the United States. The first, the Federal Bureau of Investigation's Uniform Crime Reports (UCR), is based on crimes reported to police and has been maintained since 1930. The other is the National Crime Survey's Victimization Rate, which is determined by polling 100,000 people annually. It includes all crimes, whether they were reported to the police or not, and has been taken every year since 1973, after the big spike in crime rates occurred. Unless otherwise noted, the UCR is used in this book, principally because it picks up the rising criminality of the 1960s and early 1970s. It also includes homicides, the ultimate violent crime, which cannot be self-reported in a victimization survey.

INDICATORS: CRIME

When criminals expected to spend less time in prison the crime rate increased. When expected punishment increased, the crime rate decreased.

Expected Punishment for Crimes of Violence and Burglary

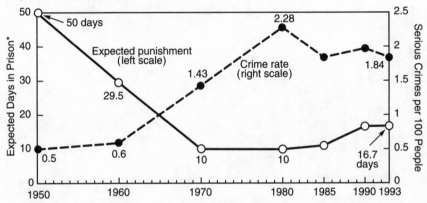

* Median prison sentence for all serious crimes, weighted by probabilities of arrest, prosecution, conviction, and imprisonment.

Source: Morgan Reynolds, National Center for Policy Analysis, from federal data.

The violent crime rate went up sixfold from 1957 to 1993.

Violent Crime Rate per 100,000, 1957–1993

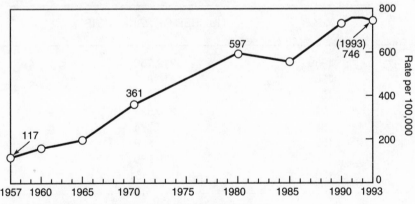

Source: FBI Uniform Crime Reports, *Crime in the United States.*

143

The rate of increase of violent crime has decreased and now may be dropping in real terms.

Rate of Increase of Violent Crime, 1960–1993

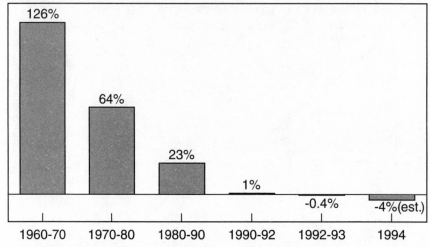

| 1960-70 | 1970-80 | 1980-90 | 1990-92 | 1992-93 | 1994 |

Source: Bureau of Justice Statistics: Federal Bureau of Investigation; *Uniform Crime Reports, 1994.*

There are more prisoners in America today than at any previous time.

YEAR	NUMBER OF PRISONERS
1960	212,953
1965	210,895
1970	196,429
1975	240,593
1980	315,974
1985	480,568
1990	739,980
1994*	1,012,851

* A midyear figure.

Source: Bureau of Justice Statistics, *Prisoners in State and Federal Institutions* on December 31, and *Correctional Populations in the United States.*

144

Violent criminals typically serve only about one-third of their sentence.

Time Sentenced versus Time Served Among State Prisoners, 1988–1990 (in months)

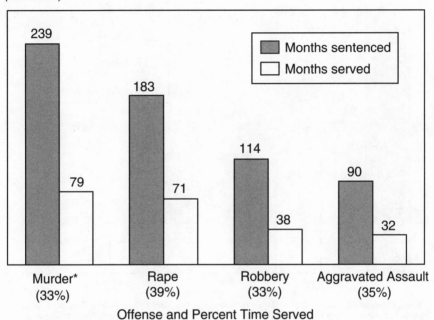

Offense and Percent Time Served

* Includes manslaughter.

Note: Figures in parenthesis represent percentage of sentence served.

Source: Bureau of Justice Statistics, *Violent Crime in the U.S. 1988–90.*

Criminals are less likely than earlier to spend time in prison.

Percentage of Crimes Resulting in a Prison Sentence, 1950 and 1983

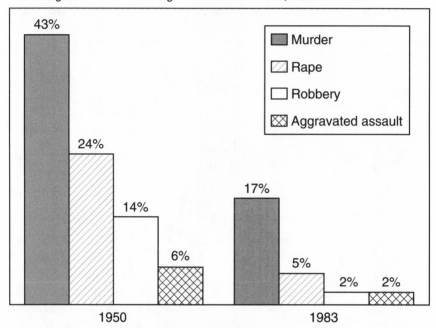

Source: Morgan Reynolds, National Center for Policy Analysis, *Crime Pays, But So Does Imprisonment,* 1990; Federal Bureau of Investigation, *Crime in the United States, Uniform Crime Reports for the United States;* Bureau of Justice, Bulletin NCJ-110331, April 1988.

146

The number of men on probation or parole almost tripled in thirteen years.

People on Parole or Probation as a Percentage of the Adult Male Population

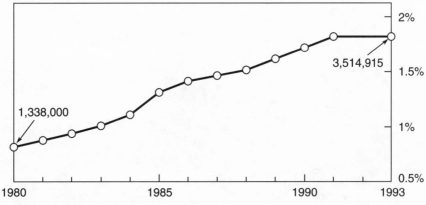

Source: U.S. Bureau of Justice Statistics.

Black and white inmates received roughly similar sentences for similar types of offenses.

Median Sentence of State Prison Population by Offense (Months)

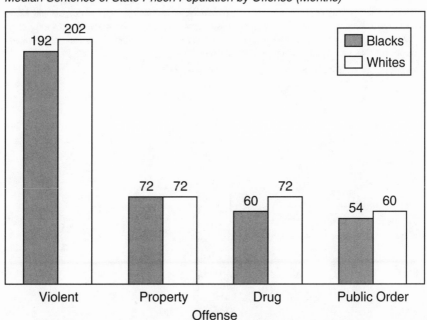

Source: Bureau of Justice Statistics: *Survey of State Inmates,* 1991.

147

Less than 7 percent of prisoners are nonviolent, nonrepeat offenders.

State Prisoners, by Offense

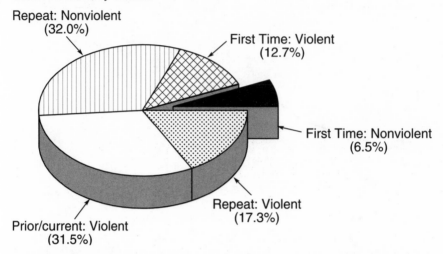

Repeat: Nonviolent
(32.0%)

First Time: Violent
(12.7%)

First Time: Nonviolent
(6.5%)

Repeat: Violent
(17.3%)

Prior/current: Violent
(31.5%)

Note: Roughly 90 percent of prisoners in the United States are in state prisons. Criminals in federal prisons are less likely to be violent offenders.

Definitions: Repeat violent offenders have served more than one sentence and only for violent crimes. Prior/current violent offenders have served time more than once and at least once for a violent and nonviolent offense. Repeat nonviolent offenders have been incarcerated more than once, but only for nonviolent offenses. First-time violent offenders have not been previously incarcerated and are currently serving time for a violent offense. First-time nonviolent offenders have not previously been incarcerated and are currently serving time for a nonviolent offense.

Source: U.S. Bureau of Justice Statistics, *Survey of Prison Inmates, 1991.*

Black men are the most frequent victims of crime.

Violent Crime Victimization Rate per 1,000, age 12 and over, 1991

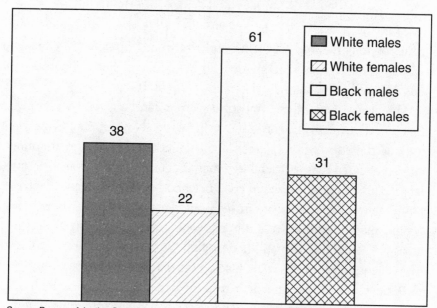

Source: Bureau of Justice Statistics, *Criminal Victimization in the United States, 1991.*

Then, in the early 1990s, the increase in the rate dipped further and went into *negative* territory. The 1994 data showed a 4 percent decline. The lastest data look promising. Comparisons of the number of homicides in the first six months of 1995 and 1994 showed homicide declines of 32 percent in New York and Houston, 19 percent in Chicago, 18 percent in Atlanta, 10 percent in Washington, and 71 percent in Los Angeles. (The Minneapolis rate was up by 108 percent.)

The biggest part of this statistical picture can be given the acronym DITROI (Decrease In The Rate of Increase). Now, of course, no one walking the streets thinks much about DITROI. Mothers in the inner cities are scared that their children may get gunned down from stray bullets; suburban home owners in good neighborhoods worry about robbery; businesses still fear to locate in high-crime areas, no matter how many goodies might be put in an "enterprise zone"; television reporters in many areas of the country can still honestly fill the screens with blood almost every night; many whites think blacks live by a different moral code.

A decrease in the rate of increase when the baseline is high still means a very high crime rate. And so, DITROI has sometimes been a laugher in political terms. That's what New York City mayor David Dinkins found out in the 1993 elections, when he stressed that crime in Gotham declined during his tenure. It was, as Casey Stengel used to say, a "true fact." But Dinkins lost, in some large measure because his opponent, Rudolph Giuliani, was able to show that crime in New York City was still horribly high.

But laugh-at-able, or politically unsayable, or counterintuitive, is not the same as wrong. It does seem as if we are making some slow but real headway against the crime wave.

Why? One big reason is that more criminals are in prisons. How does this cut the crime rate?

Putative solutions to the crime problem abound. We hear regularly about gun control, drug rehabilitation, welfare reform, alternative incarceration, a Marshall Plan for the cities, greater use of the death penalty, habeas corpus reform, more cops in community policing, boot camps, and boarding schools for offenders.

As it happens, I approve of most of the above catalog (and might even sign on to a Marshall Plan, if I could design it). But there is this sad fact: No one has a clue about whether such proposals would seriously cut the rate of violent crime. The existing criminological studies are thin and often contradictory. On balance so far, the results of the studies have not been encouraging. There is no magic bullet in that list, or anything close.

What probably works best is what nearly everyone intuitively knows: incapacitation. A thug in prison cannot shoot your sister.

Is that theory valid? Consider the flow of the (incapacitated) prison population as shown in the Indicators.

In 1960 there were 213,000 criminals in state and federal prisons. Crime was surging, but there was that pervasive and regnant liberal idea of American guilt. Society opted for a mushy social welfare response to increased crime. There was a search for root causes. From *West Side Story*, written in 1957, we hear juvenile delinquents serenading Officer Krupke, saying, "We ain't no delinquents, we're misunderstood, deep down inside of us there is good, . . ."

That mushy theme is reflected in the "expected punishment" data: There was a softening of deterrence. And while crime was going *up* during the sixties, by 1970 the number of prisoners actually went *down*, to 196,000.

By the late 1970s (just before Ronald Reagan became president) the enormity of what was happening sunk in. Society began to toughen up. The number of prisoners *climbed* to 316,000 in 1980—a 61 percent increase in a single decade.

By 1990 there were 740,000 prisoners—a 134 percent decade-to-decade increase!

In one year, 1989, the number of inmates in state prisons grew by 63,000. To be able to accommodate that pace of increase means creating a new 1,000-bed prison every six days.*

This tougher tendency, too, was also in play in *West Side Story*: "Officer Krupke, you've done it again, this boy don't need a job, he needs a year in the pen."

If the rate of crime increase went up because (in part) punishment and criminal incapacitation went down, and the rate of crime increase is

* The estimate is by Patrick Langen of the Bureau of Justice Statistics, writing in *Science* magazine.

now going down because the rate of punishment and incapacitation has gone up, a precedent question arises: Why did punishment go down in the first place?

To some large measure, it happened because of how government, in its many faces, changed its policies.

We can begin with that now-mythical assembly, the Warren Court, named for Earl Warren, who served as chief justice of the Supreme Court from 1953 to 1969. The Warren Court did much good. For one obvious example, the end to school segregation was a noble turning point in American life.

But on the issue of crime, the legacy of the Warren Court is under challenge. The case is made that Warren placed a federal blanket over state criminal procedures, softening such procedures, interpreting the Constitution as if the criminal was the victim and the police and the courts (and America) the oppressors. All of which, it is said, pushed down the rate of expected punishment, directly or indirectly.

Consider a brief time line of how the Supreme Court changed the nature of criminal justice in America:

- In 1961, in *Mapp* v. *Ohio,* the Court ruled that evidence obtained illegally could not be used against a defendant in court, that is, it must be excluded—hence the so-called exclusionary rule.
- In 1963, the Court ruled in *Gideon* v. *Wainwright* that Florida's policy of not providing a lawyer to poor defendants denied such defendants the due process of law.
- In 1964, in *Stovall* v. *Denno,* the Court ruled that all confessions had to be independently assessed to determine if they were voluntary.
- In 1966, *Miranda* v. *Arizona* coalesced many Warren decisions into a universal set of rules for every law enforcement official in the United States. *Miranda* established, among other things, an absolute right to an attorney and an absolute right for the defendant to remain silent.*

---

* Mr. Miranda, charged with rape, was freed by the Court and later committed robberies, which put him behind bars again.

- In 1967, in *Arizona v. Gault,* the Court ruled that the Bill of Rights applies to minors the same as to adults. (In the view of Judge James Lincoln, the former head of the Juvenile Judges Association of the United States, the Court "took a ball bat and virtually clubbed the Juvenile Court out of existence" because states could no longer emphasize reforming rather than punishing young offenders.)
- In 1972, in *Papachristo v. City of Jacksonville, Florida,* the Court (after Warren had retired) struck down a city ordinance that essentially allowed police to roust anyone they thought looked suspicious, particularly "rogues," "vagabonds," and "dissolute persons." (It was easier to be "homeless," which constituted one stepping-stone toward the creation of a massive homelessness problem in America.)

What's wrong with the Warren Court rulings? Taken alone, it appears that most of the specific decisions make at least some sense. There is a theme to the Warren pudding, and it is certainly not all bad: Defendants have rights.

It is in its totality rather than its specificity that the Warren rulings may fall short. A vast web of extra hearings, more lawyers, more paper, more appeals, and tougher standards of evidence certainly made it *seem* harder to arrest likely criminals, to indict them, to prosecute them, to convict them, to get them into prison for an extended period of time, from which spot they cannot mug your sister.

Did the law of Warren actually push up the crime rate? We do know that crime went up sharply after Warren, and we know that "expected punishment" went down. The word was out on the street: You can beat the rap (i.e., something for nothing). Many criminals believed it; so did many cops. It tended to embolden the former and demoralize the latter. Whether this was a coincidence or a cause is a matter that has been debated for a quarter of a century. I vote mostly on the causal side.

Warren may have made sense as 1950s law, set against a backdrop of low crime rates. But courts must also give society the tools to defend itself. When the violent crime rate increases sixfold in the course of the three decades following Warren, it is not premature to reassess the fruits of Warren and the seeds of the fruit.

Had Warren occurred in a vacuum, perhaps it would not have caused much trouble. But other forces in the society were also diluting the potency of the criminal system, sometimes flowing directly from the elected political system, sometimes not. The numbers of males on parole and probation soared from 1.3 million in 1980 to 3.5 million in 1993. Crimes were less likely to result in prison sentences. Violent prisoners were serving only about one-third of their sentence time before release. (See Indicators charts on pp. 145 and 147.) Because the recidivism rate is high, there is never a shortage of credentialed plunderers and predators on the streets.

As the babies of the leading edge of the baby boom grew into their later teenaged years the crime rate started going up more seriously. There is a close relationship between crime and the number of young men aged sixteen to twenty-four in a society. Starting in the 1960s there was no shortage of young males.

As shall be examined in the next chapter, the percentage of children growing up without fathers in their house soared. Here is what Daniel Patrick Moynihan wrote in 1965 in "The Case for a Family Policy" in *America* magazine:

> (A) . . . community that allows a large number of young men to grow up in broken families, dominated by women, never acquiring any rational set of expectations about the future—that community asks for and gets chaos. Crime, violence, unrest, disorder—most particularly the furious, unrestrained lashing out at the whole social structure—that is not only to be expected; it is very near to inevitable.

As shall be examined, discipline eroded in schools. Drug use became much more common. (Statistically, drug use is not a victimless crime, as it was too often described in the 1960s. Drugs are a powerful multiplier of criminal activity.) If violence on television and in the movies causes more crime, be it noted that the amount of on-screen violence increased and intensified. Nor did Warrenism end with the retirement of Chief Justice Warren. In a dramatic and symbolic decision in 1972, the successor Court temporarily banned the use of the death penalty. That ban remained in effect for four years. In 1970 no prison system in America functioned under court orders, often dealing with alleged "overcrowding." By 1990 there were 1,200 state prisons and 500 municipalities operating under such orders, which have the effect of pushing prisoners out of confinement, allowing them to mug your sister.

Society is a living organism. It responds to stimuli in many ways, and certainly through its political system. Over the years, many liberals stuck to the idea that the proper response to the rising tide of crime was to deal with root causes. From the 1960s onward, America spent several trillion dollars in government programs, in education, welfare, health, and so on, to deal with root causes. While some specific budget line items fluctuated over time, the totality of root cause programs have been funded at ever-increasing levels. Political flimflammery aside, this has happened during the course of both Democratic and Republican administrations. Some root cause activities made sense and have been good in their own right. Others have been clunkers. In either event, crime did not go down as we spent more money on root causes. It went up.

In politics, as in life, two things can happen at the same time. America did root causes. Then, after a while, America also began to intensify incapacitation. Prison populations increased. The number of sworn law enforcement officers, including police, went up from 450,000 in 1983 to 600,000 in 1992. Laws began to change. In the early 1980s Congress passed legislation regarding "mandatory minimum" sentencing for "career criminals," which tended to increase the amount of time served before parole.

High violent crime rates fed the television news. The public became more frightened. The case is made now, with more vigor than ever, that punishment works. This view stimulated some of the most important parts of the 1994 crime bill, at least for a while.

The public has been angered by the crime situation. By an 81 percent count, respondents told pollsters that courts do not deal harshly enough with criminals, with the response rate of blacks somewhat lower (76 percent) than the white rate, but still overwhelming. When asked whether the government should make greater effort to "rehabilitate" criminals or to "punish" them, respondents go 49 percent for punishment and 32 percent for rehabilitation.*

From the 1960s onward, crime never left the public agenda. The public believes, as does the author, that we have not been sufficiently severe about criminality. Insofar as Democrats were seen as not fully responsive to this view, it cost them at the polls.

High rates of criminality in America, and its perception, is near catastrophic. Think of the repercussions: It helps create an exodus from the inner city, it destroys commerce in the inner city, it sets black against white, it is a costly public expense, it takes fathers away from their children, it virtually imprisons some law-abiding citizens in bad neighborhoods, particularly the elderly. It gives America and democracy a bad name, and it can sap the will and the spirit of a nation.

Moreover, although crime rates are coming down somewhat now, many criminologists believe something ominous is just down the road. John DiIulio of Princeton and the Brookings Institution says: "Between now and the year 2005, we're going to have about a 30 percent increase in the number of 14–17-year-old males in this country, a 50 percent increase among Latinos, about a 30 percent increase among black males—those most at risk of being victimized by crimes and committing crimes." It's a very important issue. It is more important than whether the federal budget is balanced in 2002 or 2004.

No other Democrat understood all this better than Bill Clinton as he ran for president in 1992. His stock lines on the stump were:

> Those who commit crimes must be caught, those who are caught must be convicted, those who are convicted must be punished.

> We have to prevent crime and punish criminals, not explain away their behavior.

As the campaign tightened in the final weeks, the Clinton campaign commercials stressed that Clinton and Gore had sent a strong signal to criminals by supporting the death penalty. (Unlike Michael Dukakis.)

---

* Roper Center, 1993; the *Los Angeles Times*, 1994.

Clinton ran against the standard liberal idea of crime and punishment. It was central to his strategy of showing himself as an acceptable moderate to American swing voters, those Reagan Democrats who had demolished Democratic candidates for a generation.

But did he govern that way?

Chapter 8

THE WELFARE WAVE

A woman needs a man like a fish needs a bicycle.
　　—Ancient feminist adage, overtaken by events

I don't think AFDC undermines values, I think it destroys them.
And it destroys them because it says to a person work is not important. . . . It destroys the person. . . . We probably have to do something we're pretty scared to do as a country: eliminate AFDC. But
we're pretty scared to do that, because we immediately say, "Well,
what's going to happen to the kid?" And I would say, "What's happening to the kid right now?"
　　—Eloise Anderson, Director, California Department of Social Services, interviewed July 1995 for PBS television version of this book

Nowhere else do the themes of this book come together more cleanly
and obviously than in the realm of that broad and haunting catch-all
topic of welfare.

　Consider the familiar circle sketched out in this book: liberal guilt,
yielding perceived victimization, yielding something-for-nothing coun-

terproductive government payoffs, yielding values erosion, yielding worsening conditions, yielding—again around the circle—more guilt and perceived victimization, more counterproductive government pay- offs, more values erosion, and ever-worsening conditions for those caught up in the cycle, while some slip the noose and move upward.

All of which eventually yields, I hope, a political course correction. Such a new direction could be put into play in several ways. Well- meaning but chastened liberal perpetrators, pushed by a liberal presi- dent who was elected on the strength of nonliberal votes, could change their minds and change the government. Or conservatives could beat liberals at the polls regularly. Or there could be a combination of both.

Michael Harrington, writing in *The Other America* in the early 1960s was prominent among those arguing that poverty came from the na- ture of the American economy, that therefore we all were guilty, and that the poor *deserved* welfare because they were victims. Their "com- pensation," he said, was a matter of "justice, not charity." Later that decade, roughly the same thought was put forth by George Wiley of the National Welfare Rights Organization; his slogan was, "Welfare is a right, not a privilege."

But it was not a brilliant new idea suddenly conjured up by either Harrington or Wiley that changed the nature of thinking about wel- fare. It was in the air, heavy with guilt. Soon, many welfare officials and community activists began calling welfare an entitlement, or compen- sation, or even reparations. To many, it was seen as a remedy for vic- timization in a guilty society.

But, of course, it can be put in a different light. During the presidential election campaign of 1992, Bill Clinton chose to characterize aspects of what was happening in the context of a society with a tendency to give away something for nothing. And his general prescription, mentioned endlessly, was "No More Something for Nothing." More specifically, he favored an end to welfare as we know it, keyed to time limits—two years and out—and working in concert with reciprocal responsibility.

However it is described, the monies involved in welfare—which are officially called "income-tested benefits," or "means-tested benefits," and will often be called here Greater Welfare—have soared in recent decades, totally and on a per recipient basis. The Indicators tell the story.

The program that is too often thought to make up the entirety of welfare is Aid to Families with Dependent Children, usually known as AFDC. In a little more than three decades, the number of persons on AFDC has climbed from about 3 million to almost 15 million. But the average AFDC benefit has remained about stable: $134 per person per month in 1960, and $131 in 1993, after having moved somewhat upward in the intervening years. That is, a mother with two children—three persons—gets almost $400 per month in cash, which is not much.

No more money per person disbursed from the most prominent welfare program. Many more welfare recipients. But much more spending per capita on Greater Welfare. What happened?

What happened was politics. There was a public cry against too much welfare. At the same time, legislators would be held responsible for any heartless cutoff of benefits destined for innocent children. And, of course, liberals kept up a drumbeat about spending more for poor people. So at various levels of government, lawmakers figured out ways to accommodate the apparent political contradictions.

If AFDC could not be directly cut, lest a politician be accused of heartlessness, it could be frozen—allowing inflation to erode its value over the years—thereby accommodating those who felt welfare was going too far. And frozen it was in many places—but with a trick, to accommodate the appetites of liberals.

As AFDC spending on benefits per person was frozen in place, almost all the other federal means-tested programs climbed. Again, observe the Indicators, all shown in constant, noninflated annual dollars, from 1968 to 1992:

- The amount of money disbursed to the needy for food benefits, particularly food stamps, soared from $3 billion to $33 billion. (The number of food stamp recipients went up from 16 million in 1975 to 27 million in 1992. More than 10 percent of the population now receives food stamps.)
- Funding for medical benefits, mostly Medicaid, went up from $10 billion to $79 billion.

- Housing benefits for the needy went from $3 billion to $21 billion.
- Education benefits for the needy went from $3 billion to $15 billion.

All the numbers above were neatly put together by the Congressional Research Service back when Democrats ran the Congress and exercised oversight of CRS. The total of all federal Greater Welfare spending rose from $43 billion to $207 billion (in constant dollars) between 1968 and 1992. In addition, state and local spending for Greater Welfare climbed from $17 billion to $82 billion. (Roughly speaking, had federal Greater Welfare not climbed there would be no annual federal deficit today.)

Aggregated, the real dollar increase goes from $62 billion to $290 billion in the quarter century from 1968 to 1992—a 468 percent rise. (Some modest fraction of these sums goes to the elderly poor, not really our topic here, but the increase has been enormous no matter how measured.)

These increases did not come about because America was growing in population or because more people were in poverty. During that time (1968–1992) the total population grew by 27 percent, the number of people in poverty climbed by only 10 percent, and the rate of people in poverty declined mildly, from 17 to 14 percent. Moreover, Greater Welfare spending as a share of the gross domestic product went up by 270 percent and as a share of the federal budget up by 230 percent.

The expenditures for Greater Welfare are not tightly linked to economic conditions, to political party, or to ideology. Expenditures went up during Democratic and Republican years, during booms, recessions, and normal times, when liberal ideas were regnant and when conservative ideas were in the saddle. They went up rapidly in the seventies, up slowly in the early eighties, up rapidly again since the late eighties. Always up. (And up again, way up, in the first Clinton budget.)

America is spending vastly more per poor person. There is no secret about where the ever-increasing amounts of money come from. They come from government, mostly the federal government but from state and local governments as well. It is governments that are providing the "something" in "something for nothing." Those are government welfare checks going out, government food stamps, government reimbursement for medical care, and so on. There are now more than eighty separate means-tested federal programs. And across the country the verdict is:

welfare isn't working, welfare is a disgrace, and, sadly, welfare recipients are ripping off the system. (See public opinion Indicators, Chapter 6.)

The vast increase in the amount of government payoff didn't just happen. Laws and programs had to change. In the case of welfare, and in most of the other areas that come to our attention in this matter, the evolution of the laws and programs do not seem to have been planned as part of a grand design, other than to help the unfortunate. But, too often, what happened was not what was supposed to happen. The famous "Law of Unintended Side Effects" (LUSE) was in the saddle.

LUSE has been much commented upon. The phenomenon also relates to the acronym BOI—the "Best of Intentions," as in, "With the best of intentions, the government made it much easier for young girls to have babies without getting married." Or, "With the best of intentions, America made its laws much more accommodating to accused criminals" (a situation which could yield a headline TEEN KILLS SHOPKEEPER. BOI LUSE).

Mentioning the BOI phrase makes everyone feel better, and it will be used here, sometimes seriously. But BOI deals with original intent. It does not deal with subsequent culpability or whether there is any. It should be asked: Was there a point at which liberal governmental activists understood that many liberal programs had aspects of great counterproductivity? At what point did they act to change direction? I'm not sure of the answer to the first question and in any event, I sort of swore off the question of motivation in the first chapter of this book. The answer to the second question is, "Not yet."

Or to put it all in a more recent formulation: What did they know, and when did they know it? And now, most important, When will they start doing something about it? Or, worse: Will they ever do something about it?

———

To give a flavor of what has occurred in many realms of government, we might pause here for a moment to consider the sad history of two important programs, AFDC and SSI (Supplemental Security Income).*

———

* Some of the AFDC historical material here is based on Mickey Kaus's book *The End of Equality* (Basic Books, New York, 1992). Some of the material about SSI comes from Carolyn Weaver of the American Enterprise Institute, who has written extensively on the matter.

Our central welfare program, originally called Aid to Dependent Children (ADC), was established in 1935. America was in the midst of a great economic depression, with a 25 percent unemployment rate. Many millions of Americans received "direct relief," the infamous "dole," which President Franklin Roosevelt abhorred.

Indeed, in words that could be uttered today, Roosevelt said, in his 1935 State of the Union Address:

> Continued dependence upon relief induces a spiritual and moral disintegration fundamentally destructive to the national fiber. To dole out relief in this way is to administer a narcotic, a subtle destroyer of the human spirit. . . . I am not willing that the vitality of our people be further sapped by the giving of cash, of market baskets, of a few hours of weekly work cutting grass, raking leaves, or picking up papers in the public parks.

For those who could work, Roosevelt had the Works Progress Administration, a big jobs program. ADC was established for those who could not work and who had minor children, typically families whose head of household was "dead, disabled, or absent."

In the startup year of 1935, the vast majority of recipients—81 percent—were widows. Aid to illegitimate children was legally permitted in the original program, although such aid was banned by some states and was, in any event, generally rare. (The provision was quietly put into the law without the knowledge of FDR's secretary of labor, Frances Perkins, whose agency was responsible for drafting the original legislation. When Perkins found out later that such assistance was actually allowed in the legislstion she was outraged.)

By 1937, two years after the enactment of the program, only 3.5 percent of the children receiving assistance were illegitimate. But in 1939, encouraged by the Federal Bureau of Public Assistance, all states allowed illegitimate children to receive benefits from the ADC program.

Over the next twenty years, the nature of the program changed, as America changed. By 1960, the proportion of widowed families in the program had shrunk from 81 percent—to 8 percent. The makeup of the welfare population shifted, first to families sundered by divorce and marital separation (as those trends grew), and then to female-headed households created by out-of-wedlock births.

As the proportion of households in the renamed AFDC program changed from those who were on welfare due to an "involuntary" situation (widowed) to the more voluntary end of the spectrum (divorced, separated, and born out of wedlock) the numbers and rates of recipients went way up. Many states grew concerned by the strain on budgets, and some tried to crack down on welfare, often by attempting to impose so-called suitable-home restrictions. This included night raids on welfare households where "male callers" might be found in violation of the so-called "man-in-the-house" rules. After all, the reasoning ran, that man in the house might be the father of the children, and if he was, why should the family be on welfare if there was a working father? The crackdown appeared to be directed primarily at blacks. It became a civil rights issue.

Here is how Charles Murray describes what happened:

Until the 1960s, American welfare was stigmatized not only in the public mind but operationally. The AFDC mother was subject to a variety of restrictions. First, the recipient was in fact always a she; married couples were not eligible for AFDC payments. Furthermore, she could not live with a man. She could not hold a job. She might have to wait through a residency period before becoming eligible for assistance. Her caseworker was as much an enforcer of the rules as a source of guidance and help. *During the 1960s, all of these restrictions were relaxed or eliminated.** (Italics mine.)

As author Mickey Kaus sees it, the continuing liberal response to the welfare situation could be summed up in one word: "more." And, he writes:

Thus began a decades-long process in which liberals tried to eliminate the perverse incentives of welfare by broadening its coverage. Unfortunately, each extension of welfare created new problems, which in turn could seemingly be solved only by extending welfare still further. If the problem

---

* Charles Murray, "Welfare and the Family: The U.S. Experience." *Journal of Labor Economics* (January 1993).

was that unemployed fathers were deserting their families, then (liberals argued) you should offer welfare to poor families with unemployed fathers who hadn't deserted. But that created an incentive for fathers to become unemployed. To eliminate that incentive, you had to extend aid to families with fathers who were employed but were nevertheless poor, which created another perverse incentive for the family to split up if the husband began earning enough to move out of poverty.*

Lawrence Mead of New York University offers a cosmic political approach to the issue, quite in keeping with the theme of this book:

> Since the mid-1960s, the competing claims of economic interests and classes have ceased to be the leading domestic issues in national politics. . . . Politicians used to divide over whether government should be larger or smaller. They still do, but the question of whether to enforce social values is more contentious. Dependency at the bottom of society, not economic equality, is the issue of the day. . . .
>
> . . . Traditional approaches to social reform have been exhausted. Government has failed to overcome poverty simply by expanding opportunity, the traditional American solution to social problems. This is because most of the poor do not work, so they cannot take advantage of most benefits that government and the economy offer. . . . In response, social policy has become paternalist, increasingly seeking not to reshape society, but to manage the lives of the dependent.†

Consider next the bizarre case of the Supplemental Security Income program. Like AFDC, the program began for one set of reasons and ended up doing something else. (LUSE BOI strikes again.)

AFDC started out mostly for widows; it ended up mostly for out-of-wedlock mothers. SSI was designed to offer help to poor elderly people and, as a lesser matter, to disabled adults in order to replace lost income. It ended up, in too large a part, as a program for drunks, druggies, and nondisabled children whose parents sometimes teach them to lie.

---

* Kaus, *End of Equality*.

† Lawrence Mead, *The New Politics of Poverty* (New York: Basic Books, 1992).

The idea of disability payments for children (who had no lost income to supplement or replace) was never debated when the original SSI legislation was passed in 1973, during Richard Nixon's presidency. It was slipped into the law, apparently unnoticed, by a senior welfare official (with the BOI) in a twenty-six-word amendment. (Interesting: just as aid for out-of-wedlock mothers was slipped into AFDC legislation, in Roosevelt's time.) By 1990, about 350,000 children were receiving benefits. Not unreasonable; there surely are severely disabled children who need help.

Then, in 1991, a full eighteen years after the law was passed, the Supreme Court ruled (*Sullivan* v. *Zebley*) that the Social Security Administration should relax the criteria relating to the disabilities of children.

Which they did, for example, in regulations allowing benefits for kids who did not display "age-appropriate behavior." This decision landed just at a time when new items like the controversial diagnosis of attention-deficit disorder were coming into vogue in some parts of the mental health community. To make a long story short, the number of "disabled" children on SSI climbed from the 340,000 of 1990 to 652,000 in 1992 to an estimated 900,000 (!) by 1994 and is still climbing.

Stories of massive fraud surfaced, including those of children who had been coached to appear disturbed. A child in Arkansas plaintively asked his teacher if his "crazy money" would be cut off if he did well on a test. (A woman with two children on SSI will receive three times as much in cash as an AFDC family of similar size.)

Moreover, the number of drug users and alcoholics on SSI has also soared, to about 250,000 in early 1994, with half of those substance abusers coming on the rolls between 1989 and 1994. All this with the best of intentions.

Both the AFDC and SSI systems are drenched in fraud. In late 1992 the ABC program "Prime Time Live" ran a segment dealing with welfare cheating. It went far beyond anything Ronald Reagan ever said about "welfare queens." The portrait was one of systematic and widespread cheating and swindling. A number of the perpetrators appeared on-camera, faces unhidden, and said they felt no guilt at receiving more than one welfare check, or traveling interstate (Chicago to Milwaukee) to gain welfare benefits while holding down full-time jobs. It was part of the system, they said, and the welfare payments were their just due. Just the way George Wiley said it was twenty years earlier. Diane Sawyer was the correspondent on the piece. Her conclusion:

> The official government line is that welfare fraud is tiny, but we discovered that even welfare recipients say that's preposterous, as do a lot of welfare workers who told us that anywhere from one-fifth to one-half of recipients are cheating.

When Rudolph Giuliani became mayor of New York City and initiated a careful screening of welfare cases, it was found that half of the applicants did not live at the residence address they put on the form and that 60 percent were not eligible for welfare. A 1994 study discovered that 25 percent of a sample of welfare recipients were double-dipping in New Jersey.

This is no secret to the public. In 1994 the CBS/*New York Times* poll asked: "Do you think most welfare recipients really want to work, or not?" By 63 percent to 27 percent the answer was, "Not." The same poll asked whether welfare families were getting too little welfare or too much. By 58 percent to 21 percent the answer was, "Too much."

And so spending on Greater Welfare, including state and local programs, climbed by 468 percent during a turbulent quarter of a century and will probably reach *half a trillion dollars per year* within a few years unless some major changes are made.

What are the fruits of all this spending? Some are very good, clearly. For example: SSI provides a degree of economic dignity for needy elderly persons. Medicaid gives health care to those who can't afford it. When AFDC and food stamps are used to help either the long-term disabled or those temporarily out of work or out of luck, such aid is humanitarian and necessary. But something else often hitched a ride with our humanitarianism: long-term purposeful dependency.

INDICATORS: WELFARE

Each of the five major Greater Welfare functions has at least doubled since 1968.

Federal Spending for Income-Tested Benefits by Form, 1968–1992 (1992 Dollars)

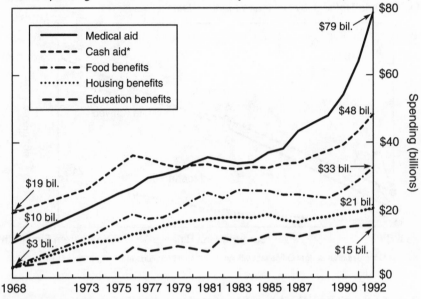

* Aid to Families with Dependent Children and Supplemental Security Insurance.

Source: Congressional Research Service, *Cash and Non-Cash Benefits for Persons with Limited Income 1990–1992.*

Total federal spending on Greater Welfare has increased almost fivefold.

Total Federal Spending for Income-Tested Benefits, 1968–1992 (1992 Dollars)

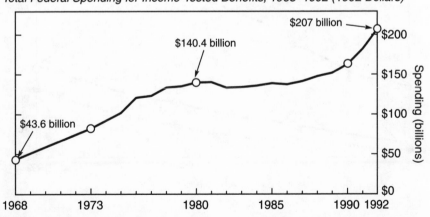

Note: Total includes, cash aid; medical, food, housing, and education benefits; job training; energy aid; and other services.

Source: Congressional Research Service, *Cash and Non-Cash Benefits for Persons with Limited Income.*

Teenagers who give birth out of wedlock are likely to go on welfare, regardless of race.

Cumulative Entrance Rates to Aid to Families with Dependent Children for Teenage Mothers, by Race and Marital Status

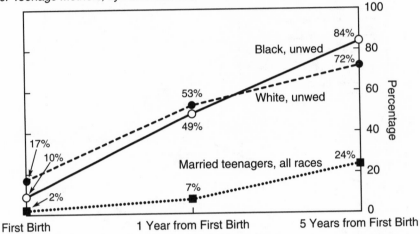

Source: Congressional Budget Office tabulations of National Longitudinal Survey of Youth, 1979–1985.

Out-of-wedlock births have gone up dramatically for whites and blacks.

Out of Wedlock Birth Ratio (percentage of live births), 1960–1992

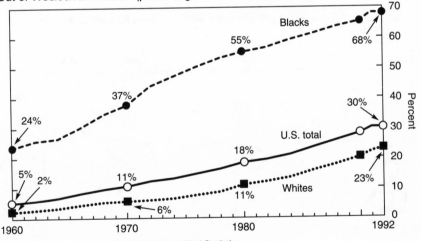

Source: National Center for Health Statistics, *Vital Statistics*.

170

Seen as a share of America's economy and budget, spending on Greater Welfare increased, ebbed, then resumed its increase.

Share of Gross Domestic Product and Federal Budget Used for Needs-Tested Benefits, 1968–1992

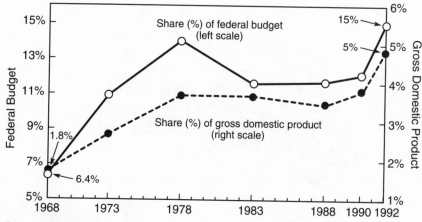

Source: Congressional Research Service, *Cash and Non-Cash Benefits for Persons with Limited Income 1990–1992.*

Aid to Families with Dependent Children (AFDC) benefits (cash) have stayed about level since 1960, but participation has increased greatly.

Average Monthly Recipients and Benefits for AFDC (1993 Dollars)

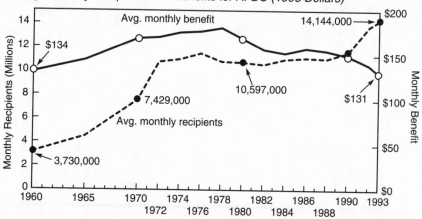

Source: 1960 and 1965 data from U.S. Department of Commerce, *Historical Statistics of the United States: Colonial Times to 1970.* Post-1970 data from Office of Financial Management, Administration for Children and Families: House Committee on Ways and Means, *Green Book,* 1993.

The majority of adults receiving disability payments claim mental disorders.

Adults on Supplemental Security Income Rolls by Leading Cause of Disability, December 1993

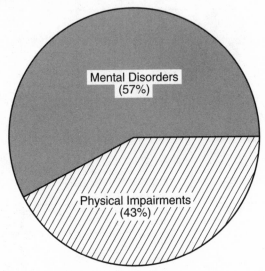

Source: Carolyn Weaver, American Enterprise Institute, congressional testimony January 27, 1995; *Social Security Bulletin, Annual Statistical Supplement, 1994.*

The number of children being compensated for "disabilities" has skyrocketed since 1990.

Children Receiving Supplemental Security Income

YEAR	NUMBER (THOUSANDS)
1974	71
1980	229
1985	265
1990	340
1994	900

Note: Calendar years 1975–1992; fiscal years 1993–1994. Estimate for 1994.

Source: Carolyn Weaver, American Enterprise Institute, congressional testimony, January 27, 1995; Congressional Research Service, *Status of Disability Programs of the SSA, 1994.*

Typically such dependency starts with birth. It was once called "bastardy." Then "illegitimacy." Then "out-of-wedlock birth." And now, frequently, wholly sanitized, "nonmarital birth" or even "alternative parenting."

The largest part of the growth in Greater Welfare comes from women bearing nonmarital children. Nationally, the rate of out-of-wedlock births climbed from 5 percent of all births in 1960 to 30 percent in 1992 and is still rising. Among blacks the rate has reached almost 70 percent. (See Indicators.)

The situation in the black community is particularly staggering and has often been described. But the fastest *rate* of the increase in illegitimacy has been among whites. As Charles Murray has pointed out, the white rate is now about as high as the black rate was in 1965 when the so-called Moynihan Report appeared, which documented the climbing and destructive rate of black illegitimacy.

There is no doubt that out-of-wedlock birth is pushing up the welfare numbers. The Congressional Research Service reports that from 1987 to 1991, of the new cases in the AFDC program, 71 percent were headed by a never-married mother.

And make no mistake about it. It is not often noted, but this explosion of illegitimacy is *voluntary* reproductive behavior.

- It happened as abortion became legal. (Black abortion rates are almost twice the white rate.) Many of these out-of-wedlock pregnancies could be voluntarily terminated among those who do not find abortion morally impermissible, if there was a desire to terminate them voluntarily.
- It happened while contraception became more available, more sophisticated, and easier to use.
- It happened while publicity campaigns against illegitimacy flourished featuring the heroes of the black community, including Jesse Jackson ("It doesn't prove you're a man to have a child, it proves you're a man to support a child"). It happened while an even bigger publicity campaign warned young people that if they had unprotected sex, they might well die from AIDS.
- Most remarkable, the proportion of illegitimate births *went up* while fertility rates in America *went down* across the board, for all races.

Consider the Total Fertility Rate (TFR), roughly defined as the number of children born by women over the course of their child bearing years. In 1957, when the baby boom peaked, the TFR in America was 3.7 children per lifetime per woman. By 1970 it was 2.5, and in 1976 it touched an all-time low of 1.7. In the early nineties, the rate was between 1.9 and about 2.0 (and apparently running about flat). Fertility went down in every segment of American society—among whites and blacks; in the North, South, East, and West; among Catholics, Protestants, Jews, and Mormons.

Black fertility rates fell proportionally more rapidly than white rates. Even black fertility rates among never-married women fell. Women— black and white, married and unmarried—who a generation earlier were having four or three children were opting to stop at two children or one. Think back, if you are old enough, to the television stories of the recessions of the late fifties and early sixties, showing black welfare families with six or eight children on the linoleum floor of a dingy apartment. That is rarely seen today.

This offers further evidence that the increase in illegitimacy comes essentially from *voluntary* behavior. After all, if a woman on welfare can control the birth of a fourth child, or a third child, it is not illogical to assume that she could (usually) also control the birth of a first or second child. Young women know about contraception and abortion. There is a solid body of evidence showing that much illegitimate child-bearing is not principally accidental. In short, we are often dealing with purposeful behavior.

Purposeful. In late 1993, I went to Kansas City, Missouri, to gather some material for the PBS television version of this book. A focus group was set up with six welfare mothers, most in their mid-twenties, all enrolled in a local self-help program called "Futures." Most were African American, most of them going to school, beginning to work or getting ready to begin work, trying to get out of a tough personal situation. They were deeply and tenderly concerned about the well-being of their children.

After about a half-hour of conversation, I started to ask this more-or-less standard neoconservative question: "Some people say that teenage girls are having out-of-wedlock babies in order to get welfare.

Now I don't believe that's so. But isn't it likely that the package of welfare benefits reduces the restraints against such births, and therefore makes them more likely?"

I never did finish the question. Most of the women were vehement as they jumped in right after the first sentence. As transcribed from the videotape:

Woman 1: Right, there are women out there just having children just to get it.

Woman 2: That's what they'd rather do, is sit at home and do nothing.

Woman 3: Young girls out there will brag that "I have four kids so I get this amount of money and this amount of food stamps."

Often purposeful—and with terrible consequences. The available data show clear correlations: Illegitimate children are much more likely to die in infancy, drop out of school, be poor, use drugs, commit suicide, go on welfare, have emotional problems, experience abuse or neglect, become violent criminals, and, tragically, as the circle goes around again, bear out-of-wedlock children.*

Thus, the stark illegitimacy rate touches, and helps shape, every problem discussed in this book. The missing father of the house does not insist that his son stay off the streets in the evening. That contributes to criminality and drug use. It also leads to diminished educational standards: A boy on the street is not doing his homework. If he is black or Hispanic that same undereducated boy later becomes a walking argument for the need for quota hiring. It leads to loose sexual standards, which, starting the cycle afresh, leads to more

---

* How bad is it? Very bad, but perhaps not quite as grim as portrayed. A study in the late 1980s by Larry Bumpass and James Sweet of the University of Wisconsin showed that almost half of out-of-wedlock mothers marry within five years after birth and about 70 percent within fifteen years (although subsequent divorce and separation rates are very high.) About a fourth of out-of-wedlock births occur among unmarried couples who are living together. Sociologist Frank Furstenberg, Jr., of the University of Pennsylvania has tracked several cohorts of teenage out-of-wedlock mothers and found that it can be a "disadvantage," not necessarily a "disaster." Of course, in so many cases, putting already poor teenagers at an additional disadvantage can yield disaster.

out-of-wedlock children. It does not seem to be an accident that the erosion of the inner cities in America coincided with the stunning rise in out-of-wedlock birth.

It is a very serious matter. It is more serious than whether the budget is balanced in seven years or in nine years.

———————

Is there a way to cut the vicious circle? Is welfare the place to do it? Do our welfare policies actually buy more illegitimacy through perverse incentives?

Policy is pedagogy. We are teaching young girls and women that if they have a child, don't have a husband, don't have savings, and don't have a job, the friendly government will step in and provide cash, medical care, food, help on the rent, and possibly day care, job training, and education, altogether worth at least $16,000 to $18,000 per year, according to some estimates and higher in others. That can look quite appealing to a teenager living in an inner city.

Illegitimacy causes more welfare. But does welfare cause more illegitimacy?

There is a big debate about that in the community of welfare scholars. Surely the lines on the Indicators charts show that welfare and illegitimacy went up at roughly the same time, but are these coincident indicators also causal?

Charles Murray notes in the *Journal of Labor Economics* that "Ellwood and Bane, Duncan and Hoffman, and An et al. found no significant effect of welfare on illegitimacy, whereas Winegarten, Ozawa, Bernstam and Plotnick did find significant effects." (Which tells you more than you want to know about the state of social science today.) I intuitively agree with the causal group, although what is statistically "significant" may not be monumental. It may be an impossible idea to validate one way or the other. Where is the control group that has zero receipts from Greater Welfare? After all, a 10, 20, or 30 percent differential in per recipient Greater Welfare expenditures from state to state, cost adjusted, might not change out-of-wedlock fertility rates by much, but a 50 or 75 or 100 percent cut might provide an enormous change.

James Q. Wilson examines the data somewhat differently. He says the evidence is mixed and believes that a small part of the rise in illegitimacy is caused by the availability of more welfare, but likely only a small part. The remainder, he says, comes from the ongoing erosion of values.*

Fine. But if values matter most, what influences values? And particularly, what influences on values can politics and government influence?

Values, and morality, come from many places: the family, the culture, religion, and neighborhood, to begin a long list. I leave much of that aspect of the situation to theologians and social philosophers. Readers interested in these subjects can begin an education by checking the recent works of Wilson, Michael Novak, John Neuhaus, and Gertrude Himmelfarb. Changes in morality are needed—about honesty, selfishness, manners, perseverance, punctuality, and self-denial—but typically cannot, and should not, come about by change in law or by government fiat.

This book, on the other hand, deals with politics and policy, and looks for places where government can intervene most quickly, most effectively, and with political plausibility.

Good welfare policy should send a message to young men and women that if they have children before marriage it's not going to be very easy. It's going to be difficult. Ideally it should not be a retroactive system that gets too tough with those who have already fallen into a welfare trap we have baited. "Workfare" might be the best we can do. But a year or so after the signing into law of welfare reform no *new* teenage recipients coming into the system should receive any cash benefits, for mother or children. (Food stamps and Medicaid would continue.) If out-of-wedlock childbearing is mostly voluntary or controllable behavior, then the system must signal all prospective welfare recipients that they should control that voluntary behavior, or be prepared to face the consequences.

---

* James Q. Wilson, "Culture Incentives, and the Underclass," Brookings Institution Seminar Series on Values and Public Policy. In an interview for the PBS television version of this book, Wilson made a somewhat finer distinction: "We would have out-of-wedlock births if we didn't have welfare, but they would be fewer in number, and they probably would be more confined to the affluent who in the process of their own self-emancipation have talked themselves into the view that there is nothing wrong with having a child with no father."

How much does it really matter, in the policy world, in the political world, whether there is a causal or only a coincident relationship between illegitimacy and welfare? After all, if there is causality, or even some causality, *then we should clearly act to stop it and change it.* And if the causality has not been proved *we should still stop it, and change it,* because it *may* be so. If it turns out that way, and we didn't act, weren't we playing fast and loose with the lives of youngsters by not cutting down on the incentives? Finally, if the relationship between welfare and illegitimacy is wholly coincidental—which I find hard to believe— *we still shouldn't be paying for it.* Illegitimacy, as Wilson stresses, is immoral. Government should not subsidize immorality.

In any event, a dramatic change in welfare would be good politics. Most voters hate the welfare system as it now exists. So do most welfare recipients.

The focus group of Kansas City welfare mothers vigorously volunteered the information that many teenagers were bearing children in order to gain the package of current welfare benefits. They were outraged about the situation.

On that same visit to Kansas City, I conducted another focus group. The participants were welfare fathers. They vehemently resented the term "deadbeat dads." They were a part of the "Futures Connection," a self-help program related to the Futures program mentioned earlier in this chapter. The men were either at work and paying child support, or studying to prepare for jobs so they could pay child support for their children on welfare. There were six of them, four blacks and two whites, most in their late twenties.

They were well spoken. Clearly, as the discussion progressed, it was apparent that they wanted to help take care of their children and that they loved them. After a while, I turned the discussion to politics and asked a long question, which I present here almost verbatim. I began:

BW: Let's say there is an election. Candidate A says something like this: "The welfare situation is a real problem. But we're going to have to keep up those taxes, because we have to give people education, and some cash to live with. It's true, some of this help falls through the cracks; it's true, the rate of out-of-wedlock births keeps going up; it's true, the government screwed it up in welfare. But there are little children involved, and we have to keep paying for it."

Then there is Candidate B. He has a one-word slogan: "Enough." He says, "We have created some kind of Frankenstein monster in the welfare program. It is encouraging out-of-wedlock birth, creating a comfort zone for it, pulling people into welfare. We have to cut back welfare in order to stop this. Enough!"

In that election who would you vote for: A or B?

Suddenly, among the six welfare fathers in the room there was what can only be described as an eruption:

Many persons at once: B, B, I vote B.

BW: You would vote for the guy who says stop it?

Many persons at once: Yeah. Yeah. Yeah.

Man 1: At some point you gotta do something. The buck stops here. I can't say I condone everything he suggested, but he had the right attitude.

BW: Which is, "Enough, cut it off?"

Man 2: Sooner or later you got to bite the bullet and start getting back to making the country what it was.

Man 3: No, no, not necessarily cut it all off.

Man 2: Otherwise it gets so out of control that everybody suffers.

BW: Loosely speaking, Democrats take the position of Candidate A. Republicans say what Candidate B says. People in your situation are not usually voting Republican.

Man 3: [a black man in his late twenties who had served prison time for armed robbery and is now employed]: Well, you know, I've been listening to the show—Rush Limbaugh. So I figure I'm turning conservative at least. I don't know about being a Republican or not. But he's got a lot of good views. He's saying the same thing, you know. People ought to get up.

There's no sympathy for people just sitting around doing nothing . . . you know free food for somebody who just wants to go around just living off someone else.

All this, mind you, from people whose loved children are being supported by the welfare system!

The political window for serious welfare reform was wide open, open for big change. Back in 1972, nearly a third of Americans (31 percent) wanted to *increase* welfare, while only 18 percent wanted to *reduce* welfare. In 1994 only 10 percent wanted to *increase* welfare, and 44 percent wanted to *reduce* it. Tinkering at the edges, which is what previous welfare reforms had attempted, would not assuage that kind of sentiment.

Of course, one hates to get political on this matter, but the headline on Barbara Dafoe Whitehead's article in April 1993, got it just right: "Dan Quayle Was Right."* Of course Quayle was right—not necessarily about Murphy Brown, but about out-of-wedlock birth, which was the central topic of that speech. Everyone knew it, even at the time, even as the issue that Quayle highlighted caused such great consternation. It's no secret: A child without a live-in father has a big problem, which will hurt him or her, and us.

Quayle's speech was given in May 1992, an election year. Candidate Bill Clinton also knew about the politics and the policy of the issue. His welfare sound bites were quite tough: "End welfare as we know it," "Two years and out," "A helping hand, not a handout."

In 1995, in his State of the Union Address, President Clinton called teenage pregnancy "our most serious social problem."

Clinton knew it. But did he govern that way? Did he try to end welfare as we know it?

---

* *The Atlantic Monthly,* April 1993.

Chapter 9

THE EDUCATION SLIDE

The education situation is not anywhere near as bad as that in crime or welfare. What has been noted in those realms is dangerous, ugly, and sordid.

There are some very nice aspects to American education. Our universities are the best in the world. We win most of the Nobel prizes. College enrollment is up. The high school dropout rate is down. There are some nice reasons for these nice facts, which will be discussed toward the end of this chapter.

Still, everyone knows our education system is deeply flawed. I believe the defects relate directly to the sort of something-for-nothing liberalism under discussion here. And President Clinton, as a candidate, made it clear that he understood that. He promised to fix it.

———

We have heard that our education system is dreadful, that we can't compete with those Japanese and Germans, and that our test scores are terrible. We are told that we will not be able to compete globally unless our education system improves. Ross Perot twanged it: "World class schools for a world class economy"—or we'll become a third-rate, Third World country.

What's the problem?

Is it money? Per student expenditures, after adjusting for inflation, have climbed by 81 percent since 1970. This includes an increase in teacher salaries of 45 percent, a faster rate of increase than for most other occupation groupings. It isn't money. (See the Indicators.)*

Some years ago it was said that technology would be the savior of education. There was a rage for something called "teaching machines." That would do it! The teaching machines evolved into computers. Lord, if only we had computers in the classroom, and "computer-literate" students, by George, that would do it!

We did it. We're doing it. In 1981, only 18 percent of our schools had some classrooms with computers. By 1990 the rate was 97 percent, and there was already one computer in school for every twenty-one students, with the ratio shrinking rapidly. We now have more computers per square child than any other nation in the world. Has it helped? Perhaps so, but why do we keep hearing about how poorly we're doing?

If it isn't money and it isn't technology, what is it? It's surely not due to overcrowded schools. In 1955 there were twenty-seven students per teacher; in 1992 the number was at seventeen, a drop of 37 percent. The pupil-to-teacher ratios in the big inner cities are not much differ-

---

* As is the case in almost every aspect of social measurement, arguments abound in the education realm. Advocates of public education say that historical data series regarding spending should be adjusted for the new role that schools have been asked to play in recent years. Today, public schools may well be asked to handle "special ed" students in mainstream classes, including blind, deaf, and mute students, manic depressive and schizophrenic students, catheterized students and students with attention-deficit disorder. In earlier times such services were not typically counted within the academic budget. Moreover, teachers today are asked to deal with classrooms with higher proportions of children from single-parent families than in earlier times. This adds to problems in school, which may need costly expenditures in time and personnel. So, the case is made: It takes more teachers to handle that sort of education, and more money too. It's a good point. Still, no matter how adjusted, there is not much argument that we are spending much more money per student on education than before, and that the results (as we shall see) are, at best, mediocre.

ent: New York City, seventeen; Baltimore, nineteen; Philadelphia, eighteen; Washington, D.C., seventeen; Los Angeles, twenty-three; Dallas, sixteen.

In 1965 only 27 percent of children from ages three through five were enrolled in nursery school or kindergarten. By 1993 the rate was 55 percent, more than twice as high. And that doesn't count the 714,000 kids in Head Start.

It's not that students aren't staying in school. The high school dropout rate is at an all-time low. By age twenty-five, almost 90 percent of young Americans have graduated from high school. The black dropout rate has fallen particularly rapidly, from 22 percent to 11 percent over a twenty-year period, close to parity with the white rate (a remarkable and little-reported development). Only the Hispanic population lags, as the Indicator page shows, and there is movement there as well.

It's not just that students are staying in high school until graduation. College enrollment rates are at an all-time high.

In short, so many of the things that nice people once wanted to happen in our schools have happened. But schooling isn't the purpose of school. Learning is. Learning has apparently diminished or, at best, gained no ground.

The problem in our schools concerns changed values. Everyone knows it. While the true origin of the changed values may be the subject of lengthy argument, we can pinpoint one medium by which the changed values came to the schools: changed public policy. And changed public policy is either driven by, or accepted by, the political system. Values. Politics. Policy.

When I was going to school, there was a pretty clear (if silent) value system deeply embedded in every aspect of the education system. It might as well have been written on the blackboard: *Hard work and disciplined behavior gains a reward.* That is a fairly elemental notion: something for something. In real life, in real time, that is usually how the world works, and everyone knows it. But too many of our schools have been working double session to corrode that value. And it shows.

The trouble can be observed in many places in the school system, and probably most clearly in public secondary schools. Consider some recent trends in American education during the past few decades, particularly in secondary schools. What follows is not wholly applicable everywhere—there are many good, tough school systems still around—but too much is all too applicable in too many places—probably most places.

Take the example of grades. Grades become a matter of greater seriousness to students when they enter high school. Back in 1972, according to the College Board, *28 percent* of college-bound seniors reported that they had A or B averages. By 1993 the figure was *83 percent*. How nice; perhaps the students were getting better educated. No. During the same time, the average combined Math and Verbal SAT scores tumbled from 937 to 902. A similar trend is apparent at the college level. Columnist John Leo of *U.S. News and World Report* reports about the Harvard student who says, "In some departments 'A' stands for average."

In short, we have witnessed what is called "grade inflation." Why did it come about? Specific reasons are hard to uncover; there was no official directive in the 15,025 school districts that suddenly mandated, "Thou shalt inflate the grade."

But there are some things we can divine about the move toward grade inflation. The marshmallow mentality of 1960s guilt-mongers could not tolerate the idea that a bad grade might scar a youngster's self-esteem. The bad grade was likely the fault of a sick society. Wasn't that obvious? Prominent victim groups were hurting. Blacks got lower grades than whites. So did Hispanics. Girls scored lower than boys in mathematics. The easy fix was too apparent: raise everyone's grade. In America these days, something for nothing starts early.

But how were the sixties ideas actually incorporated into the educational system? Politics.

Any serious discussion of education in America begins with a central fact: The vast majority of the 52 million American students—almost 90 percent—are in public schools. The schools are typically run by those 15,000 local school boards. The school boards are typically *elected* by voters. The costs of the schools are paid by taxes, most of which are usually legislated and levied by a variety of *elected* officials.

This means that although educational policy may originate from hothouse elites in times of turmoil, or that such policies may bubble up from the public more generally, or that such policies may be inculcated in naive teacher-training students attending courses in liberally oriented teachers' colleges, or that the inculcation may proceed from teachers to students in the classroom—the changes in educational policy are (at the very least) *ratified* in the political marketplace.

Politics is the gatekeeper that allows certain ideas to enter the classroom and keeps other ideas out. If educational policy has changed for the worse, as it apparently has in the case of grade inflation, the most important place to look, and the most logical place to lay blame, is at that place called politics. And, class, repeat after me: If the cause is political, the cure should be political.

Grade inflation is only one small example. Not so long ago it was common educational policy that if a student did not reach a certain level of proficiency in a given grade then that student would not advance to the next grade.

That changed. Now there is "social promotion." An idea had blossomed: It was bad for students—any student—ever to be denied promotion to the next grade, even if that student was doing so poorly that an inflated grade wouldn't help. After all, what sense did it make to bruise the self-esteem of the worst students? Moreover, a disproportionate rate of previously unpromotable students were black. If they were not promoted, wouldn't that indicate a discriminatory school system? Might not an *elected* school board be called racist?

In earlier times most public high schools "tracked" their students. The more accomplished youngsters were put in one class, the less accomplished in others, enabling teachers to gear teaching to the level of the class. But it turned out that in many schools too many black and Latino kids ended up in the lower tracks, and too many white kids in higher tracks. That became a political issue in some communities. So in some school districts, tracking was eliminated or diminished. That meant that teachers had to water down course content to accommodate the slowest in the class, to the detriment of the more accomplished students. Message: We don't care; don't bother to work hard; get something for less.

The courts played an important role. The court-ordered remedy of busing to achieve racial balance was one way to deal with the perceived educational inequality, and it tended to exacerbate all of the trends cited above. Moreover, courts ordered certain expensive forms of "special education," politically correct codes of school discipline, and "ESL," that is "English as a Second Language," which ignited a major argument about bilingualism in American schools.

And so—grade inflated, socially promoted, merit-ignored, politically pawned, linguistically short-changed, court-coddled—even the worst students marched up the ladder. That tended to deal, ostrich-like, with yet another problem. After all, it was reasoned, it's better to keep unruly kids in school than to have them drop out and roam the streets. Grade inflation plus social promotion was linked to another education buzz phrase: "social warehousing." Some schools became warehouses for a class of students who saw no need to work hard or to master much of anything. All of which was approved by, ignored by, or encouraged by, the school boards that were *elected* by the public, and/or by public officials who were appointed by *elected* officials. By omission and/or commission, what happened was political.

Not only was the "work hard" part of the original values formula in school eroded by political misfeasance, so too was the "behave yourself" part.

In the good old days, when a "bad boy" misbehaved in class, he was typically warned, then disciplined, and then asked to bring his parents to school. If his disruptive behavior did not cease, he could be suspended from school, or expelled, or sent to a special school for incorrigibles. In extreme cases there was reform school—I recall it pronounced as a single word, "rfawmskool"—an almost unimaginable place, and yet real enough to keep students scared.

Today when teachers are asked what constitutes their biggest problems, one common answer is "discipline." What happened? The rights revolution hit the schools as it hit the rest of the culture. The unruly boy today may be sent to a psychological counselor and then back to class. After all, it was obvious that a disproportionate number of problem children were blacks and Latinos. What would it look like if a separate school for disciplinary cases was made up mostly of minority youngsters?

Scholastic Aptitude Test scores trended downward and have not recovered.

Scholastic Aptitude Test Score Averages for College-Bound High School Seniors, 1966–1992

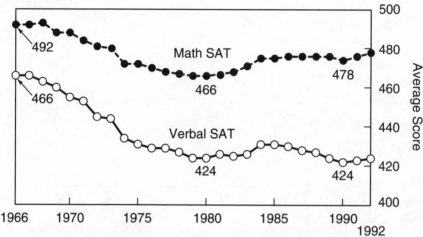

Source: College Entrance Examination Board, *National Report on College-Bound Seniors,* various years.

Spending per student has gone up; the ratio of students per teacher has dropped.

Pupil-Teacher Ratios and Expenditures per Pupil in Public Elementary and Secondary Schools, 1955–1993 (1993–1994 Dollars)

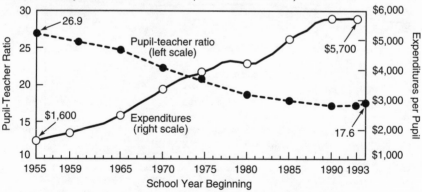

* *Note:* Data unavailable for 1960–1961 school year. Data for 1993–1994 are estimates.

Source: U.S. Department of Education, National Center for Education Statistics, 1994.

Total federal spending on elementary and secondary education has more than tripled since 1965.

On-Budget Federal Support for Elementary and Secondary Education, 1965–1994 (1994 Dollars)

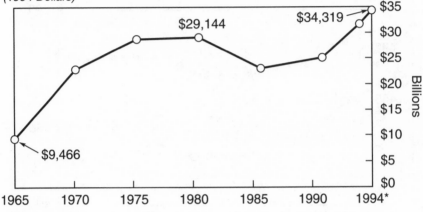

* *Note:* Estimate.

Source: National Center for Education Statistics; Office of Management and Budget, 1994.

The share of young people enrolled in school is at or near all-time highs in every age category.

Percentage of Population 14–29 Years Old Enrolled in School, by Age, 1950–1993

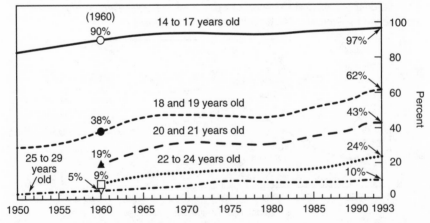

Note: Includes enrollment in any type of public, private, parochial, or other schools. Trade, business, and correspondence schools are not included.

Source: U.S. Department of Commerce, Bureau of the Census, 1994.

The number of students going to college has almost tripled since 1964.

Total Fall Enrollment in Institutions of Higher Learning 1963–1992

YEAR	NUMBER (MILLIONS)
1964	5.3
1965	6.0
1970	8.6
1975	11.2
1980	12.1
1985	12.2
1990	13.8
1992	14.5

Source: U.S. Department of Education, National Center for Education Statistics, 1994.

The United States is ahead of only Jordan and Ireland in international science tests.

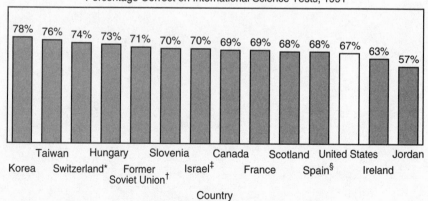

Percentage Correct on International Science Tests, 1991

* *Note:* Fifteen cantons.

† Schools in fourteen republics where instruction is in Russian.

‡ Schools where instruction is in Hebrew.

§ Schools where instruction is in Spanish, all regions except Catalonia.

Source: U.S. Department of Education; National Center for Education Statistics.

Today, blacks and whites complete high school at about the same rate.

Persons 18–29 Years of Age Who Have Completed Four or More Years of High School 1920–1993

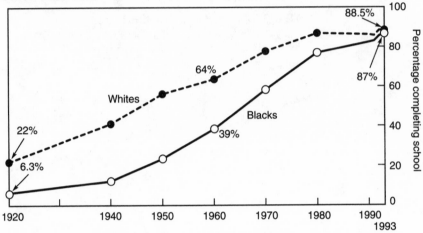

Note: Includes other nonwhite races prior to 1970. Hispanics are included, as appropriate, in the "white" category. The 1940, 1950, and 1960 surveys were taken in April. Subsequent surveys were taken in March.

Source: U.S. Bureau of the Census; Bureau of Labor Statistics, 1994.

190

How could a politician get reelected if minority activists call him a racist and such a denunciation appeared live in a voter's living room? Don't ask again if politics drives educational policy.

And so discipline eroded. The felony is compounded and perpetuated when the parents of the better-behaved students—by no means exclusively white—become disgusted, pick up stakes, and leave for a suburb or a farther-out suburb.

Something else changed in the classroom. It became almost impossible to *teach* values. How did it happen? No surprise. Politics, in a variety of forms, did the deed.

Consider the holy war against religious expression in schools, going back many years. It may have reached its apogee in Rhode Island in the spring of 1989 at the Nathan Bishop Middle School, when Rabbi Leslie Gutterman polluted the minds of graduating eighth graders with the following wildly theological remarks:

> God of the Free, hope of the brave, for the legacy of America where diversity is celebrated and the rights of minorities are protected, we thank you. May these young men and women grow up to enrich it. For the liberty of America, we thank you. May these new graduates grow up to guard it. For the political process of America in which all of its citizens may participate, for its court system where all may seek justice, we thank you. May those we honor this morning always turn to it in trust.
>
> For the destiny of America, we thank you. May the graduates of Nathan Bishop School so live that they might share it. May our aspirations for our country and for these young people who are our hope for the future be richly fulfilled. Amen.

The courts that Rabbi Gutterman thanked in his invocation did not respond, "You're welcome." Deborah Weisman and her father, Daniel Weisman, sued on grounds that the prayer violated the 1962 Supreme Court ruling that banned prayer in public schools. The Court sided with the Weismans, thusly: "The government involvement with religious activity in this case is pervasive to the point of creating a state-sponsored and state-directed religious exercise in a public school."

How does this happen? How does it happen in a nation where ACLU attorneys carry coins in their pocket that have "In God We Trust" engraved on their face, where the president ends his speeches, carried on publicly chartered airwaves, with the words "God bless America," where the chaplain of the U.S. Senate opens the proceedings with a prayer, where the phrase "endowed by our Creator" appears in the Declaration of Independence, and where 74 percent of the population favors nonsectarian voluntary prayer in the school?

It happens through the courts, and through politics. It wasn't just what could no longer be stressed in a school—like religious belief—that changed the values. It was what now could be stressed. As education became politicized, greater class time was devoted to environmentalism, disarmament, feminism, and racism—the standard fare of victimology and guilt. Publishers changed their textbooks to reflect these issues and that viewpoint.

Perhaps the logical culmination of all this politicization happened in New York City, when, to the standard green/peacenik/feminist/multicultural feast, was added an activist homosexual agenda. Under the influence of a vigorous gay lobby, the New York City school system deemed it appropriate to add to the books made available to first graders these: *Heather Has Two Mommies, Daddy's Roommate,* and *Gloria Goes to Gay Pride.* First graders, recall, are six years old. Still, it was seen as important that they quickly learn about alternative lifestyles, and that such lifestyles are normal and acceptable. In the fourth grade in New York City, it was deemed important to teach ten-year-olds about AIDS and anal intercourse. In many high schools, free condoms are made available to students.

One City Council member in New York had the temerity to recommend that abstinence be taught along with safer sex. Many educators rejected the idea; it was, they said, unrealistic. Funny; you can try to convince teenagers that the world is overheating, that nuclear weapons are likely to go pop in the night, that quotas don't exist, that teachers are underpaid—but not that premarital sex or sexual promiscuity is unwise.

And so some public schools, taxpayer funded, subject to policies put forth by *elected* officials, have gone from prayer in school to anal intercourse. And then it is wondered why crazed, zealous, members of the "religious right" get upset. It might better be wondered why it is the left that complains that the right wants to change the school curriculum.

———

The something-for-nothing curriculum doesn't end when high school ends.

What happens when students finish their high school course of study? They either look for a job or go on to college.

If they look for a job, they must try to find an employer. All dressed up, our new high school graduate goes for a job interview. The employer interviews the applicant. But, hold on, something strange is going on. The employer does not ask the applicant about grades.

Why not? Because those grades have been inflated. And the applicant has gone to a school that practices social promotion. What might a grade transcript actually tell a prospective employer? That the applicant graduated? Sure. But did the diploma mean anything? Or was it perhaps merely a certificate of social warehousing? There are high school transcripts that might just as well read, "Dear Mr. or Ms. Employer: This graduate has been kept off the street for four years."

There is another reason the employer doesn't look at the transcript. The employer may be violating the law. The Civil Rights Act of 1991 indicated that hiring on the basis of grades might be evidence of racial discrimination. Why? A bus driver may not need to know geometry or history to drive a bus. If the employer takes grades into account when hiring bus drivers, and whites have better grades than blacks, the employer may end up with too many white bus drivers, which can trigger a suit based on "disparate impact." The applicant gets the reward (the job) with little regard to academic achievement. Hard as it may be to believe, that law passed just when the Congress couldn't stop telling us how important it would be to promote American competitiveness and educational excellence.

What is the first thing the new bus driver tells his little brother, who is just entering high school? He says: "There is no payoff for hard work. Don't be a sucker, kid!"

Suppose the new high school graduate wants to go on to college. In the superior colleges, the applicant's high school transcript, extracurricular activities, and a personal interview are all weighed. But that procedure is less common than it was. Many public colleges—once the ultimate gate-keeper of standards for all schools that sent students their way—now accept any student with passing grades. After all, so goes the reasoning, it would be unfair to keep black or Latino students disproportionately out of a taxpayer-funded institution. Yet if grades were the central criterion, that is what would happen.

Now, in itself, it is not a bad idea that any young American who wants to go to college should be able to do so. There are lots of late bloomers, lots of young people who never took high school seriously, and who do not deserve to be punished forever for their shortsightedness. It is particularly important that minority students be encouraged to get on track, no matter how late in the educational process.

And so, the grade-inflated, socially warehoused, socially promoted student goes on to college. Once there, he or she is—what? Too often grade inflated and socially warehoused and socially promoted.

Young people are not idiots. They learn the rules of the road quickly. When the rules were work plus discipline equals reward, they worked, and they behaved themselves. When that equation was shattered, they understood that too. And they worked less hard, and behaved less well, content to get something for nothing.

———

Of course, there are days of reckoning. The books must be balanced. Students who don't work hard, because they aren't rewarded when they do, or punished when they don't, don't do as well in school as they could.

So it comes as no surprise to learn that American students do not do as well on standardized tests as students in most other countries. That record is shown in the Indicators section. American youngsters remain at the bottom end of the international spectrum in math. We are mildly lower than average in science. At the top of the math and science lists is South Korea. We trail Slovenia. But we do consistently beat the Kingdom of Jordan. We are about average in reading.

There is some argument about these sorts of international comparative results, particularly at the high school level. America (appropriately, in my judgment) made a commitment some decades ago to try to get all of our children graduated from secondary school. That means that children from the lower ranges of the socioeconomic scale are more likely to be represented when a sample of seventeen-year-old Americans take an achievement test for international comparison than when seventeen-year-old Italians or English take the same test. Accordingly, there may be some rationale for the lower scores Americans get on these international comparisons.

That would offer some comfort were it not for the fact that Americans also score lower when tests are administered for thirteen-year-olds—presumably before the elite systems in other nations do much winnowing out of their less capable students.

Perhaps most disturbing is the attitude of American students: They *think* they are doing just fine. When asked if they thought they were "good at mathematics," 68 percent of thirteen-year-old American students answered in the affirmative. When the question was asked of thirteen-year-old Koreans, only 23 percent answered "yes." What can one make of these data? We surely want confident young people, brimming with self-esteem. But we do not want self-deluded young people. After all, it is the South Koreans who score well in math and the Americans who score poorly.

The international comparisons are in concert with American data. Look at the National Assessment of Educational Progress (NAPE) scores, presented in the Indicators section. They show that proficiency in reading, mathematics, and science has remained about flat from the 1970s. There has been a small decline in writing proficiency since 1984. At best, things haven't gotten worse. On the plus side, there has been an increase in reading proficiency among black and Hispanic seventeen-year olds.

The Scholastic Aptitude Test (SAT) scores have gone down and stayed down. Perhaps most ominously, there has been a declining rate of high-scoring students—those who score above 650 or 750 on both the verbal and mathematics sections of the SAT. The College Entrance Examination Board, which runs the SAT, "recentered" their scores in 1995, which had the effect of giving each student a bonus of about 100 points. Education scholar Denis Doyle of the Hudson Institute says: "The SAT re-centering is a bad joke that even the College Board has trouble explaining. Clearly it was an attempt to raise the scores of bad students to make them, and their teachers, feel better." Score inflation.

We should not be surprised. It would be surprising if less demand for hard work and less demand for discipline would yield anything other than mediocre results. It would be particularly surprising if we saw anything but mediocre results in school in an era when so large a proportion of children live in one-parent homes as a result of divorce, separation, or out-of-wedlock birth. Social issues link up, with the whole worse than the sum of its parts.

Alas, it is not only the mediocre students who think they are doing smashingly when they are not. Their parents think so too. Poll after poll shows that Americans think the educational system is generally bent out of shape, but *their* schools, which *their* children attend, are doing well. Because regarding values, politics matter most, and because parents vote, and students don't, self-delusion on the part of parents may be the more serious matter.

The education establishment works hard to see to it that the notion of my-kid's-school-is-fine stays in place. A fight goes on in Washington about whether schools should be ranked; the answer so far has been no. The educrats also say that even *states* cannot be ranked in terms of the achievement of their schools. At the present time only *regions* are ranked. That's certainly useful: "Oh Jane, I think we should send Johnny to the West Coast for third grade; the schools here on the East Coast aren't ranked so highly."

The final reckoning, of course, is reality, which often shows its true face after the school years. In the real world hard work and discipline pay off. Sloth is a loser.

That lesson, if not learned in the early school years when it should be, is usually only delayed, not eliminated. Ill-equipped students learn, later in life than deserved, what many schools have tried to hide: there is no free lunch. (These days, often not even in the school cafeteria.)

Beyond a certain point, it is hard for either an employer, or a union, or government, to save a mediocre student, even if the attempt is made. The rush toward a global economy puts American students in competition with students elsewhere, who are still taught that reward requires hard work. Moreover, that economy is in a spasm of corporate Darwinism. Restructuring and the drive to be lean and mean are surely not always pleasant, but they do serve clearly to reestablish the links between hard work, competence, and reward. The old value system, of merit and accomplishment, ultimately reasserts itself, and there are winners and losers.

At this point the reader should be asking this still-optimistic author a question: If there is so much silliness going on, how come America is still the wealthiest country in the world and the most productive? If everything is so bad, how come so much of everything is at least fairly good?

There is a massive saving grace in our system. Ironically and paradoxically, it is the very value system I am criticizing. With all its flaws, American society is the most open in the world. The American economy is the freest in the world. This combination of open sociology and a free enterprise economy yields some great benefits.

On the educational side, the ill-educated student, who finally gets the message, is not shunted aside forever, as in some of the more class-oriented European societies, or in Japan. He or she can get back on board the education train. On the economic side, such a student is aided by the fact that the relatively free American economy, with all its flaws, is forgiving. If a student who hasn't worked hard, who hasn't learned enough, who has been babied through the system finally senses the error of his or her ways, there is often an economic accommodation available.

I visit some American pockets of poverty—Palm Beach, Palm Springs, Scottsdale—addressing corporate executives. If you don't believe the data, belly up to the bar and you can hear it from them: "The kids who apply to work for us can't write. They don't know math. They don't read well."

But in an open society with free economics, there have been salutary responses. There are estimates that private corporations spend
$50 billion per year to reeducate the ill-educated students turned out
by American schools, give or take $10 or $20 billion either way. Many
of the youngsters involved are relearning the 3Rs. It works pretty well,
according to the executives I have spoken with.

This is a stupid way to run a railroad. Obviously it would be better if
the secondary schools did it right the first time. But economic and social freedom yields a safety net. The corporations need literate workers; if the schools won't provide them, the private economy often does
it on its own.

There is something else. College enrollment has been going up. This
should not make much sense when you look at recent demographic
trends in America. If you subtract 18 (the age at which students typically enter college) from 1995 (the year this book is published), you get
1977. That was a year when only 3.3 million children were born, one of
the lowest totals in American history, when the total fertility rate was
1.8 children per woman, also one of the lowest in American history. In
theory, then, college enrollment rates should be going down.

Why are the enrollment numbers up? In some large measure because
adults are going back to college. Americans who were ill educated, bored,
or restless in school the first time have matured and decided to go back to
school. Young women, whose little children are entering preschool, are
deciding to start, or continue, their college education. Today, 41 percent
of the students in American higher education are above the ages normally associated with college. That is the highest rate ever in the United
States and higher by far than in any other country. America has the only
serious system of continuing education in the world.

This is part of something larger, which is our national treasure.
Shortly after the cold war ended, I met with a group of East European
teachers visiting Washington. We sat around a table, and I asked what
America could do to help. Their message was simple: We need American education, send us teachers, teach us English, establish branches
of American universities.

I asked the obvious questions: If the test scores in Hungary and
Slovenia are higher than in the United States, why do you want Amer-

ican education? If Americans are so upset with their education system, why do you want it? The Germans, the French, and the English are beating American kids in international competition, why don't you turn to them for help in this area? The answer was stunning: "Only Americans know how to make things work."

In Japan, too, there has been an interesting reaction to American education. While we stand in awe of the vaunted Japanese education machine, the Japanese are saying something else: They know there are big problems with American schools, but in certain ways they want Japanese schools to be more like American ones. Japanese schools, say many Japanese education reformers, concentrate too much on learning by rote, on getting good test scores, on discipline, and end up snuffing out the spark of creativity in their children. America's openness allows that creativity to flower. (How about a Jamerican school system?)

As I divine what is being said, it is this: Enlightened foreigners don't want the American education system; they want the American culture—or at least what the perceived American culture was some years ago: meritocratic, open, upwardly mobile, individualist, and free.

———

Is there hope for American kids? You bet there is. These are mostly good kids. We are properly concerned about the thugs and mugs, the druggies and drunks. But recent attitudinal data collected by the U.S. Department of Education show that a majority of high school seniors (58 percent) say that religion is "very important" or "pretty important" in their lives, a rate that hasn't changed. High school seniors are much less likely than at earlier times to smoke cigarettes, drink alcoholic beverages, or use drugs. Huge majorities (over 75 percent) still believe that success at work and marriage and family are "very important." Much more than before, a solid majority of both whites and blacks aspire to a college or postgraduate degree; other millions seek to go beyond high school to junior college or vocational school.

———

What should we do about American education? The answers are not so difficult and are well known.

The buzz phrases to remember are these: "output over input" and "standards, tests, and consequences." Another word, "choice," is in the air, but consensus on that one has not been reached.

A major turning point in American education came about with the publication of *A Nation at Risk* in 1983. Overstated, almost wholly negative, it announced that America was being overwhelmed by "a rising tide of mediocrity" and that the deterioration of our education system in a competitive age was an act of "unilateral disarmament."

As the report was digested, a general agreement emerged. America had concentrated on inputs, such as lower pupil-teacher ratios, better school buildings, higher teacher salaries, and so on. But the inputs—strangely—hadn't yielded better outputs. Test scores were down, American students were showing up poorly in international comparisons. What was needed was better outputs, possibly designed to meet a federal, but voluntary, set of standards.

Governors in every corner of the nation, particularly in the South, took on education as a principal cause. One of those governors was young Bill Clinton in Arkansas, who with his wife, Hillary, went to every section of his state to sell the outputs idea. Another was Dick Riley, then governor of South Carolina, who later became secretary of education in the Clinton administration.

The principal mechanisms of reform involved setting *standards* (that is, curriculum and content design), *testing* to see whether students had actually learned the material, and *consequences* or *stakes* (that is, seeing to it that if a student couldn't pass a well-designed achievement test at certain grade levels, that student would not be promoted). Similarly, a teacher who couldn't pass a test to demonstrate competency could not continue teaching.

These ideas, simple but potent, were saluted by most but opposed by some. School boards, civil rights leaders, unions, conservatives, educrats, and bureaucrats were nervous. Would teachers be fired? Would blacks do worse than whites? Who would design the test? Who would design the curriculum that was to be tested? Would new standards just enshrine more of the goo of political correctness? Would the federal government trample on the central right of the state government to educate? (One perhaps unexpected champion of the argument about "stakes" was Albert Shanker, president of the American Federation of Teachers.)

The standards movement took on momentum, and in 1989 its leaders met with President Bush. A new plan, called America 2000, was announced. Governor Clinton, then co-chair of the Governors' Education Summit, was a prominent player in the runup to the plan. Clintonites like to recount one incident in the byplay at the final session. Friendly George Bush looked up and said, "Nice job, Bill." When Clinton ran for president against Bush, he pledged to establish tough standards and a national examination system.

Standards make sense, but there are problems too. Even with standards, the players don't change much. There are still the unions, school bureaucrats, politicians, and the special-interest political activists. With those dullards still in place (so goes the argument), how much can really change?

Enter "choice." What changes institutions best? Competition does. The argument is made that American schools suffer from a lack of competition. Why should they get better? Nothing bad happens to them if they don't.

A movement toward school choice emerged. Let the parents decide which schools will do best for their kids. If a school isn't delivering, the parent will yank the kid, which will cause suffering among teachers, principals, and bureaucrats. Such potential suffering, it is argued, will upgrade performance.

School choice took two forms. The public education establishment was prepared to try out public-public choice: Give students the opportunity to choose schools, hopefully new and innovative schools, but only within the public system. Of particular interest within this concept was the idea of the charter school, that is, new public schools chartered for specific goals for specific sorts of students—gifted, retarded, musically inclined, highly disciplined, whatever.

Many conservatives feel that isn't nearly enough, and seek an option for full choice: public-private choice. A poor or middle-class child, say the conservatives, should have the option of doing what a well-to-do child now has the option to do: choose either a public school or a private school, but in the case of private, some funds would come from the *public* treasury. The chosen method of distribution of such funds is the voucher. The idea is that parents get vouchers to cover the whole cost of public education, or some or all the cost of private education and the parents make the choice, theoretically in the best interest of the child.

Public-public choice has a solid constituency. Public-private choice generates controversy. Conservatives are attempting to address the voucher issue piecemeal, with some state and local demonstrations of the concept, which makes sense.

Those are the problems. Those are the proposed remedies. The problems were brought to us courtesy of our politics. The remedies of standards with tests and consequences, to yield greater output, have solid support in the country. Such a remedy can only come to us courtesy of our politics. That sounds simple. If it were simple, it would have happened long ago.

Clinton promised to change it.

Chapter 10

THE PREFERENCE PROLIFERATION

I wish our own leadership, I wish the black leadership would understand that removing affirmative action is the way to something more real, is the way to ideas and values that will sustain us in the long run, that will enable us to develop. That's certainly my reason for resisting it. . . . To protect against the fear of failure, we celebrate failure as authentic blackness . . . the real black is poor and uneducated. What a pathetic, self-destructive form of identification! I think I'm the real black. I think Colin Powell is the real black.
—Shelby Steele, interviewed July 1995 for PBS television version
of *Values Matter Most*

Almost everyone is in favor of the original conception of affirmative action which went beyond plain antidiscrimination to "outreach," involving (for example) advertising for jobs in black newspapers, sending college admissions officers to inner-city schools, and providing special tutoring for minority students who needed help to catch up.

But over the years, affirmative action has turned into something else: "affirmative-action-as-now-practiced," which is often called "preference," "proportionalism," or "quotas." The Q word is regarded as inflammatory by the civil rights community, but too often it is accurate.

I wrote a column late in 1993 that looked at affirmative-action-as-now-practiced, grimaced at the direction in which we were headed and asked, perhaps superciliously, whether we soon would have quotas for Sri Lankans, Lebanese, and Russian Jews. In a few days, I received a letter from George R. LaNoue, a professor of political science at the University of Maryland, Graduate School, Baltimore. Here is an excerpt from Dr. LaNoue's missive:

> I imagine you regarded the question rhetorically, but in fact, there is government policy on this issue. During the Eighties, the Small Business Administration made a series of decisions on which groups were eligible for its 8(a) program and these decisions became the model for affirmative action programs all over the country. Through Freedom of Information Act requests, I have been able to acquire for the first time the bureaucratic papers explaining which groups were to be included and excluded from affirmative action.... The SBA included Sri Lankans and for that matter Tongans, while excluding Middle Easterners (Lebanese) and (Russian) Jews.

Tongans? Sri Lankans? This sounds bizarre. It is not. It is everywhere. Russian Jews may be excluded in the SBA realm, but as it happens there is protected-class status for Hasidic Jews in another governmental arena.

The affirmative action/preference/proportionalism/quota issue is both different from and similar to the three issues that have been previously discussed.

Different. There is, first, the important matter of promises made and elections won. Clinton made clear promises about crime, welfare, and education. He promised to "end welfare as we know it" and offered a formula for it: "two years and out." In the educational arena, he was a known quantity, vigorously supporting standards, with tests, and consequences. To fight crime, he promised community policing, 100,000 new cops on the street, and boot camps for convicts. All this fit neatly beneath the rubric, "No More Something for Nothing."

That's what Clinton said; that's how he ran. There were times after he assumed the presidency when questions, often complex, arose about whether he could, or would, deliver on these items. This will be examined later.

The promises on the issue of affirmative-action-as-now-practiced are somewhat different. It is true that Clinton spoke out in a general way about the issue of proportionalism. Clinton became chairman of the Democratic Leadership Council in March 1990. The first full meeting of the DLC under his aegis was in New Orleans that same month. It was a critical moment for the organization. A presidential election was looming. The time was deemed ripe to put forth a statement of principles, drawing a line in the sand, that at once linked the DLC to earlier mainstream Democratic party values and yet separated it from the liberalism that had become the corrosive identifying hallmark of the party. And so the DLC nailed its theses to the door in the form of the New Orleans Declaration.

A list of principles was proclaimed, manifesto style. The very first one, and first not by accident, read this way:

> We believe the promise of America is equal opportunity, not equal outcomes.

Clinton's DLC hit the antiproportionalism theme more than once. In May 1991 at a major Cleveland meeting, a resolution regarding the issue was put to a vote, resulting in a harsh floor fight that was won easily by the antiquota forces. That, too, was not mere happenstance. The combat was anticipated, and used to make a point. The text of the resolution read:

> We believe in guaranteeing equal opportunity, and in affirmative action and developmental programs to assure that opportunities are in fact equal. But government should not mandate equal outcomes; therefore, we oppose quotas that create racial, gender or ethnic preference.

There was some interesting byplay regarding the Cleveland declaration. What was big news, and salutary news from the DLC perspective, was that the Reverend Jesse Jackson had purposefully not been invited to scold the group, as had been earlier DLC custom. This was regarded as a snub by the journo-political establishment. (Reciprocity is no test in these matters. Rest assured that the DLC's Senator Sam Nunn was not automatically invited to harangue Reverend Jesse Jackson's Rainbow Coalition.)

What happened in Cleveland turned out to be a precursor. Clinton and his DLC stalwarts received media confirmation of an old simple political precept: It's often easier to define a political position negatively than positively: Anti-busing, anti-NAFTA, anti-Reagan, anti-Clinton, anti-abortion, anti-Mexican bailout, anti-Jesse Jackson.)

Later, in June 1992, the moment came for a high-profile reprise of the Cleveland DLC meeting. Clinton, preparing for a national campaign, appeared before the Rainbow Coalition and went out of his way to denounce antiwhite remarks made by the black rap singer Sister Souljah, who had addressed the Rainbow meeting earlier. Clinton said: "She [Sister Souljah] told the *Washington Post*. . . . 'If black people kill black people every day, why not take a week and kill white people?' If you took the words 'white' and 'black' and reversed them, you might think David Duke was giving that speech." Reverend Jackson took the bait and denounced Clinton, which was what a Democratic candidate needed most to get elected.

Jackson, in the course of two presidential campaigns, had engaged in scores of debates with twelve Democratic candidates without any public attack on him. Clinton's tough remarks, and his subsequent brushoff of Jackson during the campaign, went a long way to certify Clinton as an authentic nonliberal, prepared to stand up to the far-left wing of the party.

Clinton was antiquota, right? Well . . . Clinton is so adept at the political game that he can use an antiquota position to accommodate the proquota views held by many activist liberal Democrats. Consider this thigh slapper from a candidate forum held in Denver on February 29, 1992. The five active candidates were asked:

> Q. If elected, will you smash the glass ceiling and guarantee that half of your appointments will be women, and if not, why not?

Jerry Brown: Well, since I've already done that, I have no difficulty making that commitment.

Bill Clinton: I wouldn't restrict myself to having just half the cabinet be women; I might want more. . . . [Laughter] Now wait a minute, I'm being serious. Why are you laughing about that? . . . I think it is not appropriate to say, "If there are fourteen, I'll be sure there are seven." I don't believe in that. But I do believe—so I'm not going to say half, but I'll say this. I wouldn't restrict myself to half. Women have held most of the important positions in my administration. I've been raised by a working grandmother, a working mother. Half of the people in the country now think that I ought to begin by putting my wife in the cabinet, and I wouldn't restrict myself just to 50 percent.

Bob Kerrey: Well, I'll be fairly direct on this thing. I've acted affirmatively as governor and as senator to hire, but I don't believe in quotas. I don't believe in imposing and adhering to an artificial quota. I just don't.

Paul Tsongas: My cabinet must reflect America. It's not only women but minorities.

Tom Harkin: I can answer that by saying yes, it could be more than that.

(Thus, the Democratic presidential candidates in 1992, by four to one, refused to come out against a proportional representation of women in high level government jobs—a sad indicator of such sentiment within the party.)

It's nice to have all this material—some mushy and some clear—on the record. But it would be a stretch to mark it down as a solid commitment by Clinton. It is not in the same league as what was said about crime, welfare, or education. To the best of my knowledge Clinton made no specific promises about ending affirmative-action-as-now-practiced in America, and certainly no formulas about how to do it. He did not acknowledge that we have quotas. He did not say we have to quit quotas. He did not say we have to end proportionalism as we know it. There were no campaign commercials about it. The issue is not mentioned in his announcement speech in Washington in late 1991 or in his acceptance speech to the Democratic convention in New York in July 1992.

In any event, the issue of proportionalism did not become salient in 1992. That is mostly the fault of George Bush and the mushy Bushy Republicans. They should have raised it, and easily could have. It is too bad they did not. The debate about preference was one that America deserved in 1992. It is a debate that America deserves in 1996. It is true that it can be a divisive issue—but an honorable public argument, with a possible resolution in sight, is not unhealthy for a troubled electorate.

Different. Unlike the issues of welfare, crime, and education where possibilities of political headway within the Democratic party are plausible, the political equation concerning quotas in the Democratic party is grim. After all, it is a party that has sets of rules and regulations requiring goals, timetables, and priority of consideraton to ensure that proportional numbers of women, blacks, Latinos, Asians, and Native Americans serve as members of each state delegation to the Democratic National Convention. (Those regulations, according to the DNC, are now "under review" as a result of President Clinton's speech on affirmative action delivered in mid-1995.)

Remember, too, that in recent presidential elections, about 90 percent of the black vote has gone for the Democratic candidate. That sort of number has appeared in many races for Congress as well. Such a massive proportion of one-way voting is almost unheard of in American psephological history. Today the Jewish vote, regarded as Democratic, is still about 20 to 30 percent Republican. Latinos vote about 40 percent Republican. Women too are more likely to vote Democratic; the so-called gender gap is real but small. In 1994, among all females, the vote was 54 to 46 percent for Democrats while males voted 58 to 42 percent for Republicans. (The majority of white women voted Republican.) With that sort of black vote, it is very difficult for most Democrats to vote against what can be portrayed as an elementary issue of fairness to many black voters.

Different. Unlike our other issues, a serious case is made for proportionalism, at least by some in the intellectual community.

INDICATORS: RACE AND ETHNICITY

The white majority has declined. It will continue to decline. It will remain a majority for the forseeable future.

Percent Distribution of Population, Projections 1990-2050

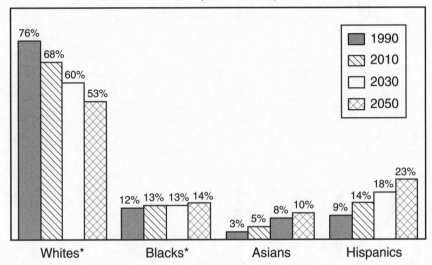

* Counted as non-Hispanic whites and blacks, respectively.

Source: U.S. Bureau of the Census.

Public attitudes concerning racial matters have improved.

SCHOOL INTEGRATION		NEIGHBORHOOD INTEGRATION		INTERRACIAL MARRIAGE	
Responses of whites to the question, "Do you think blacks and whites should go to school together?"		Responses of whites to the question, "Would you mind if a black person with equal income and education moved into your block?"		Responses by whites to the question, "Do you approve or disapprove of marriage between blacks and whites?"	
YEAR	PERCENTAGE ANSWERING "YES"	YEAR	PERCENTAGE RESPONDING "NO, WOULD NOT MIND"	YEAR	PERCENTAGE APPROVING
1942	30	1942	38	1968	17
1956	48	1956	54	1972	25
1965	68	1963	67	1978	32
1970	74	1966	72	1983	38
1976	83	1970	79	1991	44
1980	86	1972	86	1995	51
1985	92	1995	96		
1995	92				

Source: School integration and neighborhood integration: National Opinion Research Center, *Newsweek*, February 1–3, 1995; interracial marriage: Gallup Poll, ibid.

In recent years a number of predominantly white constituencies have elected blacks to represent them.

ELECTED OFFICIAL	OFFICE	STATE OR CITY	PERCENTAGE OF BLACK CONSTITUENTS
Douglas Wilder*	Governor	Virginia	18
Carol Moseley-Braun	U.S. senator	Illinois	15
Gary Franks	U.S. House of Representatives	Connecticut	4
J. C. Watts	U.S. House of Representatives	Oklahoma	7
Alan Wheat*	U.S. House of Representatives	Missouri	24
Ronald Dellums	U.S. House of Representatives	California	32
Walter Tucker	U.S. House of Representatives	California	34
David Dinkins*	Mayor	New York	28
Tom Bradley*	Mayor	Los Angeles	14
Norman Rice	Mayor	Seattle	10
Emanuel Cleaver	Mayor	Kansas City	30
Freeman Bosley, Jr.	Mayor	St. Louis	48
Elihu Harris	Mayor	Oakland	44
Wellington Webb	Mayor	Denver	13
Sharon Belton	Mayor	Minneapolis	13
Robert Nix	Chief justice, state supreme court	Pennsylvania	9
Roland Burris	State attorney general	Illinois	15
Pamela Carter	State attorney general	Indiana	7
Carl McCall	State controller	New York	16

* Have recently left office.

Source: Joint Center for Political and Economic Studies.

From a very low base, the number of black elected officials in the United States has grown dramatically since 1965.

NUMBER OF BLACK ELECTED OFFICIALS		PERCENTAGE OF BLACK OFFICIALS AMONG ALL ELECTED OFFICIALS*	
Year	*Number*	*Year*	*Percentage*
1965	300		
1970	1,629		
1975	3,503		
		1977	0.5
1980	4,112		
		1984	1.2
1985	6,056		
1990	7,370		
1993	8,015	1993	1.6

* *Note:* Blacks constituted 12.3% of the United States population in 1993.

Source: Joint Center for Political and Economic Studies.

There are many more blacks in college than previously and many more black college graduates than previously.

YEAR	NUMBER OF BLACKS ENROLLED IN COLLEGE	TOTAL NUMBER OF BLACK COLLEGE GRADUATES
1950	114,000	150,000
1960	227,000	281,000
1970	522,000	457,000
1980	1,007,000	1,115,000
1990	1,127,000	1,902,000
1993	1,545,000	2,335,000

Source: U.S. Bureau of the Census.

The rate of blacks employed in the better occupations has increased.

Percentage of Employed Blacks

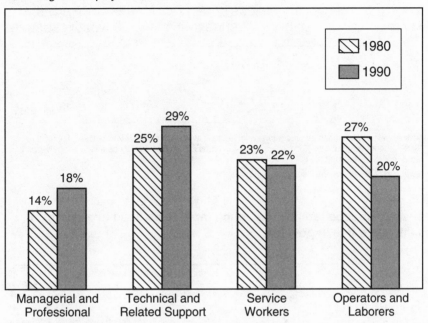

Source: U.S. Bureau of the Census.

The ratio has narrowed, but whites are still much more likely than blacks to own their home.

YEAR	BLACK HOMEOWNERS	WHITE HOMEOWNERS
1940	23%	46%
1950	35	57
1960	38	64
1970	42	65
1980	44	68
1990	43	68
1993	43	68

Source: U.S. Bureau of the Census.

For both whites and blacks the percentage of the population living in suburban areas has increased substantially since 1970.

YEAR	BLACKS LIVING IN SUBURBS	WHITES LIVING IN SUBURBS
1970	15%	31%
1980	19	36
1990	26	48

Note: Suburbs are defined as percentage of population living in Standard Metropolitan Statistical Area (SMSA), "not in central city." For 1970 numbers, suburbs are percentage of population living in urban areas, not in central city.

Source: U.S. Bureau of the Census.

Female-headed families are much more likely than two-parent families to live in poverty.

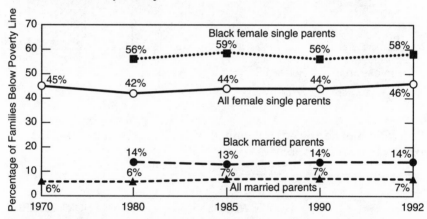

Source: Congressional Budget Office, *Trends in Family Income: 1970–1986,* February 1988, and unpublished data; U.S. Bureau of the Census, *Current Population Survey.*

Black families are much more likely to be headed by female single parents than are white families.

Percentage of Families Headed by Single Mothers

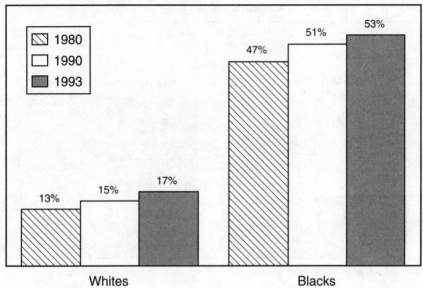

Legend:
- 1980
- 1990
- 1993

Whites: 13%, 15%, 17%

Blacks: 47%, 51%, 53%

Source: U.S. Bureau of the Census.

215

For both whites and blacks, the income earned by married house-holds is substantially greater than the income earned by single mothers.

Median Income, 1992

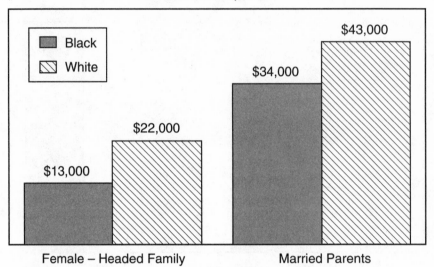

Household Type

Source: U.S. Bureau of the Census, *Current Population Reports,* P60-184.

216

There are not many policy experts who claim that our welfare system makes sense. That negative view is emphatically echoed by the public. The policy critics of our school systems make up a large battalion, and there are few wholehearted defenders. The public agrees, at least on the national dimension of the problem. Crime in America is a disaster. Everyone knows it.

Not so with affirmative-action-as-now-practiced. While the public is in opposition, many serious people in the elite policy community believe that proportionalism, preference, or quotas, or something akin to those notions—beyond the original benign concept of affirmative action—is a path that must be taken to achieve America's true destiny.

But if the quota issue is different from the other three social issues in some respects, it is very similar in other ways.

Similar. Like the other three issues, it is in the values realm, the stated terrain of this exploration.

Similar. Like the other issues, it is both important, and potentially harmful. A phrase from the Vietnam War comes to mind: "We are destroying the village in order to save it."

Similar. As with the other social issues, a vast majority of Americans have clear feelings on the matter: They dislike the very idea of proportionalism, be it in jobs, education, or elsewhere. Most blacks don't like quotas either, although at much lower levels of distaste than whites, and there may be a difference of view about what constitutes appropriate affirmative action. (See public opinion Indicators in Chapter 6.)

Similar. Like the other issues, even more so in some respects, what happened has been driven by government. Affirmative-action-as-now-practiced, comes to us courtesy of rules, regulations, court decisions, and a rare law or two.

What's wrong with proportionalism, or affirmative-action-as-now-practiced? Ask this: *What would a white racist want?*

- Surely to set race against race. Proportionalism, particularly in employment and education, has done that.

- Surely to set young whites and young blacks against each other. Preference in college admissions practice has done that. Almost every white college student in America knows that the black student walking across the quad is likely to have received preferential treatment in admissions.
- Surely to convince young black college students to self-segregate themselves. This is a complicated issue, but systematically admitting less-qualified blacks to colleges has encouraged it.
- Surely to rob successful blacks of their dignity, always wondering if they deserve their success. Yet that is the effect of proportionalism. (Do read *Reflections of an Affirmative Action Baby* by Stephen Carter.)
- Surely to set in motion a situation where whites will not want to trust blacks with responsible tasks. After all, whites may reason, did Mr. Jones, who heads a department in the XYZ Corporation, get that job on his merits or on his color? If a better and important slot opens up, wouldn't it be smarter to shunt the black executive off into a cosmetic job with a title, and give the serious promotion to a white executive who is known to have moved ahead by merit?
- Surely to establish the idea that blacks are inferior. That is one root of a preference policy and of a belief that blacks can't do it on their own.
- Surely to set blacks on an unproductive path. Playing the victim card is pernicious policy, harming blacks more than whites. (Read Shelby Steele's book *The Content of Our Character*.)
- Surely to establish special black congressional districts. That means that black voters will hardly be present in majority white districts where they might influence the vote and voice of 80 to 90 percent of the members of Congress.
- Surely to promote the idea of separatism, which now often flies under the flag of "diversity" and "multiculturalism."

We have made racists happy. Proportionalism as now practiced is the ultimate something-for-nothing program.

————————

There was a moment, and not long ago, when well-meaning whites had every reason to embrace the agenda of the civil rights leadership.

It was moral. It made economic sense. In some broad areas, it has been a smashing success. But because of the issues we have explored—crime, welfare, education—and now proportionalism—it may well be that in some ways African Americans have come to be perceived as more threatening to whites than in earlier times.

Make no mistake about it: The something-for-nothing syndrome described in this book applies across the board to the American population. And in most aspects it is by no means mainstream within a black community that in some aspects is moving upward in a somewhat traditional American way. But in every instance something for nothing is particularly acute in the black community. In each instance it is harmful, or perceived to be harmful, to many whites.

Thus: The crime rate among blacks is disproportionately high, and whites feel threatened. This violence spills over to schools, scaring parents and students. Because of very high illegitimacy rates,* blacks are disproportionately on welfare, which costs taxpayer money, undermines public morality, and creates conditions for more crime and welfare. To this is added affirmative-action-as-now-practiced, seen to be subverting the merit system in America, telling some whites that the deck is stacked against them when it comes to looking for a job or getting into college. That threatens the cohesiveness of the nation.

Learned scholars, afraid to articulate what is plainly to be seen, sanitize and euphemize it. Thus, it is said there is an "underclass" problem. It is said that there is a bad situation among "minorities." It is said that there is a crisis in the "inner city." We ought at least to have the guts to say what we are talking about. Mostly, not entirely, we are talking about American-born blacks.

Not only are the effects of proportionalism bad. The original reasons that set it in motion have become much less relevant.

There was a time when a much more solid case for proportionalism could be made. Consider the year 1964, when the Civil Rights Act was

---

* For example, the rate of Hispanic out-of-wedlock birth is 39 percent, very high, but much lower than the 68 percent for blacks. The Hispanic crime rate is high, but much lower than the black rates.

passed. In that year, about 15 percent of America was "minority." And more than 75 percent of those minorities were, by census designation, "Negroes," as African Americans were then classified.

Moreover, and most critical, the particularly troubled and tragic history of African Americans was mostly unredressed. Public segregation by race was legal in the United States. In the nation's capital, public drinking fountains were marked "white" and "colored." In many areas of the South, blacks were denied the central right of a democracy, the right to vote. Lynching happened occasionally, not as a matter of course, but it happened.

This general history is unique in America. It is not what happened to Hispanics, Asians, Native Americans, Caribbeans, Sri Lankans, Jews, Poles, Italians, Irishmen, and Tongans. It is not what happened to women. (It is our worst-case situation, which is why most of the discussion here centers on blacks.)

Under such conditions, it could be argued that this was the moment to institute some form of proportionalism in America, temporarily. A powerful case was made for bending over backward to help blacks. Still, even that was not promulgated as a preference, and certainly not as a quota. During Senate debate on the Civil Rights Act of 1964 Senator Hubert Humphrey, "Mr. Liberal," said, "Title VII does not require an employer to achieve any sort of racial balance in his work force by giving preferential treatment to any individual or group." Just warming up, Humphrey went on to say that if anyone could find in this bill language for racial preferences, "I will start eating the pages, one after the other, because it is not in there."

The situation in 1964 was crystal clear: a situation that was unfair, unredressed, unique, and tragic.

Things have changed. We can look first at the demographics.

From 1960 to 1992 the number of Hispanics in America shot up from 7 million to 24 million, from 4 percent of the American population to 9 percent. By the year 2010 the number of Hispanics is expected to surpass the number of African Americans.

The number of Asian Americans increased by 1,072 percent from 1960 to 1992, from 800,000 to 8.4 million.*

There has been a large, new legal immigration of blacks from the Caribbean and a smaller one from sub-Saharan-Africa. (From 1971 to 1992 an estimated 1.9 million Caribbeans immigrated to the United States and about 330,000 newly arrived African blacks.) The literature and anecdotal evidence suggests that the new black immigrants share many sociopolitical views and socioeconomic conditions with other immigrants, and not with American-born blacks descended from slaves.

In the 1980s the number of persons of Native American descent, formerly called American Indians, went up very sharply: from 1.4 million to 2.1 million. How interesting. Population can grow by only two means: natural increase due to more births than deaths, or by immigration. The reported increase of Native Americans far outstrips any plausible growth due to natural increase. And, by definition, there can be no new immigration of Native Americans. What caused the stunning increase? Many Americans with even a trace of American Indian heritage declared themselves Native American in order to qualify for the various goodies of affirmative-action-as-now-practiced.

It goes beyond all that, beyond the well-recognized black-Latino-Asian-Native American protected classes. Since 1964 the number of Muslims has gone up from an estimated few hundred thousand people to an estimated 5 million to 8 million. The Asians who have come in are usually perceived to be of Chinese descent—mainland, Taiwan, Hong Kong, or from Korea. But 500,000 Indians have arrived since 1964 and 1.1 million Filipinos. There has been a large, new immigration from Eastern Europe and the old component parts of the Soviet Union. Some of these are Jews; most of them are not. It is estimated that about 1 million Poles emigrated to the United States during the 1980s, mostly illegally.

---

* When Attorney General Robert Kennedy was asked, in testimony before the Congress, how many Asians were likely to come to the United States as a result of the new immigration bill of 1965, he said, "Approximately five thousand . . . in the first year. . . . We do not expect there would be any great influx after that." Asian immigration is now running about 350,000 per year.

In some important respects, native-born American blacks of early American descent are no longer unique. They no longer make up 75 percent of the minorities in America. They make up less than 50 percent, and the rate is steadily sinking. There are many growing minorities in America. If we are going to go down the route of proportionalism—and until very recently America seemed to be headed that way—it would likely involve a huge proportion of the population on racial and ethnic grounds alone. Add in gender and handicapped status and the situation becomes somewhat bizarre: More than 75 percent of Americans are now "protected."

———

It is not just demography that has changed in the last thirty years. This book concentrates mostly on what government has done wrong and how to fix it. But what government has done right is a monumental story as well. Legal segregation began to crumble in 1954 when the Supreme Court unanimously decided, in *Brown* v. *Board of Education,* that school segregation by race was unconstitutional. The Civil Rights Act of 1964 was passed, then the Voting Rights Act (1965), then another one dealing with housing (1968). Discrimination in every aspect of American public life is not only illegal now but pretty well enforced by a wide array of governmental and nongovernmental institutions. (Indeed, much of the argument is now about reverse discrimination, or as Nathan Glazer of Harvard has called it, "affirmative discrimination.")*

With the dwindling of segregation and discrimination, blacks have been succeeding as never before. The rate of blacks graduating from high school has now—for the first time in American history—almost reached parity with the white rates. The rate of growth of blacks living in suburbs has climbed enormously, as shown in the Indicators. Of critical importance: Census Bureau data shows that young married African Americans in two-earner families have roughly the same incomes as their white counterparts.†

———

* Nathan Glazer, *Affirmative Discrimination* (Basic Books, New York, 1975).

† It should not be assumed that economic and social progress among African Americans has been *caused* by affirmative action. In *This U.S.A.,* published in 1965 (before the advent of

In the course of a decade or so we saw that America's most famous and most admired military officer was black (Colin Powell). So was America's most universally acclaimed athlete (Michael Jordan), top-rated comic performer (Bill Cosby), most popular talk show host (Oprah Winfrey), best television anchor (Bernard Shaw), and most popular singer (Michael Jackson). In 1965 there were 300 elected black officials in all of America. Today there are 8,000. If General Powell becomes president there will be one more.

Two things should be said about such facts. The first is that they tell a remarkable story, and severely undertold, much to the dismay of many blacks who are furious at the constant media drumbeating about crime, illegitimacy, poor test scores, and so on. The second is that the downbeat aspects of the black condition are also true and very important. It is those social inequalities that lead to the demand for proportionalism.

The case in favor of proportionalism, insofar as it ever had merit, is based in some large measure on the facts of yesteryear. Blacks are not a majority of American minorities. Thirty years have passed, long enough to fulfill the idea of a temporary bending-over backward. (A man fifty years old today was entering the labor force when the Civil Rights Act became law in 1964.) There has been enormous black progress. The major barriers to black advancement are no longer *externally* imposed factors such as segregation or discrimination but *internally* driven factors like the high rate of black single-parent families.

Based on facts that are less and less relevant, a system has been perpetuated far beyond its original design, infuriating most Americans and harming some of them.

We can go about changing what has happened only if we know how it happened. Government did it. How? According to Glazer, by "lies and evasion."

---

affirmative action), Scammon and I examined census data and showed that solid catch-up by blacks had been made in the 1950s and early 1960s. In 1974, in *The Real America*, I reported similar positive results for the 1960s and early 1970s, a time period mostly uninfluenced by affirmative action, which wasn't even promulgated by Executive Order until 1965 and then took a considerable amount of time to filter through the system.

The 1964 Civil Rights Act had several explicit statements against proportionalism, including one that *prohibits* "preferential treatment to any individual or to any group because of the race, color, religion, sex or national origin of such individual or group on account of an imbalance which may exist with respect to the total number or percentage of persons of any race, color, religion, sex, or national origin of such individual or group." Preference is against the law.

Even President Johnson's famous Executive Order 11246, promulgated in 1965, which has become the fount of proportionalism run amok, stipulates only equal opportunity, specifically not preference. In the course of engaging in contracting, the federal government is told to *"take affirmative action to ensure that applicants are employed, and that employees are treated during employment, without regard to their race, creed, color, or national origin."* As Glazer points out, the language is color-blind, but the implementation has been color-conscious.

From such acorns of affirmative action, the oaks of proportionalism have grown. Consider some landmarks:

• In 1968 in Green v. County School Board, the Supreme Court let go of the Brown decision that barred racial discrimination in education. Race-based integration could now be required as a "remedy" for past unconstitutional segregation of schools.

• In 1970, in *Contractors of Eastern Pennsylvania v. Schultz*, a federal court ruled that "specific [hiring] goals and timetables" were "no more or less than a means of implementation of the Affirmative Action obligations of Executive Order 11246."

• In 1971 in *Swann v. Charlotte-Mecklenberg Board of Education* the Supreme Court upheld the practice of busing—that is, assigning students to schools on the basis of race—because it was a remedy to past wrongs rather than an end unto itself.

• In 1971 in *Griggs v. Duke Power* the Supreme Court unanimously upheld Title VII guidelines stating that any test that distinguishes among individuals would also distinguish among groups. Thus, high school diplomas, literacy, and math tests were ruled to be potentially or actually discriminatory. Tests, it was ruled, disproportionately discriminated against blacks. Even if the test was "fair in form" and even if there was no discriminatory intent on the part of the employer, such criteria served as a "built-in headwind" for minority groups. This could be proved by showing "disparate impact" in the existing workforce. And so employers were barred from ignoring race and forced to consider it. The numbers had to come up right, or close to right.

Threatened by law and potential adverse publicity, the corporate community moved toward proportionalism. Why not? The corporate executives wouldn't suffer much from reverse discrimination. And if they didn't go along, one day they might get a nice call from the folks at the Equal Employment Opportunity Commission telling them all about the *Griggs* doctrine of "disparate impact."

• In 1978, in *Regents of the University of California* v. *Bakke* the Court held that Title VI of the Civil Rights Act did not apply equally to discrimination against whites.

• In 1979, in *U.S. Steel Workers* v. *Weber*, the Court ruled that Title VII's prohibition against discrimination toward "any individual" did not apply fully to discrimination against whites.

These measures were compounded by programs intended to aid minority businesses. The Small Business Act, for example, provided that a portion of all government contracts be reserved for minority-owned firms—"set-asides."

So many laws, decisions, rules, and regulations. Naturally enough, a federal bureaucracy grew up to enforce them all. At the top of the heap, the process of affirmative action operates through the office of Federal Contract Compliance Programs, situated in the U.S. Department of Labor, and through the Equal Employment Opportunity Commission. Other departments do heavy lifting in their own realm. In the Department of Defense, for example, the Director of Contractor Employment Compliance at one point had an authorized staff of 565!

Affirmative action came to encompass goals, timetables, and sanctions. That yielded affirmative-action-as-now-practiced, which many Americans believe to be shorthand for preference, proportionalism, and quotas.

Nothing better illustrates the corruption of affirmative action than the race norming of tests in America. Officially, race norming is known as "within-group percentile conversions." The idea is to load the dice in favor of minorities and women, and thereby against those who are not—white men. As described by Jared Taylor in *Paved with Good Intentions*, race norming was conceived at the end of the Carter administration at the Department of Labor in response to a variety of Supreme Court decisions. Ironically, race norming was fully implemented after Ronald Reagan took office in 1981. It was the Gipper's Department of Labor that ordered that test scores for hiring purposes be reported only in percentiles and that minorities be scored only within their own cohort. Soon state governments and many private businesses were race-norming their tests. More than 15 million people were scored this way; few knew about it. If a company hired through state employment agencies, and many companies did, they got race-normed candidates. At one point, the Equal Employment Opportunity Commission threatened to sue companies that did not race-norm. Testing companies came up with new ways to make it happen. It was an out-and-out quota deal with hardly a disguise.

Slowly, in some places, resistance grew. In a number of cases in the 1980s the Supreme Court whittled away at the reach of *Griggs*.

All during this period the civil rights leadership maintained that there was no quota hiring in America. That was stressed during the debates about proposed laws to reinstate *Griggs* in all its grandeur, particularly during the arguments concerning the 1990 civil rights bill (which did not pass, because George Bush vetoed it). The no-quotas-in-America idea was stressed again by activists during the debate about the 1991 civil rights bill. But it was then pointed out that the federal government itself hired people on the basis of race-norming. Oops! Even the Democratic Congress, when confronted with such a clear example of discrimination, had to reconfigure. And so, the Civil Rights Act of 1991, which passed into law and apparently restored much of *Griggs*, also banned race-norming. Disparate impact, however, was left in a gray area.

You may ask: How can disparate impact be avoided without something akin to race-norming? I do not know.

Even after Supreme Court decisions limited certain aspects in 1995, proportionalism remains widespread. The "temporary" remedy has lasted for three decades. Long-time civil rights activist Professor Roger Wilkins, of George Mason University, has said that the civil rights law and guidelines could be reviewed "every fifteen years."

In 1991 President Bush's counsel, C. Boyden Gray, met with William Coleman, distinguished Washington attorney, black Republican, former secretary of transportation, and civil rights leader. Here, from a *Louisiana Law Review* article published in 1994, is how Gray describes the meeting:

> There were private indications that a desire to codify a quota regime was the principal motivation behind the (1991) legislation. William Coleman, the bill's principal author, was quite candid with me about what he wanted. "What I need is a generation of proportional hiring, and then we can relax these provisions."

"Fifteen years," "a generation." Coleman and Wilkins are mainstream black leaders. Other civil rights activists talk privately about a century, or simply see no end in sight.

How long is forever? Thomas Sowell, in *Race and Culture: A World View*, makes the point that quotas always start out as temporary and are never voluntarily given up by proponents. (Can you imagine, in your mind's eye, twenty-five years from now, and an aged Jesse Jackson saying the time has come to end affirmative action?) In the *Bakke* case Justice Harry Blackmun, who supported preferential treatment, worried that such a policy might continue too long. He thought it could be eliminated in about ten years, which would have been 1986. It wasn't. If anything, until very recently it was ascendant.

In *Commentary* of June 1995, Arch Puddington, a senior scholar at Freedom House, writes: "Because it got into this business, the United States has been moved dangerously close to a country with an officially sanctioned spoils system."

So then: At least four big, harmful, something-for-nothing problems: crime, welfare, education, and affirmative-action-as-now-practiced. And on election day 1992, Bill Clinton won. He had campaigned on a platform of no more something for nothing. Yet he would operate within a political party that had created most of the something-for-nothing policies, and developed huge constituencies based on such policies.

What happened?

Part Four

VERIFICATION

Chapter 11

WHY CLINTON AND THE DEMOCRATS ALMOST BLEW IT, OR DID

So that was the state of play with respect to the social issues—the most important issues we face—when the Democrats, with the best of intentions, began their presidential transition after the 1992 election.

For the first time in sixteen years the Democrats had pulled off the political hat trick: a Democratic president, a Democratic House of Representatives, and a Democratic Senate. In addition, a majority of governorships were in Democratic hands, as well as a huge majority of the big-city mayors, and an apparently permanent majority of state legislators and state legislatures. Other than the fizzled Carter term in the late 1970s, it was the first all-Democratic moment since Lyndon Johnson left office in early 1969, almost a quarter of a century earlier.

Democrats were ecstatic. Gridlock was broken! Finally, things would get done! Arthur Schlesinger, Jr., a distinguished historian of Democratic persuasion, saw a new Democratic cycle of activist government. Some seers even knew the details of how this activist progression would work out: eight years for Clinton, eight years for Gore, eight years for Hillary.

And why not? Clinton had just amassed 370 electoral votes to George Bush's 168 and Ross Perot's zero. Clinton had captured 43 percent of the popular vote, a nice six-point margin over Bush's 37 percent, with Perot getting 19 percent. Exit polls showed that if Perot had not run, Clinton would have picked up about half the Perot vote, thereby maintaining his margin. Shortly after the election, Clinton's approval rating was in the neighborhood of 62 percent.

Then something happened. As had been noted before, and will be noted again, Democrats were devastated. What happened? Such a dramatic electoral turnaround would usually be associated with a suddenly tough time in the economic realm or perhaps an unpopular war. But the nation was at peace in 1994. The economy had improved markedly since Clinton took office.*

The good economy during the 1994 election cycle tends to verify what has been said here several times: Economics isn't the only game in town, and it may not be the most important one, either tactically or substantively. The economy was healthy, yet the in-party got trounced.

Some verifying evidence about the primacy of the values issues in 1994 has been presented earlier, in chapter 6 and in the Indicators preceding that chapter. Consider now the work of Fred Steeper, a veteran Republican pollster who analyzed the only two national exit polls taken on November 8, 1994, one by Voter News Service and a second by Mitofsky International. Steeper writes:

> [The results] . . . strongly suggest that the old paradigm of the parties as aggregations of economic interest groups has been eclipsed by the politics of shared cultural values. Many, if not most, of the cutting issues of today defy an interpretation based on economic self-interest.

Accordingly, Steeper sees the formation of a new Republican party based on noneconomic factors:

> When a new party system emerged in our past, it was because a new set of unresolved concerns came to the fore, commanding at least as much

---

* Clinton partisans maintain that there is some evidence that many voters hadn't fully noticed the good economy and therefore didn't give the Democrats credit they deserved. Perhaps. But a good economy is hard not to notice; it affects a voter's everyday life.

voter attention as the older issues. Violent crime, a permanent welfare population, and lagging student performance have led many to conclude there has been a breakdown in important traditional values such as personal and family responsibility, self-reliance, individual merit, and religious principles. Specific cultural issues such as capital punishment, school prayer, abortion, illegal immigration, gay rights, and affirmative action, together, form a new continuum in our politics.*

In the fall of 1994 pollster Lance Tarrance asked respondents: "What is the biggest issue facing the middle class?" The number one response was "declining moral values." Republicans were seen as much stronger than Democrats in promoting morality (42 percent to 26 percent) and individual responsibility in society (43 percent to 29 percent).

If values mattered most in the election of 1994 and the Republicans won big in 1994, then it is plausible that the Democrats must have done something wrong about values from 1992 to 1994, or the Republicans done something right, or both.

The Democrats certainly had first crack at the issue. President Clinton campaigned on that no-more-something-for-nothing platform. He could have pursued the high goal of "Nixon-to-China," that is, the presidential art of gently convincing his own party, that it has been wrong on an issue. Clinton could have been Nixon-to-China on social issues. He could have been Clinton-to-Crime, showing Democrats that thugs must be incapacitated by means of long sentences. He could have been Clinton-to-Welfare, showing Democrats why it was necessary to break down the incentives for out-of-wedlock birth. He could have been Clinton-to-Education, showing Democrats how to devalue the funny money in education and go to standards-tests-consequences. He could have been—maybe—Clinton-to-Affirmative Action.

---

* Fred Steeper, "This Swing Is Different," Market Strategies, Inc., January 1995. The theme expressed in this book was in manuscript long before the 1994 election, and thus long before Steeper wrote. Steeper did not see this manuscript before he set down his thoughts. Moreover, until May 1995, when we conducted some focus groups together in Dayton, I don't recall meeting or talking with Steeper. Before I talked with him, Steeper had amended his thesis to split the values issues in two, "national morality" issues and "religious morality" issues, which roughly corresponded to the "social" and "cultural" rubrics discussed here.

Clinton and the Democrats could have shown America how to break up the something-for-nothing state. Did he? Did they? They had control of government; they are the ones who can be judged. (Republicans may well get their turn in the dock soon.)

I have neither the space, nor the inclination, nor the knowledge, to write a plenary history of the first two years of the Clinton presidency, from election day 1992 to election day 1994.* I propose here to explain what happened in the values realm, and what happened regarding some important items that touch on that realm. Put that way, it's still not plenary, but it turns out to be plenty.

The most important of those items related to a values agenda concerns *personnel*. A president's first acts are ones of appointment. The question to think about is: Who will run the government? After all, in the high reaches of the executive branch of government, only Clinton and Albert Gore were elected. Just about all the rest were appointed, by Clinton.

It is a truism of life in Washington that there is always "a battle for the mind of the president." Less attention is paid to the idea that victory in the battle of ideas often depends on the political and ideological nature of the battlers. Liberal advisers give liberal advice. Hence it is true, as the saying goes, "Personnel is policy."

A president does not sit in splendid isolation making decisions by checking the "yes" or "no" box on a memo. Nor is it as simple as having honest brokers presenting policy menus with three or four neat options. Who are the brokers? What do they believe about how the world works? Who calls them on the phone? Whose phone calls do they answer? Whom do they call for guidance? Most specifically in this context: Are they "New Democrats" or "Old Democrats"?

Party warfare, party warriors. New Democrats? Old Democrats? For almost three decades it has been said that there was "a war for the soul of

---

* Elizabeth Drew's book, *On the Edge: The Clinton Presidency* (Simon and Schuster, New York, 1994) does an excellent job on that topic, through July 1994.

the Democratic party." That intramural combat in the Democratic party did not end with Clinton's election.

The labels describing the feuding factions have changed over the years, in an often amusing and convoluted way. The Democratic split goes back at least to 1968, when the terms of polar disendearment were elemental, if not precise. There were many highly publicized "antiwar" Democrats, a few publicly professed "prowar" Democrats, but lots of "anti-antiwar Democrats." There were "pro-Johnson" Democrats and "dump Johnson" Democrats. After LBJ decided not to run, there were "pro-Humphrey" Democrats and "dump the Hump" Democrats. There were "Bobby" Democrats and "Clean for Gene" Democrats (for Senator Robert Kennedy and Senator Eugene McCarthy). There were, somewhere, a significant number of "John Connally Democrats," but they were mostly unreported on by the national press. There were also lots of unreported-on "George Wallace Democrats" or "George Wallace ex-Democrats."

There were also garden variety liberal, moderate, and conservative Democrats. But with President Johnson vigorously engaged in Vietnam and vigorously pro–civil rights, even those simple labels could get confusing.

Gradually a term entered the vocabulary that seemed to capture the spirit of the fray: the New Politics. Who supported the New Politics? Most were Democrats of the left who had signed on to most of the liberal guilt-peddling. Typically, they hailed from the cause movements of the time: antiwar, civil rights, environmentalist, consumerist, and feminist.* (Gay rights activists openly came on board somewhat later.)

Who, within the Democratic party, opposed the energetic New Politics left wing? There were many players with many gradations of views. Most vigorously, the labor unions were "anti–New Politics" and "anti-McGovernite." Indeed, the AFL-CIO, under the leader-

---

* When George McGovern captured the Democratic nomination in 1972, many of the New Politics types were identified as "McGovernites." But it was a transitory and overblown designation. Later, McGovern himself would deny that even *he* was a McGovernite, as the term was used. (At the Gridiron dinner in late 1972 McGovern said, "We opened up the doors of the Democratic party and 30 million Democrats walked out.").

ship of the late George Meany, did not endorse George McGovern's 1972 presidential bid against Richard Nixon. Given the tight linkage of labor with the Democratic party, that was a remarkable political repudiation.

A "Scoop Jackson wing" of the party formed, allied in many ways with the anti–New Politics and anticommunist views of the labor movement. I am familiar with this part of the political spectrum due principally to a small organization that I co-founded and later chaired, the Coalition for a Democratic Majority (CDM), which started up in late 1972 after McGovern's defeat. (And drifted out of existence in the mid-1980s.)

Among the principal political personages during the early life of CDM were Senators Henry Jackson, Hubert Humphrey, and Daniel Patrick Moynihan and Representative Thomas Foley, a former Jackson staffer and then a young congressman from the state of Washington.[*]

To follow the label game, it is interesting now to recall that CDM sought to help shape the climate of ideas in favor of what were then called "Traditional Democrats." But the New Politics liberal Democrats became ever more powerful within the party. Young Vietnam-era activists matured and sought public office. Some won. After a while some of them, not us, were being called traditional Democrats. In the Democratic party parlance, "traditional" had become "liberal." Thus, Senator Edward M. Kennedy, once a leading exemplar of the New Politics, is now often cited an exemplar of a traditional labor-liberal Democrat, which Republicans would call a "big government liberal."

The struggle for the soul of the party has continued over the decades, but the labels seem to migrate like geese in winter. Liberals continued to gain influence in the party, but they lost national elections because voters didn't like what liberalism had come to stand for.

---

[*] Among the signers of the original CDM manifesto were Jeanne J. Kirkpatrick, Zbigniew Brzezinski, civil rights activist Bayard Rustin, a number of presidents of AFL-CIO unions, Richard Schifter, Penn Kemble, Ambassador Peter Rosenblatt, Midge Decter, and Norman Podhoretz. Somewhat later, during the mid- to late 1970s, Elliot Abrams was among the most active members. (Kemble was the first executive director of CDM and is now in the Clinton administration as deputy director of the United States Information Agency.)

Attacking the "L word" became standard Republican practice. So, in camouflage mode, liberals began calling themselves progressives. That, for example, was the word associated with the 1976 presidential candidacy of Representative Morris Udall, a liberal. Then in 1984 and 1988 the P word was used by the Reverend Jesse Jackson to describe his own very-left spot on the spectrum.

And now what? Well, the newest incarnation of those who reject—yes, reject—the New Politics Democrats are called—believe it or not—"New Democrats"! That makes it "New" versus "New." It's a little silly, but that's the way it is. The central clearinghouse for the new New Democrats is the Democratic Leadership Council (DLC). Its related think tank is called, ironically enough, the Progressive Policy Institute (PPI). That also makes it "progressive" versus "progressive."

Enough of labels. The point is this: There has been a fight, the labels change, the fight goes on. It has not been an idle or sterile fight. The stakes have been huge: influence within the oldest and (until 1994, at least) the most powerful political party in the world, in the oldest and most powerful democracy in the world, the only true superpower in the world, whose culture, including its political culture, is a model for the rest of the world.

To keep things simple here, I shall, following the most familiar contemporary label usage, call the two arguing teams "New Democrats" (the right wing of the left-leaning party) and "liberals" (the left wing of the left-leaning party). Occasionally, liberals will be called "Old Democrats."

The DLC was set into motion during the 1984 Democratic convention in a San Francisco hotel suite at a meeting of New Democrats. It was clear to most of the participants that although the brass bands were playing for Walter Mondale in the Moscone Arena, he and his party were seen as too liberal to be elected.

The DLC was formed to change that sort of politics. The group was soon attacked by liberals, who denigrated it as the "southern white boys' caucus." But it grew and evolved, and it developed a coherent set of beliefs. The DLC stressed the themes of opportunity, community, and responsibility. It called for "empowering" citizens, not "entitling" them. It looked for market-oriented solutions not governmentally based ones. It sought to "reinvent" government, and sometimes to cut it. It promulgated the idea of a "third way," to succeed liberalism and conservatism, which was necessary because, as candidate Clinton said on the stump, both parties were "brain dead." The DLC did not shrink from defining itself by its adversaries; DLC president Al From often calls his Democratic opponents "liberal fundamentalists" or occasionally even "liberal Ayatollahs."

In terms of a list used earlier in this book, the DLC understands what happens when a party is perceived to be in favor of vagrancy, murderers, crime, promiscuity, drugs, pornography, and quotas and perceived to be against the neighborhood school, single-family homes, work, prayer, merit, and Christmas.

The DLC is an interesting group. Most of its members who are elected officials are moderates or right of center in the Democratic party. Some elected officials, however, who joined the DLC were from the mildly liberal side of the spectrum (apparently seeking political cover from a straight L-word affiliation).

An early member of the DLC, and later its chairman, was Governor Bill Clinton. He helped shape the DLC philosophy, and in turn was shaped by it, ran on it, and won on it. So it came to pass that the DLC became the measuring rod of whether President Clinton was governing as a New Democrat or whether he was reverting to traditional New Politics special interest liberalism.

I repeat two thoughts: (1) the fight within the Democratic party is old, ongoing, and sometimes bitter, and (2) personnel is policy. If Clinton had hired and properly employed his DLC shock troops to reinvent the Democratic party then the idea of Nixon-to-China, Clinton-to-Liberals would have been off to a good start.

———

He didn't.

What went on regarding personnel in the first part of the Clinton administration was no case-by-case accident nor easily remediated after the fact. Those early appointees shaped the policy that was to come and will probably continue to shape it, although perhaps to a somewhat lesser extent.

Under the rubric of picking an administration that would "look like America," a remarkably rigid demographic quota system to fill jobs was quickly established. Blacks, Latinos, and women were hired for preordained slots, even when apparently better-qualified white males sought appointment. It got tough, and nasty. Within the administration, jobs were described as earmarked for "a skirt." There was infighting among the quotees. "Non-Hispanic white females" complained they were losing out to "twofers," that is, black or Latino women.

Apparently, in some instances the quota mentality extended to sexual preference as well. There was this story:

> When the head of one of the transition teams that shaped policy for Bill Clinton asked the White House recently why it had not offered him a job in the new administration, the reply was baffling.
>
> "Your transition team had no OGs and this is considered unacceptable," he was told. Translated, the message was clear: because his team included no openly gay men, he was judged unwilling to encourage diversity in government.*

At one point Clinton angrily denounced the "bean counters" who were pushing him. In fact, his administration was handing out beans by the bushel. President Clinton gave an excellent imitation of President Quota.

At first glance, quota mongering may not sound like a policy initiative or an ideological thrust beyond the realm of group preference itself. But it is. Of course, there are women who are liberals or moderates or conservatives. Of course, there are blacks who are liberals or moderates or conservatives. So too with Hispanics. But when, in the Democratic party, people are picked *because* they are women, blacks, or Latinos, they are much more than likely to be swinging from the activist liberal side of the plate. (Insofar as there is a gay quota, the same idea applies.)

---

* James Adams, "Hillary Clinton Causes Chaos in the Politically Correct Manner," *Sunday Times* (London), February 28, 1993.

Alas, there were no quotas for moderate Democrats, or conservative Democrats. Appointees chosen because they look like America do not think like America.

Why did this happen? A major player in the Clinton White House was Hillary Rodham Clinton. She was not only the main enforcer of proportional picking in the abstract, but was active in the day-to-day appointment process.

One of her key advisers in this matter was her old friend and mentor, Marion Wright Edelman, chair of the Children's Defense Fund, one of the most active, and potent, liberal advocacy groups in Washington. Another alleged big player in the appointments game was Susan Thomases, a New York liberal who met Bill Clinton at a 1970 antiwar demonstration, and met Hillary Clinton in 1974 while working on Bill's unsuccessful campaign in Arkansas for a seat in the U.S. House of Representatives. This Hillary-Edelman-Thomases troika was tightly interlinked with the feminist and civil rights activist groups, which meant that candidates from the liberal activist wing of the party were inevitably pushed forward.

Then there was the powerful office of the White House counsel, which vetted many candidates for key jobs throughout the government. It was headed by Bernard Nussbaum, a wealthy and generally liberal lawyer from New York City. In New York he had worked on political campaigns for Elizabeth Holtzman, a very liberal politician. Nussbaum had been Hillary Rodham's boss when she served as a young attorney on the House Judiciary Committee staff preparing the case for the impeachment of Richard Nixon in 1974.

Nussbaum's deputy was the late Vincent Foster, who had worked closely in Little Rock at the Rose Law Firm with his good friend and law partner, Hillary Clinton. William Kennedy, also an attorney from Rose, was second in command in the counsel's office. So the liberal and activist Mrs. Clinton had many ways to shape the emerging Clinton administration.

Consider, too, the rest of the White House staff. These are the people who have the most immediate and regular access to the president. Many of the new White House staffers were young—the so-called Under Thirties. Their principal experience came from work in the liberal Democratic Congress and in election campaigns, particularly the 1994 Clinton campaign. What were they supposed to know about the substance of ancient battles between the rad-libs versus the trad-libs? They had come of age smirking about the Evil Empire and believing that Ronald Reagan was out to make life miserable for poor people and minorities. (As conservative humorist P. J. O'Rourke likes to point out, Reagan used to slip out of the White House at night to sell crack and get young girls pregnant.)

George Stephanopoulos was appointed director of communications at the White House. Stephanopoulos, then thirty-one, a self-described liberal, had been a congressional aide to House Majority Leader Richard Gephardt. Working with Stephanopoulos were David Dreyer, age thirty-six, formerly Gephardt's press secretary, and Mike Waldman a young, former Nader's Raider. A key economic aide was the liberal Gene Sperling, thirty-three, a former economic adviser to Governor Mario Cuomo. Also present was Ricki Seidman, a former staff aide for Senator Ted Kennedy and former legal director of People for the American Way, who had been active in the assaults on Supreme Court nominees Clarence Thomas and Robert Bork.

And there was Ira Magaziner, serving as the principal aide in a legislative venture to plan and pass universal health coverage for Americans. The czar—or czarina—of the project was Hillary Clinton. Magaziner was an energetic activist liberal from his college days. It is no wonder that the plan that emerged was tagged as "too liberal" and "a government takeover of one-seventh of the economy." Magaziner ended up being called "Rasputin-like" in his interaction with Mrs. Clinton. (The quote comes from a high Clinton administration official.)

To that team was added the influence of the political campaign staff that did not officially go to work in the White House but had easy everyday access to it, actually holding permanent staff passes. Key players included Stanley Greenberg, a liberal pollster and a former Yale Law School professor; Paul Begala, a speechwriter on Gephardt's 1988 presidential primary campaign; and the superstar campaign manager, James Carville. Carville had gained national prominence by managing the 1991 Pennsylvania Senate race of liberal Harris Wofford, who won a surprise victory on an issue that would haunt the Republicans and later the Clintonistas: health care.*

To all this must be added a Himalayan fact. A majority of the Congress was Democratic, and a majority or a solid plurality of the Democrats in Congress were liberals. The congressional liberal wing had been growing and then took a big jump in 1992 when, because of court-ordered reapportionment of congressional districts by race and ethnicity, the number of black and Hispanic legislators jumped from thirty-nine to fifty-eight.

Back in the mid-1980s, I had asked then majority leader Tom Foley how he would ideologically characterize the Democratic members of the House. He said: "One third liberal, one third moderate, one third conservative." In early 1995, shortly after he left the House speakership (with great dignity), I asked him the same question, concerning the Democrats of the 103d Congress (Clinton's first two years). The answer was quite different from his earlier estimate: "About a half are hard-core liberal, about a third conservative, the rest moderate." Foley believes that the Democratic caucus in the current House (104th Congress) is somewhat more liberal yet.

At the start of Clinton's term, the House had 261 Democrats—amounting to 60 percent of the whole body. In the Senate, there were

---

* Clinton's chief White House speechwriter (for other than foreign policy issues) was David Kusnet, who had written speeches for the presidential campaigns of Walter Mondale and Michael Dukakis, and was chief speechwriter on the 1992 Clinton campaign. Kusnet comes out of the labor movement and had been a public relations consultant and speechwriter for many liberal activist groups. He is the author of Speaking American, subtitled How Democrats Can Win in the Nineties. His greatest achievement, by far, was marrying my daughter Ruth. When David started to work for Clinton, he told his nosy columnist father-in-law next to nothing about what was happening on the campaign or inside the White House. He believes in the old code that a president's staff should keep quiet and work for the president. I salute him for that, but he wasn't worth much as a source. Kusnet left the White House to become a syndicated columnist for the Creators' Syndicate. He likes to describe himself as "of the left," which I am happy to record here, but with one unusual caveat: He makes a great deal of sense. In any event, as I have divined it from others, the speechwriting shop under Clinton was not often a principal combatant in the ideological struggles that went on.

57 Democrats out of the 100 total. Almost all of them, disproportionately liberals, had run better in their districts or states than Clinton had. Clinton needed almost all of them to help pass his program, and they would press him to make his program conform to their views. Many of these 318 Democrats had allies or staff members who sought jobs in the new Clinton administration. Many of them got those jobs and were able to advance the ideas they had come to believe in while in service with Democratic members of Congress, disproportionately liberal.

Moreover, the Clinton White House, unlike most other recent White Houses, had no ideological czar. (Reagan was his own ideological czar, with Ed Meese for backup. John Sununu czarred for Bush.)

Consider the case of Thomas "Mack" McLarty. A boyhood friend of Clinton, a former chief executive officer of the Arkansas Power and Light Company, McLarty was an early participant in the DLC, and in fact was probably the person most responsible for bringing Clinton into the organization. McLarty is a moderate. When he was appointed Clinton's chief of staff, there were hopes that he might keep Clinton pointed in the DLC direction. It was not to be; McLarty, known as "Mack the Nice," is neither an ideologue nor a policy man. (There is a story in circulation, perhaps apocryphal, of McLarty's walking out of a White House staff meeting, muttering, "I would feel a lot more at home as chief of staff in a Republican administration.")

In the old Soviet Union there was a formal position in the Central Committee of "Secretary of Ideology." For many years the spot was occupied by Mikhail Suslov, an old communist war horse whose job was to set out the party line. The Clinton White House had no apparent Suslov. If there was one, it was Hillary Clinton, a lady of the left, who was never called Hillary the Nice. In the Democratic party when there is no Suslov, a certain law of political gravity takes over: *Whatever isn't nailed down slides left.*

Of course, there was one man who might have reshuffled the stacked deck: Bill Clinton, the man ultimately responsible for the deck stack in the first place. A president with iron in his soul could confront the forces of (1) a strong-willed and liberal wife, (2) a White House staff tilted toward youth and the liberal side, (3) a Democratic Congress tilted left, and (4) a bean-counting quota system for appointments, with a built-in ideological leftward bias. Clinton could have been Clinton's Suslov. And maybe he was.

Inevitably we must consider the question of where Clinton's political heart is located. In the Washington shorthand about Clinton the question is, "What does he *really* believe?"

I had pretty well sworn off political psychiatry when I read *First in His Class*, by David Maraniss. A first-class biography of Clinton from his birth to his 1991 announcement of candidacy, it offers a sense of an answer to the What does he really believe? question: *Clinton is a tactical moderate and an ideological liberal.* (His supporters say labels don't mean anything anymore, which is what liberals say these days.)

The past is prologue. Drawing from Maraniss, what would Early Clinton and Early Hillary look like if made into a movie in the *Forrest Gump* style? Watch the screen: There go Bill Gump and Hillary Rodham Gump popping up at most every watering spot along the liberal wagon trail.

Thus, Bill gets his ticket punched: (1) working for the leading opponent to the Vietnam war (Senator William Fulbright, also a segregationist), (2) at the antiwar hothouse that was Oxford University (on a Rhodes scholarship), (3) as "a full-blown anti-war organizer," (4) as an artful draft avoider, or evader, or dodger, considering selective conscientious objector status, (5) at the liberal Yale Law School, where students are encouraged to do their own thing, (6) which for Clinton was the 1970 Senate campaign of Joe Duffey in Connecticut, which drew young, liberal, antiwar activists from across the country, (7) as an early supporter, then organizer, in liberal George McGovern's 1972 presidential bid (while most of his political friends went to work for the more moderate Senator Edmund Muskie).

Meanwhile, Hillary pays her dues (8) at the very liberal Children's Defense Fund, (9) as a lawyer for the Watergate investigation that drew up the Nixon impeachment charges and later, (10) serving on the board of the Legal Services Corporation, an organization which was designed to help poor people use the law, and periodically, allegedly, used its personnel for quite liberal political purposes, which would be contrary to their charter and federal law.

Following Maraniss's tale, we see the boy prodigy from Arkansas bloom in the fertile soil of the New Politics. There is passion everywhere: joy, rapture, despondency. Clinton is described as a young man who hardly sleeps, who consumes food, books, and women in prodigious quantities, who will talk to and listen to almost anyone, anywhere, anytime, who fits easily into any scene. (Maybe the right movie model is Woody Allen's *Zelig*.) Amid the passion, Clinton builds an acquaintance card file to help him run for high office later in life. He marries. His wife is smart and ambitious. They shout at each other a lot.

This young man is an impressive piece of work. He returns to Arkansas and runs for Congress at age twenty-eight (loses), for attorney general at age thirty (wins), and for governor at age thirty-two (wins). Over the years Clinton is seen as a man who is tardy and indecisive; sometimes dissembling, fudging, and fibbing; seen increasingly at "racy nightclubs" (Maraniss) as stories about his extramarital sexual activity grow to legendary proportions.

During his first gubernatorial term (1980) Clinton comes to be known as a know-it-all liberal. Arkansas voters sense what's going on; he loses his reelection race.

Ex-Governor Clinton then transforms himself into a Not-Liberal, launching what Clintonistas call, then and now, the "Permanent Campaign." This includes an ongoing devotion to public opinion surveys and focus groups, taking the poll results "to shape the substance and rhetoric of policy debates," according to Maraniss. In a most revealing passage, Maraniss describes pollster Richard Morris and ex-Governor Clinton massaging survey responses and speaking them aloud until "Clinton would shout, 'You know, I feel it! I feel it! I'm out there and that's just what I feel! That's absolutely right!'" He regains the governorship in 1984. He never loses again. (Morris and Clinton later split, and then reunited in late 1994 after the anti-Clinton Republican congressional sweep.)

What does Clinton really stand for? Reading Maraniss, one senses that Clinton's conversion to Not-Liberal New Democrat beliefs was a tactical shift designed to win elections and perhaps an intellectual shift as well. His liberalism, on the other hand, is more deeply embedded and more passionate.

That was the background against which the appointment process worked. The early high-level appointments seemed quite evenly balanced. Six of the sixteen cabinet members were DLC members. So was Vice President Gore. So was President Clinton. But the DLC membership roster of elected officials covered a broad array of office-holders, including many somewhat liberal types who had joined up for political convenience. Moreover, some of the DLC-type appointees, like the late Les Aspin, secretary of defense, were in the foreign policy realm. (So too with James Woolsey, director of the Central Intelligence Agency.)

The director of the Office of Management and Budget is a critical position. Former congressman Leon Panetta also was a DLC member and a deficit hawk, but more technocrat than an ideologue. Former Arizona governor Bruce Babbitt, secretary of the interior, seemed to be a complicated mixture: half DLC-style ideologue, half environmental activist. Richard Riley, secretary of education, former governor of South Carolina, was an authentic DLCer, but he, like the rest of the cabinet, had to cooperate with a liberal Democratic congressional majority.

Senator Lloyd Bentsen was a genuine moderate DLC-style Democrat, and his job, secretary of the treasury, was surely an important spot in the government. His deputy, Roger Altman, came from a Wall Street career as an investment banker. Robert Rubin, the head of a new Office of National Economic Policy, was managing partner of Goldman Sachs. Not exactly the hotbed of radical economics (although Laura D'Andrea Tyson, chair of the Council of Economic Advisers, was regarded as tilting toward the academic left). It was said, accordingly, that the conservatives captured the key financial spots of the Clinton administration. (For the record: That is almost always said of the financial appointments in a new administration, regardless of party.) And yet when Clinton's first budget came out, it was attacked—appropriately, I believe—as "more taxes, more spending, more regulation," hardly the hallmarks of a conservative viewpoint.

Much of the cabinet was far from where the DLC philosophy had come to. Donna Shalala, the secretary of health and human services, was known as the high priestess of political correctness. (Although, by my lights, she turned out to be all right.) Robert Reich at Labor was— what?—a neoliberal industrial planner turned labor liberal? Ron Brown at Commerce had come into national politics as a protégé and associate of Senator Ted Kennedy and was later a key operative for Reverend Jesse Jackson.

But the cabinet was the least of it. Most government policy is formed at the subcabinet level. Keep your eyes on the under-, deputy, and assistant secretaries. Watch the under-card. Where were they coming from? Who were they?

Al Kamen was a veteran national affairs reporter for the *Washington Post* when he was asked by his editors, following the Clinton election, to write regularly about personnel appointments. His extremely popular thrice-weekly column, "In the Loop," appears on the widely read Federal Page of the *Post*. What was thought to be a brief interim assignment has been running for almost three years as this book goes to press.

I asked Kamen what he thought about Team Clinton, and he told me:

> It was inevitable. Activists and liberal cause groups make up the base of the Democratic Party. The Friends of Bill (FOB) and the Friends of Hillary (FOH) came from the same sort of backgrounds. In addition there were the Arkansas cronies and bureaucrats who had no strong ideology. That's why we got an over-whelmingly liberal government.
>
> The Carter people had told them "don't lose control"—which is what happened to Carter when he allowed Cabinet Secretaries to pick their own staffs. So they appointed down to micro level. The President signed off on deputy assistant secretaries and on down to members of the Fine Arts Commission. Everyone had to check off on an appointment, Hillary, Gore, the diversity patrol, the interest groups.
>
> Not much got done. In the Counsel's office, Nussbaum didn't know Washington. Nor did Vince Foster. Nor did Bill Kennedy, also from the Rose firm and going through a tough divorce.

Enviros were put in just about every key slot, at Interior, the Corps of Engineers, OMB (Office of Management and Budget), and the White House Counsel's Office.

At Justice the key players included Webb Hubbell, from Arkansas; Frank Hunger, assistant attorney general of the Civil Division and Al Gore's brother-in-law; Sheila Anthony, assistant attorney general for legislative affairs, and former Arkansas Congressman Beryl Anthony's wife and Vince Foster's sister; Anne Bingaman, assistant attorney general of the Anti-Trust Division and wife of Democratic Senator Jeff Bingaman; Eleanor Acheson, assistant attorney general for legal policy, and Hillary Rodham's classmate. The solicitor-general was Drew Days, a liberal law professor from Harvard and former head of the Civil Rights Division in the Carter administration.

Kamen has it right, particularly about the cause groups. A quick riffle through a solid source book* shows important appointed Clintonistas hailing from the American Civil Liberties Union, the Wilderness Society, the National Center for Lesbian Rights, the National Abortion Rights Action League, the Women's Equity Action League, the National Committee to Save the Menominee People and Forest, Inc., the Women's Employment Program, and the National Resource Defense Council, the folks who told you to stop eating apples when there was nothing wrong with apples.

And what happened to the DLC wing of the party? The two principal DLC players, Al From (president of the DLC) and Will Marshall (president of PPI), ended up without jobs in the administration. The chief economic theoretician of the DLC, Rob Shapiro, ended up without a job. There was hope in DLC quarters that young Bruce Reed, a DLC policy aide who had traveled with Clinton during the campaign, would end up as director of the White House Domestic Policy Council. He didn't; the job went to Carol Rasco of Arkansas, of whom it was said, "she works for Hillary." (Later, when there was talk of a staff reorganization, it was said categorically that "Rasco can't be replaced.")

---

* Jeffrey B. Trammell and Gary Osifchin, *The Clinton 500: The New Team Running America* (Washington D.C., Almanac Publishing Inc., 1994).

Reed became a deputy director of the Domestic Policy Council, principally handling welfare and crime issues, not unimportant ones. William Galston, one of the DLC chief theoreticians and a man of unusual wisdom, was also appointed a deputy director of the Policy Council, dealing mostly with education issues. Jeremy Rosner, a DLCer, became the foreign policy speechwriter for Clinton, working for the National Security Council. After a long delay, political scientist Elaine Kamarck, a DLC and Democratic party veteran, ended up working on Vice President Gore's staff, a key player in the "reinventing government" project.

And that was about it for the New Democrats around the president and around the White House. Good people, smart people, in tune with the New Democrat thinking that had elected Clinton. But they were numerically swamped by liberals. By the time the president was inaugurated, a simple message was in the Washington air: The DLC has been stiffed. Later it became clear what happened to the few DLCers who did go into the administration. They were "wonked," said one former DLC operative. That is, they worked on specific policy issues, against the grain, but not on grand themes or grand attitudes.

So that was the lay of the land around the president as he took office on January 20, 1993. There were a few DLC-type players with an idea structure in place, roughly reflecting the stated upfront 1992 campaign philosophy of Clinton. And there were a multitude of liberal Democrats, many of them young, most of them campaign activists and ex-congressional hands. These are the young men and women who grew up believing the 1980s was a decade of greed, that real income had declined for twenty years, that America was going into decline (and that only they could save it), that Republicans won elections by playing the race card, that linking Willie Horton to Democratic softness on crime was so unfair, and, of course, what they had learned by rote from their elders, that America was, like, guilty.

When there is no fixed ideology in the White House, or when the lack of an ideology yields an inchoate ideology of the left, or when there is a hidden agenda of the left at work, things soon happen that shouldn't. Two examples: Lani Guinier and Janet Reno.

When Professor Lani Guinier was nominated as assistant attorney general for civil rights, she was vetted by the office of the White House General Counsel, headed by Bernard Nussbaum. Among the materials reviewed were Guinier's academic writings in the realm of "critical race theory."

Soon the *Wall Street Journal* ran an article mostly about her writings by the Institute of Justice's Clint Bolick, under the headline "Clinton's Quota Queens." The press pack went in full pursuit. Later, one columnist referred to Guinier as the "Quota Queen, the Princess of Proportionalism, the Duchess of Diversity, the Vicar of Victimization, the Czarina of Czeparatism." (That was me.)

Preparatory to writing about Guinier, I spent the better part of a weekend reading some of her articles in law journals (some written as recently as 1991). To me, it could be adduced from these writings that she: (1) favored quotas for minorities in local legislatures, (2) believed quotas weren't enough, (3) thought that minorities should have the right to veto many significant laws passed by the majority, (4) felt that the minorities must be "authentic" and not "middle-class blacks," (because "black representatives are not just physically black"), and (5) believed that minorities should be entitled to enact, alone, a proportionate share of legislation, for example, establishing set-asides.

In theory, many of these actions would require amendment of the Constitution, or at least new legislation. But voters would oppose that. So Professor Guinier mentioned a different procedure in her articles: to administer and reinterpret the existing Voting Rights Act to make such things happen, putting federal resources behind a court defense. If she had been confirmed, she would have been in charge of all that, and although she could surely not have acted alone, she would surely be in a position to make the case, with vigor.

It was later maintained that Guinier's articles were mostly and merely academic speculation. Perhaps so. To me, they read like the strong views of a strong and smart woman who believed in what she wrote.

Now, had there been a DLC-type ideologist on the vetting team, or high up in the White House ranks, he or she would have spent ten minutes on Guinier's writings before saying, "No way" and arguing that position with vigor when the advisability of her appointment was under consideration. Without such an ideologist, White House vetters apparently saw no big problem. And, of course, the Guinier nomination blew up, to the president's dismay, because it seemed as if he supported her views.*

Or take the appointment of Janet Reno as attorney general. (Please.) With the possible exception of Ramsey Clark, she is probably the most liberal AG ever to serve the United States (General Reno continued to support Guinier, even after the president deemed her unacceptable). How did she get there?

Through the efforts of the feminists, working with Mrs. Clinton, it was determined that a female would get one of the Big Four spots—State, Defense, Treasury, or Attorney General. The nomination of Zoe Baird crashed in Congress when it was learned that she had employed illegal aliens as housekeepers—she had what came to be known as a "Zoe Baird problem." Interestingly, Baird, under fire in Congress, was not supported by the feminists. After all, it was said she was "a moderate," and that's not what activates political feminists. Under pressure, Clinton dumped her. The almost-nomination of Judge Kimba Wood crashed when it was maintained that (arguably) she too had a Zoe Baird problem, although of a much lesser variety.

Reno was plucked from the relatively obscure office of Dade County district attorney in Florida. She came to the attention of the Clintons through Hugh Rodham, Hillary's brother. In south Florida she had been known as "Root Causes Reno." The way the White House was staffed, it is doubtful that anyone went to the president and said, "This is a very liberal woman." When she came to Washington, she acted like, well, like "Root Causes Reno."

---

* Subsequently, Lani Guinier made a number of appearances on my public television program, "Think Tank." I have come to know her in person, which I did not when I wrote that column. She is a warm and intelligent woman, highly articulate, and—as our "Think Tank" staff have discovered—dynamite on television. I still don't generally agree with her, but I must say that her case on certain aspects of voting rights, as I hear her now expressing it, is more persuasive than I had thought when reading her academic work.

Chapter 12

GOVERNING

Such was the nature of Clinton's starting team. We now move ahead to observe the team on the field, in action. The time frame is 1992 to 1994, a political moment when the Democrats still controlled the major executive and legislative parts of government—federal, state, and metropolitan. And it was a political moment when the tide of the values issues was high and rising.

For several decades the influence of gays in American politics had become ever more important. The activist homosexual community is generally well to do, with high levels of voter participation, dispropor-tionately but not monolithically liberal, and with some passionately held causes that can energize vigorous political action. This was a nat-ural constituency for Democrats. Exit polls would later show that Clin-ton received 70 percent of the gay vote in a three-way race. It has been estimated that about one-seventh (14 percent) of Clinton's total vote came from the gay community, which is an astounding figure.

Fast-forward to November 11, 1992, just one week after the elec-tion. After a Veterans Day speech in Little Rock, Clinton was asked by

NBC correspondent Andrea Mitchell if he would keep his promise about lifting the ban on homosexuals in the military. Clinton said he would issue an executive order to do that. The story ended up on the front page of the *New York Times*.

A press feeding frenzy ensued, and a roar of displeasure about their president-elect was heard from the citizenry. Most Americans were not in accord with Clinton's stated position that "affectional orientation" was irrelevant to service in the military. The issue became fodder for the talk shows. Clinton's view was opposed by Sam Nunn, chairman of the Senate Armed Services Committee and a powerful and senior Democrat. The president appointed a commission to study the matter. Sailors on aircraft carriers with crowded dormitory areas, with bunks stacked like cordwood, and with open public showers were interviewed by network television correspondents. They were not happy sailors. Ultimately Clinton, under pressure from Congress, accepted most of the basic Nunn position of "don't ask, don't tell, don't pursue," a policy far short of what gays wanted.*

Almost two years later, in the Republican landslide, pollsters and journalists were still hearing about gays in the military as an indelible memory that helped define Clinton and, by extension, the Democratic party.

Several thoughts:

1. Traumatized by press reports of intolerance at the Houston convention, the Bush campaign was inept and misguided in not making an issue of gays in the military during the 1992 general campaign. It was, after all, a matter of executive policy, brought up by the opposition candidate.
2. The things that stick against a politician and a party are the items that tend to confirm what the public already senses or fears. If Ronald Reagan had directed the Department of Defense to change the policy regarding homosexuals in the military, I suspect

---

* A full and fascinating account of the journalistic aspects of the gays-in-the-military issue appears in the book *Media Critic*, written by Carl M. Cannon, White House correspondent for the *Baltimore Sun*.

it would have been a much lesser matter. But coming from Clinton, who was seen as a draft dodger, in a party that was often seen as backing far-out cultural interests, it was murderous. And so it remains.

3. Earlier, the mostly conservative idea that cultural issues yield social issues was examined (page 17) and found that while such a link may well exist, it is hard to deal with substantively in a political context because on many issues there is little public consensus and/or morality is generally hard to legislate. In the gays-in-the-military issue, we see cultural issues linked to other cultural issues—like President Clinton's behavior when he was vulnerable to the draft during the Vietnam War. There is also a linkage from social issues to cultural issues. If Clinton had been seen as tough on crime, tough on welfare, tough on education, tough on quotas, he might well have lowered the static he was to receive regarding gays in the military. He wasn't; he didn't.

4. What is it with Democratic presidents and the military? Jimmy Carter's *first* act in office was to grant unconditional pardons to draft evaders, setting up a public firestorm, particularly from Vietnam veterans.

In early 1993 the new president prepared his first budget. This is the document that should give meat to the president's governmental philosophy. It lays out a plan. Among other things, the president's plan, as expressed in the budget, can use government to try to remedy the problems that government has caused.

Recall that Clinton ran for the presidency claiming that both parties were "brain dead." He maintained that there was a "third way" between Democrat and Republican, between liberal and conservative. He pledged a "New Covenant," which endorsed the ideas that he had helped develop as chairman of the Democratic Leadership Council. He promised a different political pole star based on the idea of "No More Something for Nothing."

The American public had every reason to expect something new from Clinton's first budget. What they got was this: At the first meeting of the major budget planners, it was said, allegedly by Vice President Gore, and others, that "the only way to pass a budget was to get all the Democrats." Not exactly a third-way scenario.

Think about that. "All the Democrats" means designing a budget that will be approved by the Progressive Caucus, the Black Caucus, the Latino Caucus, and the 68 percent of the Democrats in the Congress whose rating from the liberal Americans for Democratic Action exceeded 70 percent approval on the ADA litmus issues. To get those votes you not only have to "raise taxes on the rich" (which Clinton had pledged to do) but also come up with a budget that hands out large amounts of federal largesse to liberal constituency groups. That largesse, of course, is just the root of the governmental part of the something-for-nothing mentality.

In theory, to offer a New Covenant budget Clinton should have had substantive task forces report to him—on health, welfare, crime, education, and so on—and *then* offer Congress a budget that reflects an allegedly New Democratic outlook. Alas, that is not the way the timing of the budget or the legislative process works, nor did Clinton try to do anything to change it. As one Clinton aide said, "The budget outran its supply lines." (For example, Clinton's welfare task force wasn't even appointed until June 1993, four months after the budget proposal had been submitted and debate was already underway. More than another year would pass before the task force actually made its recommendations.)

Of course, it was not necessary to get all the Democrats to pass a budget through the Congress. Suppose Clinton had stuck to a solid idea of a third way. After all, the idea of getting all the Democrats represented one of the earlier two ways that he said had failed.

There was an alternative strategy. The president was urged by centrist DLC types to build his coalition "from the center out." Passing a budget, after all, means getting 50 votes in the Senate and 218 in the House. They don't all have to be Democrats. The inside-out strategy would have started by corraling the votes of centrists, that is, moderate Democrats and moderate Republicans, and then built outward along the political spectrum until the requisite number of votes were available. (Clinton had pledged to include Republicans in his administration, up to and including the Cabinet.)

That would have angered two groups: conservative Republicans and liberal Democrats. The Republicans would have seen their party cleaved as if it were an overripe melon smacked by an axe. The liberal Democrats would have cried "betrayal," thus certifying to the rest of America that Clinton was an authentic New Democrat. The resulting budget would have ended up looking something like the original plan put forth by Clinton's budget director Leon Panetta: two dollars in spending cuts for every one dollar of new taxes.

Alas, a coalition of the center did not materialize. The Republicans weren't consulted about a budget designed to get all the Democrats through a formula with a balance of much greater tax increases and much smaller spending cuts than the Panetta plan. And so not a single Republican in either house of Congress ended up voting for the critical budget reconciliation bill. Why not?

We former speechwriters believe that rhetoric helps shape reality. A president's budget is not just numbers; it has words and themes as well, and these often express what the numbers really mean. In early 1993 the key thematic chapter of Clinton's budget message to Congress was entitled "A Legacy of Failure." (That's a good way to get Republicans.)

It was an economically illiterate rewrite of the 1980s designed to shape the 1990s. Here was its central thought: "Reaganomics eroded family structures, offered succor to the greedy privileged few who engaged in financial scheming, while ordinary Americans were left behind and could no longer dream the American dream." (The key phrases are from the document, in context, consolidated for brevity.)

All that, mind you, describing the world's premier economy, which had added 19 million jobs in the 1980s, when real family income among rich, poor, and middle class had increased.

When the budget was published in 1993, Michael Boskin, the former chairman of the Council of Economic Advisers in the Bush administration, looked at the Clinton plan and said that its direction was toward "social engineering, big government, high taxation, interventionism, regulation, re-distributionism, and industrial planning." Boskin, of course, was not necessarily viewing Clinton's budget with total dispassion. But the budget did include *increased* funds for existing, often tired, programs for food stamps, weatherization, parenting, trees, forests, immunization, mass transit, worker profiling, one-stop career shopping, and clean water, just for starters. Also present was Daddy-knows-best high-tech planning: "information highways," "cross-cutting high performance computing," and entities like NIST, FCCSET, CRADA, acronyms for agencies mostly designed to let wise government bureaucrats play a role in picking commercial winners and losers.

That first Clinton budget was trimmed and reshaped as it made its journey through the Congress. Centrist Democrats in the Senate were instrumental in stripping out the so-called stimulus program, a $16 billion catchall including jobs programs, AIDS funding, and infrastructure for the inner city. (It was said to be the price that liberals demanded to vote for the budget. It was also said that the stimulus plan was necessary to revive the economy, which subsequently managed to revive nicely without it.) Even that cut was not sufficient to bring spurned Republicans on board. By then they had dug in. Unless Clinton was seriously willing to reshape some of the precepts promoted by the left wing of his party, the Republicans would not play, indeed could not play.

What does such a budget, shaped without a Suslov, shaped by reflexively liberal Democrats—sometimes grinding an ideological axe, sometimes just going along with the gang—mean in terms of the thesis of this book?

The most egregious damage can be seen in the realm of what has been called here Greater Welfare—(the AFDC program of about $25 billion per year plus other means-tested programs such as food stamps, Medicaid, Supplemental Security Income, and subsidized housing).

The total amount of such spending (as calculated under the rubric of income-tested benefits by the Congressional Research Service) was $156 billion in fiscal year 1992. Under the Clinton budget those benefits would have risen to $252 billion by 1998. That would be an 8.3 percent per year rise, as opposed to "only" a 6.6 percent per year increase in the previous decade. Seen another way, under Clinton's plan, Greater Welfare would have increased by 3 percent per year *more* than it would have risen if no changes had been made in then-current law.

So much for the early plan from the president who opposed something for nothing. In too many ways it was the classic budget of an Old Democrat, not a New Democrat.

By the accounting procedures of baseline budgeting, it did cut $496 billion from the budget deficits that would have accrued had existing law continued over the next five years. When the budget reconciliation bill passed with the narrowest of margins, Clinton claimed credit for those half a trillion dollars of deficit reduction, and still does. But many of the claimed cuts were already foreordained from previous budget deals, and in any event the total *debt* of the nation would *grow* by more than a trillion dollars during the five years.

Jodie Allen, editor of the *Washington Post*'s "Outlook" section,* is a long-time budget watcher. She says: "The 1993 deficit reduction came almost entirely from the tax increase and defense cuts. Social spending was actually accelerated. Clinton missed the mood of the voters."

All this was too bad from the perspective of what we are talking about here. The moment was golden. There was a potent national feeling in favor of serious budget cutting, in part generated by the 1992 campaign of Ross Perot. A new president had been elected to deliver new merchandise. It might well have been a doable deal if he brought Republicans in from the beginning. Building the third way coalition, from the center out, including center and moderate Republicans, at least should have been tried. That, in fact, was the advice Clinton was getting from DLC-style legislators like Senators Charles Robb, Sam Nunn, David Boren, John Breaux, and Joseph Lieberman. Moderate Republicans like Senators John Danforth and John Chafee were ready to play.

Americans were prepared to rally around a plan that would have shown some fidelity to Panetta's original formulation of two-for-one spending cuts over tax increases. It would have included some of the spending cuts and recissions that Republicans would later propose in 1995, which many congressional Democrats were to condemn. But had Democrats originally proposed them, the cuts would likely have sailed through Congress, as America applauded the vision of the New Democrats.

---

* Formerly with the Department of Labor, the Department of Health, Education and Welfare, the Executive Office of the President, the Department of the Army, the Brookings Institution and the Urban Institute.

It was not to be. And so by the time the budget passed the Congress, Clinton had come to be viewed as a liberal president, and not a very popular one. The budget reconciliation bill passed by the margin of a single vote in the House and by Vice President Gore's tie-breaker vote in the Senate. It was the first time that a budget passed without any opposition votes. When the deed was done, the American people did not cheer, "Huzzah for President Clinton." No sir. His poll ratings went tumbling down—to a 39 percent approval rating in the early summer of 1993.

What happened? Too liberal. A liberal Congress. A fat budget. Tax increases (mostly on the well to do, but not entirely). Tax decreases for the poor and near-poor. A generically and genetically liberal White House staff. A bureaucracy staffed and stuffed with liberal activists. No third way reaching out to Republicans. Ideological warriors from the DLC marginalized. Not a Suslov in sight. Gays in the military.

All this played against a backdrop of scandal, semiscandal, media firestorms, and feeding frenzies regarding scandals, semiscandals, and nonscandals. These included alleged financial misbehavior (Whitewater), alleged sexual misbehavior (Troopergate), and alleged cronyism (the White House Travel Office). There was the tragic suicide of Clinton's close aide and friend, Vince Foster. There was Clinton's penchant to hobnob with the glitterati, including famous and famously liberal movie stars, just the sort who would get $200 haircuts (alleged to have taken place upon Clinton's locks, on the tarmac of Los Angeles airport, allegedly holding up passenger traffic—with the charges vigorously denied by the White House).

Added to this mix was the case of Hillary Rodham Clinton's trades in the commodity futures market. In 1979, with an investment of $1,000, she had made $100,000 trading cattle futures. How? She got friendly advice from an old friend, Jim Blair, who also happened to be the outside counsel to Arkansas's largest business, Tyson's Foods, a firm with deep political and financial connections to Clinton. The commodity orders were placed through a broker who earlier had been charged with attempts to manipulate the egg market. There were those who thought these transactions were nothing more than a marginally legal gift to the wife of the state's rising political star, her husband, Bill, soon to be governor. It appeared to be nothing less than "succor to the greedy privileged few who engaged in financial scheming," to quote from the president's economic message.

The painting of Clinton in harsh cultural colors was a process, not an event. Over time the separate issues blended to form a portrait of Clinton that was quite harmful, to him and to his party. Negative cultural issues erode a politician's standing, making it more difficult to deal with serious issues of substance, particularly on social issues. The public senses a linkage, probably correctly.

In the winter of 1994, after the anti-Clinton earthquake election, David Osborne (coauthor of *Reinventing Government* who had worked on the Clinton-Gore plan to reinvent government) wrote a long, tough, open letter to the president that appeared on January 8, 1995, in the *Washington Post* magazine. It included these lines: "Most Americans see you and your administration as members of a cultural elite— people who graduated from Yale and Harvard and Oxford; people who attend Georgetown dinner parties and Renaissance Weekends; people who hang out with movie stars and vacation in places like Martha's Vineyard."*

In the same article Osborne criticized Stephanopoulos and his staff of liberal Stephoids, and wrote, to Clinton: "The lesson is simple: if you want New Democratic politics, get New Democratic advisors."

Clinton, as perceived by many, was a smooth, lying liberal, who betrayed the voters who had made him president, the Reagan Democrats. To some of those people, he and his wife had become walking personifications of the worst aspect of 1960s social liberalism.

President Clinton is a very knowledgeable public servant and political wunderkind. He knows much more about politics than is written in this book. And so, in mid-1993, as all this anti-Clinton feeling was fermenting, he went out and tried to fix what was wrong. He hired David Gergen.

---

* Author's note: I've been to Renaissance Weekend on three occasions.

Gergen has since become a verb. When one "gergenizes," it is said that "spinning" is taking place. To be sure, Gergen is a spinner of the first magnitude. To be sure, he had served conservative Republican presidents, and it was a little weird seeing him in Democratic garb. But something was missed in the furor and fascination about the Gergen appointment. Gergen's reputation was that of a communicator. But Clinton had hired a semi-Suslov.

I've known Gergen for many years. He had moved beyond mere communications. By the early 1990s he was flitting from conference to conference, serving on blue-ribbon commissions. He became a student of public affairs with a coherent set of views. His general view was moderate mainstream/establishment/business, somewhat hawkish on both defense and the deficit, mixed with some residual liberal southern guilt. When he joined the Clinton staff, Gergen was characterized as a hired gun with an ideology for sale. That was unfair. After all, he had been well to the left of the Reagan staff and was now well to the right of the Clinton staff. That's not necessarily a huge leap.

In 1992 Gergen and I collaborated on two one-hour television programs dealing with American political parties, aired by the Public Broadcasting System. Here is an excerpt from Gergen during one of the documentaries, which aired shortly before the 1992 election. It gives a flavor of where he had come to:

> I'm struck by the idea that Bill Clinton sounds a lot like Jack Kennedy, and that Jack Kemp, the Republican, sounds a lot like Jack Kennedy. Both parties . . . are pro-business, they're pro-growth, they want to cut capital gains, they want to bring choice to school.

In short, Gergen had become somewhat of a DLC surrogate. His appointment to the White House gave him immediate access to the president on a full range of issues, domestic and foreign. His new position was reported this way on May 30, 1993, in the *Washington Post*:

> Gergen will be part of a five-person senior circle, including the President and First Lady Hillary Rodham Clinton, McLarty and Vice President

Gore. While the rest of the staff will report to Clinton through McLarty, Gergen is said to have sought and received a pledge of direct access to the president.

In the same story, "a senior White House official" was quoted as saying that the hiring of Gergen

is not targeted at George [Stephanopoulos]; it is targeted at the idea that we need some adults here. We are concerned about this rap . . . that the operation is too young, too inexperienced, a little too cocky.

Later on Gergen noted, as quoted in the *New York Times* on January 2, 1994, "I didn't take the job to do P.R. . . . . . I am more interested in substance, in issues of governance, than communications."

One staff man does not an administration make, particularly when all of the earlier staff problems still existed. But at least the *attempted* spin had changed.

There was a question I had wanted to ask Bill Clinton for a long time. I got my chance, unexpectedly, on Tuesday afternoon, June 15, 1993, shortly after Gergen had joined the White House staff. I was in the White House for a ceremonial announcement concerning American international radio broadcasting when I was invited to interview the President in the Oval Office. My question to the president was: "If you were forced to give a one-word answer, would you describe yourself as a liberal or a moderate?"

In answer to my question, Clinton paused momentarily and said "moderate." He quickly added that, of course, it was complex, because he was liberal on civil rights and conservative on crime.

Clinton said he had been mistakenly portrayed as a liberal largely because of the issue of gays in the military, although he had actually spent little time on the issue since taking office. He said he did not regard it as liberal or conservative. "To me," Clinton said, "it's an issue of civil liberties." He said he was very pleased that conservative Barry Goldwater had also gone public in support of gays in military service.

In general, Clinton thought he had been unfairly typecast as governing from the left side of the political spectrum. I asked why, if he saw himself as a moderate, there were so few moderates on the White House staff. The president responded that he had asked Al From, the head of the moderate DLC, to work at the White House but that From had turned him down. (From had headed Clinton's domestic policy task force during the transition. He confirms the invitation, noting that it had been offered immediately after the election but was not reextended after that.)

Clinton then elaborated, turning to Gergen (who was present at the interview, along with columnist Fred Barnes and senior adviser George Stephanopoulos, who never quite left the inner circle of five, making it six.) "My conservative adviser, no my centrist adviser, David, says I made a mistake by cutting the White House staff levels by 25 percent." Clinton's context seemed clear: Alas, it was only a shortage of White House slots that was now making it difficult to bring moderates aboard. (When I repeated this remark to an active DLC leader he said, "Of course, he could always fire some of the liberals.")

The president also said he thought that the perception of him as a liberal tax-and-spender would soon fade. He says that everyone was agreed that the current round of tax increases was as much as the economy could afford. He was expecting important budget results from the report of Vice President Albert Gore's National Performance Review task force, whose job it was to offer recommendations to streamline, slenderize and "reinvent government." Clinton emphasized that the Gore report could trigger "a big round of spending cuts."

In response to Barnes's question regarding the process by which he chose Judge Ruth Bader Ginsburg for the Supreme Court, Clinton said he had started with a pool of about forty potential candidates. He narrowed the list to seven, and then to two fully qualified finalists, Judge Stephen Breyer and Ginsburg, stressing that "both are moderates."

So the president had plenty of answers for his moderate and conservative critics. But President Clinton is a man of many political faces. Not long after, he was interviewed by liberal reporter William Greider of *Rolling Stone*. As the session ended, Greider mentioned that people were saying the president seemed as if there was nothing he would "stand up and die for." Then, as *Rolling Stone* (December 9, 1993) describes it:

> [The president, standing a foot away from Greider, turned and glared at him. Clinton's face reddened, and his voice rose to a furious pitch as he delivered a scalding rebuke—an angry, emotional presidential encounter, the kind of which few have ever witnessed.]
>
> *Clinton:* But that is the press's fault, too, damn it. I have fought more damn battles here for more things than any President has in 20 years, with the possible exception of Reagan's first budget, and not gotten one damn bit of credit from the knee-jerk liberal press, and I am sick and tired of it, and you can put that in the damn article.

Thus: He was a self-described moderate complaining bitterly that he had not gotten one damn bit of credit from the knee-jerk liberal press.

A Japanese reporter may have come close to the mark about Clinton when describing a trade negotiation between Clinton and the Japanese. The reporter said that upon close examination, the final agreement turned out to be a *tamimushi*, which is a Japanese insect that changes color to match its surroundings. Like a chameleon.

The important thing was not that Gergen was hired but that Clinton wanted to hire a Gergen. There is a great deal of argument about the many facets of the personality and beliefs of Bill Clinton—but little argument that he likes to win elections. Mrs. Clinton also likes winning. They both know that Clinton-seen-as-a-liberal is a loser.

Things changed, for a while. The Lani Guinier nomination was abandoned. The nomination of Ruth Bader Ginsburg, the putative moderate, sailed through the Senate confirmation process.

Then came the passage of the North American Free Trade Agreement. It was a monumental political achievement. Clinton was late in getting started. A high-profile left-right anti-NAFTA, sometimes populist coalition formed: How could Ross Perot, Pat Buchanan, the Sierra

Club, Ralph Nader, and Lane Kirkland, president of the AFL-CIO, all be on the same side? But they were, and they pounded the airwaves about how NAFTA would steal jobs from America. In September 1993, the public opinion polls about NAFTA showed the "anti" leading the "pro" by 41 percent to 35 percent.

I was at the White House ceremony when Clinton launched his public rebuttal with a brilliant and emotional speech. Three other presidents—George Bush, Jimmy Carter, and Gerald Ford—were present, and each made a pro–free trade pitch. I have never seen the East Room so crowded. CEOs were wall to wall.

Gradually, led by Clinton's virtuoso politicking, the tide of public opinion turned. Still, only a few days before the vote, there was doubt about the outcome. It was said by shrewd observers that NAFTA would win by one vote or else go down by forty.

NAFTA passed with a margin of thirty-four votes. This meant that not only had Clinton worked and wheedled the Congress, but that he had wrought a change in public opinion.* After all, the idea of a victory by one vote was predicated on the belief that NAFTA would be a very unpopular vote—like the budget. The thought was that Members would have to be sold on the idea that the Clinton presidency had to be "saved," and that it would be bad for America if the president was "embarrassed" in the international arena. As it turned out, though, congressmen clamored to get on board the train before it left the station.

Had NAFTA lost, there would have been a clear lesson: When Clinton coalesces with the liberals, he wins, as he did with the budget. And when he coalesces with conservatives, as in NAFTA, he loses. But something else happened: A majority of Democrats voted *against* NAFTA, and a majority of Republicans voted *for* NAFTA. The moral seemed clear: Clinton could not only win with the center-out coalition he had earlier eschewed but could win by a bigger margin than the one provided by the all-Democratic coalition designed to "save the president."

---

* With an assist from Vice President Gore's solid victory over Ross Perot in a nationally televised discussion on CNN's "Larry King Live."

Interesting. It could be done. Liberal special interest groups could be beaten back by center coalitions. It makes good politics. It makes good policy.

Good politics and good policy makes a great strategy. Was Clinton able to replicate this strategy, regarding the four social issues stressed in this book? Did he try? Was he foiled? Why was he foiled?

Chapter 13

THE ISSUES IN PLAY

Crime, welfare, education, and affirmative-action-as-now-practiced are all complex substantive and legislative issues. What happened on these fronts during the 1992–1994 season was, as might be expected, confused by the fog of political combat. You could write a book about each topic (you, not me). In this chapter I try to tell a brief story of what went on in each realm. In each of the four major issue areas I picked one or two critical aspects where substance, symbolism, perception, politics, and policy met. The examples give a sense of how it came to be that Democrats were rebranded as painfully liberal. That's not the way this book was planned. It is where I came out while following the No More Something for Nothing idea.

CRIME

The crime issue could have been a slam-dunk for Clinton. He had run with tough anticrime rhetoric in 1992, stressing his support for the death penalty and community policing. Along with welfare reform, it was crime that most nearly defined his status as a New Democrat.

269

During the course of his first year in office, a series of well-publicized and horrible crimes captured the headlines. In 1993, the problem of crime vaulted to number one in public opinion polls. (See Indicators, page 119.) Clinton ended up presiding over the passage of what might have been the most important federal crime bill in American history, a bill that appropriated not the $2.5 billion (over five years) that he had originally requested, but over $30 billion.

How could it be that he received little credit for what had transpired on the crime front? How could it be that in the minds of many Americans, Clinton and his party were seen backing the wrong dog in the fight?

Consider some crime chronology:

- On July 23, 1993, it was reported that basketball star Michael Jordan's father, James Jordan, was asleep in his car just off a North Carolina highway when he was shot dead by two local thugs, Larry Demery and Daniel Green, both eighteen. Both were within the criminal justice system when the crime was committed. Demery was *awaiting trial* for the robbery of a convenience store and smashing the head of a sixty-one-year-old store clerk, leaving her with a fractured skull and brain hemorrhage. Green was *on parole* after serving two years of a six-year sentence for attempting to kill a man with an axe, a crime which put the victim into a coma for three months.

    Questioned about Green's early release, the Robeson County (N.C.) prosecutor said that most state prisoners serve about 20 percent of their sentences before parole, and Green had served longer than usual. The county sheriff, Hubert Stone, said, "Mr. Jordan would now be alive if the [legal] system worked the way it should."

- In the thirteen months prior to the 1994 election, nine foreign tourists had been murdered in Florida. In September 1993, a British tourist was slain. Several suspects had been identified as black male youths. When police concentrated their search principally on young black males, the American Civil Liberties Union objected.

- On October 1, 1993, in Petaluma, California, Polly Klaas, age twelve, was kidnapped from her home during a slumber party. A national and well-publicized search for the young girl was initiated.

Two months later, Richard Allen Davis was arrested for a *parole violation* on a tip. He was later convicted of the murder of the girl. Davis, as it turned out, had a twenty-year rap sheet that included burglary, assault, robbery, sex offenses, and two convictions of kidnapping. He had been imprisoned on three separate occasions, each time getting out early. In 1984 Davis was sentenced to sixteen years in prison for kidnapping, assault, and robbery. He was released after eight years. Had he served his full term, he would have been imprisoned until the year 2000, when Polly Klaas would have been a sophomore in college.

- Two young Japanese exchange students were killed—one in California, one on Halloween night in Louisiana. The Halloween incident occurred when the student, seeking directions to a Halloween party, was shot by a homeowner, who, fearing a burglary, had yelled, "Freeze!" The Japanese young man did not understand the context.
- In October 1993, four gunmen shot and pistol-whipped the Asian-American owners of a jewelry store in Washington, D.C. The crime was videotaped by security cameras in the store. Over and over, the tapes played on Washington local news shows. National publicity followed. Three of the four robbers had previous convictions. One of them *was wanted on a bench warrant* for skipping out of a halfway house. (Halfway to what?) Another was free on $5,000 bond on eight theft charges and simultaneously *awaiting further court action* on an armed robbery charge.
- In December 1993, Colin Ferguson opened fire on a commuter train headed from New York City to Hicksville, Long Island. The deranged gunman killed five and wounded nineteen.
- On June, 12, 1994, Nicole Brown Simpson and Ronald Goldman were found brutally murdered in Los Angeles. Five days later, football hero O. J. Simpson was arrested and charged with murder. The case was well covered by the media.

Events like these resonate with particular harshness in a video society. We saw Michael Jordan going to his father's funeral. We saw the identification pictures of Polly Klaas while she was missing. We saw the families of the slain Long Island commuters. We saw the fearful reactions of European tourists—who some years earlier had sneered when American tourism to Europe fell off because of the threat of anti-American terrorism.* We saw the reaction in Japan to violence in America. We saw so much of O. J. that the case became macabre grist for comedians.

Much of what we saw conformed to the general perception (and reality) regarding criminality in America: More criminals ought to spend more time incapacitated. Such a thought, intertwined with ghastly national events, cannot, and should not, be kept outside politics.

The year 1993 was an off-off-year election, with neither congressional nor presidential contests. But four high-profile races were in play:

- In Virginia, voters picked a new governor, George Allen. He won big (58 percent to 41 percent). His major theme was that he would end the state's parole system.
- In Los Angeles, with Democrat-to-Republican registration of 64 percent to 36 percent, Republican Richard Riordan was solidly elected mayor in a nonpartisan election. His key theme: safety in the streets.
- In New York City, with a five-to-one Democratic registration, Republican Rudolph Giuliani, a former prosecutor, beat the incumbent mayor, David Dinkins, a Democrat. Giuliani stressed crime.
- In New Jersey, Republican Christine Todd Whitman beat Democratic Governor Jim Florio. Florio was unpopular due to a massive tax increase but took an early lead as a crime hawk, attacking Whitman for being soft on certain aspects of crime and welfare. Whitman then went to a tougher-than-thou campaign coupled with a pledge to cut state taxes. She caught up and won, narrowly (50 percent to 48 percent).

Suddenly the two biggest cities in America, each with big Democratic majorities, were governed by Republican mayors. A long string

---

* In 1994 the number of international arrivals to the United States dropped by 0.6 percent, despite a weakened dollar that made America a travel bargain. "Safety and security clearly were an issue. . . . It'll take time [for Europeans to get over their fear]," said Greg Farmer of the U.S. Travel and Tourism Administration. Yes, social issues cause economic harm.

of Democratic statewide victories in Virginia, just across the river from Washington, D.C., had been shattered. New Jersey almost reelected as governor a much-scorned tax hiker who was tough on social issues, and who lost only when his opponent, who started out as a perceived softie, changed her angle of attack.

The public had sent a message. Who received it?

Apparently not General Reno, she of the root causes. Throughout this time, she was talking to the public at great length. An examination of her speeches and interviews from that moment shows an interesting pattern. While so many Americans were afraid to walk around the corner at night, the AG chose to chat endlessly about theories of early child development and their link to our crime problems. She was fascinated that "50 percent of all learned human response is learned in the first year of life. But there are too many of those one-year-olds that have no rights, no law, no structure, no fabric whatsoever." And that "zero to three is the most formative range of life, because it's during that time that you develop a conscience." (An interesting case, one worthy of high-profile dissemination by the secretary of health and human services, and which was, in fact, then being pushed forward by Secretary Shalala.)

Occasionally touching on the issue of here-and-now crime, Reno put forth an interesting view of prisons. Yes, she would say, career criminals should spend more time locked up, because they serve only 20 to 30 percent of their sentences. Alas, our prisons are overcrowded, and there is no space for them. But, she would say, we don't have to build more prisons because so much prison space, 40 percent of it, is occupied by "nonviolent drug offenders." Who, she said, should be offered early release after serving just 10 percent of their sentence and then be treated, rehabilitated, detoxed, job trained, job placed, after-cared, followed up, random drug tested, and put in "residential nonsecure" places, where they will be watched over and certified by public officials who feel their pain. All that would provide prison space for the really bad boys. (Columnist Chris Mathews calls Democrats the "Mommy Party.")

Reno's theory is not taken too seriously by most serious students of crime, who believe that "nonviolent drug offender" is a world-class oxymoron. Truly nonviolent folks who make a career of selling drugs are very often very dead very soon. And only about 7 percent of prisoners in America are nonviolent nonrepeaters (see crime Indicators). With very few exceptions, people in prisons these days have done very bad things, repeatedly.

Reno not only had a problem with prisons, but with police. It took six months for the attorney general to endorse President Clinton's call for 100,000 more cops on the street. White House staffers put pressure on her to do so, but when she resisted, she was regarded as "untouchable"—because of her quite remarkable role in the Branch Davidian shootout in Waco.

Remarkable indeed. With Reno's approval, FBI agents surrounded the compound and subjected it to a CS gas attack. Under circumstances still not fully understood, the buildings went up in flames. A total of eighty men, women, and children perished. President Clinton temporarily ducked comment on the tragedy. Reno stood before the television cameras and took "full responsibility," without indicating that any mistakes were made by the FBI and without offering any apology. She did a full round of talk shows offering reasons for the action (such as ongoing, contemporaneous physical abuse of the Davidian children), which she later said turned out to be false.* For all this, Reno immediately became the best known of the new Clinton cabinet and was enshrined as a folk heroine. From that position of public lionization—while Clinton's popularity was in sink-like-a-stone mode—Reno was able, for quite a while, to speak for the Justice Department without having to bend much to direction from the White House.

Soon an interagency group was set in motion to concentrate on the administration's position on crime. It was run by Peter Edelman, a quite liberal Washington lawyer. Interestingly, Edelman operated out of an office at the Department of Health and Human Services, not typically the locale of premier crime-busters. Edelman's early pronouncement prefigured where the Clintonistas would end up:

---

* The charge regained some credibility during congressional hearings in the summer of 1995.

"Law enforcement officials tell us in unison that they can not do the job by themselves, that there has to be an investment in prevention." (As shown in the Opinion Indicators, voters value punishment over prevention.)

Let us grant that all America was not hanging on every word of Janet Reno or Peter Edelman. But what was Clinton himself saying from the bully pulpit? Roughly this: An ounce of prevention equals a pound of punishment. (Would that it were so!) Clinton's speeches made the case that Brady bill–gun control was a big deal (I favor it)— but it isn't. We already have 200 million firearms in America, and a five-day waiting period for new ones won't change that. Clinton also made it clear that he favored more community policing and boot camps. They too are good ideas, but probably limited.

In mid-1993, crime legislation was being negotiated and debated in both the House and Senate with the issue of more prisons high on the agenda. Clinton talked frequently about crime but remained mute on prisons. Then, in August 1993, Clinton announced his own "crime package" at a grand ceremony on the White House lawn. There was no mention of more prison space. I spoke to deputy attorney general Phil Heyman at the time. He said not to worry; it would be in the Clinton bill when it was sent to Congress.

The Republican response to Clinton's plan was quick. "Unilateral disarmament in the form of . . . cutting prison construction is no way to fight a [crime] war," said Congressman Dick Armey (R-Tex.), then the GOP conference chairman. A House Republican briefing paper entitled *Getting Tough on Crime?* was put forth by Bill McCollum (R-Fla.), then ranking member of the House Subcommittee on Crime. The key to the title is the question mark. The report included this sort of language: "If we want to bring the crime rate back down to the levels of the 1950s, we must raise to 1950s levels the deterrent to commit crimes."

A formal Clinton crime bill, the one that was supposed to have prisons in it, never was sent to the Congress. Clinton could, however, have still pushed the comprehensive Senate version of a crime bill, which included many billions of dollars for more prison space. He didn't. He first chose to back the much more limited House bill, which did not have any provision for more prisons. And why did it not deal with more prison space? Because, according to an impeccable House Democratic source, Attorney General Janet Reno didn't want it! (After a while Clinton said, Clintonesquely, that he was for both bills.)

Of course, given the mood in the country and the Congress, there was little chance that a crime bill would pass the 103d Congress without some provisions for more prison space. The House and Senate bills would have to go to conference, provisions would be added and subtracted, traditional chaos would ensue, and there would be titles for more prisons in a final bill, if a final bill was ever to be agreed upon, which never was a certainty. In the course of the next year, the crime bill grew and grew as it went through a series of partisan machinations.

A key part of the struggle involved money. President Clinton had appointed Vice President Gore to set up a task force to "reinvent government." In September 1993 the task force report appeared, detailing how 252,000 federal jobs could be cut in the course of the next five years. (Many of the cut jobs came from civilian employees of the Defense Department, a downsizing that had begun earlier.)

At the time the Senate was negotiating Senator Joseph Biden's crime bill, which had grown to $5.9 billion. Senator Phil Gramm (R-Tex.) quickly noticed that Gore's personnel cuts would free up billions of budget dollars and started thinking about putting that money into the crime bill. Senator Robert Byrd (D-W. Va.) got there first and proposed to sequester the Gore money—$22 billion—into a special trust fund earmarked only for crime control.

Biden had only $5.9 billion worth of ideas. He decided to raise it to $9.6 billion, with the new money targeted for more police.

The race was on. Hard-line Republicans added in more money for punishment, most of it earmarked for more prison cells to accommodate their "truth in sentencing" idea, which would keep criminals locked up at least 85 percent of their terms instead of the current 35 to 40 percent average. Another central, but little-noticed provision concerned stripping away from federal judges the power to issue court orders that declared prisons "overcrowded," which often pushed prisoners out the door, from which point they could mug your sister. Democrats added money for prevention—including some parts of an alternative crime bill, the Racial Justice Act of the Congressional Black Caucus—which had failed passage previously.* The monies for prevention included funds for drug rehabilitation, youth job training programs, direct aid to high-crime neighborhoods, and recreation programs, including the soon-to-be-infamous "midnight basketball" program that provided for athletic teams in inner-city neighborhoods.

Word went out that additional crime programs were suddenly fundable, a situation that guaranteed a stampede of politicians anxious to get in on the action. In the Senate, the bill was ultimately increased to $30 billion.

At about the same time a key White House economic aide, Gene Sperling, was quoted as saying it's more important to spend money on poor kids than on prisons. Stout heart, Gene. But poor kids were getting shot at by people who should be in prison. And the parents of those poor kids couldn't get jobs in the inner city because businesses flee from high-crime areas.

Clinton and the Democrats had started out with a strong hand: They favored community policing, boot camps, a "police corps," gun control, a "safe-schools" proposal, and drug rehabilitation, to only begin a long and serious list. But a funny thing happened on the way to what should have been the most important crime bill in American history.

First, the legislation was amended by Republican pressure to strip out some, but not all, of what they called "pork." About $900 million for job training programs was taken out of the bill. Also out was $10 million for a Criminal Justice Center at Lamar University, in the Texas congressional district of Jack Brooks, the Democratic Chairman of the House Judiciary Committee, which had jurisdiction over crime legislation. (Of Brooks it is said: "He doesn't like police

---

* The original Black Caucus bill said that prosecutions for murder should, in effect, be proportionalized by race because too many black murderers were being executed. John DiIulio of Princeton and the Brookings Institution has studied the issue and makes a solid case that blacks and whites are treated equally within the criminal justice system. (See the Indicators chart in Chapter 7.) Neither Clinton nor the congressional Democratic leadership accepted the provision to execute by the numbers.

officers.") Midnight basketball, actually not such a bad idea, stayed in the bill. So did the ban on certain semiautomatic assault weapons, a hot-button political issue. Some new Democratic prevention items came back into the bill and further antagonized pro-incapacitation theorists. Some Republicans supported the amended bill but most announced their opposition, characterizing it as a vast social welfare spending scheme masquerading as a crime bill.

Both sides claimed the moral high ground. Who was right? Consider the testimony of John J. DiIulio, Jr., a working criminologist, who makes more sense talking about crime than anyone else in the business. At thirty-seven, DiIulio is a professor at Princeton University and a Senior Fellow at the Brookings Institution. He is "tough on crime," but he supports gun control and the assault weapons ban. He was born a Democrat and, he says, "I expect to die a Democrat." Until about three weeks before the passage of the crime legislation he was a supporter of the bill. Then things went on that led DiIulio to later call it "a rotten legislative oyster." Here is how he saw it:

I had thought the bill was a big step in the right direction, not perfect but good. I appeared on the Brinkley show and said that. Then, just before it passed, behind closed doors, some of its toughest and most important parts were watered down so much as to make them almost worthless.

They changed the fine print in the "Truth in Sentencing Incentive Grants." Instead of pushing the states to reform their penal codes to make violent prisoners serve at least 85% of time sentenced, they allowed the states to spend money in ways which do little to keep prisoners in prison longer.

They watered down a provision to put an end to liberal federal judges issuing orders that declare a prison "overcrowded," which then ends up putting criminals out on the street, and lets judges run the prisons. That's the chokehold on the whole criminal justice system.

The anti-incarceration lobby was calling the shots, acting through Democrats on the House Judiciary Committee and through the Justice Department. Janet Reno, who is the Ramsey Clark of the 1990s, and a bully, buys the whole line. The White House did nothing.

The anti-prison people have been at this for years, trying to make Americans believe that prisons have failed and that we're not much threatened by violent criminals. The big players are the ACLU, the National Council on Crime and Delinquency, The Sentencing Project, and the Justice Project of the Edna McConnell Clark Foundation.

Most Americans believe we have "revolving door" justice, and that violent criminals belong in prison, where they stay incapacitated for a serious amount of time They're right. Violent criminals who should be in prison are committing crimes on the street. In 1993, according to Bureau of Justice Statistics data, there were 11 million violent crimes committed. Only about 200,000 resulted in felony convictions, about 90% of those were plea-bargained, and only about 120,000 criminals ended up behind bars, where they typically served well less than half their terms.

The anti-incarceration lobby believes that too many people are in prison. These are same people who said "the rich get richer and the poor get prison." They've had enormous influence on the Clinton Justice Department.

The Democrats also messed up the "100,000 cops on the street" plan. That only can work if the cops are concentrated in high crime areas. They aren't.

Too bad. It could easily have been the most important crime bill in American history. Over a six-year time period it provided for $13.4 billion for police, $9.9 billion for prisons, $5.5 billion for prevention, and $1.4 billion for antidrug efforts. There were thirty titles in all, including a ban on the sale of semiautomatic assault weapons, a "three strikes and you're out" policy,* a provision allowing juveniles aged thirteen

---

* "Three strikes" legislation has swept the country, peddled by liberals and conservatives alike. It leaves much to be desired. Figure it out. Under a "three strikes" provision, a young thug gets convicted of a violent crime, serves a couple of years, and gets paroled. Then he's on the street again, thugging. Then he's caught, and is imprisoned, for a longer stretch. Then he's paroled again, and once more a predator at large. Only when caught for a third crime, would he get *life imprisonment*. Ultimately the government gets the bill for his geriatric medical needs, long past the age when he is likely to commit violent crimes.

Violence is a young man's racket. So "three strikes" lets some young predators be in and out of jail when they're most likely to commit crimes. And imprisons middle-aged and elderly people who are much less likely to commit violent crimes. A smarter law would hand out tough, long sentences, 15–20 years, for the young violent predators, and then let them out.

and fourteen to be prosecuted as adults for certain violent crimes, tougher rules regarding sex offenders, and a ban on the sale of handguns to juveniles. Instead, it turned into an inviting target for Republicans to reform in 1995.

Recall that Clinton's campaign text on crime was: "We believe in preventing crime and punishing criminals, not explaining away their behavior." But there was little emphasis on punishing in Clinton's original crime package. Democrats mostly ignored the idea that incapacitation yielded prevention as well as punishment. By letting Reno-ites at the Justice Department, and the Congressional Black Caucus (CBC), play a large role in defining the legislation, by coming out squarely on both sides of the punishment debate, by gutting key provisions late at night, the Democrats ended up, at best, politically neutral on an issue that could have been a big winner for them in the 1994 election.

The Democrats never did get the idea of the punishment–prevention debate. In the real world, alas, prevention programs (such as job training) do not have a good track record at cutting crime. Incapacitation may be the Neanderthal way of going at the problem, but, by definition, it works: A thug in prison cannot mug your sister, or the *twelve* other people *per year* that are harmed by that thug out of prison (according to an estimate in a Brookings Institution study.) Incarceration and subsequent long-term incapacitation is also a form of prevention. As shown in the Indicators, it is clear that voters understand that.

WELFARE

In the welfare area, as with crime, Clinton started out with a clear advantage. He had run for the presidency with all the appropriate rhetoric, unheard of for a Democratic candidate, and even unheard of for a Republican candidate. He said we should "end welfare as we know it," and that "welfare should be a helping hand, not a way of life." He promised changing a "welfare state" to an "enabling state," that would no longer purvey "rights" without asking for "responsibility," in a society where people would no longer get "something for nothing."

He had a somewhat specific goal in mind: "Two years and out." It was a clear and prominent political promise, from a self-styled "different Democrat." It could not have been clearer if he had said, Bush-like, "Read my lips: Two years and out."

It was sweet music to voters' ears. The welfare system has become a disaster that makes it irresponsible to be responsible. Clinton's idea, as used and perceived in the public dialogue, went something like this:

> Welfare recipients will be told in advance that there is a cut-off point. There will be support—additional support—for recipients for two years, including education, job training, and child care. (Which will cost the government more money.) Then, after two years of such help, if they have not been able to get off the welfare rolls with a private sector job, they will be offered a public sector job, with a low, but living wage. At which point they will then be cut off from welfare payments. And should they not perform on the job, or not show up, if they are healthy, they are on their own.

Elementary. And radical. That was the word—"radical"—that I heard again and again at a conference at UCLA, "Reducing Poverty in America," in mid-January 1993, just before Clinton's inauguration. The presenters and participants represented a wide variety of perspectives, from quite liberal to quite conservative, with many scholars from the black and Latino communities, some in favor of the idea, some against. It was said, by all, that even Ronald Reagan could not have gone quite that far.

The radical aspect of the idea goes to one central point: If you legislate a cutoff point, it means that at some point the federal government will be prepared to tell poor mothers and—indirectly—poor innocent children that their benefits have ceased or been sharply diminished. That is tough stuff. After all, it is argued, the children did nothing wrong. Why should they suffer?

There is an answer, and Clinton seemed to know about it. Unless there is a disincentive, like a cutoff point, the younger sisters of the young mothers already on welfare may well think to themselves, "Welfare is not a bad deal." Arguably (but logically), the existence of that thought tends to perpetuate welfare, directly or indirectly. Thinking there are no hard times ahead if she gets pregnant while unmarried, the younger sister may soon get sucked into the welfare trap, perpetuating the cycle of dependency.

The early jousting regarding welfare reform was interesting. In December 1992, at a Little Rock press conference, Donna Shalala publicly accepted her appointment from Clinton as secretary of Health and Human Services. She listed her five top agenda items. Welfare reform was not one of them. (Shalala was formerly the chair of the Children's Defense Fund, which, over the years, had characterized the idea of welfare phase-outs as "punitive" to poor people.)

A month later, when Shalala's confirmation hearings were held before the Senate Finance Committee, her prepared opening statement devoted exactly one sentence to welfare reform. That prompted Senator Daniel Patrick Moynihan, chair of the committee, to say that he heard "the clatter of campaign promises thrown out the window." He also charged that Shalala was ignoring "the largest commitment the President made."

Clinton's task force on welfare reform was late, very late, in getting started. It wasn't even appointed until June 1993, seven months after Clinton's election victory. Why so late? The Clintons feared it would derail their health-care extravaganza. (Many aspects of a welfare bill would have to be handled by the same congressional committees that dealt with health care.)

If late, the president's public charge to the task force was right on the money. He directed that legislation be devised "to end welfare as we know it, to break the permanent culture of dependence." And just before leaving on a trip to Asia, President Clinton met privately with the task force and told them this: "Get the values right; if you get everything else right, and get the values wrong, it won't work."

I interviewed Senator Moynihan shortly after. He is the man in politics who probably knows the welfare issue best, and he was not happy. He said that if the Clinton plan embodies some of the principles that have been ascribed to it, it would be "a political train wreck waiting to happen." That, explained Moynihan, is because "there is a dirty little secret to it."

Indeed a proposal was on the task force table, advanced by one of the group's cochairs, Harvard professor David Elwood, to establish a "child support assurance system." That new program would give extra *government* monies to children whose absent fathers were not paying child support. The politics of it, said Moynihan, were potentially catastrophic: "What an awful surprise voters will get when they find out that ending welfare means being able to retire on a court-awarded child support grant!"

(Elwood was something of a mystery. Was he the tough academic who originally helped formulate the "two years and out" concept? Or is he the soft "government as Daddy" proponent? He was described by some as a sheep in wolf's clothing, which, as things turned out, seemed about right. Even during the transition time in late 1992, it was clear to many on the welfare transition team that Elwood, and fellow future cochair of the commission Mary Jo Bane, thought that the Clinton two-years-and-out program was not viable. Elwood's child support assurance system did not survive the task force's scrutiny, perhaps because of Moynihan's public objection.)

There was another secret. The Clinton plan—at least based on what had been said about it by Clinton and others—would not have ended welfare as we know it. Not even close, according to welfare expert Douglas Besharov of the American Enterprise Institute.

How so? The theme of the plan was "two years and out." That ostensibly meant that for up to two years, able-bodied welfare mothers would get (in addition to the cash grant) major support for education, job training, and child care but then must get a job. But what happens if a welfare recipient doesn't go to work? Or starts work and quits? Based on the original ideas discussed by the Clintonistas, the only penalty would be a loss of the *mother's share* of an AFDC cash grant. And that's only a small part of her Greater Welfare support. The welfare mother would continue to get AFDC grants for *her children*. And she would get *food stamps, housing grants, Medicaid,* and *Women, Infants, and Children* (WIC) *benefits.* She also would remain eligible for more than seventy smaller programs—in fact, the whole Greater Welfare portfolio. She would still receive an estimated 85 to 90 percent of her current benefit. There would be little incentive to work even if a cutoff happened.

I attended the first press conference of the welfare task force. It was not a reassuring session. Despite the fact that more than 70 percent of new AFDC cases are headed by a never-married mother, the thirteen pages of briefing material put out by the task force did not mention the concept of out-of-wedlock birth even once. Happenstance, you say? Was it happenstance that the task force handouts also did not mention Clinton's four magic campaign words, "two years and out," although that pledge was what validated Clinton's promise to "end welfare as we know it"? Was it happenstance that the task force did not even use words like "sanction" or "termination," even though those are the terms of art that point to tough-minded solutions like a serious cutoff plan?

The task force's nonspecific euphemism of choice was "time-limited transitional support system." Only upon questioning did the briefers endorse the two-year limit.

It was not happenstance. Indeed, serious discussions were taking place inside the task force about values and behavior issues, of which illegitimacy is paramount. So why the reticence in public? I cannot prove it, but I can divine it. The truth about illegitimacy, the Clinton-appointed commission feared, would cause displeasure among liberal Democrats, who would claim that such a view is merely "blaming the victim." Could agents of a Democratic president really say that voluntary choice regarding reproductive behavior is the principal agent driving welfare and many of our other social problems? Could they even intimate that perhaps out-of-wedlock births could be reduced by a threat to end benefits?

Although there was some tough-minded thinking going on about welfare inside the Clinton task force, the public timidity seemed to foreshadow where the plan would end up, and why Republicans were later able to capture the issue. If political leaders remain uncomfortable mentioning illegitimacy, it will continue to be condoned. As long as it is condoned, it will be subsidized. When it is subsidized, it is bought. By us. By now it's our fault. If Americans should feel guilty about something, that's a good place to start.

———————

After a year in office, there was still no welfare proposal from the White House. Both the president and Mrs. Clinton had determined that health care was a "crisis." Further, it was said that congressional hardball liberals would hold health care legislation "hostage" unless welfare reform was delayed.

Moynihan reentered the fray. He said on a national television talk show that "there is no health care crisis in America; there is a welfare crisis in America." And further, that although Clinton himself was sincere about ending welfare as we know it, many members of his task force had "no intention of doing it."

Moynihan was right on the substance. It wasn't being said that we have the best welfare system in the world, so let's fix what's wrong with it. Yet that is what was being said about health care.

We may have the worst welfare system. Through a set of perverse incentives, we are encouraging fatherless homes. And as Moynihan pointed out, "That is a terrible thing to do to a child." He was also right about the Clinton task force. They were mostly mildly liberal welfare experts from massive federal agencies who were prepared to tinker, mostly via job training and public service jobs, with a wholly failed system. They seemed to miss what the voters heard in the call to end welfare as we know it. The voters believed that "ending" meant ending. It was an issue, like crime, ready to erupt. Besharov said to me of the Clinton task force: "They are mostly Old Democrats commissioned to come up with a New Democrat plan. They don't get Clinton's idea of 'tough love.' "

Health care, not welfare, became the central preoccupation of the Clinton administration. The plan involved federal direction of about one-seventh of the entire American economy. It crashed so badly it never even came to a vote.

It was not until June 1994, almost a year and a half after Clinton was elected, that a welfare proposal emerged from the White House. Given the health care calendar, it was too late for serious consideration before a busy Congress. Just as well. On welfare, Clinton could have gone for the long ball. He bunted. By my lights, this was foolish. The long-ball strategy not only would have been better for the country and for potential welfare recipients but better politics for a president and a party in trouble in an election year.

Solid welfare reform should revolve around this larger question: Can government action modify human behavior in a salutary way? Recent evidence provides a clear answer to the question: Sometimes.

Thus, the number of people who smoke cigarettes is way down, partly because of government research and public education programs. Government-sponsored education campaigns have somewhat lowered drug use. Automobile accident deaths are down substantially, partly because of government safety regulations dealing with mandatory seat belts, air bags, highway construction standards, speed limits, and partly because of private public relations campaigns against drunk driving. And, of course, after hearing from segregationists that "laws can't change what's in the hearts of men," the civil rights laws did change both the hearts of many people and certainly their behavior.

But there was something more than your friendly government at work in these partial successes: a disincentive. We were told on every cigarette pack that smoking can kill us. We saw television commercials that told us that drugs could fry our brain like an egg on a skillet. Drunk drivers, we were told, could end up in the slammer. Civil rights laws were enforceable, and enforced, even by President Dwight Eisenhower, who was not happy about the school desegregation decision of the Supreme Court, but, following the law, ordered troops into Little Rock in 1957.

Did Clinton's welfare plan promise to change behavior through disincentives, in order to fulfill his pledge to end welfare as we know it? Not much.

A wise welfare reform proposal should deal with two sets of people: those already on welfare—identifiable mothers with children—and those who might be on welfare in the future, who for the moment are only statistical abstractions.

Regarding people now on welfare, Clinton's bunt strategy may have been barely acceptable. The idea in the Clinton proposal was to get mushy-tough on young welfare mothers, those born after 1972, only about *one-fifth* of the case load and that phased in gradually, due to the heavy costs of federal job creation. Among other things, they are told to prepare to get a job within two years, typically by going to school or to a job training program. Under the Clinton plan, the new jobs would be in the private sector, if possible. Alas, most would probably end up in the public sector. Moreover, the plan does not put a firm time limit on those public jobs, raising the possibility of *permanent* government make-work jobs and if the jobs don't pay as much as the original welfare payment, then AFDC payments would make up the difference. So much for two years and out. Welfare mothers would still get cash stipends for their children, plus the full array of Greater Welfare benefits. Plus expanded stipends for day care even if the mother did not show up for work. If enacted as written, the Clinton plan would have cost the federal government an additional $9.3 billion over five years, mostly for jobs.

It did not match Clinton's original rhetoric about welfare. Newt Gingrich, somewhat of a partisan, put it this way, "The President is brilliant at describing a Ferrari, but his staff continues to deliver a Yugo." But both Republicans and conservative Democrats called the plan "billions more for welfare as we know it."

Forget for the moment that government jobs programs have a history of failure. Forget that if the training is for "good" jobs, that could lead to situations where qualifying for welfare by having an illegitimate child can become yet another desirable entitlement ticket. Forget that the last patch-up welfare reform bill, in 1988, engendered a New York state commission report a few years later which concluded that the new program was not helping.

But remember this: In that first category of people, those already on welfare, we are dealing with young children, in trouble through no fault of their own. It might be worth one more try to help them out of the welfare trap, Clinton style—or, better yet, Clinton style with some extra backbone.

It is in its treatment of the second group—those unidentifiable abstractions of people who will come onto welfare in the future—that

Clinton's plan fell down. They were treated the same as real people now on welfare. So where was the disincentive to reduce those illegitimate *first pregnancies* that begin the whole cycle? That is the only serious way to start ending welfare as we know it.

The Clinton plan did provide $300 million for an education and public relations campaign, through schools, targeted on illegitimate births, and using the president's bully pulpit. How effective this might be is a matter of conjecture. After all, the great rise in illegitimacy occurred after school sex education courses became common in America and after popular politicians and athletes gave warnings on television programs. In any event, there was a political risk: Bill Clinton talking about sex might just end up as fodder for David Letterman and Jay Leno.

How could we roll back *future* welfare? The best plan I saw during this time was put forth by Congresswoman Jan Meyers (R-Kans.). It already had fifty cosponsors, including some Democrats, when Clinton's draft bill was put on the table in 1994. The Meyers proposal stipulated that new teenage mothers of illegitimate children, *and the children* be denied any cash payment from the AFDC program. That could be a true disincentive: zero dollars. (Meanwhile, the food stamp, Medicaid, day care, and other programs would continue, thus providing some support for innocent children.) Moreover, it froze AFDC funding levels and returned the program to the states, which would remove AFDC from ever-growing entitlement status.

The Republican House conference thought (at that time) that the Meyers plan was too tough and went in a more moderate direction; call it Clinton Heavy.

As it turned out, all the plans were softer than what came to be debated after the Republican congressional victory. That vision, in the Republican Contract resembled the Meyers plan but went somewhat further. It sent the AFDC program back to the states. It ended entitlement status. It denied any cash benefits to unmarried mothers under age eighteen. It also cut back food stamps, cut SSI eligibility making it more difficult for kids to get "crazy money," and led Newt Gingrich to say the word "orphanage," which wasn't even in the Contract, but caused a media firestorm.

On December 5, 1994, the *New Republic* ran a cover with no art-work, only stark type introducing an article by Mickey Kaus:

THEY BLEW IT.

"The fundamental STRATEGIC MISTAKE of the CLINTON PRESIDENCY is now clear. If President Clinton had pushed for WELFARE REFORM rather than health care reform in 1994, we would now be talking about a great DEMOCRATIC REALIGNMENT, rather than a great REPUBLICAN REALIGNMENT . . ."

The text of Kaus's article continued inside the magazine. Here are some excerpts:

Even the President's chief of staff admits that "in hindsight, it would have been better if we had taken on welfare reform," before tackling health care. . . .

Welfare reform is not just any initiative. When NBC and the *Wall Street Journal* polled voters right after the (1994) election, reforming welfare was the issue most often listed as a top priority for the new Congress. Health reform came in a distant second. Among the heavily wooed independent voters, welfare reform beat out such Perotian staples as a balanced budget amendment (by a nearly two-to-one margin) and Congressional term limits (by a nine-to-one margin) . . .

Nor did it really take hindsight to recognize welfare's salience. How, after all, had Bill Clinton gotten elected in 1992? By promising to "end welfare as we know it." That was the main message of the television ads his consultants ran in contested states. It was a central applause line in both his State of the Union addresses. . . .

Poll-takers will tell you that welfare reform is a "values" issue. The values involved are work and family. Both AFDC and Food Stamps flout the work ethic, offering support to able-bodied Americans whether they work or not. . . AFDC also seemingly undermines families, because it is available, by and large, only to single parents (mainly mothers).

But more than symbolism is involved, since welfare is implicated in America's most difficult social problem—the existence of whole neighborhoods, mostly African American, where there are precious few intact, working families. Welfare may or may not have caused this underclass, but welfare is clearly what sustains it. And the underclass, in turn, drives the crime problem, the race problem, the "urban crisis" and the general sense of social decay ("12-year-olds having babies, 15-year-olds killing each other").*

My sense is that Kaus probably overstated the political reward of welfare. I'm not sure welfare alone would have made for a Democratic realignment. But overstatement is not the same as wrong. Far from it in this case. Welfare is a big, big, player, for all of the reasons that Kaus says. And Clinton had a handle on it first, in a manner that defined his 1992 campaign. And then he blew it.

EDUCATION

Why, by November 8, 1994, did the Clinton administration, and by extension the whole Democratic party, look like Old Democrats, not New Democrats? Some reasons have been mentioned: Clinton's personal views, his wife's views, the liberal Democrats hired to staff the new government, the general cause-group liberal tilt of the Democratic party, the "look-like-America" hiring quotas, and the role of the liberal Democratic Congress.

What happened to Clinton's education program is one case history of just how tough that Congress can be, even with a Democratic president. Recall that Clinton had committed himself to the central national goals of the educational reform movement. He believed that the state educational system must stress outputs, not inputs. This meant a variety of tough nationally certified nongovernmentally produced

---

* Excerpted with permission from *The New Republic*, copyright © 1994 *The New Republic*, Inc.

content standards, from which the states could voluntarily choose or not, as they saw fit. It meant that the whole deal wouldn't be worth much unless the states would apply tests and stakes to the newly developed curricula. Without such stakes, it would just be the same old funny money game.

In his campaign document, "Putting People First," we find Governor Clinton pledging to "establish tough standards and a national examination system." Speaking to education groups during the campaign, he said America needed "a meaningful set of national exams." He continued to bring up this theme as late as the 1994 State of the Union Address.

Clinton was unable to make it happen, although he tried and had some of his best people working on it.*

Clinton's original version of an education bill, entitled "Goals 2000," embodied the standards-tests-stakes idea. It was drafted by Secretary Richard Riley's Department of Education, working in coordination with Bill Galston at the White House. It was sent to the House Committee on Education and Labor, chaired by William D. Ford, a sixteen-term Democrat from Michigan.

To give a flavor of the regnant philosophy in the Democratic liberal realm, consider what happened at a closed meeting with a number of education professionals not long before the bill was drafted. Chairman Ford's chief counsel on the Education and Labor Committee, Jack Jennings, said this: "The chairman is unalterably opposed to assessments with consequences." Translated into American: "Billy Ford is against tests that count." (Jennings told me that he said no such thing, but several people in the room have verified the account.)

Now, this interesting comment does not mean that chairman Ford is a nasty man. He is a liberal Democrat, with a recent rating of 95 out of a possible 100 in the liberal Americans for Democratic Action ratings. The liberal position in this matter is that any sort of stakes or consequences that are connected to tests will hurt inner-city black and Hispanic children because they will likely do poorly on the tests. Therefore, say the liberals, don't do it.

---

* Some of the material here is detailed in an important book, *National Standards in American Education*, by Diane Ravitch.

Others say otherwise: Minority children need tests with stakes even more than suburban students; minority students won't be able to compete in the real world without hitting such marks; tests without standards are something for nothing—they are not only worthless but harmful to poor and minority students.

In any event, there was a tough interchange between House heavyweights and Clinton subalterns about the draft education bill. The Clintonistas were told that the draft bill would be DOA if it were not changed substantially.

That is a tough abbreviation in the world of Washington. "Dead On Arrival" was the harsh greeting extended to Republican legislation by the Democratic Congress during the time of Presidents Reagan and Bush. DOA informs the executive branch that its legislative proposals are to be scrapped and that any work on an alternative would start from scratch. But this was different: These were *Democratic* barons of Congress quietly telling a *Democratic* president to stuff it or play ball.

Clinton played ball, at least early on. The White House and the Department of Education did what they were told to do. They revised the bill. What was ultimately sent up to the Congress was legislation that chairman Ford and his liberal colleagues would deign to consider before attempting to change it. In effect, such a congressional strategy tended to give the most liberal group of congressional Democrats not only veto power over a Clinton proposal, but shaping power as well.

For example: The liberal Democrats, particularly on the House side, didn't like outputs over inputs. After all, outputs might show that minorities, an important part of their constituencies, weren't doing well. On the other hand, inputs—like more teachers and more money—bring goodies to their voters and solace to supporters in the teachers' unions, particularly the liberal National Education Association (although, as seen earlier, rising inputs do not seem to improve outputs).

The bill that finally went forward from the Clinton administration had lots about inputs in it, officially now called "Opportunities to Learn Standards." Liberals hoped, and moderates and conservatives feared, that such input standards could be invested with a force of law and turned into a new round of massive spending on schools, possibly court ordered. It was said by moderates and conservatives that OTL really stood for "Opportunity to Litigate." And that could happen without doing anything at all to bring about the trinity of standards, tests, and consequences—the very criteria designed to bring intellectual rigor and discipline back to the schools.

Clinton pushed back on the liberals' view of OTL, and a compromise was reached. Ultimately, "Goals 2000" *encouraged* but did not *demand* states to set up OTL programs.

There was no compromise concerning testing and consequences. The Senate wanted language in "Goals 2000" that would permit the use of standards-related tests three years after the enactment of the bill (the delay appropriately deemed necessary so that students and teachers would have time to prepare before any "consequences" came into play). The Clinton White House also wanted that sort of a provision. Alas, the House version of the bill had a very different provision in it. What emerged, apparently without White House knowledge, was a provision that stipulated:

> (C) The [National Education Standards and Improvement] *Council shall certify State assessments only if:* . . .
> > (ii) such assessments will not be used to make decisions regarding graduation, grade promotions, or retention of students for a period of 5 years from the date of enactment of this Act.

Of course, the bill had only a five-year term. In other words, in the final version, *tests could not be used with consequences.* Team Clinton never knew what hit them. Clinton signed the bill into law. Later, I asked Al Shanker of the American Federation of Teachers what he thought. "Stakes have to be the centerpiece of any serious move to standards," he said. "The failure to get stakes in the bill undermines everything else. It's an educational tragedy."

In all, from the point of view of pro-standards advocates, it wasn't even half a loaf. Voluntary academic standards (outputs) might be encouraged in many states (although many states have acted on their own). Inputs would also be encouraged. There could be testing. *But the test results could not be used to hold students accountable.* The funny money standard was not repealed. A student could still go through school, socially promoted, grade inflated, socially ware-housed, and undisciplined.

Shortly after the passage of the "Goals 2000" legislation, the Congress took up the once-every-five-years business of renewing the Elementary and Secondary School Act (ESEA). Unlike the mere $400 million in "Goals 2000," ESEA is America's principal federal education program, disbursing $7 billion per year, ostensibly to poor schools, but in fact land-ing at about 90 percent of all schools.

The original intent of the president, his education aides, and Secre-tary Riley was to take the standards-tests-stakes ideas that were to be embodied in "Goals 2000" and link them nonoppressively to the big money of ESEA. What happened instead is that what got linked to ESEA was the mush that emerged in "Goals 2000." Many moderate education experts felt a sense of great letdown. There had been a chance, they believed, to get outputs, not inputs, and consequences and stakes, thereby breaking up the something-for-nothing situation in the classroom.

Prostandards Republicans such as Governor Carroll Campbell of South Carolina and former Secretary of Education Lamar Alexander were driven to a point where, by 1995, they ended up working hard to repeal the bill. Other Republicans, mostly conservatives, who had been working against the standards concept all along (on anti-Washington control grounds) intensified their opposition.

Clinton loyalists made the case that despite its flaws, the bill moved one more step toward the goals set up by the standards move-ment. States, schools, and parents would think about serious world-class standards and there would be some additional federal money to help develop such curricula, with stakes and consequences if the states wanted it that way.

How did Clinton get into this particular mess? It was the Con-gress—the Congress driven by a Democratic majority, a Democratic majority driven by a liberal majority, rolling a rollable president.

The "Goals 2000" bill was signed on March 31, 1994. It received scant attention in the press and on television. Later in the year Presi-dent Clinton referred to it a few times in speeches, but there the story ended. Insofar as it was at least a partial step in the right direction, the president never managed to get the standards idea recognized by the voters. A chance to kick-start the concept of standards was missed.

————

The size of the loaf shrank further, due to a strange set of events. An early set of draft standards, "National Standards for United States History: Exploring the American Experience" (NSUSHEAE), was published in late 1994. Perhaps the most important statement in the document appeared up front: "This paper does not necessarily represent the positions or policies of the United States government, and no official endorsement should be inferred."

Moreover, even if the standards did represent the U.S. government, they would have represented the administration of George Bush, not Bill Clinton. The grant money for the preparation of the standards was given to the UCLA Center for History in the Schools by the Bush administration, largely by the National Endowment for the Humanities, whose Bush-appointed chairman was Lynne Cheney. Although the history standards were published by a Bush-funded private group, they were published on Clinton's watch and created a mini-tempest, which offered Clinton an opportunity to show where he stood.

The first blast at the history standards appeared on the editorial page of the *Wall Street Journal* in late 1994, written by Cheney, who was surprised by the results of her grant. She described the content of the standards as an exercise in political correctitude, noting that Senator Joseph McCarthy was mentioned nineteen times and Senator Daniel Webster not at all. Soon nonliberal columnists were on the attack.

> The whole document strains to promote the achievements and highlight the victimization of the country's preferred minorities, while straining equally to degrade the achievements and highlight the flaws of the white males who ran the country for its first two centuries.
>
> Charles Krauthammer, *The Washington Post*, November 6, 1994

> The standards are . . . crude anti-Western and anti-American propaganda. . . . (The standards) are beyond salvage and need to be junked.
>
> John Leo, *U.S. News and World Report*, February 6, 1995

There is nothing more important than teaching America's story to American children. The standards had big problems, although by my lights perhaps they were not quite as terrible as portrayed.

NSUSHEAE did, in fact, cover key aspects of American history. Its turgid prose dealt with far more than students from grades 5 through 12 could be expected to absorb, which turns the idea of some limited national voluntary criteria into an unlimited national cafeteria. It touched on the peopling of America 30,000 years ago, and compared "The Simpsons" with "Ozzie and Harriet." A student is asked about the African political kingdoms of Mali, Songhai, and Benin; about "reverse discrimination"; about how "white land hunger" shaped pre-Revolutionary times; and about what they thought of the idea that "Ronald Reagan's defense and military initiatives led to the collapse of communism." Shays's Rebellion, the Whiskey Rebellion, Jay's treaty, and the Monroe Doctrine all make their appearance.

The problem was in the point of view. One was prevalent. Another was missing.

The one that dominated stressed those who were left out of earlier histories. It's true that until recently American history books did not pay much attention to women, blacks, Native Americans, Hispanics, and Asians. There is surely room for a kind of multicultural sensitivity that would deal with the roles of American minorities and women.

But in the NSUSHEAE history standards, the tales of oppression seem to be the principal themes on a politically correct stage, with each honored group taking its turn in the spotlight. Harriet Tubman, a black woman (in modern personnel hiring parlance, a "twofer," as in two-for-the-price-of-one) who rescued slaves, was mentioned six times. Robert E. Lee (a dead white male "nofer") got none. Paul Revere, Thomas Edison, and the Gettysburg Address are not mentioned. The Ku Klux Klan gets seventeen mentions, the American Federation of Labor gets nine mentions, and Seneca Falls (origin point of the women's movement) also gets nine mentions.

Defenders of the NSUSHEAE draft standards say that is mere bean counting. Perhaps. But the downplaying of traditional American heroes does reflect an important idea: There was no single broad, *positive* theme to define the American story. After all, the academic New His-torians dismiss such thinking as "triumphalism." The codirector of NSUSHEAE, Gary B. Nash, a history professor at UCLA told me flat out that the document was "against triumphalism." He said too many nations suffer from viewing themselves "as us, the good guys versus them, the bad guys."

Us good guys have a different notion. America is not just another nation. That subversive thought even slipped into NSUSHEAE. Nearly buried, it is reported that the voyages of Columbus "led . . . to the planting of English settlements where the ideas of representative government and religious toleration would grow haltingly and, over several centuries, would inspire similar transformations in other parts of the world." (Tsk tsk . . . triumphalism.)

At issue is this: What will our children be taught? That America is just another country in the us-versus-them game? Or that we have changed the world, mostly for the better? Should the American story be told to American children as value-neutral and with lots of aton-able guilt on display? Or as the great country of recent history, whose record is surely less than perfect?

Clinton stood mute on the issue. Why? The case made within the administration was that, after all, these were *draft* voluntary standards for the *states* (although handsomely produced and widely disseminated to schools) and the president shouldn't be intervening. Marshall Smith, the U.S. undersecretary of education wrote: "The Department of Education took no position on the standards, but not because we wanted to duck the issue. The Department simply isn't in the busi-ness of endorsing any set of academic standards. Setting standards is the job of the states and local school districts." Fair enough, the admin-istration had kept support for the standards idea by stressing that they would be voluntary and that Big Daddy government would not be run-ning the show from Washington. Neither Smith's comment, nor the explanation, received any attention. Clinton never explained it either.

It didn't take long for this educational sizzler to end up on the floor of the Senate. Senator Slade Gorton, a moderate Republican from Washington State, denounced the standards as an "ideologically dri-ven, anti-Western monument to politically correct caricature." Senator

Joseph Lieberman, a moderate Democrat from Connecticut, said during Senate debate that the standards described the cold war as mere "swordplay of the Soviet Union and the United States," a characterization he called "insulting." And further, that "because America has dramatically and positively affected the course of world history . . . we ought not let that be disparaged. We ought not let that . . . be lost in a kind of 'everything is equal, let us reach out and make up for past exclusions' set of standards."

A "sense of the Senate" resolution was introduced, stipulating that if any further funding would be forthcoming regarding history standards, any "recipient of such funds should have a decent respect for the contributions of Western Civilization, and United States history, ideas, and institutions, to the increase of freedom and prosperity around the world." In other words: don't trash America with federal dollars. The vote squeaked through, ninety-nine to one.

Remarkably, President Clinton, a man with a finely attuned political antenna, who manages to comment on most items in the news, didn't comment on the Senate resolution. A few months later, the Christian Coalition joined the battle. Their Contract with the American Family came out against the concept of voluntary federal standards on the grounds that such standards would end up as "politically correct." Their evidence was adduced from the NSUSHEAE standards, in which, they said,

> the United States Constitution was never mentioned in any of the 31 standards, and was relegated to the supporting materials; the establishment of the National Organization for Women and the Sierra Club were viewed as notable events, but not the assembling of the United States Congress; [there was] only one quotation from a Congressional leader, and that was Tip O'Neill calling Ronald Reagan "a cheerleader for selfishness."

Do the views presented in the UCLA standards really represent those in the education-history community? Gary Nash says they certainly do; it was a communal effort that blended the voices of nearly every important academic organization or institution connected with the topic. It's a bad-news story either way. If the standards do not represent the history industry, then a grand hustle is afoot, perpetrated in NSUSHEAE. If they do represent current academic thinking (more likely), then there are bubbleheads in the professoriate, and they are teaching our kids.

At the end of the day, the movement toward no-more-something-for-nothing educational standards had taken two body blows. The first was delivered by the liberal Democratic Congress, diluting the concept almost beyond recognition. The second was administered by runaway multiculturalists in the academy, unanswered by the president. Two body blows may be enough for a knockout, which would be too bad.

PREFERENCE

In Chapter 10 it was explained how politically treacherous it would be for a Democratic president to bite the bullet on the issue of racial preference. Accordingly, perhaps the fair question to ask about President Clinton in the 1992–1994 time frame is this: Did he make it worse?

Yes he did.

It is not that Clinton didn't understand the issue of quotas. As we've seen, he understood it from more angles than there are. (See: "Why are you laughing?" page 207.) We noted earlier how President Clinton began to look like President Bean Counter by appointing an administration to look like America, rather than to think like America.

It got worse. Secretary of Defense Les Aspin's recommended appointments were repeatedly turned down by the White House on the grounds of race/gender/ethnicity. Soon he was being called the *"Home Alone* secretary." Ultimately the Department of Defense snapped to attention. On August 10, 1994 (after Aspin had been pushed out as defense secretary), Undersecretary of Defense Edwin Dorn put forth a memorandum to his subalterns that he said was implementing Secretary William Perry's demand for "vigorous action" to increase the number of "women, minorities, and persons with disabilities." Dorn wrote: "I need to be consulted whenever you are confronting the possibility that any excepted position [i.e., political appointment] or any career position at GS-15 level and higher, is likely to be filled by a candidate who will not enhance . . . diversity." Dorn went further. If this procedure did not work, he wrote, then "we will need to employ a more formal approach involving goals, timetables, and controls on hiring decisions." In other words, all top-level Pentagon hirees must be minorities or women unless Dorn allows otherwise. Or else there will be quotas.

Question: Does the threat of quotas yield self-imposed quotas? Answer: Of course.

After the Lani Guinier nomination crashed, a long search for a new appointee as assistant attorney general for civil rights ensued. After many months, word came out that Clinton was considering the appointment of John Payton, the highly regarded corporation counsel of the District of Columbia. But Payton, who is black, was not acceptable to the activists of the Congressional Black Caucus. And so Payton was dropped. Why? A White House official told the *Washington Post* that "we've got to assess for the President whether he risks more by going forward with someone the Black Caucus won't support for the post. People just don't want to take on a battle on the left for this position." And so, with the functional equivalent of veto power granted to the Black Caucus, the search for a new nominee went on.

It took the Clinton administration more than a year after Guinier was dropped to propose a new appointee. He was Deval Patrick, a former colleague of Guinier at the NAACP Legal Defense Fund. Unlike Guinier, he had not written provocatively about civil rights issues. At his confirmation hearing, he pressed all the reassuring buttons. Responding to a question from Senator Strom Thurmond (R-S.C.) the nominee-designate noted that affirmative action "has to be reserved for limited circumstances and has to be flexible."

Patrick was confirmed. He appointed Kerry Scanlon, also of the Legal Defense Fund of the NAACP, as a deputy. The other deputy slot went to Isabelle Pinzler, director of the American Civil Liberties Union's Womens' Rights Project. No surprise, really. Just about every other appointee in charge of the various civil rights bureaucracies within government came from the activist ranks of the quota-pushers.

The new commissioners of the Equal Employment Opportunity Commission (EEOC) came from the Puerto Rican Legal Defense and Education Fund, the Asian Law Caucus, and the Western Law Center for Disability Rights. The new legal counsel at EEOC came from the

National Women's Law Center. The civil rights slot at the Department of Education went to a regional counsel for the Mexican-American Legal Defense and Education Fund.

Roberta Achtenberg was chosen as assistant secretary for fair housing and equal opportunity at the Department of Housing and Urban Development (HUD). She had previously worked as executive director of the National Center for Lesbian Rights. The choice for chair of the U.S. Commission on Civil Rights was the all-time, all-star quintessential queen of the quotacrats, Mary Frances Berry. It was Berry who had written that "civil rights laws were not passed to give civil rights to all Americans . . . [but only] to disfavored groups [such as] blacks, Hispanics and women."

Clint Bolick is the litigation director at the Institute for Justice in Washington. Of these appointments he says: "[Clinton] has given over the entire civil rights apparatus to ideologues who cut their teeth in left-wing advocacy groups, unleashing them to pursue militant, in-your-face policies in areas touching the lives of every American. . . . He [Clinton] is satisfied to let them have their way, as what he mistakenly perceives a low-cost appeasement of those who dwell at his party's left boundary."

Bolick is an alumnus of EEOC and the Department of Justice during the Reagan years. The Institute for Justice is a conservative-libertarian organization. Accordingly, his opinion must be tested against the reality of the policy of the Clinton administration. What sort of policy did these civil rights activists, and the president, actually pursue during the first two years of the Clinton term?

- Deval Patrick described the Supreme Court's ruling against racially drawn congressional districts as "alternatively naive and venal" and vowed to fight "every single challenge." Patrick organized a new seven-member legal team at Justice charged with that function. (Clinton saluted the idea of African-American and Hispanic voting districts for Congress.)
- The Clinton Justice Department supported the retroactive enforcement of the 1991 Civil Rights Act, which the Supreme Court then rejected, eight to one.

- A 50 percent quota for women and minorities for the issuance of 2,000 new licenses for personal communications services (PCS), at 60 percent below market value, was promulgated by the Federal Communications Commission, headed by Clinton appointee Reed Hundt. The *New York Times* said it was "the biggest affirmative action program in decades." A financial analyst estimated the value of the bestowed benefits at $500 million. Hundt says he is against quotas. But what is he for? This: "Due to market failures, and taking account of other social goals, sometimes societies must stimulate the growth of networks beyond the private-market optimum to a social optimum." Not quotas, only a "social optimum," which, of course, comes about through set-asides and economic giveaways that are deemed not to be quotas, but have the effect of quotas.
- Under pressure from Achtenberg at HUD, the Chevy Chase Savings and Loan was forced to approve loans for minorities at below-market rates, with special grants to cover down payments. (That has the effect of raising the price of unsubsidized mortgages.) With the handwriting on the wall, the Mortgage Bankers Association surrendered and promised to "encourage development of a workforce that reflects the cultural, racial and ethnic diversity of the lenders' market." (Does that mean that a black banker should not work in a white suburb?)
- Achtenberg also led a crusade to muzzle the free speech of citizen activists in Berkeley, California, who protested the siting of a homeless shelter in their nice neighborhood. HUD admitted that such pressure was being exerted in many other places. Ultimately HUD backed down and acknowledged that the First Amendment was still in the Constitution, but Achtenberg reminded the public to "anticipate more actions of this kind."
- The Clinton health care plan proposed quotas for minority doctors to get specialist training, while prospective white doctors would be pushed to serve as general practitioners.
- The Clinton Justice Department switched sides from the Bush Justice Department in a New Jersey case that gave preference to a black teacher over a white teacher (equally qualified) regarding

who would get laid off during a reduction in force. The Bush department opposed reverse discrimination; the Clinton department supported it.

To the surprise of the Clinton administration and the Democratic Congress, but not to many others, 1994 became known as the "year of the angry white male."

On Election Day 1994, Clinton's approval rating was 44 percent (after having sunk as low as 39 percent). The Republicans carried the U.S. Senate, where for eight years they had been in a minority. They carried a majority of the state governorships, something they had not accomplished since 1970. They ended up holding gubernatorial power in states with 70 percent of the population. They gained 500 seats in state legislatures, to come within striking distance of a majority, something they had not had since 1957. And for the first time in forty years, they captured control of the U.S. House of Representatives.

Exit polls showed that in 1994 only 18 percent of voters selfidentified themselves as liberals. More than half, 51 percent, thought that Bill Clinton was a liberal.

There were scholars and pundits (even me) who talked about how the 1994 election could be a realigning contest that could turn control of the American political apparatus over to conservative Republicans for a generation. (Or more. By some counts, Franklin Roosevelt's New Deal didn't wholly run out of steam for sixty years, that is, until 1994.)

And Clinton was complaining. The gist of his comments were: The voters don't understand what we have done for them; we haven't been able to get our message out. For a while some of his spinmeisters spun thusly: Voters were anti-Washington and anti-incumbent, Clinton had run in 1992 as an agent of change, and he still represented that spirit and mandate, therefore the 1994 vote actually ratified Clinton's 1992 mandate. Could the spinmeisters really believe that?

Soon reality set in. Many congressional Democrats were mowed down by the scythe of voter indignation. Moderate Democrats were particularly hard hit, tarred as liberals in some large measure because of an early connection to Clinton. The Mainstream Forum, a group of moderate House Democrats founded and chaired by Congressman Dave McCurdy (D-Okla.), had seventy-two members before the 1994 election—and only thirty-one afterwards. (Some lost their re-election bids, some ran for higher office and lost, some retired.) McCurdy himself ran for the Senate from Oklahoma, was linked to Clinton in a series of cartoons in the state's largest newspaper, and elsewhere, and was solidly beaten. One of the cartoons showed McCurdy carrying Clinton piggyback, with Clinton carrying two placards, "Gay Rights" and "Gun Control," with a caption coming from McCurdy's lips: "He ain't heavy, he's my mentor."

(McCurdy recalls a party at Pamela Harriman's house shortly after the 1992 election, in honor of President-elect Clinton. All the great and near-great of the Democratic establishment were in attendance. McCurdy, remembering that Clinton had given speeches pounding the brain-dead Democrats, said to Clinton, "These are the people you ran against." Clinton responded, "They are the people who will determine my success in Congress." McCurdy thinks that Clinton is a failed president—because he had his eyes on a political box score, not on a political philosophy. Operationally that leads to a stance that "any deal is a good deal"—and to voters who ask, "What does he stand for?").

Not a single incumbent Republican senator, congressman, or governor lost. It became apparent that what happened was much more than random drive-by shootings committed by angry voters.

It was a hectic and exciting two years. Journalists had a great time. Clinton was hot copy. To Clinton's great credit, many important new ideas surfaced. For those of us in the column writing trade, it was a bonanza. Gone, for sure, were the boring days of President Bush.

When the two years were over—after all the hoopla about gays in the military, midnight basketball, $200 haircuts, Hillary, Somalia, Gergen, Haiti, Whitewater, trade with China, troopers, talk radio—there were three big items of substance pushed by the Clinton White House. The budget. Health care. NAFTA. None was a values issue or a social issue.

Chapter 14

THE REPUBLICAN
REVOLUTION

It was hard to see at first. Later it became more clear.

The tableau is already frozen in our mind, in the part reserved for American political history. September 27, 1994, is a sunny day in Washington. And there they are, more than 300 Republican candidates for Congress, assembled on the steps of the Capitol, forming a backdrop for the stout man with a shock of white hair. The stout one is orating with gusto. That is Newt Gingrich, Republican minority whip, promulgating the Contract with America, pledging enactment in one hundred days after the start of a House of Representatives with a Republican majority.

The Contract was a twin-edged knife aimed at the heart of the something-for-nothing state. It was both tactics and substance, intertwined. In this case it is hard to know which was more important.

For a full generation, an iron rule put forth by Speaker of the House Thomas P. "Tip" O'Neill shaped the political universe. *"All politics is local,"* said Tip. That was seen by most observers as a natural and neutral law of political tactics, hardly arguable, hardly ideological, widely trumpeted by the punditocracy. And, indeed, what else could explain how it was that the Democratic majority in Congress, particularly in the people's House, was far more liberal than the nation, and yet was returned to power like clockwork, every two years?

It seemed so clear. A congressman should take good care of a constituent's micro problems with the Social Security Administration or the Veterans Administration. A congressman should bring back boodle for a federal courthouse or a mass transit system. If the congressman did well at those personal and local concerns, why, then, he could vote any damn foolish liberal way he pleased on national macro issues like welfare, crime, education, affirmative-action-as-now-practiced, as well as a few dozen other items.

"All politics is local" was a tactical notion that helped make possible the substantive nature of modern liberalism. The Contract was an in-your-face challenge to O'Neill's law of localism and personalism. In surfacing the Contract so prominently, Gingrich tried to "nationalize" the elections.

The Democrats, in suicide mode, did what they could to help Gingrich. Led by Bill Clinton, they savagely and publicly attacked the Contract. Tony Coehlo, former congressman and congressional Democratic whip, working as a political adviser to the White House, saw the Contract as "our big break . . . a gift from heaven . . . I think we can win on it." Coehlo saw the congressional race as between "Clintonism and Reaganism." Democrats around the country echoed this view.

After the huge election victory by the Republicans, Coehlo told the *New Republic*'s Ruth Shalit that he was actually right but got ambushed by Alzheimer: "I haven't seen this written anywhere," he said. "I think the Reagan announcement on (the) Friday (before Election Day) [that he has Alzheimer's disease] is basically what did it. . . . Our polling showed the numbers were moving with us. But when he announced he had Alzheimer's . . . it was all over the evening news. And the country reacted. All of a sudden sympathy set in for the guy. I think it really stopped us. I don't know what else could have happened."

Interviews with a number of Congressional candidates, of both parties, indicate that whatever the "what else" was, it started moving toward the Republicans from four to eight weeks before Election Day. As for Reagan, almost two months before the election and the announcement of his illness, and several weeks before the announcement of the Contract, a *Times Mirror* poll (September 9–11, 1994) asked an interesting question:

> *Of all the U.S. presidents who have been elected* SINCE YOU FIRST STARTED FOLLOWING POLITICS *which* ONE *do you think has done the* BEST *job?"*

Reagan finished in first place with 22 percent. President John F. Kennedy, who has usually led such polls, finished second with 19 percent. The results were devastating to Clinton. He finished in seventh place with 6 percent. George Bush beat him with 11 percent.

Coehlo had been interviewed earlier by Michael Kelly in the *New Yorker* and said, "Ideas are not the issue." (That is another recent liberal line, logically paired with "all politics is local." It also theoretically allows liberals to vote liberally and pay no price on election day.)

Ideas were surely the issue *after* the election. Gingrich pounced. By making the case in advance that the Contract was a covenant with the voters regarding ten specific items, he was able to claim somewhat credibly that most prized of political rewards, a "mandate."* Moreover, the Contract mandate set up a chain reaction into issues far beyond what was in the Contract itself.

———

But a mandate for what? Without stretching the point of this book beyond where it will go, let us consider the Contract in our terms. It was a blatantly antiliberal document; every item in it concerns something that conservatives have believed for a long time. It did not deal with cultural issues. Prayer in school was not mentioned. Neither was abortion. Not even gays in the military.

———

* Even though it is true that only a minority of voters had heard about the Contract. Of course, even a small minority of voters, changing their minds, can create a landslide. Lincoln and Kennedy were elected by minorities.

Many of the items, although important, were procedural. The two thoroughly substantive issues concerned crime and welfare. The proposed Contract *crime* bills concentrated on more prison space to enable more incapacitation. The Contract *welfare* proposal sought to turn the system over to the states, thereby removing it from entitlement status, sure to reduce its value over time. It further sought to eliminate cash benefits for out-of-wedlock families if the mothers are under eighteen, setting up a strong disincentive for out-of-wedlock birth. Thus, regarding both crime and welfare; no more something for nothing.

During the campaign, and after, Gingrich had a trademark line that came to embody the Republican charge, and whose theme should be somewhat familiar to readers of this book:

> No civilization can survive with 12-year-olds having babies, with 15-year-olds killing each other, with 17-year-olds dying of AIDS, with 18-year-olds getting diplomas they can't even read."*

Hmm . . . Not a word about the economy.

Not by accident many of the other items of the Contract also touch on the intertwined themes of responsibility, discipline, and something for something. Consider: (1) The proposed balanced budget amendment, which in theory means that the government could no longer irresponsibly spend more than it receives; (2) a balanced budget, which would do that in seven years; (3) tax reduction, which drives deeper spending cuts, which reduce the amounts available to government to offer something-for-nothing goodies, and specifies a $500 per child tax

---

* There were several variations on Gingrich's riff, including this one from Jo Baylor, a Republican black woman from Austin, Texas, who ran (and lost) for Congress in 1994: "It is impossible to maintain civilization with 12-year-olds having babies and carrying coloring books to the delivery room, 14-year-olds taking guns to school to feel safe, 15-year-olds dying of AIDS because they haven't learned the meaning of abstinence, 18-year-olds getting diplomas they can't read, 21-year-olds who are grandmothers, 31-year-olds who've never held a job, and 65-year-olds who sleep on the floor out of fear of drive-by shootings."

credit, a favorite of the Christian Right because it helps out in raising a family; (4) legal reform, which limits the irresponsible use of litigation, by reducing the bonus for something-for-nothing nuisance lawsuits; (5) unfunded mandates, which deny the federal government the right to irresponsibly make laws that the states have to pay for; (6) regulatory reform which makes it harder for federal guideline writers to demand something for nothing.

The Contract was mostly seen as an attempt to reduce the role of government. Many Republicans often expressed that view: The voters, they said, were "antigovernment."

I think what voters heard during the dialogue was a bit different. How about: "Anti-what-government-has-been-doing-that-doesn't-work-and-has-been-hurting-us." This will be explored later. In any event, these can be closely related concepts, at least in the early stages of reform.

What was hard to see on that September morning in 1994 became much clearer by mid-1995. The contract wasn't about ten items in a hundred days. It was about the whole realm of government and about the American way of life. It was less about 100 days than 100 months, or more.

———————

Most Republicans and conservatives saw the difference—both tactical and substantive—between social and cultural issues. If there was much doubt about the correlation of forces between those matters it began to get clearer shortly after the landmark 1994 election.

Speaker-designate Gingrich said that as soon as work on the Contract was finished, he would bring up a prayer-in-school amendment. Then he backed off. Here is a sample of the reaction he got from Republicans:

Ralph Reed [executive director of the Christian Coalition]: "I want to make it perfectly clear that this is not our top priority. . . . I, for one, don't think we'll turn the country around by having public acts of piety. Our priorities are tax relief and welfare reform."

Beverly LaHaye [president and founder of Concerned Women for America, a group that favors the agenda of religious conservatives]: "I don't know what magician is going to write this language. But it's going to be interesting to see. We have a huge problem here. Prayer is not supposed to divide people but to bring them together. So if prayer is going to be the battleground, maybe we should sit back and take a long look at it."

Sen. Robert Dole: Said the Senate should concentrate on legislation it can pass, rather than get "bogged down" in protracted debate over a school prayer amendment.

And so, for quite a while, Gingrich stopped speaking about prayer in the schools.

What happened regarding abortion was an even greater tip-off. Prayer in school had been sort of a sidebar issue among conservative Republicans. Not so abortion. For millions of Americans who care deeply about it, the antiabortion posture of the Republican party was a large part of its defining essence.

Yet, surely, this cultural issue was divisive among Republicans. The Houston convention had been unsettling. Bush's subsequent loss was a big loser for the prolife movement. No longer could prolife Republicans say the party wins when there is a tough antiabortion plank in the platform, as was the case with Reagan twice and Bush once. Moreover, President Clinton's subsequent appointment to the Supreme Court of two prochoice justices meant that *Roe* v. *Wade* was not going to be overturned any time soon. The prolife forces would (at least temporarily) have to work mostly within the parameters of the Supreme Court ruling in *Webster* v. *Reproductive Health Services*, which allowed states to limit only some aspects of legal abortion.

There was another reason that Republicans moved very slowly on the cultural issues. Something potent was in the air that Republicans sniffed: the intoxicating aroma of presidential victory. And, it was obvious, the way to maximize Republican chances was through coalition politics.

The religious right had already moved a long way in that direction. In 1992 a strange situation occurred in Georgia. The Democratic senatorial incumbent, liberal prochoice Wyche Fowler, won a slight plurality of the vote on election day but not a majority, as required under Georgia law. This meant a runoff election between Fowler and Republican challenger Paul Coverdell.

Coverdell was quite conservative, but he was also prochoice. The Christian right, vigorously prolife, had to make a call, and they made it. They solidly supported Coverdell, the prochoice conservative who, on November 24, 1992, narrowly won the runoff against Fowler.

Lesson: The Christian right is not a single-issue group.

A similar situation occurred in Texas in 1992. Kay Bailey Hutchinson was a conservative prochoice Republican. She was not the first pick of prolife Republicans in the primary election. But when she won, the prolifers backed her enthusiastically over Bob Kreuger, a Democrat more liberal than Hutchinson.

With this sort of background, we can understand the frustration of the antiabortion Republicans. They felt they were compromising and coalescing when necessary, but mainstream Republicans would not often cooperate with them. (As in Virginia in 1993 when Michael Farris, a fundamentalist lawyer, ran for lieutenant governor, and in 1994 when Oliver North ran for the U.S. Senate. In each case moderate Republicans gave little support to these Republican nominees or abandoned them completely.)

Early in February 1995, Ralph Reed of the Christian Coalition had made this tough prolife statement:

Pro-life and pro-family voters, one-third of the (Republican) electorate,* will not support a party that retreats from its noble and historic defense of traditional values and which has a national ticket or a platform that does not share Ronald Reagan's belief in the sanctity of human life. . . . There are still those who claim to be our leaders, and even those who aspire to be

---

* One-third may be a somewhat high estimate for the "religious right," according to some public opinion analysts. Karlyn Bowman, AEI's expert on survey research, thinks that depending on how the term is defined 25%–30% is closer to the mark. Either way, it's a lot.

our president, who state that the social issue must ride at the back of the bus, and that innocent life simply doesn't matter. And they even propose that they balance the ticket in 1996 by choosing someone who is liberal on the issue of human life.*

Reed's comment was interpreted to mean that the Christian Coalition would not support the GOP if even the *vice-presidential* nominee was prochoice. As fate would have it, the first GOP "cattle show" of potential 1996 candidates was scheduled on February 19, 1995, in Manchester, New Hampshire, just nine days after Reed's comment, and one year before the 1996 New Hampshire primary.

The rhetoric that came forth that evening could not have been mistaken for Houston 1992. Nine putative Republican candidates for president appeared in Manchester. Three candidates, Senators Bob Dole and Phil Gramm and Governor Lamar Alexander, each said he was prolife but welcomed prochoice voters into a big GOP tent. Senator Arlen Specter and former Secretary of Labor Lynne Martin announced that they were prochoice and supported a big tent, such tent to be made truly large if the 1996 Republican platform would please remain silent on abortion. And—reach for your Richter Scale—even Pat Buchanan preached GOP inclusion, while mentioning that he was pro-life in a quite subdued way. Only two bottom tier candidates, Alan Keyes of Maryland, hell-and-brimstone orator, and Congressman Bob Dornan, a fiery prolife right-winger, made a strong prolife case.

Soon Reed let the word out that his remarks had been taken out of context. (Later, Reed gave a dramatic speech to the B'nai B'rith's Anti-Defamation League, acknowledging that Christian fundamentalists had on occasion been insensitive to Jewish concerns and that the phrase sometimes used by some on the religious right, a "Christian nation" was inappropriate. He also stressed that evangelicals, much like Jews, were often caricatured unfairly.)

Professional Democrats were not speaking publicly during this by-play, but they were not happy. It was becoming plausible that the 1996 Republican platform would (A) drop the plank for a constitutional

---

* Reed's use of the term "social issue" would coincide with the use here of "cultural issue."

amendment making abortion illegal (unlikely) or, (B) water it down (likely). If that happened, the moderate prochoice suburban wives of conservative Republican businessmen, some of whom defected in 1992, would be more likely to stick with the GOP this time.

In mid-April 1995, Pat Robertson commented that even he could live with a platform plank that no longer contained a call for a consti-tutional "human life" amendment. Quoted in the *Washington Times*, he said:

> There is no way, given the present makeup of Congress, that we could get a two-thirds vote for a constitutional amendment banning abortion. It's just not possible. . . .
>
> I don't want to make any statements about the platform right now, but I certainly will work with people to craft something that's significant.

Surprisingly, in the early months of 1995, the Republicans were showing every sign of intelligent political behavior. They had maxi-mized their remarkable congressional victory by linking it to a mandate for major social, procedural, and budgetary change. They dominated the political agenda and, through that, the political media. They had abjured the cultural issues like prayer and abortion. They had ex-panded their social program by endorsing only affirmative action with-out the as-now-practiced part of it. They understood that values matter, and social issues matter most of all. Nine of the ten Contract items were passed by the House by the ninety-fourth day of the session. The Republican Revolution had turned the bow of the ship of state to the right.

Let us look at the Democratic situation in early 1995 with two thoughts in mind. Democrats are not complete idiots. Politicians, like generals, tend to refight their last successful war.

How could the Democrats deal with (1) an apparent conservative tide, (2) a 100-day Contract agenda in which each item ran above 70 percent favorable in the public opinion surveys, (3) an incredibly productive and publicized conservative Speaker of the House, and (4) a probable Democratic presidential ticket that would likely be headed by an unpopular and untrusted incumbent president who wants to run for a second term?

How? One way was to reunify Democrats left and center. Another way was to refight Houston, trying to redemonize Republicans and split them apart, center from right. A third way was to do all of it at once, which seems to be what happened.

Reunification. At the Democratic Leadership Council annual dinner in December 1994, Clinton urged DLCers to "join me in the arena, not in the peanut gallery." That left two unanswered questions: Who had put the Democratic centrists in the peanut gallery for two years? Who wasn't putting them in the arena now? (No DLCers were appointed to important jobs in the aftermath of the 1994 election. Still, White House leakers kept saying the president was moving toward the center. And, in fact, Clinton's pollster/consultant of yore, Richard Morris, now mostly a *Republican* pollster/consultant, was soon in regular touch with the president. Privately, after the trouncing by the Republicans and the press comment that he was becoming "irrelevant," the president was saying "I want my presidency back.")

Redemonization. Just as Republicans wanted America to forget abortion, Democrats, Clinton especially, wanted America to remember abortion.

Like most other successful politicos, Clinton believes in the adage that it is wonderful to turn chicken shit into chicken salad. He had his shot at such alchemy when the nomination of Dr. Henry Foster, an apparently wise choice, ran into deep trouble. Clinton had a problem: how could he get voters to forget the cultural liberalism of his first appointee as surgeon general, the outspoken Arkansas fireball, Dr. Jocelyn Elders, recently fired by Clinton? (Elders had denounced Catholic priests, said we should think seriously about legalizing marijuana, thought condoms for kids were swell, and had enunciated a hands-on view of masturbation.)

Who could be better than Foster, a soft-spoken, distinguished black obstetrician-gynecologist who had spent much time promoting a program to discourage teenaged out-of-wedlock birth? Alas, following his nomination it was revealed (alternatively) that he had performed one, fewer than ten, thirty-nine, or perhaps seven hundred abortions. Further (according to his detractors) Foster had participated in involuntary abortions on mentally incompetent women and had been aware of the infamous medical experiment at Tuskegee Institute where black syphilitics had been denied medication in order that doctors might study the progress of the disease. Dr. Foster vigorously denied any wrongdoing.

The Clinton vetters had obviously messed up, and not for the first time. In a way it was Guinier redux. The vetters, so immersed in a liberal cultural commune for so long, apparently did not think it relevant to delve thoroughly into the abortion issue with a nominee who was an OB/GYN.

Many Republicans in the Senate thought they had a free vote. They could come out against Foster on the grounds of both his apparent dissembling about his background and the White House bumbling regarding his appointment. This would (they thought) gain them a gold star from their prolife supporters, without much alienating their prochoice voters.

Shrewdly, Clinton stuck with Foster, an obviously decent man. Clinton made the case that the Republicans were, in effect, outlawing abortion, by turning down a distinguished doctor who had performed about *one abortion per year, legally,* over nearly forty years of practice. Republicans, by Clinton's scenario, were zealous right-wingers on this cultural matter. It was a Democratic wedge issue.

After much political tambourine-rattling, Foster was denied nomination when he could not muster the GOP votes necessary to prevent a filibuster. But Clinton had turned Foster into chicken a la king. He drove a wedge into the Republican party, trying to separate prochoice Republicans from the GOP, just the tactic executed in Houston.

Stall. 'Twas the season for wedges, perceived wedges, and reverse wedges. The liberal media have a big problem with wedges. Not this author. So-called wedge issues are usually good for the polity. If people are angry, it is usually best to air that anger in the political marketplace.

The issue of wedges surfaced in earnest when affirmative action and quotas came onto the table. On a Sunday talk show, Senator Dole said he had asked the Congressional Research Service for a review of all affirmative action laws. At the New Hampshire cattle show, Lamar Alexander said, "Equal opportunity in this country does not mean treating people as groups." In his announcement statement at College Station, Tx., candidate Phil Gramm said that if elected, he would immediately issue an executive order that would "overturn quotas, preferences and set-asides." Dole then announced he was against the current application of affirmative action (acknowledging that he had earlier fought in favor of the policy). A political tide, long dormant but always present, was gathering strength.

In California, the speaker of the California House, Willie Brown, a long-time dynamic liberal black leader, denounced the racial climate as akin to Nazism. On television, Congressman Charles Rangel described what was happening as "like Hitler."

Democrats were deeply concerned. This was a potential wedge issue of nuclear proportions. A solid majority of white Democrats are opposed to affirmative-action-as-now-practiced. The black Democratic leadership, speaking for the most solid bloc of Democratic voters, said there were no quotas in America, everyone hated quotas, and affirmative action was being demonized, although it was doing so much good for minorities, for women, and for white male Americans, even though most of them might not realize it.

It didn't take long for Clinton to enter the debate, on several sides, trying to keep his coalition together. At a press conference right after the New Hampshire Republican meeting, Clinton said that he too "had ordered a review of [his] Administration's support for affirmative action programs" and that "we shouldn't be defending things we can't defend. So it's time to review it, discuss it, and be straightforward about it." But, said President Straightforward, he was determined to prevent the debate over affirmative action "from becoming another cheap, political, emotional wedge issue."

Affirmative action was a wedge-hedge special. Clinton was accusing his nasty opponents of using a wedge issue by playing the race card. That became his wedge issue. Meanwhile, his hedge was to look for ways to adopt at least some of the views of his opponents.

Sure enough, the Clinton Justice Department soon sued Illinois State University for reverse discrimination. At issue was the case of a white male Illinois resident who sought admission to a six-month program in which learners are certified as "probationary building service worker," a job that often used to be called "janitor." ISU had refused to consider applicants who were neither minorities nor females. In a press release, Assistant Attorney General Deval L. Patrick said, "Cases involving employment discrimination against white men are rare, but no less important, than cases involving minorities and women." (Existing guidelines and court decisions have effectively made it legal to discriminate against white males, which makes such cases "rare.")

The potency of the quota wedge issue within the Democratic party soon became apparent. Under intense pressure from black and feminist leaders, the Clinton White House started leaking word that their review wouldn't really roll back anything significant in the realm of affirmative action. (In fact, one purpose of Clinton's study of the issue was to set up a holding action while waiting to see how the politics developed and how certain Supreme Court cases would be decided.)

The old splits and schisms within the party soon surfaced anew. The chairman of the Democratic Leadership Council, Senator Joseph Lieberman (D-Conn.) weighed in. Taking questions at a press conference, Lieberman said he favored "outreach" but "group preferences are wrong, it's just not consistent with American values."

I interviewed Reverend Jesse Jackson in mid-March 1995, shortly after Lieberman's statement. He said that on the issue of affirmative action, "Lieberman and Helms are indistinguishable." (Senator Jesse Helms, R-N.C., former segregationist, and arch-conservative.) Jackson, who heads the national Rainbow Coalition, said that members of the Connecticut Rainbow were holding rallies against Senator Lieberman, in his home state. That is not a trivial act in American politics.

(Contacted about Jackson's Helms-Lieberman comparison, Lieberman said: "If we can't find a way to discuss these problems without polarization, this country really will be in trouble. I am as committed as ever to civil rights and equal opportunity. I support some forms of affirmative action. But some of it has gone too far." In an op-ed piece in the *New York Daily News* DLC president Al From wrote, "The country would be better off if the debate on affirmative action were not framed by the two Jesses.")

Jackson offered a bleak picture of America and a potential party-splitting horror show for Democrats. He said he felt that America may well be jumping ship on the cause of racial justice. It had happened before in American history he noted, following post–Civil War Reconstruction, and it brought about a "separate but equal apartheid." By putting "affirmative action" on the table, Republicans had shown themselves as "opportunists" who were "scapegoating."

Jackson reserved his toughest scorn for those Democrats who would not support the current application of affirmative action, particularly those of the DLC persuasion. He was not a happy camper in the Democratic party. He noted petulantly, "It's been twelve years since I first ran for president and I've only been invited to two Jefferson–Jackson Day dinners."

Jackson said that if Clinton didn't hang tough on affirmative action *and* start up a big program for urban infrastructure, he would likely run for president on a third-party line. Asked how he could handle the sure-to-come comment (if Clinton loses) that "Jesse Jackson brought down the party," Jackson was not troubled. He said that he had campaigned in more states than Clinton did in 1994, and that he's the one, not Clinton, who had brought in 6 million new voters to the Democratic ranks.

It's a no-win situation for Democrats. If Clinton (or any other Democratic candidate for president) follows the track Jackson outlined, he will be seen as a liberal Old Democrat, still favoring racial preference and big government spending. Such a perception would bolster the view that Democrats have become the party of minorities and would further erode Clinton's center constituency, including Reagan Democrats. Without such voters, it is hard to see how Clinton can win in 1996.

If Clinton rejects the Jackson approach and Jackson then runs an independent candidacy, the results would likely drain off at least some black and hard-core liberal Democratic votes in important states. Even a small loss of such votes could close down most plausible paths to reelection.

Clinton continued to play both sides of the issue. In April 1995, he appeared before a convention of the California Democratic party. He said, "We need to defend, without any apology whatever, anything we're doing that is right and decent and that lifts people up," but also that "affirmative action supporters must understand that this is psychologically a difficult time for a lot of white males—the so-called angry white male."

More reunification. A politician in trouble has to protect his "base." In April 1994, an anonymous Clinton aide told columnist Morton Kondracke that what was going on at the White House was a "panderama." In early May, columnist Paul Gigot of the *Wall Street Journal* labeled the phenomenon the "Pander Primary." (And back in 1992 candidate Paul Tsongas had called candidate Bill Clinton a "Pander Bear.")

Indeed. In the spring of 1995 Clinton began touching all his bases, in a quite remarkable pander parade: promises to farmers, veterans, Jews, blacks, trial lawyers, the elderly, unions, and educrats, all of which broke the hearts of DLC-type Democrats. In apparent further deference to his pro–big government pro-special interest base, Clinton, the self-styled budget cutter, decided to ignore the budget deficit for a while and submitted a fiscal year 1996 budget unbalanced as far as the eye could see. President Pander.

More redemonization. The Clintonistas and the Democrats said that extremist Republicans had declared a "war on children."

After all, Democrats said, if cash welfare to teenaged mothers of illegitimate babies is cut off, some of those babies may suffer. If SSI for disabled children is cut back, poor disabled children would be harmed. If welfare is devolved back to the states and "capped," there won't be enough money for welfare when America next goes into a recession, and innocent children will suffer. If school lunch programs are cut back, kids go hungry. If food stamps are capped and not allowed to grow as an entitlement program, kids also go hungry as the population increases and inflation takes its toll. Vice President Gore said that proposed Republican cuts for the Public Broadcasting System (PBS) were part of the war on children. It would hurt kids because they would no longer see Big Bird and Barney.

And so it went. Of course, Republicans saw it differently. Some of the school lunch monies were going to middle-class children, not poor ones. The use of food stamps had been growing wildly, to a point where (in 1993) about one in ten Americans received food stamps. Moreover, they said, Big Bird would surely survive in a private television system.

Republicans made the case that welfare as we know it isn't helping the poor: it's hurting the poor. Children born out of wedlock have the cards stacked against them. Stopping cash payments to unmarried mothers under age eighteen would cut back the enabling legislation that had (with the best of intentions) contributed so much to the cycle of dependency and illegitimacy.

Republicans said it was the Democratic welfare state that had waged war on kids. Democrats said the welfare state had saved kids and proposed Republican solutions were draconian. It is a big, long argument, probably worth several elections to sort out.

––––––––––

The demonization strategy by the Democrats is focused on the proposition that Republicans have become more conservative, to a point of zealotry. If Democrats can make that case stick, it's a winner.

On balance, I don't believe it's true. At early points in the ongoing argument, conservative Republicans do often sound very tough. Tarzan-like, they grunt, "Ugh, watch out, we big tough guys, we cut government, we roll back welfare state, we make Great Society go away."

But in reality, compared to what conservatism used to be in America, most conservatives today are teddy bears. The tough-guy stuff covers up a much-disguised fact of American politics: Contrary to common belief, in many important respects conservatives are more liberal than they used to be.

The country is moving rightward toward a new center, while conservatives have moved leftward on many issues, toward that new, righter, center.

Thus, when the conservatives put the issue of quotas and/or affirmative action on the table, they supported it in an interesting way: by quoting Martin Luther King, Jr., and Hubert Humphrey in support of a color-blind society that will not judge people "by the color of their skin, but by the content of their character"—just as intoned in Dr. King's soaring cadences. This is not how most conservatives stated the issue in the early 1960s.

Or consider immigration. It's said that Republicans are against it, which proves how truly retrograde they are. Look at how terrible Proposition 187 was in California! But what Republicans (most of them) are against is *illegal* immigration. Listen someday to Newt Gingrich talk about (legal) immigration; he thinks it's the magic stuff that makes America the greatest. So does the majority leader, Dick Armey. Phil Gramm too. (He's married to a Korean-American.)

This not-really-very-conservative posture can be seen even in the Contract with America. The heart of the crime proposals could have easily been summed up with a sentence like this: "We have to prevent crime and punish criminals, not explain away their behavior." That line comes from the 1992 Clinton campaign, but the Republican language is just as good. The welfare part of the Contract proposes to—what?—end welfare as we know it. That's what Clinton said he would do. If Clinton ran that way in 1992, how conservative could it be?

(A former colleague of mine on the LBJ staff says, "Newt uses the word 'opportunity' almost as much as Johnson did.")

In fact, a good deal of the Contract, and subsequent Republican proposals after the first hundred days, could fit under Clinton's pledge of "No More Something for Nothing." The Republicans seek to shut down that part of the something-for-nothing state that has proved harmful: criminal justice without sufficient incapacitation, welfare without sufficient disincentive, quotas without merit, and education with political correctness.

Still, Democrats say Republican proposals confuse "No More Something for Nothing" with just plain "No More." That's what much of the 1996 election will be about.

Chapter 15

THE REPUBLICAN EVOLUTION

A new entry to the PCHF (Political Cliché Hall of Fame) made an appearance in the early part of 1995. It was said by some observers of the political scene that "there is no center."

If so, this would be very troubling, for America. When sages and pundits say there is no center they mean there is both a very conservative element and a very liberal element at work in our politics—and not much in the middle. That can easily lead to polarization, divisiveness, and tumult. Perhaps worse.

I have a double-vested extra interest in explaining and demonstrating why this is not so. In *The Real Majority* Scammon and I put forth three main ideas: (1) that the social tide was rising; (2) that the bulk of the electorate was middle aged, middle class and middle minded; and (3) *that elections are won at or near the center of the politico-ideological spectrum.*

About item 3, we noted that "the winning coalition in America is the one that holds the center ground on an attitudinal battlefield," that "the only extreme that is attractive to the large majority of American voters is the extreme center," and (largely ignored in the controversy about the book) that this middle ground was not a constant but a *"moving attitudinal center."* The shifting center, we believed, tended to move slowly, but it did move and the process underwrote both healthy stability and healthy change in America. But if now "there is no center" then *The Real Majority* might have been wrong—or might not have stood the test of time. It was not wrong. It has stood the test of time.

In this book I maintain that values issues have become paramount. I say that they have reached such an exalted state because they reflect the views of the broad middle ground of the American electorate, just that very moving attitudinal center of *The Real Majority,* composed now of voters fed up with some of the excessive fruits of liberalism, particularly in the realm of social issues. If now "there is no center," it might be that the victories of values we have seen in recent politics have been won on extremist grounds, perhaps by demagoging to angry white men. If so, the executors of such victories might seek extremist remedies. That's not what happened as America's new politics revealed itself through most of 1995.

Successful societies do not need revolutions, but they do demand vigorous evolution toward the moving attitudinal center.

What happened during the spring and summer of 1995, after the first hundred days in the time of the Newtoids, offered fine examples of that political tropism toward the moving center—in the Congress, the Presidency, the Courts, and the country. Such a tropism illuminated the ideas stressed here—that values matter, that social issues matter most, that what politics caused politics can cure, that what liberals caused conservatives can cure, that (perhaps) what liberals caused liberals can cure, all the while governing within the ever-changing consensus of the great American middle.

Wouldn't it be most unusual if "there was no center" at a time when voter self-identification as "moderate" had climbed eight points from 33 percent to 41 percent while "liberal" had declined by six points and "conservative" rose by three points? Wouldn't it be unusual if "there was no center" when the number of voters identifying themselves as "independent" was at an all-time high? (See public opinion Indicators.)

What we saw in 1995, through the end of August, is a foretaste of the political struggle we will be hearing and seeing, weighing and judging, until Election Day of 1996, and for many years to come after that—I bet well into the next century.

Let us look at a few examples of what went on in 1995, after the 100 days of the Contract were concluded in early April. The values issues were front and center.

SCENE-SETTER

In late June I went to Dayton, Ohio, and one night spent four hours talking to nineteen people, divided into two focus groups. The key "voter screens" for recruiting the panels were total family income no lower than $25,000 nor higher than $75,000, suburban residence, registered voters, ideological and party balance, with an education level no higher than a bachelor's degree. (Pollster Fred Steeper, who organized the sessions, believes that participants with advanced degrees tend to lecture other participants too much and mess up a focus group.) We were looking for the kind of voters who swing elections one way or the other in America.

There are no typical Americans, but these nice folks were surely not *un*typical. Here are some sentiments and opinions that emerged:

- *Washington.* "All they do is bicker." "Why don't they stop bickering and do something?"
- *The Economy.* It's harder to make a living these days. You need two earners. Balance the federal budget. Don't cut Medicare. Instead, cut out all those silly government studies. *But that won't balance the budget.* Don't cut Medicare! (Not asked, alas: Should Medicare be saved to prevent it from going broke? Note: Only a few of the panelists were elderly people.)
- *America.* It's on the wrong track. *Why?* (Boom! Here the conversation became animated.) Because there is a moral decline. People aren't taking care of their children, we're asking the schools to do

that, and they can't. Too many Moms are working. Most families don't really need two earners. That's greedy. Live on less and take care of your kids. That's a big reason we have crime, welfare, illegitimacy. Foolish government policies contribute to this. We need more discipline and personal responsibility. America is still the greatest country.

- *Race.* It's not a racial problem. There are plenty of whites ripping off the welfare system, plenty of white illegitimate births, plenty of white criminals. Affirmative action is OK in principle but quotas are terrible. Some panelists offered case histories of quota hiring. (One panel had no blacks on it, the other had one. The tenor and texture of the conversation was roughly the same in each group.)

- *Cultural Issues.* Hollywood better clean up its act. Television is too violent, too sexual, disgusting. *Should there be censorship?* Yes. Sure. You bet. *By the government?* Well, no, not by the government. The movie companies and the television networks ought to do it. It's our fault, really, we're the ones who watch the stuff. *Homosexuality?* Let people live their own lives. *Gays in the military?* No problem, said most of the women. Big problem, said most of the men, particularly veterans. *Should abortion be legal?* Most thought so, but no one is going to change the minds of those who didn't.

- *Politics.* We need more toughness. Economic issues, jobs, and social services are important, but moral, social, and cultural concerns are more important. Republicans are more likely to understand that than Democrats. But the Dayton 19 would probably have voted, grudgingly, for Clinton against a Republican. The Daytonites saw Republicans as the party of the well-off. (Everett Ladd, Director of the Roper Center, thinks the luke-warm Clinton sentiment is misleading. "This is exactly what we saw in 1979 for Jimmy Carter. But that was a presidency in deep trouble, and so is Clinton's.")

- *Candidates. Newt Gingrich:* seen as a cartoon character. *Bob Dole:* known by all, but standing for what? *Jesse Jackson:* seen as a showboat. *Bill Clinton:* got sympathy, "He tried to do something"; "He's doing the best he can"; "Get off his back about Whitewater and sex." *General Colin Powell:* will be discussed in a minute.

The Dayton 19 were smart folks. They hadn't noticed much of the big change going on in Gingroid Washington. (In fact, almost all the change was still on paper, typically passed by the House, still under negotiation in the Senate, with the President and his veto pen still to play a part.) There was little racial animosity (it may be taboo to mention it). The Republicans had not yet convinced the Dayton cross-sectional panelists that they can get tough but not mean, and think about plain people. The Democrats had not yet convinced them that they can be tough too.

Nineteen swallows do not a summer make. But these nineteen panelists were people of the moderate middle, not wing-nuts or extremists, deeply concerned about values.

THE POWELL POTENTIAL

By mid-1995, the Colin Powell for President idea was getting serious, and very interesting. Unremarked upon, but unmistakable, planned or unplanned, Powell occupied a unique spot on the political turf: a values candidate, of the political center, from outside the political system.

At the Dayton focus groups, Steeper asked each panel who they would like to see as president in 1996, and mentioned a list, including Clinton, Dole, Gingrich, Jesse Jackson, and Colin Powell. Both panels favored Powell. In one panel, the instant Steeper finished asking his question the panelists erupted, almost in unison, "Powell," "Powell, "Powell."

In late June the ABC program "Nightline" presented Powell with a Valentine of the first magnitude. Correspondent Jeff Greenfield noted that Powell was "probably the single most compelling speaker in the United States today." Greenfield went on to say that "the message of (Powell's speech) absolutely resonates with everyone from inner-city black kids to Midwest conservative religious white folks, and the message is a blend of sacrifice, hard work, pride, humor, inspiration, love of country, 'we're all one family . . .' it's a brilliant political message." Yes it is.

The Powell potential is serious because some of the arguments against it are not. It's said that third party or independent candidacies are unusual and must be taken with a grain of salt. It's said that it's very hard to get a new party or a new candidate qualified on fifty state ballots. It's said "sure, he's popular now, but wait until he has to take a hundred positions." It's said that voters flee from third party candidates as Election Day nears because they come to believe that "he can't win" and then choose between those who can.

Major third party candidates are not unusual. In this century they have been almost commonplace: Theodore Roosevelt (1912), Robert LaFollette (1924), Henry Wallace and Strom Thurmond (1948), George Wallace (1968), John Anderson (1980), and Ross Perot (1992).

Ross Perot didn't say he was interested in running until just nine months before the election. It can be done, even late in the season.

Don't buy the idea that Powell would have to take a hundred specific positions. A candidate who can talk credibly about "sacrifice, hard work, pride, humor, inspiration, love of country . . ." doesn't have to get too specific. Clinton ran by saying he'd "end welfare as we know it." Is that specific? And Perot's best thought was, roughly, "there are lots of good ideas around Washington. I can sort 'em out without being pushed by special interest groups." Running as an independent, Powell could accomplish that, better than Perot.

Don't believe that a third party candidate can't win. A June 1992 Gallup poll showed Perot with 39 percent, Bush with 31 percent, and Clinton with 25 percent, making Clinton the third man out. In an ABC poll in June 1995 Powell beat Clinton, head-to-head, 47 percent/39 percent.

In July of 1992 Perot dropped out of the race. Then he re-entered. Three weeks before the election Perot's poll ratings were averaging about 11 percent. Experts expected further shrinkage as voters said, "he can't win." He got 19 percent.

It is true that third party, new party, or independent candidates rarely win. It has only happened in 1860, when Abraham Lincoln won, with 39 percent of the vote, carrying the standard of a party that had fielded a national candidate only once before.

Powell has one obvious constituency, and a couple not so obvious. He is black, and he would get some of the black vote, from Democrats. Powell is the child of Jamaican immigrants, and could easily become the darling of many recent newcomers, some seventeen million of whom have arrived in America since 1970. He is a retired four star general, and Chairman of the Joint Chiefs of Staff during the Gulf War. He served two tours in Vietnam.

Some years ago pollster and social philosopher Daniel Yankelovich described American attitudes toward Vietnam as an "undigested lump." If you think it's since been digested, read Robert Timburg's truly wonderful book *The Nightingale's Song*. When you're finished you won't doubt that there is still smoldering anger among many of the nine million Americans who served in the military during Vietnam— veterans who, I bet, would disproportionately flock to Powell's banner.

If Powell runs as a Republican, or ends up as the Republican vice presidential nominee, he could get more-or-less locked into a platform that opponents would characterize as "conservative." That might well dilute his image as an iron-tough centrist and "outsider." Moreover, he would surely face some opposition from conservative Republicans, either in primaries, or at the Republican convention, particularly if he surfaced as a prochoice candidate.*

Hmmm . . . A good slice of thirty-three million blacks, seventeen million recent immigrants, nine million Vietnam-era veterans. Add to that an incalcuable number of white Americans who would like to vote for a black candidate to prove they are not racists and subtract a lesser number who wouldn't vote for a black, period. Then add a piece of the Americans who honor "sacrifice, hard work, and love of country . . ." which is most of us. A values candidate, of the center, from outside the political system, which has not responded to values issues. Take Powell seriously.

FROM LEFT TOWARD CENTER: CLINTON'S FLAVOR OF THE MONTH

By spring, Clinton had mostly (not entirely) de-emphasized the presidential pander primary, and looked to where the voters were, in the center of the political spectrum and attuned to the values issues.

---

* "He has told audiences that elements of the House Republican agenda are 'a little too harsh' and that he would not completely dismantle affirmative action. He has also suggested that he supports abortion rights." (Richard L. Berke, *New York Times*, July 30, 1995.) There is a word for candidates who say the House agenda is "a little too harsh," that they "would not completely dismantle affirmative action" and that they support abortion rights. They are called centrists.

Because it has appeared in book form, we can get a sense of what kind of advice Clinton had been getting from his old campaign staff. Early in 1995 *Middle Class Dreams* by Clinton's pollster Stanley Greenberg, was published. It's an interesting work, particularly if you want to find out what is still wrongheaded about the Democratic party in the era of Clinton.

Greenberg says that Americans have been doubly betrayed by their political parties. The Democrats betrayed the people with the "Great Society." And the Republicans betrayed the people with "Reaganism." (Wrong twice.) The Democrats betrayed America because "bottom up" economics hasn't worked. And the Republicans betrayed America because "top down" economics hasn't worked. (Wrong two more times.)

Bill Clinton, said his pollster, would be able to fix it. Greenberg's remedy/slogan: "accountable government with public investment."

That does not quite make it as a bumper sticker. It is also an economically driven view of politics. Whatever happened to the values-driven one of "no more something for nothing"?

Reenter Richard Morris. Because Morris did not originally hustle the media in normal ways, he became a mystery man, much sought after by the press. One Sunday morning, on the front page of the *Washington Post,* there was this headline: "Republican Advisor Stages Quiet White House Coup."

At the very end of a very long story, was this astonishing news:

One former Democratic elected official with close ties to the Clintons said the first lady as well as the President were concerned that the advice he (Clinton) was getting was "too hidebound Democrat." His influential aides are either liberal Democrats such as Harold Ickes or what the official called "congressional Democrats" such as George Stephanopoulos. Morris, with his career advising Republicans, brings "new thinking more consistent with where the country is," said the former official.

June 18, 1995

Whoa! Who appointed those people the Clintons think are "too hidebound Democrat"? Well, it was exactly "the first lady as well as the

President" who picked the mostly Johnny-One-Note liberal government, including a cause group, all-star team of civil rights, environmentalist, feminist, poverty, consumerist, and peace activists. And what about the idea that the Clintons believe that Republicans (!) have "new thinking more consistent with where the country is"? Then why were the Clintons, at the same time, scolding Republicans for advocating nasty things, like waging war on children? Did the Clintons think voters believe in terrible things like that?

It was ritual time in Clintonland again. The heralded "move to the center," or "move to the right," was back, again. Clinton promised it during his 1992 campaign. In a later incarnation (mid-1993) it involved the appointment of Republican David Gergen as White House Counselor—who was almost immediately undermined by those hidebound Democratic White House aides.*

Would Morris be Gergen redux? The same ritual seemed in play. Demoralized liberal White House staffers called Morris "the flavor of the month," and regarded him as a "one man rebellion." On the other hand the staff got older and somewhat more moderate.

In any event, Clinton moved right, toward the center.

Early in the year Clinton had proposed an idiotic budget, *with no deficit reduction.* Why? One theory was that the budget was designed so that Republicans would have to pay a full political price for every spending cut they made in the course of trying to fulfill the budget-balancing mandate of the Contract with America. The President of the United States, a man so proud of his (mostly phony) half-a-trillion-dollar deficit reduction of 1993, in effect withdrew from the economic contest in early 1995.

Soon, the buzzword on Clinton was that he was "irrelevant." In fact, on the night of April 18, Clinton gave a speech saying he was too relevant. The next morning the bombing of Oklahoma City occurred and dominated the headlines for weeks, sparing Clinton the public mockery that surely would have come to a president of the United States having to announce his relevance. (Clinton was right. Presidents are

---

* Gergen had influence for a while; by mid-1994 he went over to the State Department, and then left government service.

never irrelevant, and *will never be* irrelevant as long as the U.S. Constitution is operative.)

Another theory about Clinton's abandonment of deficit reduction held that he did it only as a Mao-like internal revolution to push the public to put pressure on his own bureaucracy to get serious about spending. Morris, so goes this theory, was Clinton's chosen instrument of reform. The liberals on the White House staff, influenced by congressional Democrats anxious to hang on to the bucks for their constituents, pushed the other way. Clinton asked for five minutes of prime time network, and on June 13, 1995 announced a *second* budget for fiscal year 1996. This one would balance the budget, not in seven years as the Republicans had, but in ten years. Liberal Democrats, who felt they had made points on items like proposed Republican cuts in the growth rate in Medicare, and could score more, felt betrayed.*

Soon, the conventional political wisdom had it that in 1996 moderate Bill Clinton would run against that easy target, liberal Bill Clinton. (Columnist and former mayor of New York City Ed Koch, reminded his *New York Post* readers that incumbent Mayor Robert Wagner, Jr., had run against his own record in New York in 1961 and won.) Liberals worried that Clinton's tropistic rush to the center would put them on the left and Republicans on the right.

Morris's hand was also seen elsewhere. In early July *sixteen months* before the general election of 1996, the Clinton campaign spent $2.6 million to put television spots on the air in 27 cities. The topic: Crime. Excerpts from the text of the commercials:

> *Narrator:* Bill Clinton did something no president has ever been able to accomplish. He passed and signed a tough law to ban deadly assault weapons.

> *Clinton:* Deadly assault weapons off our streets, 100,000 more police on the streets, expand the death penalty. That's how we'll protect America.

> *Police officer:* President Clinton is helping us make this a safer nation.

---

* The Congressional Budget Office, the official scorers, later scored the Clinton-2 budget and found no deficit reduction. Some independent budget analysts believe that the Clinton budget, based on Office of Management and Budget growth estimates, is more reliable.

Police offficer: President Clinton is right. This is not about politics. This is about saving lives.

Quite so. It is not about politics, it's about saving lives.

FROM RIGHT TOWARD CENTER:
THE CHRISTIAN COALITION

A tropism is stronger than a tendency or a trend. It is a law of nature. Clinton wasn't the only one responding to natural law.*

On May 17, the Christian Coalition issued its first "Contract with the American Family." The reaction was instructive. The Democrats chose not to play.

In the fall of 1994, not long before the Democratic drubbing at the polls, Representative Vic Fazio, the Democratic Caucus Chairman, said that Republicans were victims of a "gradual stealth takeover" by the religious right. This time, with the stealthy Christian takeover artists out there in plain sight with a ten-point program, Fazio was silent. And Mike McCurry, President Clinton's press secretary, said that while Clinton might well disagree about certain items, the President applauded the "language and the tone" of the manifesto. McCurry went on to say that "Mr. (Ralph) Reed said that the purpose of his contract is not to legislate family values, it is to ensure that Washington values families. Good quote. I think the President agrees with that 100 percent."

The Democrats were wise to lay off the demonization on this one. The Christian Coalition Contract (CCC) proposals were hard to condemn: self-described as ten suggestions not ten commandments, general not specific, without any deadline, and with many items keyed to

---

* *tropism:* "involuntary orientation by an organism or one of its parts that involves turning or curving accomplished by active movement or more often by structural alteration that constitutes a positive or negative response to a source of stimulation" (*Webster's Third New International Dictionary*).

legislation with existing congressional sponsorship, some from leading Democrats.

The CCC stand on abortion was particularly important, signaling a possible spot for compromise at the San Diego 1996 GOP convention. Gone was the controversial demand for a human life constitutional amendment which would illegalize abortion, and which has been in the Republican platform since 1980. In its place was a call to limit (not even end) "late term" abortions and "partial birth" abortions. And according to Kate Michelman, president of the National Abortion Rights Action League, only "one-hundredth of one percent of all abortions" are actually performed in the last trimester.

Hardly "extremism," even though the Christian Coalitionists viewed it as a "first step." It sets up ground where prolife and prochoice Republicans may come up with a compromise abortion platform plank.

Moderation and centrism were apparent throughout the CCC document. There was a call for private school choice, but only for twenty demonstration projects, and its existing senatorial cosponsors were Dan Coats (R-Ind.) and Joe Lieberman (D-Conn.) who is chairman of the Democratic Leadership Council. On the crime front, the keystone proposal concerns literacy and work programs for prisoners. Just who would be against that?

Prayer in the school is handled by a Religious Equality Amendment. This, say the Christian Coalitioneers, "would not restore compulsory, sectarian prayer or Bible-reading dictated by government officials." What they seek is "voluntary, student and citizen-initiated free speech in non-compulsory settings such as courthouse lawns, high school graduation ceremonies, and sports events." That's hardly language that can lead a moderate to the barricades, and in fact, a subsequent speech by Clinton covered much the same grounds, differing principally by saying no constitutional amendment was necessary to accomplish roughly the same ends.

And so it went: There was a $500 tax credit for children, a prime goal of the religious right because it provides marginal help for mothers who choose to stay home with their children; there was a provision allowing homemakers to contribute a full $2,000 share to Individual Retirement Accounts (cosponsored by liberal Senator Barbara Mikulski

[D-Md.]). The CCC also called for encouragement of donations to private charities. Those items made general sense.

Others didn't. The Legal Services Corporation has huge problems, but one of them is not that it helps poor people seeking legal divorce, which is what the CCC document chose to stress. The privatization of PBS could create a conservative nightmare—a liberal network developed with public monies. The coalitioneers trashed the notion of any federal role to help implement the idea standards-tests-stakes in public education.

In all, it was a smart and useful piece of political and substantive work. It put forth an agenda and shrank the target. It was made politically stronger when Pat Buchanan said it wasn't tough enough.

FROM HOW MUCH TO WHAT

When President Clinton decided to get back to the political center of the budget debate, he declared that he was for a balanced budget, too, but in ten years not seven, that brought Washington's budget-spinning lingo back to the megaphone: Seven years, ten years, feel the pain, get to zero, it's not really a cut it's slower growth, the Clinton assumptions are wrong, bite the bullet, be fair, don't do it on the backs of the poor, or the elderly, or the middle class. But balance it, get to zero.

There seem to be four ways of looking at the budget:

1. Deficit hawks say that we have to cut the deficit, because there is a deficit, that it's gone on too long, that if we don't cut it now it will be harder to cut later, and might grow to a ruinous proportion of the economy.
2. Liberals say don't cut it so much, don't cut it so fast, don't cut it in any way that will hurt nonrich people, and maybe don't even cut it at all.
3. Some conservatives say cut it because everything in the federal budget pertains to government and most of what government does is inherently bad. Their motto is: Starve the Tumor.

4. There are those who say cut the budget here and there because what the government is doing here and there isn't working well, or even worse, is hurting us.

Of course, there are combinations and permutations of these positions and many players subscribe to aspects of all of the above. It's a question of emphasis, and I emphasize number 4, which makes me a Fourist.

It's been more than sixty years since big government took off in the midst of the Great Depression. It's been about thirty years since Lyndon Johnson's Great Society provided a boost phase. By the late 1970s there was a growing view, often bipartisan, that it was time to review what had been done, to figure out what had worked and what hadn't.

But when the deficit rather suddenly went into orbit in the early 1980s, the emphasis changed, from "What to cut and why?" to "How much to cut and how soon?"

We are now almost fifteen years into that somewhat sterile debate. It's not only a bore, but it has stolen the emphasis from the What/Why argument the nation needs, and might even find interesting. Too bad: as it happens What/Why may well be the best way to solve How-Much/How-Soon.

I recommend Dr. Hippocrates's oath: "First, do no harm." That's good, but it's only prospective. We need retrospectivity: "First, undo past harm, gently but firmly." Accordingly, the full package of "Greater Welfare" that has encouraged dependency, illegitimacy, and crime ought to be reduced dramatically but on a program by program basis. That would help us on its merits, *and* slow down spending. Deficit hawks, alas, can't see the trees for the forest. Too bad. It's better to take down some trees and thin the forest. That's the Fourist way, and the fairest way.

DOLE GOES TO THE MOVIES

It wasn't just that conservatives of the Christian Coalition began moving *left* toward the national center, and that Clinton began to move *right* toward the national center. It wasn't just that each used values issues as their metaphors. Of course they did. Values matter most. That's what is on people's minds. Politicians want to, and often should, reflect the views of their constituents. So as election time gets closer, most elected officials try to move toward the moving center, which varies from constituency to constituency.

Senate Majority Leader Bob Dole had a particular problem with the center he was trying to find: the middle ground of those Republicans who vote in Republican primaries, a fairly conservative group, tilted toward values issues. Dole is viewed as a consummate political deal-maker, not a vision guy, not a values guy. That is not good in a values year, when the last Republican presidential nominee lost in some large part because he lacked the vision thing.

On May 31, 1995, Dole went out to Los Angeles and trashed the entertainment industry for promoting "casual violence and even more casual sex." He singled out Time-Warner for purveying the most rotten sort of "gangsta rap," ghetto music that glorifies rape, mutilation, torture, dismemberment, and murder of women.

Dole followed all the established political rules for honorable cultural politics. He named names. He delivered his lecture right in Tinseltown, the home ground of the malefactors. He dealt with a serious situation. He didn't manufacture the issue: John Leo had launched the attack on Time-Warner in *U.S. News & World Report,* and the team of Republican Bill Bennett and Democrat C. Delores Tucker already had aired television spots denouncing the company. Dole was selective, noting that, in general, "the American entertainment industry is at the cutting edge of creative excellence . . . and dominate(s) world-wide competition today." (It's even better than that.)

Dole won a political Oscar. A few days after the speech the *Washington Post* headlined:

DOLE'S BLAST AT HOLLYWOOD RESONATES—THEME HAS APPEAL
FAR BEYOND SOCIAL AND RELIGIOUS CONSERVATIVES.

Dole was lucky enough to be attacked by Hollywood liberals for endangering free expression, even though Dole abjured censorship, while peddling shamesmanship. (Similarly, Bennett and Tucker call themselves "virtual absolutists on the First Amendment.")

Dole did right. Voters deserve to know about the cultural values as well as the public policies of their potential leaders. Symbols count in politics, as in life. Worried parents can use a morale booster when arguing with their kids. And when corporate culture vultures know that political big shots will rap them publicly, they may mind their manners, particularly at companies like Time Warner, which is vulnerable to boycotts in their theme parks, retail stores, and magazines.

Fine. Sort of. Cultural politics are great signal-senders. They help politicians. They help voters who want to know that the government is on their side. But the weakness of cultural politics—and not just regarding the entertainment issue—is that it is largely ineffectual. Assume that Time Warner, under pressure, drops gangsta rap. Assume further that other big vulnerable companies do likewise (particularly German-owned Bertlesman and Japanese-owned Sony). Will that end the matter? No. Smaller companies, less vulnerable to public indignation will produce the stuff.* And if they don't, new companies will emerge to do it. Why? Adolescents buy it, yielding profits to peddlers.

That too can be stopped. By censorship. We've had it before. Except that the vast majority of Americans (69 percent to 27 percent) don't want it. They do want tighter parental supervision (93 percent to 6 percent), warning labels on records (83 percent to 15 percent), and voluntary restraint by entertainment companies (81 percent to 15 percent). But the labels tell kids it's a hot one. In perpetual rebellion mode, the kids buy the records. And new upstart culture vultures profit. That might be a plus from what we have now, but not by much.

So too with most of the stark issues of cultural politics now on the table. The proposed remedies lack either major public consensus, or appropriate governmental response, or both. There is not much the government should or could do about homosexuality. The Feds could illegalize abortion, but solid majorities don't want them to do it. The prayer in school argument, as made by the Christian Coalition, is so soft that it leads to the question: Even if you agree with it, what do you

---

* In fact, in August 1995 Time Warner was in negotiations to sell off its Interscope Records division, lead purveyors of the gangsta material. Some executives were discharged.

get from it? Any censorship laws would face tough scrutiny by a conservative court that has been quite pro–First Amendment.

Polls show that the catch-all term "values," in one form or another, is seen to be the most important issue in America. That shows voter wisdom, but not precision. The cultural part of the values issue is hard for government to deal with. Not so in the social part. In that realm there is plenty that can be done, and a broad consensus to do it. Americans want to reinstate punishment for crime, restore the disincentives to welfare, reestablish rigor in schools, and go back to an earlier nonpreferential form of affirmative action.

There is a role for cultural politics. There is a more important role for social politics. (Clinton was fuming that Dole was getting all the ink. His most widely applauded line in the 1994 State of the Union message was an attack on the entertainment business.*)

DEMOCRATIC DEFECTIONS

Also seeking their center during roughly this period of time were five Democratic members of Congress. Senator Richard Shelby, the quite conservative Democrat from Alabama, announced his switch to the Republican party in mid-November, 1994, almost immediately after the Republican landslide. That had been expected. Wholly unexpected was the turning of Senator Ben Nighthorse Campbell of Colorado, the only Native American member, who wears a bolo tie and his hair in a ponytail. It was a particularly tough defection for the Democrats, who like to regard themselves as protectors of minorities.

The three House switchers were Southern Democrats, Nathan Deal of Georgia, Billy Tauzin of Louisiana, and Greg Laughlin of Texas. It was getting harder and harder for a white Democrat to get elected in a region of the country where 61 percent of the white electorate voted Republican, and voted that way because they viewed the national Democratic party as too damn liberal, particularly on values

---

* . . . we support your freedom of expression but you do have a responsibility to assess the impact of your work and to understand the damage that comes from the incessant, repetitive, mindless violence and irresponsible conduct that permeates our media all the time."

issues, and social issues like crime, welfare, and affirmative action. Congress-watchers predicted that other Southern Democrats would join the parade, increasing the continued likelihood of a Republican-majority House. (Nine Southern Democrats voted for the GOP budget in 1995.)

When the center moves, politicians tend to move toward the new center.

CLINTON'S CULTURAL RESPONSE

There was no mistaking where Clinton was going and why he was going there. Within a blazing few weeks of political activity, Clinton:

1. Put crime commercials on the air.
2. Did not back gays in an important Supreme Court case (*Hurley v. Irish American Gay, Lesbian and Bisexual Group of Boston.*) Not long after that Clinton met with unhappy gay political leaders in the White House. (Bizarrely, when they arrived in the West Wing to pass through metal detectors and have their briefcases searched, they were met by White House guards wearing rubber gloves.)
3. Gave a speech on religion saying the Constitution did not bar most religious expression in public schools, and promised that the secretary of education and the attorney general would be sending directives to school districts explaining just what was permissible, and what wasn't, with the emphasis on what was. Clinton noted that if students went to church, synagogue, or mosque there would be less crime in America. That's probably true, but it cannot be dealt with by any law or directive that would be even vaguely constitutional.
4. Gave a speech saying that politicians should be civil to each other, and that voters were disgusted by the partisan bickering and exaggeration that has come to characterize American politics. Several days later, on a Saturday radio broadcast in mid-July, 1995, Clinton denounced Republican plans for regulation reform because they could harm and kill Americans. (Earlier he had indi-

cated that the Oklahoma City bombing might well have been engendered by "right-wing talk shows.")

5. Gave a speech endorsing the idea of a "V–Chip" for (new) television sets that would allow parents to block out violent or sexually
explicit television shows in their home, certainly those displaying
what Archie Bunker once called "noodle frontity."

6. Announced proposed new regulations to curb smoking among
teenagers.

Clinton's approval rating popped up about five points after this
flurry of cultural centrism, roughly the same amount it bounced up
after the tragedy in Oklahoma City showed Clinton in a good light.
That might sound like a ten-point increase but it wasn't. The Oklahoma City bounce wore off and Clinton's approval was about where it
had settled: in the 45 percent range. The axiom in presidential politics
is that a candidate who is lower than a 50 percent approval rating is in
serious trouble.

AFFIRMATIVE ACTION

It wasn't all cultural; it wasn't all posturing and positioning. There were
major substantive changes on the table, originating in the courts, the
Congress, and the states. All seemed to work against what the Clinton
administration had approved and applauded during the first two years
of the Clinton term.

It is said that, despite the political virginity written into the Constitution for the Supreme Court, the Justices often "follow the election
returns." In 1995, they surely did, but not the election results of 1994.
Four of the five Justices who ruled on the putatively conservative side
of the issue of affirmative action were appointed by Ronald Reagan and
George Bush, reflecting the elections of 1980, 1984, and 1988.

In *Missouri v. Jenkins* the Supremes told a Kansas City federal judge
to concentrate on ensuring that local schools do not segregate by race
but beyond that butt out: other decisions regarding magnet schools,
books, teacher salaries, classroom conditions, test scores, and white

flight to the suburbs belong to school officials, parents, and politicians. Wrote Justice Clarence Thomas: "It never ceases to amaze me that the courts are so willing to assume that anything predominantly black is inferior . . . (T)he point of the Equal Protection Clause is not to enforce strict race mixing but to insure that blacks and whites are treated equally by the state and without regard to skin color."

In *Miller v. Johnson* concerning Georgia's 11th congressional district, the Court said that districts drawn with race as the "predominant" factor are unconstitutional.

In *Adarand Constructors v. Pena* the Court said that "set-asides" for minority-owned firms are invalid unless they served a compelling national interest after strict scrutiny to determine whether any such remedy actually compensated for specific past discrimination. This is a substantially more difficult standard to meet than earlier ones, and experts believe it will limit the future range of set-asides. (Vice President Gore said that affirmative action itself *is* "a compelling national interest.")

All three decisions had certain things in common. All were seen as harmful to affirmative action, all would take years of litigation to sort out unless the Congress moved first, all were decided by razor-thin five-to-four majorities, and the two Justices appointed by Clinton (Ginsburg and Breyer) were with the minority in each case. The court rulings made things easier for Clinton in the short run, but the nature of the minority vote opened up a political opportunity for Republicans.

Clinton finally addressed the issue somewhat substantively on July 19, 1995. By the time the dust settled there was little doubt that affirmative action had become politicized and had moved to the center of the political agenda. That was very good news for the nation.

President Clinton said he was solidly in favor of affirmative action, although he did add some classic Clintonesque caveats to go with it. Governor Pete Wilson of California said Clinton was fooling us and that affirmative-action-as-now-practiced was proportionalism. Jesse Jackson said Wilson is "the Susan Smith of American politics" because he was playing politics with race. Jack Kemp said Republicans shouldn't run against affirmative action without offering something affirmative in its place. Majority Leader Bob Dole introduced legislation to do away with all federal aspects of affirmative action. Speaker Newt Gingrich said Re-

publicans will come up with an affirmative plan before cutting affirmative action. Wilson said Jackson is running for president, too. Kemp
thought Dole was moving in the right direction because he was talking
affirmatively as well as negatively. Clinton said we shouldn't play politics
with it, and after pausing for a breath, trashed Republican budget cuts.

Why shouldn't the racial issues be part of our politics? Politics is just
where the issue ought to be. One reason Americans have been so angry
about what affirmative action has become is that it came about without
serious political debate. The vast majority of practices called affirmative
action were never voted on by elected officials. Most were established by
court orders, guidelines, regulations, and political pressure applied far
from public view. Moreover, the issue has been kept out of debate in
presidential elections lest anyone be accused of "playing the race card."

There was a healthy aspect to the debate of mid-1995: Everyone
agreed it's bad to "divide America." Proponents said opponents are dividing America. Opponents said affirmative action is dividing America.

It also seemed clear where affirmative-action-as-now-practiced was
going—away. Clinton's speech showed which way the wind is blowing.
He said affirmative action has been good for America. He grew emotional as he truthfully stressed that he's always been against racism,
from his early Southern childhood (skipping over the fact that as a
young man he worked for and campaigned for a segregationist U.S.
senator, William Fulbright, to whom as president he awarded the
Medal of Freedom).

But Clinton also said what he would not "allow" in federal affirmative action procedures as he enforces the new Court rulings: (1) quotas
in theory or practice, (2) discrimination, including reverse discrimination, (3) preference for those who are not qualified. He also endorsed a
shut-down of programs that have succeeded and endorsed preference
by income and economic geography. That's pretty close to what many
opponents of affirmative action have been saying. They believe that
affirmative-action-as-now-practiced yields quotas, reverse discrimination, and preference. Proponents, of course, say most affirmative-
action-as-now-practiced doesn't do any of that at all.

How will this turn out? Play a game. It is the fall of 1996. Clinton is
running for reelection. He is being beat upon about his previously

stated pro–affirmative action view and for his choices of pro-preference Supreme Court justices. He has two ways to go. He can say that in the course of his review of federal affirmative action programs, "we have found only a few cases of abuse." Or he can say, "I've rooted out more abuse of affirmative action than any president in history." Bet on the latter. (His opponents, of course, will note that Clinton also established more quotas than any president in history.)

Certain facts will surface. Women now make up more than half of the college student population and get better grades than men. SAT scores for blacks have been climbing. New plans will surface: Republicans will say that inner city poverty is exacerbated by federal law, particularly welfare. Democrats will say it is heartless to cut welfare. Republicans will try to reform Clinton's "100,000 cops" crime bill in a way that gets the cops into the inner city where crime is highest Democrats will say that Republicans don't have clean hands on the issue of civil rights. Republicans will move more slowly than expected, trying not to alienate the center of the political spectrum, and trying to gain some black votes by showing how well conservatives can fight poverty.

It was the beginning of the right debate at the right time. One of the tragedies of the racial problems in America is that the issue has been kept out of the hurly burly of presidential politics. It belongs there because that's where America seeks its center.

CRIME

The new Republican House quickly passed six bills to reverse the items that weakened the 1994 Democratic crime bill. One bill would link federal funds to the enactment by states of serious "truth-in-sentencing" laws and increase the likelihood that violent criminals would serve longer sentences in prison. Another, called STOP ("Stop Turning Out Prisoners"), would push the federal courts to get out of the business of running prisons and diminish their ability to declare a so-called prison cap because of alleged overcrowding. It is hard to see how Clinton could veto bills so clearly in tune with mainstream public opinion. This time he will likely be shrewd enough to stare down the "anti-incarceration lobby" acting through a new activist group, called STOP STOP, formed to try to prevent any action that would limit the authority of federal judges to set prison caps.

COMES THE EVOLUTION

Writing in *The Clinton Presidency—First Appraisals*,* liberal political scientist Walter Dean Burnham of the University of Texas takes special note of the ideological fervor of the noncentrist House Republicans. He says this passion will lead to polarizing "nonincremental" changes in policy. This presumptive jolting surge to the right does not make Burnham happy.

Political scientist Norman Ornstein of the American Enterprise Institute sees things quite differently. Right after the 1994 election, when most seers were overwhelmed by the perceived rightwardness of the Gingroids in Congress and the apparent disappearance of Republican moderates, Ornstein spoke out to the contrary. "Watch the Gypsy Moths," he said, precisely the Republican moderates who were taken for dead. Ornstein also stressed that moderates of *both* political parties would hold the balance of power. That would tend to yield only *incremental* change to the center-right, not stark *nonincremental* change.

As the returns came in during the summer of 1995, through to the recess in August, Ornstein was way ahead. The center not only held, but was quite powerful. The Republican revolution turned into a vigorous Republican evolution, which is best for them, best for the country and even best for Clinton. (Truth be told, I never thought the GOP's "Contract for America" was so very revolutionary.)

For example, the tough House version of welfare reform did not survive the Senate intact. Moderates diluted it. The original Senate draft bill did not carry the House provision that would deny cash aid to teen-age mothers with illegitimate children. As the legislative process moved on, Republican conservatives and moderates tangled, and Gingrich and Dole became key players in the negotiations. The ultimate result will likely be welfare reform that is tougher than Clinton's tardy

---

* Chatham House, October 1995.

mush served up in 1994, but not as tough as the conservative House version. Vigorous evolutionary change.

That was interhouse dilution. There was intrahouse dilution going on as well. In the Senate, where some center Democratic votes are needed to prevent filibusters, Dole was not able to pass a tough regulation bill that mandated sunset clauses, cost benefit analyses and other reform ideas that some moderates thought went too far. Back to the drawing boards it went. In the House, fifty-one Republicans joined with Democrats to soften the impact of tough cuts in environmental law. Then the Republican leadership managed to push the bill through on a 210–210 tie vote, which allows passage. But tie votes do not bespeak nonincremental change as the legislative process moves forward.

There were many other straws in the moderating winds. Gingrich did not want to move forward with an anti–affirmative action bill until Republicans could replace it with a credible conservative war on poverty. White House sources kept stressing that Clinton's pro–affirmative action speech also endorsed ideas that gave preference by income and economic geography, but not by race.

The Congress was moving toward diminishing the money pot in the "Goals 2000" legislation. But states most everywhere were moving toward standards and tests, some of them with consequences.*

In Dallas in mid-August, politicians of both parties arrived to pay homage to Ross Perot and his convention of the "United We Stand" party.

Colin Powell was preparing for a book tour that would take him to every politically important spot in America and give him more television face time than all the other contenders put together.

Within the current political spectrum, both Perot and Powell should be considered centrists.

Moreover, Clinton continued to ditch or demote his populist counselors of the pro-porcine left and looked toward more centrist advisers as he continued to reinvent himself as a New Democrat for the 117th time.

---

* *Making Standards Matter—A Fifty State Report on Efforts to Raise Academic Standards* (American Federation of Teachers).

In August, *Newsweek* headlined that "A once hot Democratic political clique slips from favor," and that Stanley Greenberg, Paul Begala, and Mandy Grunwald were down or out, and Stephanopoulos was "left out of key weekly political strategy meetings with the boss." More centrist consultants, Doug Schoen and Bob Squires, joined Morris. White House spinners said there had been lots of moderates there all along, but they had been in mufti. Now, emerging from phone booths, capes flying, a small army of supermoderates would play a role. In an eleven-day span Clinton, the man who earlier sought a budget passed by "getting all the Democrats," used the term "common ground" seven times in speeches.

All this does not mean that "the center" invariably provides the best policy prescriptions. I think that the original House provision on no-welfare-to-teenage-mothers makes sense because it sends a signal that American government will no longer subsidize and encourage irresponsible behavior. But brokered end games do tend to yield safer results. The winners aren't as happy, but the losers don't go away and try to start revolutions. If it is seen that the winners are moving in the right direction, they will keep on winning, and keep on going.

America is a vastly successful nation. Such nations do not need revolutions to make progress. They do need vigorous evolutions, from the center, dealing with their most pressing problems. Amidst all the scare-talk of "train wrecks" between the Congress and the president, it seemed as if evidence was what we were getting.

A STREETCAR NAMED RETIRE

Someone else was looking for a center. In mid-August 1995, Senator Bill Bradley (D-N.J.) announced that he would not seek reelection in 1996. What he did was important. What Bradley said—that the Democratic party is ideologically bankrupt, and that he might run as an independent candidate for the presidency against Bill Clinton—was more important.

If the Democratic party goes splat!—which is not impossible—future political historians may set the clock of change ticking from the day Bradley went public with his remarkable views. Here is an excerpt from

Bradley's statement: "The Republicans are infatuated with the 'magic' of the private sector and reflexively criticize government as the enemy of freedom, and the Democrats distrust the market, preach government as the answer to our problems, and prefer the bureaucrats they know to the consumer they can't trust." That may sound like a balanced comment showing that, as Bradley also stated, all American politics "are broken." But, in fact, it is not balanced.

Bradley had been, and said he still was, a Democrat. This was a Democrat trashing his own party. And not just any old Democrat: Bradley, a former basketball star, was still ambitious at fifty-two, and hoped to have a future in public life. Moreover, in the current political climate, a party that "preaches government as the answer to our problems" is worse off than a party that "reflexively criticizes government."

Unlike most of the other elected officials who had recently jumped the Democratic ship, Bradley was no Southern conservative. He did not even quite qualify as a New Democrat of the Democratic Leadership Council stripe. Bradley had accumulated a liberal voting record: 85 to 90 percent in the Americans for Democratic Action ratings over the past few terms.

Bradley's announcement served to reinforce the image of the Democratic party as a giant colander. Jesse Jackson would probably run an independent candidacy drawing Democratic votes from blacks and the far left. By the time Bradley announced, more than one hundred elected Democrats, mostly conservatives, had already switched parties since Clinton took office—the most ever. More were on the way. Bradley's statement showed that even thoughtful liberals have reasons to look for a new political home. Politicians use political parties as vehicles. For liberal Bradley, the too-liberal Democratic party had become a streetcar named retire. (His tracks may yet cross with Colin Powell's, and Powell, running as an independent locomotive, would pull still other Democrats away from their political stations.)

The Clinton White House was not happy with Bradley's announcement. White House "sources" and "officials" promoted the idea that Bradley had voted with the president 80 percent of the time, so he couldn't be serious; that Bradley was boring; that independent candidacies are unlikely; and that by the way, a multicandidate race would actually help the president. It might. I think, but I do not know, that it is the only way Clinton can win in 1996.

THE SPEAKER AND THE PRESIDENT

By early September, Newt Gingrich's book *To Renew America* had been number one on the best-seller list for six weeks. Gingrich begins with American civilization. He sees that America is great, different, and in trouble. He writes: "We are a unique civilization. We stand on the shoulders of Western European civilization, but we are far more futuristic, more populist and more inclusive. American civilization is not merely a subset of Western Europe's. We have drawn people and cultures from across the planet and integrated them into an extraordinary shared opportunity to pursue happiness." No argument: Scholars write about "American exceptionalism."

What's the trouble? "[American] civilization is based on a spiritual and moral dimension," says Gingrich. "It emphasizes personal responsibility as much as individual rights. Since 1965, however, there has been a calculated effort by cultural elites to discredit this civilization and replace it with a culture of irresponsibility that is incompatible with American freedoms as we have known them."

Not much argument on substance there. But Gingrich is probably wrong about motivation. I don't think cultural elitists actually *calculated* a way to take America toward a culture of irresponsibility. They are neither that smart nor that sinister. In any event, it's bad politics to say so aloud. Better to call them wrong than evil.

Gingrich offers remedies for our ailments. We have to replace the welfare state with an opportunity state, decentralize the government, balance the budget, get more competitive in the world marketplace, and accelerate our entry into the information age. This can happen by getting government off our backs and letting free market individualism play a greater role. Breathlessly told, *To Renew America* offers the basic creed of what was once an oxymoron: conservative optimism.

Gingrich's best-selling themes are valid, but not brand new. In fact, in somewhat milder versions, Clinton campaigned on most of them in 1992. Clinton stressed opportunity, reciprocity, and responsibility. He wanted to end welfare as we know it. He wanted to decentralize and to get more competitive. He favored free markets. He wanted to reduce the deficit and ultimately balance the budget. His vice president was a techie. It was Clinton at his best, which is very good indeed, showing America he was a New Democrat.

But for two years Clinton did not govern that way. His any-deal-is-a-good-deal collaboration with the Democratic Congress and the liberal Democrats left him and his party reidentified with liberal big government, ripe for the repudiation at the polls that came in November 1994. In deep trouble, Clinton turned back toward those New Democrat views in mid-1995. The strategy, called "triangulation," positioned Clinton between the Republican conservatives and the Democratic congressional liberals. Better late than never. It *could* have been a great stance. Instead Clinton faces a 1996 election year in which he may come across as Gingrich Lite.

Can Clinton win as a me-too candidate? Perhaps. He is an exceptional campaigner. But neither "I Can Do It Slower" nor "Congress Made Me Do It" provides a battle call to storm the barricades. They are not even best-selling book titles.

THE CENTER TROPISM

I offer into evidence newspaper headlines that appeared in August 1995:

DOLE DEFENDING MIDDLE GROUND IN GOP RACE (by R. W. Apple, *New York Times*, August 13, 1995)

PRESIDENT DREAMS OF A MODERATE BLOC—CLINTON HOPES TO FORGE A MODERATE COALITION (by Alison Mitchell, New York Times Service, appearing in the *International Herald Tribune*, August 8, 1995)

DEMOCRATS LOOKING TO FIND THEIR WAY BACK (by Richard Benedetto, USA *Today*, August 21, 1995)

*Times*man Johnny Apple reported in his Dole story that "his message was plain: Republicanism with an ideological edge, à la Gingrich, à la

Gramm, was not for him and not, he thought, for the American people. In private, he said, they took a balanced view of Federal programs, recognizing that many were beneficial, 'but if you ask them in a big group, they all want to get up and shout about how awful the government is.' " Dole also said this about the government: "It's got to be downsized. It's gotten too big. We spend too much money. . . . But I don't think you want to leave people in the audience thinking you're some radical that's going to take them over the edge." Dole described Colin Powell as "probably moderate on social issues and fairly conservative on economic and defense issues," and according to a paraphrase by Apple, "eminently acceptable as a running mate—even if party conservatives worry about his views on abortion and affirmative action."

Alison Mitchell's story was based on an interview with Leon Panetta, Clinton's chief of staff. She wrote: "[Panetta's] remarks and those of other White House officials made it clear that the president would soon be in a struggle with Congress over which side best defined the political center and could attract the moderates."

Benedetto's piece carried a New Orleans dateline and dealt with a three-day meeting of the Democratic National Committee. He wrote: ". . . while broad support for liberal Democratic programs that tilt toward the poor and minorities is declining, some party factions refuse to back away. And it's costing them votes. . . ." But, Benedetto continued, party officials understand what the trouble is: "Largely missing from the forums here was talk of key Democratic rallying points such as abortion, homosexual rights and affirmative action. And it wasn't accidental. DNC leaders now concede that over-emphasis of such divisive issues over the past two decades caused many old-line Democrats to vote Republican, especially ethnic whites in urban areas and conservative whites in the South."

The middle of the road was getting crowded.

THE BATTLE OF THE BUDGET

In early September the talk in Washington was about a "train wreck" that would occur at the end of September when the fiscal year ended and new spending levels had to be approved by Congress and the president. Republicans in the House said major cuts were needed to balance the budget, reduce the bloat of government, and lessen the tax burden it imposes. Democrats said the cuts were draconian, that government did good things, and that the tax cuts were "for the rich."

Democrats said the appropriations bill passed by the Republican House, dealing with the departments of Labor, Health and Human Services, and Education, was the most draconian of all.

GOP: SPENDING BILL SENDS CLEAR SIGNALS ON PRIORITIES—
DEMOCRATS DECRY WORK OF "WRECKING CREW" (*Washington Post*,
August 5, 1995)

An analysis of the bill showed that the 1995 level of spending was $67 billion, which would be reduced to $61 billion for 1996, a 9 percent decrease. The appropriators made big *cuts* in the Goals 2000 program, in funds for bilingual and immigrant education, and in the Corporation for Public Broadcasting—but *increased* spending at the National Institutes of Health, in the Ryan White AIDS programs, and marginally in Job Corps. It was generally thought that most but not all of the cuts would survive in the Senate. President Clinton threatened vetoes, which would likely diminish the cuts somewhat more, down from the 9 percent proposed by the wrecking crew for the most draconian appropriations bill in a draconian season.

How did Greater Welfare make out in the process? As its five major programs—Medicaid, Food Stamps, AFDC, the Earned Income Tax Credit, and SSI—are "entitlements," they are not subject to the normal appropriations process. An estimate by the Senate Finance Committee showed that the five-year impact of Clinton's first budget, set at the "current law" baseline, would have *increased* spending 43 percent. Clinton's second budget would have *increased* it by 40 percent. The original House budget would have *increased* it by 22 percent. The final House/Senate conference bill *increased* Greater Welfare spending by 24 percent, from $187 billion to $231 billion.

The Republican entitlement cuts as of early September 1995 were only grand totals, without the specific spending allocations that would show just who would lose out with a decreased rate of increase. Those decisions were scheduled to be made public later in September, with the specifics for Medicare spending cuts promising to ignite political fireworks. Republicans sought a $270 billion budget cut over seven years—to save Medicare from bankruptcy. Democrats said the cuts would cost the elderly and harm their health.

In almost all these matters the Republicans claimed that what was happening was a "decrease in the rate of increase." Democrats said this was disingenuous because upward adjustments had to be made to account for compounded inflation and for the projected increase in the number of recipients. My sense is that the cuts, that is, the decrease in the rate of increase, are not draconian, which is in any event a somewhat imprecise term. Insofar as the cuts reduce the growth of Greater Welfare, there will be less incentive for value-busting behavior.

The arguments fueled speculation that the federal government would be closed down during that train wreck:

REPUBLICANS PONDER BUDGET "MELTDOWN"—DEADLOCK COULD HALT GOVERNMENT (*Washington Times*, August 21, 1995)

WHITE HOUSE ISSUES FEDERAL SHUTDOWN PLAN (*Washington Post*, August 24, 1995)

A BUDGET TRAIN WRECK? ALL SIDES PREPARE FOR A COLLISION THAT COULD SHUT DOWN GOVERNMENT. (*US News & World Report*, August 28, September 4, 1995)

The train wreck for which the White House was preparing concerns what happens when all or parts of the federal government legally run out of money. That occurs at the end of the fiscal year (September 30) if appropriations and entitlement spending levels are not agreed to by Congress and the president, or when the federal debt limit is exceeded (a moment that was expected to occur in November 1995).

Train wrecking is a game of chicken. The Republican Congress passes budget bills with cuts deeper than the Democratic president wants, with policy changes embedded in the cuts, and says to him, if you veto this, *you, Mr. President*, will be shutting down the government and causing people pain. The president vetoes the bill (or says he will), sending it back to Congress, saying, if you do not amend this bill in a reasonable way, *you, you Republicans in Congress*, will be causing people pain. (Roughly the same train-wrecking scenarios can come about if Congress holds the debt ceiling hostage.)

As this game goes on, words and phrases that most Americans do not comprehend are used relentlessly: "reconciliation," "current services," "discretionary spending," "entitlements," "continuing resolution," "OMB estimates," "CBO estimates," "riders," "gridlock," "conference committees," "baseline," "medical inflation."

It is very complicated even for long-term Washington hands. Readers may entertain this thought: Don't pay too much attention to it. Spend some quality time with your family. Go through this book again, line by line. When all the tumult and shouting is over (probably by the end of 1995), consider what has finally emerged from the brokerage. By how much has spending been decreased from the rate of increase, or cut? Have programs been changed or eliminated? What happened on the social issue programs, particularly welfare? Then make an assessment. I bet the bottom line will be that the America will have moved somewhat toward the center-right, about where the voters are.

Most of the cuts, under either plan, are back-ended—more painful toward the end of the time frame than at the beginning. If they are too tough, if voters rebel, they can be eased.

TICKET PROLIFERATION

The result will be all right. But the budget process will look repugnant, yielding greater disillusionment with government, which will bolster a trend already in motion:

VOTERS WANT INDEPENDENT IN RACE—POLL FINDS 62% SEE A
NEED FOR A NEW PARTY (USA *Today*, August 11, 1995)

JACKSON HINTS AT '96 RUN; PEROT LEAVES OPTIONS OPEN; 3RD-
PARTY THREATS ATTACK STATUS QUO (*Washington Times*, August 14,
1995)

BRADLEY WEIGHING INDEPENDENT RACE FOR WHITE HOUSE—DIS-
AFFECTED DEMOCRAT OFFERS FEW DETAILS, BUT MENTIONS TALK
WITH COLIN POWELL (*New York Times*, August 18, 1995)

As noted in public opinion Indicators (p. 118), self-declared independents now make up a plurality of American voters, a quite astonishing situation. Moreover, confidence in government has declined.
The strength of the parties has diminished. The Perot candidacy
proved that independent candidacies could score heavily. Polls showed
voters seeking candidates other than Clinton and Dole, and seeking
third parties. Why? In some large measure, because the system has not
responded to our most important concerns.

There may well be more than two serious candidates in the presidential race in 1996. There may well be more than three. It gets easier
as the numbers grow. The first non–major party candidate says, "I can
win the popular vote for president with 34 percent of the vote." The
second additional candidate says, "I can win the popular vote with 26
percent of the vote." The election of 1996 could be unusual.

Here are some plausible, surely speculative, presidential tickets:

1. Clinton–Gore
2. Dole–Wilson (Governor Pete Wilson of California, prochoice in a
   party where that position can hurt in the primaries but help in a
   general election)
3. Perot–Boren (former Senator David Boren, former Governor of
   Oklahoma, keynote speaker at the Perot extravaganza)
4. Powell–Bradley ("the General and the Jock")
5. Jackson–Nader (Jesse Jackson and Ralph Nader have constituencies on the left; as a fifth ticket they could win the majority of the
   popular vote with 21 percent)
6. Buchanan–Keyes (if the Republicans put a prochoice candidate
   on their ticket, these fellows would have a niche and would need
   only 17 percent for a majority)

Do not count on six tickets. Do not count on five. But do not rule
out four—which would be exciting. If more than two candidates cap-

ture winner-take-all state *electoral* votes, and there is no candidate with a majority of electoral votes, the election of the president would be determined by a vote of the states in the next House of Representatives, which will likely have a *Republican* majority.

I bet that any ticket that does not credibly stress values issues will lose.

Part Five

HOW TO WIN, AND WHY

Chapter 16

SAVING AMERICA THROUGH POLITICS

Suppose a political candidate—for any office from the presidency on down—reads this book and decides the gist of it is correct. Suppose the candidate wants to use this point of view to help win an election, and to help America. Suppose the candidate tells his campaign staff: *read this book, forget the fancy stuff in it, just tell me what to do!*

It has been touched on before, but now we enter head-on the world of ideo-political tactics.

———

First, it must be stressed that what is in this book does not supersede the normal ebb and flow of everyday parochial politics. The standard tactics of view-with-alarm and point-with-pride remain in place. I can not even advise a candidate not to "go negative." (Personal negative advertising seems to pay off, too damn often.)

Candidates, if there has been a military base closing in your state or district, by all means blame your opponent or at least his party, or the

359

Democratic president or the Republican Congress, as appropriate. In an agricultural district by all means attack a cut in agricultural subsidies as the death knell of the family farm, and explain how it is all the fault of your opponent and his party. Incumbents, including the President, should continue to brag about the new projects brought into a district or state. Sub-presidential candidates may brag about how much they enjoy helping individual voters get through the bureacratic maze at that funny farm called Washington.

Candidates, don't forget economics. Even if you believe, as I do, that values matter most, that does not mean that economics doesn't matter at all. By all means continue the silly stuff of American economic politics. It seems to work. Argue about whether Republicans or Democrats "create" more jobs, argue about who knows best how to "grow the economy" and about who cares about the "little guy." So, to both parties: be my guest, by all means use that crapola, just don't expect me to believe it.

But beyond all that—the super-issue lurks. Get on the wrong side of that and you're in trouble. Get on the right side of it and you're halfway home. Values matter. Social issues matter even more.

A word about relevance: The moment this observation is committed to paper is at the very beginning of Autumn 1995, as all eyes looked toward the Presidential election of 1996. In that context I believe that the thesis and the tactics presented here make sense. But that is not enough. A serious political thought should be relevant up and down the political scale, from the White House, to the court house, to the state capitol, to the U.S. capitol, and for local offices from mayor to school board. Moreover, if there is general validity in the thesis, then the tactics should have applicability in the 1996 election contests, and beyond, even if some details change or if unexpected events intervene. (What happens if Bill Clinton has a disabling stroke? If there are severe urban riots in the summer of 1996? If Russia invades Ukraine?) I accept all the variables of time, place, and circumstance—and I pronounce this work relevant.

Let us start with some items that apply to all the players in the game. The focus will then move to some specific strategies for Democrats, Republicans, third parties, and independents.

FOR ALL THE PLAYERS

This time around, the *economic* issue may well be the easiest. We had a recession in the early 1990s with President Bush in the White House. There was a slow recovery which continued during the election year of 1992. That recovery began to accelerate as Bush left office. The economy moved solidly ahead during Clinton's first two years with an all-Democratic government. The Republicans took over Congress in late 1994. The economy continued to improve for about six months. Then there was a dip in growth for a few months in the Spring of 1995 and then a recovery. As this is written, some economists say a "soft landing" is on the way. Others say we are heading into a recession. (I believe we are in huge, long fluctuating boom.)

The coming election is made to order for the boilerplate thrust and parry that goes with economic politics. Take credit for what is good in the economy. Blame the other team for what is bad. This vapid ritual can get only more so at a moment when the presidency and the Congress are controlled by different parties and there was change in that arrangement since the last presidential election. (Voters should remember that there are tight constraints on what politicians can actually *do* about the economy.)

Democrats will say that for twenty years prior to Clinton, the middle class gained no ground—even lost ground—mostly because of a Republican trickle-down philosophy and astronomic Reaganomic deficit spending. That view has become such an ingrown part of the national dialogue that it has political utility. Moreover, even if there was real aggregate economic progress, as sketched out earlier, that progress doesn't mean that everyone gained, or that everyone gained substantially, or that every group gained as much as every other group. Further, there are always people who would like to believe that whatever bad has happened in their lives was someone else's fault.

Many Republicans will say that what happened in the early 1990s was a typical and mild recession, that it was followed by a Bush recovery, and that the recovery is moving ahead smartly now because of the new signal of economic discipline sent out by the Republican Congress. Many Republicans will say that the 1980s were a wonderful time economically, and further suggest that Reagan would have liked to cut spending but the Democratic Congresses wouldn't let him, that the Congress put extra baubles on the tax cut bill, all of which triggered the increase in the deficit. They will promote part of the no-progress-for-the-middle-class idea and blame it on Clinton and Democratic congresses.

Republicans and Democrats will each claim that their tax simplification plans are best, and they know best how to balance the budget. Any independent running for office will surely blame both parties for whatever is wrong. He or she will commend the hard work of everyday Americans for whatever economic progress may be observable.

In 1996 the standard economic charges and countercharges may well carry less electoral weight than usual. I hope so.

There is at least one other item on the political field that applies to *all* the players: *race*. Race pervades the social issue agenda, directly and indirectly: in crime, welfare, education, and preference. Because the changes in motion run against the positions taken by most of the prominent black leadership organizations, particularly the Congressional Black Caucus, it seems as if there will be turbulent times ahead for African Americans. But if Americans (Republicans and Democrats), are smart, gentle, and firm, "turbulent" need not mean "bad."

On the *apparently bad side for blacks*: Welfare will get trimmed (Democratic) or cut way back (Republican). This disproportionately hurts blacks: Blacks are more than four times as likely to receive welfare as whites. New federal crime laws will likely increase the time criminals spend in prisons. Blacks are 12 percent of the American population but 48 percent of all prisoners. The well-educated have always made out better than the less-educated. Future economic changes and globalization will likely make that more so. The data show that whites are better educated than blacks. Affirmative-action-as-recently-practiced will not be practiced that way in the future.

The broader climate also seems tough for blacks. Democrats want to "reinvent" government, cutting government jobs. Republicans want to "reduce" government, cutting even more such jobs. Blacks are twice as likely as whites to be employed by government. Or consider defense spending. It's headed down from earlier levels, way down with Democrats in power, down somewhat less with Republicans in control.

Blacks are more than twice as likely as whites to serve in the military.

There is more than enough apparent bad news for the black community to fuel conspiracy theories that would pin the blame on racism. That, in turn, could lead to disruption or violence, which could make the conspiracy theories self-fulfilling. Any violence will be said to reveal rebellion; that is how the Los Angeles riot of 1992 was characterized.

There is a happier way of looking at the situation. No group in America will gain more than blacks if predators are taken off inner-city streets. The vast majority of blacks are law-abiding citizens and are disproportionately likely to be *victims* of crime. A tightening of eligibility for welfare, and lesser sums for it, may well help break the welfare trap. That may well reduce illegitimate birth. Blacks in the military have generally served with distinction and achieved success through merit. They will likely succeed as civilians, without any egregious affirmative action, forming a new battalion in the growing ranks of the black middle class. A phase-out of affirmative action could lead to tougher enforcement of antidiscrimination statutes, or stronger statutes, which may help blacks. It should also lead to upgraded education in the inner city, based on standards, tests, and stakes.

With the fight about affirmative action so high in the headlines, how can America best navigate through the turbulent seas? We can begin by recognizing that it is an emotional issue and *lower our voices*. We can stop attacking other people's motives and notice facts. Whites should recognize that blacks favoring affirmative action are not necessarily perpetuating a self-serving scam. Whites should recognize that the black community faces a bumpy patch. Blacks should recognize that whites opposed to affirmative action are not necessarily racists.

It seems clear that affirmative action policies will be changed. We should try to agree that such changes will be both *decisive* and *slow*. What counts most now is direction, not speed. Affirmative action can be phased out in a year, or three, or five. Many ideas are in the air. In some situations affirmative action based on *class* or geography, not *race*, make sense and would help blacks disproportionately because of their lower socioeconomic status. Judge Robert Bork believes we should phase out all affirmative action quickly, *except for blacks*, where the phase-out could go on a slower track.

The key is closure. The political window on this issue is finally open on a national scale. If all that comes of it is some tinkering at the edges, there are two bad scenarios in sight. The antiquota siege will go on, state by state, aggravating an already tense racial situation, and pro-quota forces will probably lose, state by state. If they win, and establish that preference is *not* a *temporary* solution, we had better face up to living in a society legally divided by race. Again.

If we all take it easy, and move decisively and slowly, we can get to a better place.

THE DEMOCRATS

If President Clinton is on the ballot in 1996, which is probable, the central issue as framed by Republicans will likely be reducible to a single potent word: "betrayal." The essence of any Republican campaign will resemble "Fool me once, shame on you; fool me twice, shame on me." If Clinton is not a candidate, the same line of attack will be used (with probable lesser effect) on any other mainstream Democratic candidate. Clinton and the Democrats won in 1992 by claiming a new political moderation, albeit an activist one. How Clinton and the other Democrats actually governed is debatable, but the public perception (and mine) is fairly clear: It was a reversion to liberalism. Republicans will drill that point home.

There is another factor now at work. After the congressional election of 1994, many moderate Democratic legislators lost because they were regarded as too closely linked to Clinton, the liberal. (Republican television ads attacked "the Clinton Congress.") But hard-core liberal Democrats were not hurt much because they mostly came from solidly liberal districts. And so, the remaining Democrats in Congress make up a much more liberal group than before. The case will be made, against Clinton or any other putatively moderate Democrat running for the presidency, that even a real New Democrat would have to accommodate a very liberal Democratic Congress.

How can the Democrats counter the charge of past betrayal and looming structural liberalism?

To begin, they have all their old stuff. The Democrats will attempt to redemonize and re-Houstonize the Republicans. Driven by liberal Democrats and moderate Republicans, the myth of a zealous, mean-spirited, exclusionary takeover in Houston seems to have passed almost untouched into the popular dialogue. Accordingly, Democrats will try to nurture such an image again, possibly to continued good effect.

Democrats will attack the big cultural issues. They will surely raise the issue of abortion. They will maintain that even a diluted abortion plank in the GOP San Diego platform will still represent a step toward the day when fundamentalist stormtroopers will invade the privacy of American bedrooms.

Trouble is, the 1992 Democratic plank was far from perfect. If, in 1996, the Democratic prochoice activists would allow it (doubtful), Democrats should tailor their plank to acknowledge publicly that state legislatures have the right, and perhaps the duty, to *consider* those sorts of reforms that the *Webster* decision holds legal: waiting periods, parental notification, explanation of adoption options, and so on. Such a position would put Democrats in the mainstream of American public opinion. It also happens to be roughly the view espoused by both Bill Clinton and Al Gore before they became presidential and vice-presidential candidates.

Democrats will wait for one Republican, any Republican, anywhere, any time, to say that America is "a Christian nation," and then jump up and down. It will show (Democrats will say) that conservatives don't really believe in pluralism. Democrats will say, or have others say, that Christian fundamentalists are taking over the Republican party and that they will teach literal creationism in the public schools, putting Darwin in a dumpster.*

Democrats will work the gun control issue, which has substantial support in the country. But it is a tricky item. It may raise the turnout of angry Republican gun owners. Still, it's probably a small plus for Democrats. Since the awful bombing in Oklahoma City in late April

---

* There is a prescient line in the movie *Inherit the Wind* about the Scopes trial of 1925. The Clarence Darrow character, fighting for inclusion of evolution theory into the Tennessee high school curriculum, asks the William Jennings Bryan character, whether he would like it if "only Darwin could be taught in the schools." Bryan harumphs, "Ridiculous. Ridiculous," indicating the impossibility of such an eventuality, which is now the practice in most states.

1995, the issue seems to have taken on greater saliency. The rich phrase "assault weapon" is a Democratic plus, because Republicans want to rescind the ban of 19 such weapons (out of 650) that was passed in the 1994 crime bill.

Democrats will say, or have it said, that conservative Republicans want to discriminate against gays, women, blacks, Latinos, Asians, Jews, Eastern Europeans, people of immigrant stock, bald people (foliculary challenged), and so on.

Republicans have good answers to each of these noneconomic charges (as we shall see), but the totality of all the caricatures can lend some serious weight to Democratic demagoguery. It is an important Democratic thrust, with one strong caveat: When Democrats open up the cultural warfare front, they will pay a price. It's not the Republicans that are regarded as the party in favor of gays in the military, condoms in school, or teaching kids how to masturbate. They are not regarded as the party in opposition to the death penalty, praying, and Christmas.

Democrats will attack much of the Republican congressional legislative program on economic grounds. Republicans call it class warfare, but that is because Democrats have often been able to make hay out of splitting the country between "little guys" and "fat cats." There are more little guys.

Democrats said early on that the plans of the Republican Congress represent "Robin Hood in reverse," which would "balance the budget on the backs of the poor," depriving poor children of school lunches. It is fertile political soil. Polls show that voters like the direction of the Republican program but have big problems with some of the specifics, at least when the specifics are described by Democrats.

It makes a splendid case for why poor people should vote Democratic. But there aren't nearly enough poor in a middle-class country like America to win a national election. To attract the middle class, Democrats will claim that Republican tax cuts take money from the middle class and give it to the rich, that Republican spending cuts are soft on corporate welfare, that misguided Republican policies are designed to help rich financial schemers.

In recent years, these have been strong Democratic arguments. This time, however, the public sentiment for budget balancing and spending cuts is more intense and more widespread. Despite the apparent attitudinal tilt toward primacy of spending reductions over tax cuts, remember that tax cuts have never been hard to sell. (I wonder why.)

This time, rest assured, Republicans will not only defend their tax cuts, and spending cuts, will not only counter-attack on cultural issues, but will ask this question with new vigor: "Voters, can Democrats really be the friend of the little guy if they prevented the Republicans from ending quotas, from ending welfare as we know it, from getting tough on crime, from putting discipline back in our schools?" Social Issues.

If the Democrats have wits and courage, their central response on social issues will not be negative but positive: "*We can do it better.*" There may have been a model for this in 1995 as welfare emerged as a very big issue. The Republican welfare bill that passed the House of Representatives was far tougher than anything Clinton had proposed, and was based on turning over welfare to the states. Democrats said that the plan was heartless, cruel to kids, racist, and soft on work and that the states couldn't be trusted to do the heavy lifting. Some moderate Senate Republicans objected to the House Republican bill, particularly the part about forbidding cash aid to teen-age mothers of out-of-wedlock children. As this book goes to press Republicans are trying to forge a compromise within their party. Then, pushed by the threat of a Clinton veto, Democrats and Republicans will have to come together on a welfare deal that will be substantially tougher than Clinton's original proposal and includes a devolution of welfare programs to the states.

Yes! Democrats should say, *we can do it better!* Welfare reform is necessary, Democrats should say, but the pure Republican plan would be regarded as racist and inflammatory. We can do it better. Yes, we have to diminish affirmative action but only we can do it with sensitivity. Yes, we Democrats can be tough on crime. Yes, we can be tough on education. And we can do it better than those heartless Republicans, who will divide the country. Such Democratic logic is elemental: Only liberals who feel pain can steer other liberals who feel pain away from the past mistakes of liberalism, which caused pain.

The Democrats must adopt a neo-Hippocratic oath. Hippocrates's initial rule of medicine is "First do no harm." That makes good general sense in politics as well, and fits on a bumper sticker. But it is not quite enough for Democrats. It is only future oriented. Democrats should amend it: "First, undo past harm gently but firmly." (For wide bumpers or vans, or in small type on small cars.)

"Undo past harm" means that liberal Democrats must change their minds publicly on some big and old issues. Contrary to popular belief, politicians are not great liars. Democrats should say three magic words in public: "We were wrong." That will make it easier for Democrats to believe it. Then they can reconsider incapacitation, stop rewarding illegitimacy, restore discipline to education, and roll back affirmative-action-as-now-practiced. Further extensions from the no-more-something-for-nothing idea will come easily.

A Democratic move to the center does not mean a rollback from general Democratic positions. Republicans can still be attacked as fat cats. Phil Gramm can be attacked when he says big government is bad government. It does not mean giving up on compassion.

Firmly and gently undoing past errors that still hurt us can free up funds to give more to those who truly cannot help themselves. Poverty grifters are stealing money from the poor box. Putting down educational markers for poor kids helps poor kids; less illegitimacy because of less welfare helps poor kids. Undoing past harm is the only way to calm the tide of antigovernment feeling in America. It is implausible to think that governmental solutions can be sold to an electorate that believes government is engaged in a range of activities that are making things worse in America.

A "We Can Do It Better" strategy will cause great consternation in the liberal camp of the Democratic party. They will call such a policy "me-too Republicanism." It would add a greater rationale for Jesse Jackson to run as an independent candidate, which he may well do in any event. That would be bad news for Democrats, but it could be worse. A liberal or black Democrat voting for Jackson in a general election likely costs the Democratic nominee *one* vote, sent to a candidate who does not stand any serious chance of winning. But a Democrat voting for a Republican, as the Reagan Democrats have done when they felt it necessary, costs the party *two* votes. (The same voter who *subtracts one* from the Democratic total then *adds one* to the Republican candidate, who can win.) Moreover, there are many more moderate Democrats who may move right than there are liberal Democrats who may move left to a lefter wing third party.

Democrats are damned if they do move to the center, and damned if they don't move to the center—but damned *more* if they don't move to the center. Tactically, they ought to move to the center.

There is one other (risky) strategy for Democrats: *Dump Clinton*. A careful reader may have noticed that I do not think Bill Clinton would be the best candidate for the Democrats. I have criticized policy and cited some public opinion surveys. But there is something more: anecdote. The plural of anecdote is data.

I write a syndicated newspaper column. Periodically I ask readers to participate in a contest. In 1994 I called for entries that put a name on the Clinton foreign policy. The request was phrased in an entirely neutral way. Yet, exactly 119 out of the 120 entries were negative. The winner (I was the judge) was "Lax Americana." Other entries included "Hesicrastination," "Clintonertia," "Speak Bigly and Carry a Soft Stick," "Liberté, Egalité, Stupidité," "Superpowerlessness," "Ozark Wilsonianism" (an entry that was submitted anonymously in a National Security Council envelope), "Explainment," "Flipflopcracy," "Surrealpolitik," "Stanley Greenbergism," and "Naked Digression."

In 1995 I served up another contest, this one asking readers for political slogans for various candidates in 1996. Again, the wording was neutral. Again, Clinton brought out almost entirely negative responses, such as "Four More Veers," "He Kept Him Out of War," "Don't Change Stones in Mid-Avalanche," a campaign song, "Yes, I'm the Great Big Spender" (a turn on the Platters' hit of the 1950s, *Yes, I'm the Great Pretender*, which also might be appropriate), "No More Waffling and Indecision, Probably," "Bill Chameleon for President," and "Veni Vidi Verdict." If the plural of anecdote is indeed data, this president is in trouble.*

I believe we are seeing the birth, or the rebirth, of a something-for-something society. The proverbial political train is leaving the station. The Democrats can get on board and try to shape that society according to their traditions, or watch the train go off into the future, as they

---

* In August 1995 *Washingtonian* magazine reported, "at a recent dinner with a close friend, [President] Bush was heard to say of Clinton, 'He's nothing but a bullshit artist.'" Why didn't Bush submit that one to my contest?

become history. Bill Clinton could have been the engineer on that train and a heroic American figure. He is an excellent campaigner and a smart fellow, but it will be difficult for him to win in a straight two-party race in 1996. That is so despite polls in the early Fall of 1995 showing Clinton running about even in the pairings against a Republican. He has not yet been subjected to a tough presidential campaign that will say more than that Clinton eats at a waffle house. Columnist Jack Germond, one of the most respected election watchers in Washington, noted at the time that Clinton's "reelect" ratings were quite low. He cited a poll by Republican Frank Luntz asking respondents whether they would like their children to grow up like Bill Clinton. By 72 to 16 percent Americans said no. Other polls, Democratic as well as Republican, showed Clinton with low scores on various profile issues like "strong leader," "effective," "ethical," "telling the truth," and "strong commander in chief." If Clinton is the nominee, even if he reforms and reformulates his policy message, even if the White House staff is chockful of certified neo-conservatives, the haunting questions would remain: "Isn't he doing it just to get elected?" and, worse, "Wouldn't he govern as a liberal if he didn't face another election?" (Constitutionally, Clinton could not run for a third term if reelected in 1996.)

There are other Democrats who could be better able to slip that noose, who are more likely to get elected, and, if elected, would be more likely to take the train forward, possibly by occasionally running over the liberals in Congress and some of the Democratic special-interest groups. Senators Bill Bradley, Bob Kerrey, and Joe Lieberman come to mind, even though Bradley has been eyeing a run as an independent. (House minority leader Richard Gephardt's caboose seems to be headed the other way.) If Clinton should decide peacefully not to run, that would open the door for a primary run by Vice President Gore. Remarkably, Gore has low negative ratings and high name identification, despite his high-profile association with Clintonism.

Dumping Clinton would not be easy. It will be said that a sitting president can't be denied renomination. But don't rule it out. There was a "dump Johnson" movement. Johnson never believed he was dumped. Nor do I. But he didn't end up running, did he? He said he had planned not to run, and there is evidence to support that. But might he have run if the country was in great shape and Democrats from across the spectrum said, "Please run, Mr. President, we need you"?

That, of course, is not what an important part of the party was saying to LBJ. And that is not what a large part of the Democratic party is saying to Clinton. In 1994, the Democrats lost fifty-two House seats, ten Senate seats, eleven governorships, and 496 state legislative seats. Walter Dean Burnham says it may have been the most stunning American realigning election ever, and certainly among the top three of the ninety-nine elections he examined. Exit polls revealed that Clinton was one big reason for the vast national defeat. And he wasn't even on the ballot.

Politicians are not always noted for courage, but how much courage does it take to call for the President to step aside when you know that if he doesn't step aside you'll lose your own job? Private and public pressure could conceivably push Clinton not to run for a second term in 1996. (He's a young man and could try again later.)

It's said that it's "already too late" to challenge the president in the series of "front-loaded" primaries of 1996. Perhaps so. Perhaps not. If the President changes his mind, or is forced to change his mind by Whitewater revelations, or other revelations or a party in open revolt. . . . It is not likely, only possible, and potentially beneficial to Democrats.*

Whether Clinton or someone else heads the ticket, it is likely to be a rough course for the Democrats. But that's only logic speaking. In politics luck, accident, and circumstance are always in play. Notwithstanding everything, there is still a good deal of residual loyalty to the Democratic party. About as many voters identified themselves as Democrats as Republicans in the 1994 election exit polls. So Democrats can hope and pray.

Hope and Prayer 1: Third parties. Fourth parties. Independent candidates. If Ross Perot or some other serious candidate of the center-right (although probably not Colin Powell) runs a serious campaign, Clinton can be helped. As Dick Scammon always says: "Happiness is a divided opposition." It is hard to see how the Democrats can get

---

* It might be extra hard to persuade Clinton not to run: If Clinton does not run or is defeated, he will face a civil suit by Paula Jones on the charge of sexual harassment.

50.1 percent of the votes in a traditional two-party presidential race or capture 270 electoral votes. But Democrats almost surely would be helped by a 1996 run by Perot. Unlike 1992, this time Perot would draw most of his support from anti-Clinton votes who would otherwise cast their ballot for the Republican nominee.

Hope and Prayer 2: Republican stupidity. Elections are often the choice of the lesser of two evils. Not long ago, but before the appearance of Dr. Kevorkian on the national scene, the Republicans specialized in psephological Kevorkianism: assisted suicide in the electoral arena. It could happen again. Republicans could nominate a candidate clearly out of the mainstream, as Barry Goldwater was perceived to be in 1964 (although Goldwater's brand of 1964 conservatism might play fairly well these days, and his 1995 style of more moderate conservatism might play even better).

Combining the Perot scenario with a Kevorkian Republican, even Clinton could win in a contest that would surely be called the evil of three lessers.

Hope and Prayer 3: Extraneous events. Presidents are different from thee and me. They are in the news and highly scrutinized even when they are allegedly irrelevant. Presidential popularity can go up or down based on events that presidents have little or nothing to do with. Sometimes some of that popularity, or unpopularity, can move votes on election day. Clinton got a big boost in the polls from the tragic Oklahoma City bombing by acting with great presidential dignity and sympathy. On the other hand, Jimmy Carter lost votes because the Ayatollah Khomeini took American hostages and Carter appeared helpless. Could events like these, pro or con, happen again? Of course. If they are pro, they could help Clinton.

Presidents can also get helped by just looking good. Americans usually want the president to succeed. Watching Clinton swing a golf club in front of the Grand Tetons in August made many Americans, including the author, feel good.

Hope and Prayer 4: (For all Democrats up for reelection in 1996) that Clinton is not the nominee of the Democratic party.

THE REPUBLICANS

Think now about the GOP, another party that has been arguing with itself for a long time. How should they play the game in 1996 and beyond?

The GOP split is characterized in several different ways: center-right vs. far-right, economic conservatives vs. social conservatives, country club vs. church, Wall Street vs. Main Street, Sunbelt vs. Frostbelt, with a smattering of libertarians, supply-siders, nationalists, and isolationists tossed in for good measure.

These splits can become so wide on some occasions that some moderate Republicans vote for a Democrat or an independent, so wide that many conservative Republicans stay home and don't vote, or vote for an independent. There is, however, one very big difference between liberals in the Democratic Party and conservatives in the Republican Party. American voters are about twice as likely to regard themselves as conservatives than as liberals (see public opinion Indicators). This means that if Republicans hold their conservative ideological base, both economic and social, they are most of the way toward a majority.

How can we help such a split party? Can the Republican marriage be saved? (A coalition is a political marriage.) If the Republicans can't unite, they are in trouble. Then they could not be very useful in helping to make America better, which is the aim of all the advice tendered here to all persons and parties.

In the first two years of his presidency, Bill Clinton was nice enough to unite the fractious Republicans, at least temporarily. His five-year budget plan was characterized as "more spending, more taxes, more government and more regulation." Most Republicans don't like more taxes, spending, government, and regulation. Neither do most Americans these days.

If the Republicans can make the case that Democrats believe in more spending/taxes/government/regulation, that will surely help them. It is essentially an economic case, but it can be very important.

I bet it will not be enough. With a split government, the politics of the economy are confused. So both sides will exaggerate, fib, mislead, and prevaricate. Where is Joe Isuzu when we need him? Where is the line at the bottom of the television screen that says, "He's lying"?

Moreover, with the end of the cold war, foreign policy is, for the moment at least, a lesser issue.

Republicans, like Democrats, must prepare for a values-driven campaign. This is in their best interest, and in the best interest of America. In some important respects, the GOP strategy should be quite like the one laid out here for the Democrats. The old saw still holds: the best policy is the best politics. If indeed the social issues present our most important government-caused, government-curable problems, that's where Republicans should be going to gather swing votes and to keep their coalition together.

We have explored the big four here—crime, welfare, education, and preference. It is far easier for Republicans to go with this strategy than for the Democrats. Getting tough on crime is already in the GOP playbook. So is rolling back welfare. So is restoring discipline to the classroom. So is moving away from affirmative-action-as-recently-practiced.

What's the problem? An old riddle asks: How do porcupines make love? The answer is: Carefully, carefully.

That's about the way Republicans have to deal with the social issues. There will be innocent people hurt as America shrinks the something-for-nothing state: new young unwed mothers and their babies playing by rules that had been established earlier, parents of criminals who thought they'd never see their sons in prison, high school students who thought they could coast without doing much work, blacks, Hispanics, and women who thought they might get preference from a white male society self-smothered by guilt.

The doctrine of carefully-carefully applies with particular relevance to civil rights in America. It can be an explosive issue. In recent decades Republican candidates for the presidency have not directly raised the issue of racial, ethnic, and gender quotas. Very few candidates for Congress brought it up. There were reasons: It was too hot and potentially inflammatory. It could be bad for the country. It could have backfired on Republicans. It was reserved as a risky trump ace and turned out not to be necessary. It had become so prominent a feature of the Democratic party that the issue was self-revealing.

But it now seems likely that the quota issue will come into play in the elections of 1996. It was raised in the Republican Congress in 1995. It is slated to be on the California ballot as a referendum. Several Supreme Court rulings in mid-1995 tightened criteria for affirmative action. The Court vote was 5-4 in each case with both Justices appointed by Clinton voting *not* to tighten the criteria. That opens up an obvious line of attack. Republicans will say that if Clinton is reelected, new Justices appointed by him will reinstate affirmative action. Republicans can say, "Clinton means quotas." (In 1992 Democrats said that if Bush was reelected, Bush-appointed Justices would overturn the *Roe v. Wade* prochoice decision and abortion would return to the days of back alleys and coathangers.)

Fair enough. But please, Republicans, act carefully, with attention to tonality, with gentle phase-ins and phase-outs, with compassion, with direct appeals to blacks in the inner city who hate both crime and welfare, with an understanding that many of the people who may be harmed were playing by the rules established by an elected government. All that along with the firmness that assures voters that affirmative-action-as-now-practiced is temporary and on its way out.

Republicans will appropriately stress that they have made some headway in racial matters. Until 1991 there were no black Republicans in Congress; now there are two (both conservatives). More impressive, twenty-five black Republicans ran for the Congress in 1994. The Republican National Committee has been running training sessions for black Republicans and will likely provide financial help in 1996. We may well see more black Republicans in Congress soon.

The four main social issues will likely give the Republicans a solid leg up on the elections of 1996, and probably beyond.

But they can blow it. The current up-front Republican philosophy, as typically perceived, is "against government." But that characterization gets some voters very angry, particularly when Democrats point out that "government" includes Social Security, Medicare, the folks in the control towers at the airport, and scientists trying to figure out how to treat cancer.

After sixty years of expanding government, it is surely legitimate to bring up and debate the proper role and scope of government. I suggest only that for the next few years Republicans make it as a subsidiary argument.

Republicans should first fix what the government has done that is hurting us most and is most fixable. This should be done *because it hurts us and is fixable, not because we should cut government, cut spending, or cut the deficit.* It is politically unwise for Republicans to justify shrinking Greater Welfare in order to fulfill an antigovernment ideological menu or as a means of cutting spending. The smartest Republican political argument, because it happens to be true, is that certain aspects of Greater Welfare actually hurt people. In fact, of course, cutting what hurts is still a cut, and still advances the cause of reduced government.

That becomes a better and even more credible argument if some conservative Republicans can couple it with a call for *more spending* for those parts of Greater Welfare that work well. How about *increasing* SSI payments to poor, elderly, nonimmigrant Americans? (The SSI payment for a poor elderly couple with no outside income is only $687 per month, which works out to $8,244 per year, plus food stamps and Medicaid. For a similarly situated widow or widower, the SSI payment is only $446 per month, or $5,352 per year.) Unlike AFDC there is no incentive for illegitimacy or dependency. All it would do is help poor old people most of whom played by the rules.

Another idea comes from Jack Kemp: let people coming off of welfare get a temporary tax holiday from *payroll* taxes, like Social Security, thereby increasing the value of work over welfare.

As the Democrats attack Republicans about their lack of compassion for the poor and lower middle class, Republicans will not forget to stress that the major plan for a flat tax (Majority Leader Dick Armey's) doesn't start taxing until a $36,000 level of family income is reached, thereby exempting the poor and some middle-class people from federal income tax.

Republicans should be sure that along with cuts in Greater Welfare come cuts in so-called corporate welfare (although anyone with a whit of sense understands that a subsidized agribusinessman is less of a social threat than a marauding predator). The list of corporate targets at the trough of government is long. As detailed by Stephen Moore and Dean Stansel of the Cato Institute the register of piggies runs to 125, including the following:

- Small Business Administration
- Export-Import Bank
- NASA Wind Tunnel
- Overseas Private Investment Corporation
- Agricultural Marketing Service
- Rural Business Service
- U.S. Travel and Tourism Administration
- Sematech
- Federal Railroad Administration

Early results from the congressional appropriations process have shown that conservative legislators do not want to cut programs that help their constituents and funders.

One is tempted to tell the Republicans to adopt the slogan "No More Something for Nothing." But, strange as it seems, that might engender the Democratic/media backlash of "extremist." That isn't exactly fair; Clinton used it, and it drew no criticism. Perhaps from a Republican point of view they would do best with this slogan: "Hardly Anything for Nothing." Or perhaps "Unbetrayal."

If it is necessary for Republicans to exercise caution on the social issues, there is a double need for caution on the cultural issues. Caution is needed despite public opinion surveys that reveal that a solid majority of Americans agree with the conservative side of most (not all) cultural issues: prayer in the school, antipornography, sex and violence on television, gays in the military, death penalty, instruction regarding homosexuality as a value-neutral alternative lifestyle in public schools, the pledge of allegiance, condoms in the classroom, not funding *Piss Christ,* and so on. Americans are more concerned than ever about the cultural coarseness and laxness that seems so pervasive.

Caution is needed despite the fact that a large majority of the members of the so-called religious right are upstanding people and are regarded as such. You don't see these folks, or many of their children, doing drugs or dealing drugs. They never countenanced a drug culture. Their kids don't often end up in prison or bear out-of-wedlock children. Neither they, nor their children, are likely to be found on welfare rolls. Their agenda is often much less destructive than the one preached by what has been called the pagan left. America hasn't been suffering from too much religion. I would rather have my children learn that some people believe in creationism than have them taught that America is just another guilty nation.

So what's the problem? Taken singly and expressed moderately, many of these cultural concerns are quite legitimate. But when collected together as a full agenda, when a few hotheads sound off, when they are richly publicized, the whole movement is tarred as supportive of a cultural takeover by intolerant, exclusive, antipluralist extremists. Liberal Democrats in recent years have made a career of tub-thumping about this sort of thing, just as conservative Republicans have made hay by characterizing the secular left as socialist, tree-hugging, baby-killing, anticapitalist, draft-dodging, promiscuous, utopian, anti-American nut cases.

In the past few decades Democratic liberals have made too little effort to distance themselves publicly from their own leftist extremists and special-interest lobbies. As a result, the Democrats came to be thought of as a party sympathetic to these groups, and were hurt by that perception at the polls. We shall see how the Republicans deal with a somewhat similar situation. It would be wrong, and naive, to tell the religious right to be quiet, go home, and vote Republican. Those on the right note, with merit, that they make up a solid part of the Republican vote, so why are they always the ones who have to do the compromising? But it is neither wrong nor naive to ask them to try to curb their extremists, to behave in a politically astute manner and to take note that they have been gaining ground on many issues, even among Republican moderates.

Abortion was a big issue in Houston in 1992. Since then there has been violence at clinics that provide abortion services. The religious right has gained great prominence. This time there are some prochoice Republicans running for the presidency. Rest assured the eyes and ears of the media will be attuned to the abortion debate when the Republicans convene in San Diego in August 1996.

The American people (including a majority of Republicans) and the Supreme Court seem to have reached a rough consensus about it: Abortion should remain legal but may be reasonably restricted by state laws. This may sound like splitting the difference but it is not. It is essentially a prochoice view.

Neither political party in 1992 was able to echo this nuanced prochoice view. The Republican platform called for a constitutional amendment to illegalize abortion; the Democratic platform would accept no restrictions at all. In fact, the Democrats guaranteed government-sponsored, safe, legal abortions regardless of ability to pay (which means that people who regard abortion as murder would subsidize abortion through their taxes).

From a tactical point of view, the best possible Republican platform statement on abortion would acknowledge that the party is a big tent and that good Republicans are to be found on both sides of this troubling issue; that for the foreseeable future (given the current makeup of the Supreme Court) abortion will remain legal; that most Republicans generally favor at least some reasonable state-level restrictions; and that Republicans who feel this way are encouraged to work at the state level to achieve such goals.

That is unlikely to pass. Prolife forces in the GOP are strong. The second best alternative would be to say nothing, thus eliminating the 1992 plank without replacing it. That is also unlikely to pass.

There is another option to consider. Recall that Contract with the American Family put forth by the Christian Coalition. It dropped the call for a human life constitutional amendment that would illegalize abortion. In its place was a call to limit "late-term" and "partial birth" abortions. Now, it is true that the Christian Coalition Contract (CCC) placed that quite moderate proposal in a *long-term* context of "constitutional and statutory protection for the unborn child" and that their proposal was to be seen "as a beginning to that end."

The proposal itself should not be a hard one to live with. It actually allows both sides to claim some victory. And if Republican platform writers can't finesse the idea that it is only a beginning, then the Republicans need new platform writers. ("We endorse proposals to limit third-trimester abortions, and believe that a peaceful ongoing discussion and debate of this great moral issue should continue among men and women of goodwill.")

If prolife and prochoice Republicans can come together and adopt a compromise abortion platform plank, they will bolster their chances of winning.

Should a prolife plank remain in the platform including a demand for a constitutional amendment, I expect it will be of some harm to a Republican candidate in the election. The days when a candidate can dismiss the platform as a quaint but meaningless document may be over. It was a Republican named Gingrich who "nationalized" the elections of 1994 by proposing a contract that House Republicans would honor. That *contract* was a *platform*, and House Republicans took great, and deserved, pride in living up to their platform.

Could abortion be a tipping issue? An election-losing issue? The polls say that would be unlikely, that only about 5 percent of voters regard abortion as their most important issue and most of those are on the prolife side. I am dubious. Unless gently resolved, in advance, by Republicans of goodwill, the abortion issue could cause a media feeding frenzy (showing again the potency of the values issue in all its many forms).

The leading Republican presidential candidates can help generate a process of amelioration within their party. They should try to choose their state primary delegate slates with an understanding that moderation on the abortion plank may be necessary at platform hearings and at the convention. The Bush campaign didn't bother about the views of its delegates. It wanted delegates who were pledged to Bush for president. Period. Over the years, that has been the rule, not the exception, in both parties. Presidential candidates want delegates firmly pledged to their candidacy; the hell with the issues.

Republican party leaders should call all their delegate troops together and give them the standard unity pitch but stressing the unique circumstances of 1996. They should let the delegates know they have an opportunity to change American history if they win the triple crown in

November: presidency, House, and Senate. Let's agree on the broad areas where agreement is possible (the leaders should say): economic issues, and on those social issues where Republican moderates have
moved right, like crime, welfare, and affirmative action. (Just as the
move to the left by conservatives has been barely recognized, neither has
the toughening-up of many Republican moderates, on certain issues.)

Let's get elected (they should say); we can argue about cultural details later even though we know the details are very important. History
will not forgive us if we turn San Diego into Jonestown. Republicans
drink dry martinis, or nothing; they should stay away from Kool Aid.

It would be a good idea if Republican moderates went out of their
way to praise the majority of nonextremists on the Christian right for
their sound moral principles, and for having certain items successfully
and wisely pushed onto the national agenda. After all, only a few years
ago, the idea of endorsing sexual abstinence for teenagers was regarded
as a quaint throwback to an antique era. This does not mean, by any
means, endorsement of the entire agenda of the religious right. But if
Republicans don't defend their own, it will be that much easier for
Democrats to define them in an ugly fashion, to the detriment of all
Republicans on election day.

There is one other sort-of cultural issue on which many Republicans
seem statistically out of sync with most Americans: gun control. Surveys
show that about 80 percent of Americans *favor* gun control. Most conservative and activist Republicans *oppose* it. But perhaps because gun
control is unlikely to do much to reduce crime for a long, long time, if
ever, and because Republicans are generally seen as tougher on crime
than Democrats, this usually has not been a big problem for the GOP.

In fact, it has often worked the other way. Among the 20 percent of
the voters who oppose gun control, it is an intensely held belief gener-
ating potent political activism which often helps Republicans, particularly in the western states. There are *Democratic* congressmen from the
West, where 70 percent of the electorate is *in favor* of gun control, but
who still seek the endorsement of the National Rifle Association,
which is *against* gun control. Americans favor gun *control*, but over-
whelmingly do not want their guns *taken away*. When liberal gun control advocates say, for example, that the Brady Bill is just a "first step,"

even pro–gun control gun owners can get very nervous. Suddenly, the pro–gun slogan sounds better and better: "guns don't kill people, people kill people."

This time the equation may be somewhat different. The savage bombing of a federal office building in Oklahoma City in April 1995 was apparently the work of one or more antigovernment extremists who (among other things) vigorously oppose gun control. Clinton, after an initial display of above-the-battle-sorrow, went after the National Rifle Association and radio talk show hosts, imputing guilt by association for Oklahoma City to conservatives and antigun control activists. It was a cheap shot. Still, it seemed to play well, and an intense campaign on the issue might help Democrats galvanize the pro–gun control majority.

All the other cultural issues seem to fall on the Republican side, and if used and not overused, could be helpful.

Finally, there is at least one other issue that should be considered: immigration. It is part cultural, part social, part economic, and part international—and big. It should be: Our immigration patterns today shape the kind of America we will have tomorrow.

What has been so remarkable about the politics of recent immigration to America is that until just a few years ago, it received very little high-profile attention. A major immigration bill passed into law during the closing days of the 101st Congress in October 1990. In its final form it increased *legal* immigration by almost 60 percent, from about 500,000 to about 800,000, mostly by increasing the numbers of high-skilled immigrants plus some so-called diversity immigration from countries like Ireland.

But the story was almost entirely buried by the media. Why? Because the Congress was simultaneously debating one more boring budget resolution, the one where President Bush broke his pledge of no new taxes. Which story was more important? Write your journalist!

It is not that Americans don't care about immigration. I learned this firsthand in early 1991 when my book *The First Universal Nation* was published. It deals in part with immigration. When I was doing the talk show interviews for the book, I got a very interesting reaction. Many callers thought immigration was wonderful, that it refreshed and replenished America, and that I was a swell fellow for writing about that. The other callers thought I was a first-class nut and went into detail about the Pakistani immigrant in the next apartment who threw garbage out the window, how new Latino immigrants don't learn English, and how foreigners are "taking over the country."

It is a much hotter issue now. The recession of the early 1990s played a role in heating it up. Many Americans think immigrants take jobs from Americans. (Most economists don't believe that.) Pat Buchanan's campaign in 1992 raised the issue frontally. In 1994 a California ballot proposition, Proposition 187, won big (59 percent to 41 percent). The referendum called for a cutoff of education and non-emergency health benefits to *illegal* immigrants, clearly directed mostly against illegal Mexicans. After Proposition 187 passed, its execution was held up by the courts to determine its constitutionality. As this is written, it remains in court.

I am very much in favor of continued *legal* immigration in the current moderate numerical range, or perhaps even at a slightly higher level.* But it's a long argument, and I will not restate it. We are talking politics here. And the basic politics of this issue can be gleaned straight from the public opinion polls. Almost two-thirds of respondents (63 percent) want to cut back immigration, while 27 percent want to keep rates about the same and only 6 percent want more, according to a CBS/*New York Times* poll in September 1994.

Immigration is a much better issue for Republicans than it is for Democrats. Most Republicans backed Proposition 187; most Democrats opposed it. In 1995, it was Republicans in Congress who were in

---

* I favor an additional 250,000 annual "liberty visas" to qualified persons from the former Iron Curtain area. America properly denounced the former Soviet Union when it made emigration illegal. We opened up the door to the few who managed to escape. But when the curtain was lifted, America disqualified potential immigrants from those countries because they were now "free." The bottom line was: If you can't get out, you can come in; if you can get out, you can't come in. Liberty visas would be morally and historically correct, useful to America, and would tilt the immigration ratios mildly back toward earlier European proportions. That would likely dilute some of the anti-immigrant sentiment in America today, which is largely based on heavy proportions of Latinos and Asians in the new immigrant population. (The proposed new visas would be an add-on, not a cut from existing levels.)

the forefront of the cause of lower legal immigration, led by Senator Alan Simpson (R-Wyo.) and Representative Lamar Smith (R-Tex.).

The issue of cultural nonassimilation ("they're swamping us") is a serious one when considered seriously. It also makes for hot-button politics. But Peter Brimelow's case in his book *Alien Nation,* is partly hokum, partly racialist. Brimelow maintains that non-European immigration pushes the separatist tendencies in America that fly under the flag of multiculturalism and diversity.

I don't believe it. Diversity-mongering gets its principal strength from liberal feminists, liberal Jews, liberal WASPs whose ancestors may well have come to America two centuries ago, and liberal black activists whose ancestors may well have been brought here as slaves even earlier than that. It's not a big cause among newly arrived Korean-American greengrocers or their children. Brimelow's case also downplays American exogamy, that is, outmarriage. Today more than a third of Latinos and almost half of Asians are marrying outside their group, and the rate is rising. (It's over 80 percent among Italian Americans, and 50 percent among Jewish Americans.) Demographically, America is becoming more homogeneous, not less. The issue of quotas is much more responsible for runaway multiculturalism than is immigration.

As with most of the other cultural issues, Republicans must proceed carefully. Too much heat on immigration will sound like xenophobia or racism.

That's not quite fair. Many leading Republicans fall all over themselves in their praise of new *legal* immigrants. Speaker Newt says they make the best Americans: they believe in traditional values, they are entrepreneurial, and they are patriotic. Also waxing rhapsodic are majority leader Dick Armey, presidential candidate Phil Gramm, Jack Kemp, and Bill Bennett. The conservative editorial page of the *Wall Street Journal* has even favored *illegal* immigration.

———

Republicans are in pretty good shape. The economic issue is probably a stand-off, perhaps with an edge to the president's party if the economy stays warm, probably with an edge to the GOP if it cools off. The social issues of crime, welfare, education, and quotas are natural turf for the Republicans. They can do well on cultural issues if they proceed with caution and moderation. Both parts of the values issue help them in the on-going battle of who really represents the mythical little guy in America.

Their potential weak spots concern perceived immoderation and perceived overemphasis on ideology. Perceived extremism in the cause of cultural issues is no political virtue. Perceived moderation in the campaign against big government is no vice.

Democrats will stick it to them, in any event. They will say that Republicans still favor cultural purity which leads to a diminishment of liberty. Smart Democrats—their number is indeterminant—will say its not big government that has done so much to debase our moral standards, it's stupid government that did it. Government should be reinvented to help people help themselves. That's what our political arguments should be about.

Just a few further tips for Republicans:

- If Clinton is the opponent, try to nominate the candidate with the fewest negatives. President Clinton is in deep trouble on the betrayal issue and on personal matters. This, from a Republican point of view, is not the election to nominate a candidate who is a controversial conservative. Nor, from a conservative point of view, is it terribly necessary. If a Republican wins the White House, there will almost surely be a conservative Republican majority in Congress pushing conservative policies with great vigor. To catch the greatest number of anti-Clinton votes remember this: the blander, the better. Senators Richard Lugar and Lamar Alexander seem to best fit the bill. The best possible line on the ballot for the GOP would be: "Not Clinton."
- Please, restore the suffix "ic." Childishly, Republicans like to scorn the "Democrat" party as if that was some sort of an insult. It's not a great way to woo Democratic voters. Sometimes publicans behave like juveniles.

- Make the point, endlessly, that because mostly moderate Democrats lost in 1994, the remaining Democrats in Congress make up a much more liberal group than ever before. Accordingly, the case should be made that Clinton, or any putatively moderate Democrat running for the presidency, will often have to bend to the will of very liberal Democrats in Congress. It's a good argument for the Republican presidential nominee and particularly for Republican candidates for Congress. Should the Democrats somehow nominate a candidate seen to be to Clinton's left, the case is more powerful. Only 19 percent of the electorate self-identifies as liberal.

Republicans, too, can hope and pray for good luck:

Hope and Prayer 1: That Clinton be the nominee of the Democratic party.

Hope and Prayer 2: That Clinton is the nominee after a bruising primary fight.

Hope and Prayer 3: That Hope and Prayer 2 happens *and* that Jesse Jackson runs as a third candidate *and* that Ross Perot and Colin Powell stay out of it.

Hope and Prayer 4: That President Clinton makes a few more statements like the one about how former Defense Secretary Robert McNamara's book vindicated Clinton's draft avoidance during the Vietnam War.

THIRD PARTIES

It was not as a deficit cutter that Ross Perot first came to national fame. He was the billionaire who cared about the prisoners of war left behind in Vietnam. He was the man who, often anonymously, did good deeds for servicemen in trouble. He chaired a committee to look at the problem of education in Texas, stressing higher standards, and told football-crazy Texans that their high school players couldn't compete if they didn't do well in school: "No pass, no play."* He was the dynamic CEO who set up the daredevil rescue of several of his employees in revolutionary Iran, chronicled in the best-seller *Wings of Eagles*.

Not economic issues. Not trade issues. Rather: patriotism, discipline, taking care of your own, loyalty, testing for kids in school. Values issues.

And when Perot came to run in 1992, his on-off-on campaign was something more than the single-issue, cut-the-deficit effort so often portrayed.

As journalists dug into Perot's background, some interesting things came out. He believed in marital fidelity: "If a man's wife can't trust him, why should I?" He said he wouldn't appoint a homosexual to his cabinet: "I don't want anybody there that will be a point of controversy with the American people; it will distract from the work to be done. See, as far as I'm concerned, what people do in their private lives is their business." (Which expresses two apparently opposing positions at once, hardly the mark of a political naif.)

Of the three major candidates who ran in 1992 only Perot's position on abortion coincided with that of the vast majority of the American people: legal abortion, but with moderate state restrictions.

Unlike George Bush, he approved of gun control. Not only that but:

If any human being in this country ever uses a gun to intimidate others . . . we ain't going to see him on the street anymore ever. You say, that's pretty harsh. Well do you want to fix it or not?

Perot's employees at his various enterprises, it was said, had a "uniform": suit and tie, white shirt, short hair, no beards. Many of his new hires came

---

* Perot told a meeting of the Texas High School Association, "Athletics and literacy are not equal. If I had to make a choice, it would be easy." Perot's committee issued recommendations to bolster teacher credentialing in return for pay raises, eliminate useless vocational courses, lengthen the school day and school year, reduce class size, fully fund full-day kindergarten and preschool for disadvantaged children, grant merit pay for merit-worthy teachers, equalize funding for all school districts, and, most important, test all Texas students at the third-, eighth-, and eleventh-grade levels, with no promotion unless the tests are passed.

straight from the straight-arrow military. Drinking during working hours was strictly prohibited. New employees had to take a drug test.

On the matter of drugs, he advocated house-to-house searches for certain inner city black neighborhoods, prison camps, and no bail. "You can simply declare civil war, and the drug dealer is the enemy. At this point there ain't no bail. You go to POW camp. You can deal with this problem in straight military terms . . . we don't have to have military troops to do all this, but we can apply the rules of war."

About welfare he said:

> Let me talk to men [who father babies and then abandon the mothers]: I've got no respect for you at all. As far as I'm concerned you're dirt if you create a baby and walk away from it. That's not a boy, that's a jerk . . . getting high, getting drunk, getting laid and getting pregnant.

He said it would "not be realistic" to do away with the ban on homosexuality in the military.

When he came to pick a vice-presidential running mate, it was a legendary war hero, Admiral James Stockdale. (His first choice, apparently unobtainable, was General Norman Schwarzkopf.) Perot wears a crewcut; his shoes "are shined to a polish you wouldn't believe," according to an associate. How many grown men still hark back to their achievements in the Boy Scouts? Perot advanced through the BSA ranks at blazing speed, becoming an Eagle Scout in sixteen months. His merit badges, certificates, and medals are on proud display at the Perot Scout Center in Texarkana, Texas.

But while often refreshingly straightforward, Perot has displayed a mean and ugly streak. He said that George Bush got America into Desert Storm "to prove his manhood." (Said a Bush aide: "The president is ready to deck him.")

In 1993 he said that Bill Clinton was considering taking military action in Bosnia in order to take the American people's mind off his failures with the Congress:

> My biggest concern is that anytime things get complicated in this country, we like to start a war. [For Clinton], the first 100 days didn't go so well . . . Everything's in disarray. Everything we told people during the

campaign, we're reversing now—from taxes to the medical system to you name it. The promises are just imploding. So it's a good time to distract the American people. You have all these interesting forces at work. When you're shutting down the defense industry, you can get a little war going. When you're downsizing the military, you can get a little war going.

There were other troubling aspects to Perot. He spoke to a convention of the National Association for the Advancement of Colored People, calling his audience on occasion, "you people," or calling blacks "your people," which was regarded as quite insensitive. There were rumors of anti-Semitic remarks. It was said he was a dictator and a conspiratorialist. When he dropped out of the race in August, he said he did it because Republicans were threatening to release phony dirty pictures of his daughter, timed to ruin her wedding.

All this, and more, shaped the public personality of Ross Perot during the election year. The budget was his big issue, but it was being put forth by a man, sometimes nutty, and sometimes mean, sometimes weird, but who came from an older stream of traditional American values: patriotism, fidelity, standards, family, loyalty, white shirts and short hair, tough on drugs, crime, and welfare, reasonable on abortion. A professional spit-shined Boy Scout.

There was, of course, another potent theme in the Perot mix. Here is how Clay Mulford, Perot's son-in-law and a key adviser, described it:

> Perot voters believe that . . . the government has nothing to do with their day-to-day lives, and yet they see terrible problems with politics. . . . Politics is not designed to address issues; it is designed to gain re-election. These are people who are alienated from the political system.*

But why? Why the alienation? Why the disgust? Why are the Perotistas so angry? The Perot signature answer has been: Because the government isn't working right. Just get under the hood and you'll see what's wrong. Just look at that deficit. That became Perot's

---

* William Schneider and Guy Molyneux, "Ross Is Boss," *Atlantic* (May 1993).

issue. (The deficit, of course, also represents a governmental mode of instant gratification, of something for nothing, with repayment to come later, or never.)

But we know it's not just the deficit. The crossed wires under the hood are too often short-circuiting our values. Prove this point with a simple mental exercise. Suppose the president and the Congress actually put together a budget plan that eliminates the deficit after, say, four years, or seven years, or ten years. There is no deficit! Hooray! We're running a surplus! Hooray, the national debt is receding!

Under such circumstances, do you believe that the Perot voters would then say, "Golly, now we fixed what was wrong under the hood, let's all go home"? Of course not. They would still say, rightly, what's under the hood isn't working. Our welfare system is crazy, they would say, our crime situation is criminal, preference is wrong, and where is that Perot-style Texas-style education reform, with standards, tests, and stakes?

———

Why is Ross Perot doing what he does? I am not a political psychiatrist. My experience in national politics leads me to believe that men and women in public life usually act from several motives: to help the country, to help themselves, and usually a mixture of the two.

I would maintain that Ross Perot, under either motivation or a mixture of both, ought to get off what seemed to become a narrow single-bullet campaign dealing with the deficit and the economy. If he decides to run again, he could explain how the same government that screwed up its budget has also played a role in rending the social fabric. He could even say, "What government caused, government can cure."

As a grownup Boy Scout, getting a little less nutty and a little less mean as his rough edges are smoothed by the political process, he could play a serious role in helping America where it most needs help.

Colin Powell

He has been discussed in the previous chapter. Will he run? Won't he run? Will he run for president? Or vice president? As a Republican? As an independent?

Of course, I know the answers to all these questions, but I choose not to reveal them at this moment. What I can tell you is this: General Powell could run a hell of a campaign as the values candidate, perhaps with Jack Kemp or Bill Bradley as his vice presidential nominee.

Powell was our top soldier. "The military" scores number one in the "confidence in institutions" surveys. In some large measure I bet this is so because military advancement is mostly gained the old-fashioned way, by merit. He is black; he speaks some Yiddish; he grew up lower middle class; he gets very big book advances, even by the standards of very big book advances. He seems to be the embodiment of what American life can yield to a man of responsibility, discipline, and intelligence. If he can explain that, and only that, to voters, he could get elected.

Here is how former Senator Paul Tsongas, who has promoted a Powell candidacy, described it:

> This country yearns for conviction. I meet people . . . who have heard Powell speak. To listen to white middle-aged males talk about having been brought to tears by his unabashed, old fashioned commitment to standards and values, was surprising.

Jesse Jackson

He too has been discussed elsewhere in this book. Remember this: he was never more appreciated in America than during the 1970s. His publicly visible modus operandi at that point was directed mostly to inner-city high school students. "Down with dope, up with hope," he bellowed. He also says, "Any boy can make a baby; it takes a man to support a baby."

Others

One hears, always, of other horses preening for entry into the biggest sweepstakes. They should know that values matter most to Americans; therefore, they matter most in American politics. There's room for all to play.

Chapter 17

SPIN CONTROL

Here is a summary: In The Real Majority Richard Scammon and I argued that the social issue—a broad term that included crime, welfare, race, discipline, disruption, drugs, promiscuity, pornography and much more—had become *coequal* with the then-prevalent economic issue. Here, in *Values Matter Most*, I seek to move that thesis further in the light of harsh new conditions. The values issue, the social issue, the cultural issue—call it what you will—has *gone beyond coequality* in our politics. I believe that values matter most, that values are now the *number one issue* in American politics and elections.

I can accept that this formulation of values mattering most in our politics is debatable. There are plenty of diverse data out there. Every player has a storehouse of anecdotes. I offer my data and anecdotes here, and I think they are valid. But if, by some chance, the values issues are not the *most* important political ones, it is still a close contest, and they surely *ought* to be the most important. If America founders, it will be on values, not economics.

I offer a typology here somewhat different from the one offered in *The Real Majority*. There are still economic issues. There are still for-

393

eign policy issues. But the values issues are sufficiently complex that they should be split into two parts, sometimes intertwined.

There is wide agreement about the *social issues*. They are very serious and at least partly remediable in law and public policy. Such remedies can be put into place fairly quickly, although beneficial results will surely take a while. I deal here mostly with four big ones: crime, welfare, education, and preference. There are others. Let's get cracking.

There are the *cultural issues*, which can be political firecrackers, usually dealing with concerns about liberty (as typically described by liberals) or about license (as typically described by conservatives). (Examples: abortion, pornography, prayer in school, gun control, homosexuality and homophobia.) These may be quite important concerns, but they are probably less than apocalyptic. In any event, in part because Americans often disagree about these issues, they are very difficult to remedy in law or public policy. Proposed remedies often face high constitutional hurdles.

In 1992, Bill Clinton challenged the public perception of Democrats as soft on values, and he won. Then he and the Democrats harmed themselves grievously during the next two years by going the wrong way on the values issue. It was recaptured by the Republicans and they won big in 1994. The values issue will likely reveal itself further in the elections of 1996, and well beyond that, at national, state, and local levels. It may yet vault an independent candidate into serious contention, soon.

Clinton's best slogan in 1992, by far, was socially oriented: "No More Something for Nothing." Newt Gingrich added some specificity in 1994: "No civilization can survive with 12-year-olds having babies, with 15-year-olds killing each other, with 17-year-olds dying of AIDS, with 18-year-olds getting diplomas they can't even read."

The values issue is not new in American history. Many historians believe that what is new is that in recent decades, the economy has been seen as the most important issue. The bedrock of the current view of economic primacy in politics rests on some numbers about income that have been distorted. Perhaps better-off Americans have made out better than worse-off Americans, but when all sources of income are counted, there has been at least some moderate income progress across the board in recent decades. Moreover, one principal cause of a changed distribution of income in America, probably the most important cause, concerns the stunning rise in female-headed families, often with out-of-wedlock children. That is a social problem driving an economic one.

The social issues are partly remediable through changes in public policy because, in some large part, that is where they came from. But it is politics that drives public policy, through government. So I say: What politics helped cause, politics should help cure; what politics has screwed up, politics should unscrew up. I offer a short menu of recommendations, mostly not new, often a blend of old-time Democratic policies, DLC ideas propounded by Clinton, mixed with those advanced by the Conservative Opportunity Society in the Kemp-Gingrich mold, some thoughts from a straight conservative perspective, as well as a few of my own idiosyncratic ideas.

The remedies presented here are typically presented in their elemental form and flow from the No More Something for Nothing idea. For example: reinstate punishment for crime, restore disincentives in welfare, reestablish rigor in the schools through serious standards, go back to the earlier form of affirmative action. Note the emphasis on restoration. We have made some wrong turns. Our mistakes in policy are actually harming people. That is the reason for reform, not in order to save a trillion dollars here and there, even though that adds up to real money. The Hippocratic Oath says: "First, do no harm." The Politocratic Oath ought to read: "First, undo past harm, firmly and gently." It can be done. It is not like putting toothpaste back in the tube or reraveling a sweater. It's like going the wrong way at a fork in the road, seeing unpleasant scenery, coming back, and taking a better route to the same destination.

I remain an optimist. I think we can still go back and take the right road. These social issues didn't come about in a single year. They won't be solved in a single year. But let us begin.

My proposed remedies are—only my proposed remedies. There are others around; some go slower, some faster. The important point is to try to get agreement on the cause of the problems and the direction of necessary change. Speed is then a subsidiary question. We don't need a revolution; a vigorous evolution will do just fine. It's happening.

I say here that the root causes of these issues can be tracked back to liberal ideas about American guilt and American victims. These ideas yielded a liberal politics, which yielded liberal policies, and liberal government, all of which helped erect the something-for-nothing state. These ideas represented a major change in the liberal philosophy of governance as it existed only a few decades ago. These changes turned liberalism into an ideology that dare not speak its name on a national campaign trail.

What government has caused, government can cure. What liberals have caused, conservatives can cure. What liberals have caused, liberals can cure if they see the error of their ways. Liberals may have acted with the BOI (best of intentions), but their remedies were subject to the LUSE (Law of Unintended Side Effects).

Either of the political parties can score heavily on the values issues, subset social, if they act boldly. Right now it is much easier for the Republicans. I offer some tactical pointers about how various players and parties can capitalize politically on the themes laid out here. Whichever party does it best will live on happily, in office, and deservedly so. That party will have gained the mandate of heaven by helping America in the way it most needs help. All tactics described herewith are also applicable, with appropriate shaping, to third-, fourth-, or fifth-party candidates, and independents. It could be a big year, and a big era, for third-party and/or independent candidacies— very big.

We have become accustomed to scorning our politicians, but there are times when politics, and only politics, can cure what ails us. Politics can become magical.

These issues sound like domestic issues, but they have great global relevance. What we do here so often sets the course for what they do there. The American way of life has become the most revolutionary force on earth, sweeping across a new world just aborning.

In an earlier time that American way of life was variously described as: individualistic, ruggedly individualistic, democratic, capitalist, voluntaristic, religious, egalitarian, communitarian, pluralist, meritocratic, populist, republican, libertarian, open, upwardly mobile, just plain mobile—and mostly, free, or more precisely, "much more free than other places." It is not a list that leans heavily toward "something for nothing."

I believe that, with all our problems, the cause we Americans promote today is still the best around: democracy, individualism, pluralism, and markets. We offer that American Plan freely and often with gusto. The world still looks to us, but these days too often with a squint.

When liberty beckons the retrograde voices say, "Don't do it. It doesn't work even in America. It is a country of violence, dependency, turbulence, and crudeness. We know best. Our people aren't ready for liberty."

Only if America moves smartly ahead, if we deal with our linked social issues, will there continue to be a democratic model for the world. There is an apparent paradox. The most exciting thing in the world today is the spread of American values, which push democracy, individualism, pluralism and markets. And consequently, the most troubling thing in the world today is the erosion of American values, in America.

I hope—and think—that the old American way of life, surely adjusted for modern times, will prevail again in America. I wish I were as confident of the future of liberty elsewhere. I know this: If America makes it with a flourish and a trumpet call, it will make it much easier for the rest of the world. If America falters, the world is in trouble. That will make it still worse for us.

There is an epilogue, which follows. I present some personal views about where I think I'm headed, and why.

EPILOGUE

Over the years, as either I or my party changed, I have often been asked, "Why have you remained a Democrat?" I have had a variety of answers, all heartfelt when uttered, and true at the time, I thought.

I had a cultural connection. Perhaps I may have agreed more with Republican policies, but so many Republicans seemed to be straight-arrow country club types, solid and stolid. Who would want to go out and have a beer with those guys?

I also felt: "Who says I'm going to let those liberals steal my party? More rank-and-file Democrats thought as I did than as they did!" (And still do, I think.)

Then there was the matter of the House of Representatives. We learned during the Reagan years that serious change, particularly on the social issues, is hard to come by when the Democrats hold the Congress, or even one House of Congress. For so long it was apparent that Democrats would hold the House of Representatives forever. One serious way to try to make change was to get the Democrats to change.

Yet another reason was that in our political system, sooner or later, the out-party wins, even if it is a turkey of a party. Along comes a war, a deep recession, a depression, a scandal, a three-way vote split for president, a nut-case presidential candidate. Then even an apparently popular party can lose. That, I believed, could even happen to the Republicans despite their so-called White House lock in the 1970s and 1980s. In such a case, it would be extremely useful to have some Democrats of the centrist persuasion still on the reservation. (I confess, I was a Democrat more concerned about Democrats winning than Democrats losing.)

One more reason: In this life you are dealt a hand, and you play it as best you can. As fate had it, I had accumulated some small amount of influence in the ongoing Democratic dialogue. That was not something to squander. The Democrats were (then) the most important party in the most important nation.

So I stayed a Democrat. But as time went on, many of those justifications disappeared one by one, and by midevening on November 8, 1994, most of them had evaporated.

By then there were lots of conservative Republicans who didn't know from country clubs; in fact many of the young mini-cons and baby-cons had played in rock bands. Many of my ideological soul mates had switched parties, and had done so with important effect. Many of Scoop's Troops made foreign policy for the Gipper. Meanwhile, a deadening smell of sanctimony wafted forth from too many liberal Democrats, too often.

After the big defeat of Democratic congressional moderates in 1994—tarred as liberals in some large measure because of an early connection to Clinton—it was no longer possible to look at the Democratic party and see deep ranks of kindred spirits.

It was no longer correct to think that Democrats would control the House of Representatives for forty more years. If anyone was going to control the Congress for generations, it would be the Republicans.

What about staying on the reservation because moderates could be of influence when Democrats won? Within a few weeks after Jimmy Carter's election in 1976, it was apparent that the New Politics folks would be running an allegedly centrist administration as a wholly owned subsidiary. Fool me once, shame on you. Fool me twice, shame on me. All right. Shame on me. Within a few weeks after Bill Clinton's election in 1992, it was apparent that the New Politics people (many of them the very same Carter people) would be running that administration as a wholly owned subsidiary. Who wants to wear a dunce cap labeled, "Fooled three times"?

When Democrats of my stripe think of the Clinton presidency, a single word comes to mind: "betrayal." It's not that he hasn't done some good things—some quite good, particularly in the realm of raising issues. But Clinton ran for the presidency with the DLC playbook. He proved what many of us had been preaching for many years: that a dynamic centrist New Democrat could win the presidency. And then he governed pretty much as an Old Democrat. I am usually of the mind that times make the man. On this one, I'm not so sure. Clinton could have tried to stare down the liberal Democrats in Congress. He certainly could have picked a staff with more of a DLC tilt. He could have tried seriously to roll back the something-for-nothing state, not just pass bills to get a better box score.

He didn't, or he didn't do it well, or he didn't really want to do it, or he couldn't do it, or all of the above. And because he didn't, it may be impossible for any Democrat to do so for a long time. Clinton has shown, again, that in Democratic presidential times, the center gets rolled by the left. Who wants to vote for that kind of a party? Because Clinton allowed that to happen, a tribe of moderate Democrats in the Congress lost their seats, making any real move to the center unlikely in the near future.

In reading through this book I find that it is tougher on Democrats than on Republicans. That's not the way it was planned. It was conceived as a cautious assessment of whether the New Democrat criteria were being met. The more I learned about what was going on, the more disappointed I became. Democrats, led by President Clinton, not only failed, but betrayed their promise. In any event, I write following two years (1993–1994) of all-Democratic governance. It was the Democrats who were being tested. Republicans are just beginning to make mistakes, and by my lights, they are not grievous ones yet. Unlike some people whose political judgment I generally respect, I do not fear the so-called religious right as it now presents itself. We shall see how all that plays out.

As I see the situation in mid-1995, I don't plan to vote for Clinton in 1996 if he is the nominee of the Democratic party. He is a dazzling campaigner and a knowledgeable man. He may win. But he didn't go to the center even when he had a forthcoming election to worry about. Why should I think that he would go to the center when there is no election forthcoming for him? This man could be dangerous if given a second term with no checkrein.

On the other hand, there's always an other hand in politics. These days when people ask me, "Why are you still a Democrat?" I shrug, which is not a characteristic gesture for me. Maybe down the road some new set of events or some new Democratic candidate can convince me, and other Reagan Democrats, otherwise. For now, count me as dubious.

Appendix

"WHY I'M FOR CLINTON"

by Ben Wattenberg, October 21, 1992

I'm voting for Bill Clinton for two reasons: George Bush and Bill Clinton. Bush won't attack liberalism. Clinton made a break with liberalism.

It's being said that Bush has given up. I don't think so. It is worse than that. He has reneged.

The central political issue in America since the mid-1960s has been that the Democratic party was far too liberal. That hurt Democrats (acceptable), but also hurt America (unfortunate).

Our political system self-corrects. When one party goes astray, the other takes advantage of it. Since 1968, the Republicans have taken such advantage, winning almost all the national elections. Ultimately, they perfected and stylized the process.

By 1988, all they had to say was "L-Word." The candidate could be McGovern, Carter, Mondale, or Dukakis. The issue could be defense, crime, quotas or taxes. The symbol could be Willie Horton, or the pledge of allegiance. But the theme was constant: the Democrats were too liberal, and too much liberalism hurt America.

Because too-much-liberalism still ails us, the Republicans owe America that argument. The hollow men around Bush have chosen not to offer it. Is it stupidity? Is it a failure of belief? Have they been scared off by the mindless media? Are their mushy-liberal children looking at them with sad eyes? Does it make any difference?

The Republican argument today is pabulum, mush, and saccharine. (Which exhausts my edible metaphors.) Do Republicans really think that America's big problems are "taxes" and "trust"? Give me a cake.

An intelligent case can be made that our society is still reeling from runaway liberalism. "Taxes" (read big government) may be a part of that issue, but only a part.

The other part concerns social issues. Are we heading toward a society where proportionalism rules, not merit? Are our cities turning into free fire zones? Is welfare not only wasteful, but counter-productive? Are our schools so lacking in discipline that we can't teach our children? Have we lost a moral compass, giving out condoms and pushing out ethics, moving perhaps beyond gay rights to gay glorification?

The case can be made, arguably, that all these problems, and more, stem from the ideology of post-Sixties liberalism. It can be extended to show that much of our economic difficulty stems from these values-related situations. (How do you get "world class education" for a "world class economy" with a value-free school system?)

At their Houston convention, Republicans made a tone-deaf pass at some of these social issues under the rubric of "family values." They were trashed, and giggled at, by the reflexively liberal media. Instead of expanding and explaining their theme, they "backed off."

Who needs them if they won't fight that fight?

The highest irony is that Clinton is doing a fine job of defending against an attack that Republicans are too fearful to make, or too dumb to understand. Clinton commercials deal with welfare and crime in a tough-minded way. So did the Democratic platform.

Indeed, by stressing "responsibility," Clinton shows more sensitivity to some of the conservative-style issues than Bush has. He is running as a "different Democrat." I'm nervous about it, but I trust he will govern that way. If Bush had waged a coherent ideological attack on runaway liberalism, Clinton would have set his markers even more firmly, to America's benefit.

I do not share Clinton's view that our economy is coming unglued. It is healthy at its core. I am leery of all candidates (including Bush and Ross Perot) who wave around "plans" and incant "jobs, jobs, jobs," as if their plans make jobs.

But being President is about more than plans and programs. Clinton said something at the Democratic convention that rang a bell: "We can seize this moment, make it exciting, and energizing, and heroic to be American again."

I like that heroic stuff. It is embodied in Clinton's organizing principle for an American foreign policy: the promotion of democracy. That is not only America's transcendental cause, but it can become a dynamite domestic political issue. Our two most popular recent Presidents peddled American heroism with vigor: John Kennedy and Ronald Reagan.

Clinton has a chance to be that kind of President.

Syndicated column, Newspaper Enterprise Association/United Media.

ACKNOWLEDGMENTS

Usually I am a macro thanker. Most of the books I have written contain a long section of acknowledgments thanking demographers, economists, sociologists, and statisticians. Once again I am in debt to those professionals, and many of them are cited in the text.

This book, however, also deals with politics. Crediting and thanking those sources is more difficult. Many politically connected people seek anonymity; others make no such formal request, but might be embarrassed by public acknowledgment of their help. I attribute views here whenever I can. In any event, a great deal of political information is gathered informally, at a party, conference, dinner; from a newspaper story or television; and, in my case, from colleagues at a think tank. Whom does the author thank? Because I have not come up with an answer, I limit myself here mostly to nonsource thanking—micro thanking.

I don't ever intend to write another book with as tight a deadline as was necessary for this one. I began work in late 1992; yet there is material in here through early September 1995, just a few weeks before books were scheduled to ship. The idea was to present the most up-to-date evidence available to back up the thesis.

During the final months of preparation this was an intense enterprise. Douglas Anderson and Jonah Goldberg worked nights and weekends with me. Doug exhibited a great flair for editorial logistics and research just when it was needed. Jonah, who is a budding writer, has worked tirelessly on this project since its inception, offering a top-flight editorial mind. My assistant, Lynn Hoverman, has also been engaged

405

in this venture since its beginning and has been of enormous help in editing, proofreading, opining, and a variety of other ways.

They all double in brass and work with New River Media, which produces my weekly public television discussion program *Think Tank* and several one-hour PBS specials that I am working on, including one entitled *Values Matter Most.* Many *Think Tank* guests ended up as unwitting sources for this book. The special on the theme of the book gave me the opportunity to set up focus groups and field trips that would have been hard to accomplish without such a linkage.

Andrew Walworth, president of New River Media, along with producer Ronald Bailey (author of *Ecoscam* and editor of *The True State of the Planet*), presides over a crew of dazzling young people: Jonah, Lynn, and Doug as well as Scott McLucas, Rob Schurgin, and Melissa Mathis, all of whom helped on this book that became an enterprise.

Speaking of enterprise, I am a Senior Fellow at the American Enterprise Institute. The intellectual sustenance provided by my connection with AEI has been enormous. Let me thank AEI in general by mentioning president Chris DeMuth and executive vice president David Gerson, who have done nothing but encourage me in every possible way.

Certain AEI people deserve specific mention. My long-time colleague Karlyn Bowman is a font of knowledge about American public opinion. Our librarian Evelyn Caldwell sees to it that AEI researchers learn their stuff, from almanacs to Nexis. My participation in AEI's Election Watch series along with Karlyn and colleagues Norman Ornstein and Bill Schneider has been a regular source of education for me.

I write a weekly syndicated newspaper column for Newspaper Enterprise Association/United Media. (My able editors there during work on this book were Robert Levy and Ken Kurzon.) Writing the column gave me week-to-week insight into the ebb and flow of national politics. Much of the material gathered in writing the column in turn has served as source material for this book. I also did many columns because I got interested in a topic I was writing about in the book.

This book came into being after a series of long conversations with the late publisher of The Free Press, Erwin Glikes. When he died I lost a good friend and a wise counselor. American publishing lost a pioneer who demonstrated better than anyone else that commerce in books from the other side of the ideological divide could be profitable. (Although not only from the other side.) That discovery changed not only American publishing, but American politics as well.

The tradition at The Free Press continues. Adam Bellow, editorial director, took over this project when Erwin died, understood it, didn't miss a beat, and offered important guidance to me. Adam's assistant, David Bernstein, was on top of the project every step of the way. This book was a particular challenge to the manufacturing department, headed by Iris Cohen. Edith Lewis, editorial supervisor, was the day-to-day drill sergeant, lending discipline, dedication, and intelligence to the project.

I always knew that Richard Scammon had taught me a great deal of what I know about elections. Until I got into this book, I didn't fully realize just how much. Dick is in retirement now in Somerset, Maryland.

Over the course of three summers, a number of interns have worked on this volume: Brian Renehan, Nayirah Al-Sabah, Tom Henry, Nicole Imanshah, Holly Staid, and Leila Bate. My former research assistant, Tevi Troy, helped me in the early stages of the work.

I received very useful editorial guidance, not necessarily agreement, from Daniel Wattenberg, Karl Zinsmeister, Martha Bayles, and Larry Van Dyne. As always, I argued with Ervin Duggan and Penn Kemble.

I have a great family. My father, Judah Wattenberg, almost ninety-six, is still helping me. My sister, Rebecca Schull, plays the role of Fay Evelyn Cochran on *Wings*; she is a star, as is my brother-in-law, Gene Schull. My three grown children are a delight. Each of them has helped me in this endeavor. Ruth is deputy director of the issues department at the American Federation of Teachers; Danny is a contributing editor at *George* and a freelance writer; Sarah, a clinical social worker, is director of McAuliffe House serving the mentally ill. My granddaughter, Emma, is dynamite. My brand new grandnephew, Henry Isaac Meeks, is—brand new and most welcome.

I live inside the Beltway, in Washington, D.C., with my wonderful preteen daughter Rachel and my dear wife Diane. Rachel is teaching me about the modern world. Diane and I have vigorous discussions about the issues dealt with here. This book could not have been written without her help, guidance, and patience.

INDEX